PERSONALVIEWS

Explorations in Film ———————

PERSONALVIEWS

————————————————————— Revised Edition

ROBIN WOOD

WAYNE STATE UNIVERSITY PRESS
DETROIT

Revised edition published 2006 by Wayne State University Press, Detroit,
Michigan 48201. Originally published 1976 by the Gordon Fraser
Gallery Ltd., London and Bedford. Original edition © 1976 by Robin
Wood. Advisory editor Michael Wallington. No part of this book may
be reproduced without formal permission. Manufactured in the United
States of America.

        10 09 08 07 06   5 4 3 2 1

Library of Congress Cataloging-in-Publication Data

Wood, Robin, 1931–
Personal views : explorations in film / Robin Wood.— Rev. ed.
p. cm.
Originally published: London : G. Fraser, 1976.
Includes bibliographical references and index.
ISBN 0-8143-3278-1 (pbk. : alk. paper)
1. Motion pictures—Aesthetics. 2. Film criticism. I. Title.
PN1995.W645 2006
 791.4301—dc22
2006007540

The publishers acknowledge the Kobal Collection for the stills from
The Scarlet Empress, Remember the Night, and *I Walked with a Zombie;*
and the British Film Institute for the stills from *Sansho Dayu, Les
Carabinieres, Letter from an Unknown Woman, Touch of Evil, Germany,
Year Zero,* and *Rio Bravo.*

The following essays have been previously published: "Notes for a
Reading of *I Walked with a Zombie*" first appeared in print in the Winter
1986 issue of *CineAction!* magazine, "Creativity and Evaluation: Two Film
Noirs of the Fifties" first appeared in print in the Summer/Fall 1990 issue
of *CineAction!* magazine, and "Responsibilities of a Gay Film Critic" first
appeared in print in the January/February 1978 issue of *Film Comment*
magazine.

∞

Designed and typeset by Maya Rhodes
Composed in Radiant and Minion

FOR JOHN

—— with my love

CONTENTS

FOREWORD

This is the second in a series of Robin Wood's early books, so important in the history of film studies, to be reprinted as part of the Contemporary Approaches to Film and Television series. It is particularly satisfying that *Personal Views* has followed the influential work on *Howard Hawks,* because this is the only book on cinema by Wood never to have been published in the United States. Published originally in 1976 by a small art gallery in London, England, the book received only limited distribution. The original collection of eleven essays is here augmented by three additional pieces in the spirit of the work.

The benefit for Wood is a boon for readers, who in these pages are treated to a fascinating series of essays by one of the sharpest critical minds ever to write film criticism. It is true that the essays that comprise *Personal Views* consider a wide range of films and filmmakers, from popular Hollywood directors such as (of course) Hawks, Vincente Minnelli, and Leo McCarey to recognized auteurs like Max Ophuls, Orson Welles, Fritz Lang, and Josef von Sternberg to art film icons Jean-Luc Godard, Michelangelo Antonioni, and Kenji Mizoguchi. Wood does indeed write in *Personal Views* about whatever movies or makers he happens to find of interest. Yet beyond the discussion of specific cinematic tales and tellers, films and film makers, there is one over-arching theme to this collection: the nature of (film) criticism and of the critic.

Bucking the winds of scholarly change (what he would prefer to call "fashion"), Wood remained throughout this period an anchor of critical discipline, using theory without being used by it and always attentive to textual detail. His appropriation of Roland Barthes's narrative codes as outlined in *S/Z* for his semiological analysis (at once serious and satirical) of Jacques Tourneur's horror film *I Walked with a Zombie* is a perfect example of Wood's ability to take what he needs from theory in offering a critical reading of a film.

Wood was not the lone voice of protest in the storm surge of theory. There were others. (Indeed, I like to believe that I was one of them.) But always Wood has stood apart for the power of his arguments and the sheer grace of his prose. And, despite the many theoretical discussions of the hypothetical spectator and his/her construction or positioning within the text, for his open acceptance of the experience of watching the films he discusses. This characteristic of Wood's writing should come as no surprise, given that he writes about films that, as he says, he has lived with.

Wood's overall critical project is to combine aesthetics and ideology in understanding films, for the ultimate goal of enriching our lives individually and together. In these pages he argues eloquently for this function of art generally and cinema specifically. Wood was heavily influenced by, and readily acknowledges his debt to, his teacher F. R. Leavis, who calls these critical concerns questions of "value." But if as a critic Wood is a Leavis for the cinema, he is also its John Dewey. With his emphasis on the nature of the film experience, he opens himself up to the films he discusses, applying his critical acumen to them rather than cramming them into critical containers.

In the end Wood, the proud, self-contained "unreconstructed humanist," not only offers persuasive arguments for the importance of art, creativity and personal response, but demonstrates it in his analyses of the films he discusses. He never offers his own readings as definitive—his understanding of criticism as well as of cinema precludes that possibility. But after reading them it is difficult to think of the films he discusses another way.

This is his greatest achievement and why the writing in *Personal Views* is true film criticism.

BARRY KEITH GRANT
2005

ACKNOWLEDGMENTS

The essays on Tourneur and Mizoguchi appeared in their original form in *Film Comment* and are reprinted here, revised and (in the case of the latter) considerably extended, with the permission of its editors. Other sections, written for the book, have been serialized in *Film Comment,* and the essay on Welles has appeared in translation in *Positif.*

"Levin and the Jam" developed out of lectures given for the Open University at York during the summers of 1973 and 1974. I would like to pay tribute to the stimulating and intensely creative atmosphere of Open University summer schools.

Many of the essays have developed out of lectures given during the past five years at Queen's University, Canada, at Berkshire College of Education and at the University of Warwick. Their final form, therefore, has been influenced by discussions with colleagues and students in ways too intricate and often too indirect for detailed acknowledgment of debts to be possible. Peter Harcourt, Victor Perkins, Douglas Pye, Gary McCallum, Dave Elliott, Joyce Nelson, and Tom Ryan have all been important to me during this period, by virtue of encouragements or argument; but I'm sure this list is far from exhaustive. I have tried in this book to be completely myself, as a result of which I have become much more aware of the multiplicity of influences, tangible and intangible, by which the self is determined at any given time.

I want to acknowledge, without irony, a particular debt to the editors and critics of *Screen* magazine, who have provided, over the past few years, so sustained and formidable a challenge to traditional aesthetics. If my work has developed during this period—and I think it has—that development has been in large measure a response to the challenge. Nor is the debt merely negative: I believe the reader will repeatedly detect traces of a positive influence, even if I have used ideas and interests derived from *Screen* in ways with which its writers might not wish to be associated.

I particularly want to thank The Other Cinema for their generosity in repeatedly lending me, free of charge, prints of Godard's recent films. They knew that my attitude to the films was not likely to be unequivocally favourable, and I interpret their assistance as testifying to a disinterested concern for the development of film culture; besides that, few distributors in my experience are so welcoming and friendly.

Finally, nothing in the book would be quite the same were it not for my union with John Anderson, who has affected every essay at every stage, from the first tentative formulation of ideas to the detail of their final expression.

Introduction

Of all my books, this is one of my two favorites, the other being *Sexual Politics and Narrative Film.* The reason for this preference is simple: the other books are restricted to specific subjects (in most cases directors), and in these two, with their unusually permissive editors, I have had complete freedom, seizing upon anything that captured my attention, moving freely over the entire range of world cinema. The present book even finds room for an essay on literature (mainly Tolstoy), which I regard as among my best pieces, though probably most of my readers skip it.

This also accounts, alas, for the fact that these same two books have been, overall, my worst sellers, which makes it unlikely, in today's market, that I shall ever be allowed to write such books again, since even university presses (in this age of capitalism run amok) seem today to worry more about profits than quality. As I try to write serious criticism, usually about films I have lived with over a period of years (as distinct from the ephemeral weekly journalism that passes for criticism in today's world of the instantly disposable), my books have been primarily used for university film courses, and most university film courses are about specific subjects (a director, a genre, a national cinema) when they are not about theory. There is no room in them for a book that wanders all over the place.

I hadn't read this book since it was published thirty years ago, and I was afraid that today parts of it (especially the opening essays) might seem dated to the point of being "quaint" and be of purely historical interest. In fact, on rereading them

I was pleased to find them as relevant as they ever were. They set out something of the ideals to which I have aspired (though the achievement has usually fallen short of the aspiration). My most recent work in *CineAction!* and *Film International*—a series of close readings of films by Haneke, Hou, Noe, Miike, Denis, and Kiarostami—has not, I think, been unfaithful to the critical principles I outlined in the 1970s. In some respects these opening essays may prove both timely and topical: we seem, at last, to be experiencing the beginning of a long-needed backlash in academia against the dominance of theory over criticism, and these pieces have immediate relevance to this encouraging phenomenon.

It is impossible for me to explain what may now look like eccentricities without veering into autobiography. *Personal Views* was published in 1976 by an obscure little British company (the Gordon Fraser Gallery) known primarily for its fancy greeting cards of fairies cavorting around mushrooms. They did a beautiful job—I still love the book's layout and general appearance. Its somewhat broken-backed character can be partly explained by the fact that many of the essays were written much earlier or were derived from lectures given at Queen's University, Canada, prior to 1972, while others (notably the opening essays) were written in direct response to the drastic shifts in film criticism/theory I first encountered on my return to England.

My three years at Queen's constituted my first university position. Prior to that I was a teacher of English at a high school in outer London. Today I would not even be considered for the post—I had no degree beyond a BA (and even that a mere 2.1 GPA), which would automatically disqualify me from teaching in universities today. But I had published two books (on Hitchcock and Hawks) and a few articles, which had attracted a certain amount of attention, and at that time there was no such thing as a PhD in film study—the majority of universities, on both sides of the Atlantic, had no film program at all—so I was probably as qualified as anyone. But I have always felt like something of a gatecrasher in academia.

I had left England with my wife and our three children, and I returned after the expiration of my three-year contract to try to begin a new and very different life, since in the interim my marriage had broken up, I had come out as gay, and my wife had returned to England with the children. I also returned only to be confronted with a new and alien world of film study that had already, in my absence, declared me and all my critical principles obsolete. I cannot remember, during my three years at Queen's, ever even hearing the word "semiotics," nor had I read a single word of Metz, Barthes, Althusser, or Lacan, so I was totally unprepared for the new regime that had cast me as one of its enemies before I even knew of its existence. For my first year back in London I lived in a miserable little one-room apartment and had difficulty finding part-time jobs that earned me enough to pay the rent; I don't think I have ever felt so unwanted, so outmoded. My personal situation was even bleaker than my professional outlook. I had always thought of my marriage primarily in terms of friendship and mutual respect rather than passion. I had from the outset been frank with my wife about myself, though in those days I had foolishly believed in a "cure" that of course never arrived, and I had never had sex with a man before the move to Canada. I saw no reason why our friendship shouldn't continue. My wife saw it very differently: I was allowed to visit the children once a week when she was out, and we were to meet as little as possible. (In retrospect, of course, I can see this was essential from her point of view, my own expectations mere wish-fulfillment fantasy.) It would have been the most terrible year of my life but for the presence of my lover, John Anderson, who followed me from Canada and largely supported me on his savings. I don't know, looking back, how I would have survived that year without him.

Then, miraculous as it seemed, I was appointed to start a

film studies program at Warwick University: distrusting the new trend, they wanted a "traditionalist." John and I bought a house in Coventry (the nearest city to the university) and my life started again. It was there that I wrote the new chapters of *Personal Views* as a challenge to the new regime and an introduction to (and defense of) the critical essays that followed it. It was already becoming somewhat eccentric (and probably reprehensible) within intellectual and academic circles to produce a book of film *criticism* at all: criticism was out, it was superfluous, it was just a matter of personal opinions; theory, which promised us the *truth,* was in. It is only within the past year that the supremacy of theory has begun to be questioned by, among others, the always influential Terry Eagleton.

I should confess here perhaps that though I have taught in universities for almost forty years, I have never thought of myself as an "academic." Though I still teach a graduate course each year (courtesy of York University, Toronto), I extricated myself from full-time academia as early as possible, taking early retirement at the age of fifty-nine. I usually got on well with students but very rarely with colleagues. In general (there have been, of course, exceptions) I found academic life characterized by self-importance, careerism, backbiting, and a pervasive lack of generosity, to me the most important of all human values. And I have always deplored the emphasis, so common today still in film studies, on theory. We *need* theories, of course, and we need teachers who can explain them to us (hopefully in recognizable English). But the highest aim, purpose, and justification for any university training in the arts is the eternal debate about questions of value—the value we attribute to works of art and entertainment, including films, that reflects our sense of value in our own lives and within the culture in which we live. Criticism—the ongoing, never-ending search for meaning and value—should be the highest arena of debate and education, and theorists should see themselves as its humble servants.

That questions of value are ultimately unresolvable and by their very nature resistent to "scientific" proof, their very basis subject to change from one generation to the next, is a strength, not a weakness. The debate resists any final QED, thereby developing open and flexible minds, and open minds are far more desirable than dead ends. Human progress and development depends far more on a sense of value than on theory, however apparently conclusive.

The worst (and inevitable, given the intransigence of the semioticians, who appear to wish to relate only to others of their own persuasion or to students they can intimidate and indoctrinate) effect of this has been the perhaps now irreparable break with a wider public outside academia. Any possible continuum has, of course, always been precarious, academics liking to feel and express their superiority, a pack of Lord Snooties looking down on the ignorant "out there," but at least they spoke a recognizable (if necessarily somewhat more difficult) language. The most obvious result of the semiotics takeover has been the development of what amounts to a private language and the subsequent severance of all ties, the general attitude being, "Oh, you can't even *hope* to understand what we're talking about." It's a great way to start a revolution, the aim that was the great energizing and redeeming feature of the semiotics movement in its heyday, developing directly out of the events of the students' and workers' revolution of May '68 in France. But today, when revolution has become more urgent than ever, the original fervor has dwindled into a new academicism.

Theory has proven more elusive than its practitioners ever seem ready to accept: it has shown itself a prey to fashion, with a commitment (so pervasive in twentieth-century culture) to "the latest." In the period in which this book was written, "theory" was Metz, Barthes, Lacan, Althusser—names that today I rarely encounter in classes. They appear to be passé, though at the time their conjunction was held to have resolved all our problems, provided all the answers: every film could be neatly classified upon a grid that ranged from the "radical" through the "progressive" down to the "traditional." Its value could then be readily assessed by the degree of its embroilment in, escape from, or demolition of "the dominant ideology." I was confidently informed by a leading British semiotician (I forget which one) that "all the problems are now solved." I think he was telling me that I shouldn't continue to waste my time.

But the heady excitement of that time (and it *was* exciting, as there was a sense of purpose and commitment that one rarely encounters today) couldn't be sustained. If "all the problems were now solved," the analysis of films became, first repetitive, then merely tedious. The great solvers of problems receded into the background, into history, their position of eminence usurped by a new name: Derrida, who today (or was it already yesterday?) seems to have been replaced in his turn (judging from the obligatory references and quotations in students' essays, which no longer mention Barthes or Lacan even in footnotes) by Deleuze, without whom no current essay is complete. It appears today to be of far greater importance (in the interest of academic "success") for a student to quote Deleuze (whom I haven't read) than to proffer a personal opinion or insight. I must exempt from this my own students, whom I encourage from the start to begin sentences with "In my opinion" rather than "It seems today to be generally agreed that." It takes them a seminar or two to get over the shock, but when they do the relief is palpable. I am a dangerously corrupting influence.

I should confess, perhaps, that today I read very little criticism and no theory. As I *write* about film, I feel no great incentive to *read* about it. As Ingrid Bergman so aptly puts it in *Viaggio in Italia*, "Life is so short," and it seems even shorter when you find yourself suddenly in your mid-seventies. I find it more profitable to spend my time reading and rereading literature (from, say, Chaucer to Gordimer via Shakespeare, Donne, and Tolstoy) and listening to music (from, say, Monteverdi to Stravinsky via Bach, Mozart, and Mahler)—and of course watching films, at least one a day. *That* is how to develop a sense of value.

The Future of the University

I have witnessed, during my academic career of over fifty years as both student and teacher, the perhaps now irrevocable decline and fall of the university. The typical university of today seems to me virtually indistinguishable from a career-training college—a fact very precisely illustrated in my own city, Toronto, where during the past decade an institution formerly designated a "Polytechnic" has changed its title to "University" without protest or question and without noticeable change of curriculum. As many students reading this today will not understand what I am talking about (so complete is the university's capitulation to the ethics and aims of corporate capitalism in its so-called "advanced" stage), I shall attempt to describe what a university *should* be, leaving comparisons to the reader.

The great literary critic F. R. Leavis (a direct and pervasive influence on this book) defined the ideal university as "a creative centre of culture." No actual university, perhaps, ever quite fulfilled that ideal, but the one in Cambridge, England, where I attended from 1959 to 1964 and where Leavis lectured in many ways came close. It was possible there to be a "student" in a sense in which that term cannot be used today. There were no student *loans* back then: as my parents' income was below a certain level, all my fees were paid for by the government and my living expenses were covered by a *grant*. If I fell into debt it was for precisely the reason I'm still in debt today: I spend too much on books and music. No government known to me today would finance such an institution, but anything I have achieved in my life was the direct result of those four years. Our only hope might be a socialist government (apparently more or less taboo in North America), simply because it would be the least indebted to corporate capitalism (capitalists being unlikely to finance the campaigns of a government that would, at the very least, severely limit their greed, profiteering, and devastation of the environment).

No courses were compulsory and no grades were awarded for taking them. If you chose to, you could spend all your time in discussions with your friends or studying alone in your room or the library. Today's system strikes me as essentially *anti*-educational: Why, in heaven's name, are students regularly forced to take courses in subjects in which they have no interest whatever? As George Eliot put it 145 years ago in *Mill on the Floss*, "For getting a fine flourishing growth of stupidity there is nothing like pouring out on a mind a good amount of subjects in which it feels no interest" (321). I have on several occasions in my university teaching been confronted by students asking me, the first night of a course, "What do I have to do to get a B+?" What has such an attitude (endorsed and encouraged by the system) to do with anything one might, without absurdity, term education? At Cambridge you had a tutor for whom you wrote an extended essay every week on an agreed subject, and seminars consisted of the professor, yourself, and one other student. You read your essays aloud, and the three of you then discussed them in detail. In other words, you were treated as a responsible adult. I had the great good fortune to have as my tutor A. P. Rossiter, author of a marvelous book on Shakespeare, *Angel with Horns,* now apparently out of print and forgotten. No grades were awarded for these weekly essays. At the end of the year you had a series of exams, and if you failed that was the end of your university career: you were free to leave and join the workforce. But I never heard of a student failing who had a serious commitment to study.

During my first two years I cannot recall even giving a thought to a possible future career. I studied because I loved what I was doing and what I was learning, and I had sufficient leisure to listen to music, go to movies and concerts, get involved in passionate debate with my circle of friends. I attach particular importance to the last: I believe these afternoon or evening discussions did more to help me mature and understand myself and my beliefs than the great majority of lectures. Such assets can barely survive today: most of us would be working part-time, unproductive jobs to earn money toward paying off our loans. What I am describing is something called "civilization," which no longer exists, at least not in North America. It has been replaced by what one might call a "fast food syndrome." During my third year I decided to become a teacher, and I stayed for a fourth year to work within the education department for a diploma. The courses were undemanding, and I used the year primarily as an extended study period.

The system was not perfect: too many tenured professors were lazily delivering the same old lectures year after year. During my first weeks at Cambridge I assumed I should go to everything, but after a month I generally preferred to work alone or with friends, attending perhaps three or four courses. When I glanced into the lecture rooms of the undislodgeable tenured bores, I saw perhaps a half-dozen students scattered around the hall. Leavis's lectures, on the other hand, were packed every week, with students sitting on the steps or standing at the sides of one of the larger lecture halls, everyone silent, hanging on every word of a man who never raised his voice. On principle I am opposed to tenure, but if it were dissolved in its place we would need foolproof safeguards against wrongful dismissal (for political beliefs, for example). Leavis himself, the best teacher under whom I have studied, would probably have been dismissed: he was hated by many of the other dons for his intransigence, his outspokenness, and his unspotted integrity—the very qualities that made him great.

The universities in which I've taught (Queen's, Canada; Warwick, England) prior to my present position at York, Toronto,
have retained vestiges of the past but have also been unable to
withstand contamination from the American model. There was
far less of the "fast food syndrome" ("What do I have to do to
get a B+?"), and in general I was not obliged to teach classes in
which students would ask (as has happened more than once),
"Are we going to have to watch many black-and-white movies in
this course? I *never* watch them." But the model had already established itself quite firmly; the format had become the American norm.

An Immodest Proposal

Before anyone starts yelling "Elitist!" let me make clear that if
I were to create a new model university, enrollment in "my"
university would be strictly a matter of individual choice and
would not necessarily favor those with the highest IQs or the
most money. The university would make it clear from the outset
that it had no interest in training people for the workforce and
that "success" (in the brutal but today ubiquitous sense of "making a lot of money") would by no means be guaranteed. People
(of both genders, all races, and all social classes) would go there
with the desire to steep themselves in our cultural heritage, in
the great traditions of music, literature, the visual arts (including film), with the possibility always available (in an increasingly
multicultural society) of plunging into the traditions of other
races. There would also be courses in related topics (philosophy,
social and political thought), courses that would examine critically the current state of our civilization and the urgent need for
radical social/political change, beginning with the overthrow of
corporate capitalism.

I would expect that, in a world that encourages its citizens
to be primarily interested in careers and moneymaking, enroll-

ment in such an institution would be relatively sparse. We would only need, perhaps, three or four in North America to cater to the applicants. But it would be a start: an outpost of civilization, a place in which to develop a full awareness of what is happening in our world, what is in danger of being lost, swallowed up in all the "noise" that distracts us from thinking. It would be a place committed to the critical study of the great questions of value—the values by which people live, the values by which they *might* live, the values that make human life worth living, that enrich and dignify rather than degrade. Such a university could not hope to compete with the career-training colleges that corporate capitalism demands. It would have something of the function of the monasteries in the Dark Ages (the *previous* Dark Ages), which saw their duty as the *preservation* of art and humanity in the midst of cataclysmic disaster, in the hope that a future might somehow grow out of the ruins of civilization. We live today in our own Dark Age—albeit a "dark" age of dazzling lights, constant noise and distraction, the constant novelty, the instantly disposable, the "latest" you truly must acquire or watch or listen to or wear to be "with it"—hiding from us the imminence of disaster, whether in nuclear war or the devastation of the environment and the end of life on our planet.

The likelihood of such a university coming into existence today is obviously minimal: Who would pay for it? Certainly not any government I know of or any American political party. Most universities today have capitulated to corporate capitalism and are partly funded by corporations: hence the proliferation of "business schools." They have, in other words, already sold out to the enemy, without so much as a struggle. What millionaire is going to surrender some of his millions to a university committed to a new socialism?

I see no solution short of a massive new socialist revival and revolution, of which at present there seems very little hope. There is nothing more beautiful politically than Abraham Lincoln's "government of the people, by the people, for the people," but in practice in the United States (the most powerful nation in the world, and the most profoundly irresponsible) the word's of Lincoln's Gettysburg Address would better be "government of the people, by the rich, for the rich." I am appalled by violence in any form, public or private, and would hope Lincoln's formula is still achievable by peaceful means: the formation of a new and potent Left (there appears to be none in the US—only a choice between a moderate and an immoderate conservatism) that would gain the votes not only of the workers, the poor, and the underprivileged but also of anyone interested in saving our civilization (insofar as there is one left to save) and, ultimately, life on our planet. With the realities of corporate capitalism, nuclear weaponry, and global warming before us, there can no longer be such a thing as an intelligent and responsible right-wing position.

Postscripts

A friend, reading the above paragraph, commented that he was surprised it was so "conservative." In the word's original sense, yes, it is: it pleads for the "conservation" of the great achievements of our past as our guides to a civilized and *livable* future, in an age when the future of life itself is being recklessly jeopardized by the greed of a few for wealth and power. To put it in a way that many may consider ridiculous, it is impossible that anyone who really loves and understands Mozart's music (as opposed to treating it as some kind of guarantee of one's upper-class culturedness) could support or participate in corporate capitalism. In the wise words of William D. MacGillivray (potentially the most important living Canadian filmmaker, who has been unable to make a feature film in the past decade for lack of funding) in an unfilmed screenplay, "If we lose the past, we lose the future." But my friend's remark has reminded me that there *have* been advances, however contaminated and compromised.

One welcomes the swift development of multiculturalism, visibly spectacular in Toronto (where I live), and the partial breakdown of color prejudice. Couples of different colors can now walk confidently down our main street without being molested or even receiving disapproving stares. It is still, however, unusual for persons of color to rise to positions of power, and when they do it is frequently at the cost of joining the enemy— Condoleezza Rice being the most flagrant example in North America, supporting a president in the world's most powerful, greedy, and (at the present time) ugly nation who refuses even to sign the clearly inadequate Kyoto agreement. Similarly, the gay rights movement has made great advances, but the cost of acceptance has been the loss of a wider vision and incorporation in the bourgeois world. Gays have ceased to be objects of horror and have joined the ranks of the "trendy" and "smart." In Canada they can even get married, though why they would want to is for me beyond comprehension. All marriage means today is making it more difficult to split up if you're miserable.

We can still look to the women's movement for encouragement, despite the many women who seem proud to have become business executives in the world of the enemy, seduced by the traditionally male (and predominantly heterosexual) obsessions with greed and power. They are countered by many others who are still prepared to join the battle for life, a battle that can be fought on many levels. I am currently reading Varda Burstyn's magnificent "eco-thriller," *Water, Inc.,* which is politically brilliant and, once you're hooked, very difficult to put down. It would make a terrific movie, if any Hollywood producer had the guts or the conscience to make it. There are strong and decisive roles for women (Julia Roberts? Sigourney Weaver? Sarah Polley?), and one might say that Burstyn repurifies feminism. It may yet be women (with their relative lack of greed and their capacity for caring, nurturing, and tenderness) who lead the way out of the current insanity. *Water, Inc.* should be compulsory reading, in conjunction with Joel Bakan's *The Corporation* (book and film), for anyone who still thinks our planet and our civilization are worth saving.

I should also add that I believe that not *all* rock music is worthless (its political value could stand development); that *some* television is intelligent and creative (*Buffy the Vampire Slayer, The Sopranos, Sex and the City*), though there I must add that I absolutely refuse to watch, on principle, any program that is interrupted by commercials, preferring to wait for the DVDs; and that *some* fast-food joints provide nutritious, decent, or at least unharmful meals.

Some Notes on the Original Essays

1. The essay on *Letter from an Unknown Woman* has a somewhat different (more extended, more detailed, and, above all, more "political") sequel in my later *Sexual Politics and Narrative Film.* I prefer the later reading of Ophuls's magnificent film, but I think readers may find it interesting to compare the two to see the different ways (with different emphases and at times different interpretations) films can be read at different stages in one's own development and in the world in which one lives.

2. As a matter of justice, I would not want anyone to read the essay on "Hawks De-Wollenized" unless he or she has already read Peter Wollen's original essay on the auteur theory in *Signs and Meaning in the Cinema.* His book was current at the time *Personal Views* was published, and it had significantly greater impact and influence. It remains a landmark in the evolution of film theory and criticism.

3. Of all the original essays in this book, the one on Tolstoy's *Anna Karenina* is by far the most personal, and its importance to me when I wrote it can only be fully explained within the

context of my life at the time. I wrote it during my years in Coventry with my lover after I had separated from my wife and was dreadfully missing (and feeling deeply guilty about) my three children. Always in need of money, I accepted a position teaching literature for the Open University, which offered correspondent courses during the year and a summer school at York University in England. One of the set texts that particular summer was *Anna Karenina,* with which I was already fully familiar but which, not surprisingly given its extraordinary power and my particular circumstances, completely overtook me. My identification with Anna became so strong that I developed a morbid habit of standing right at the edge of subway platforms on the London Underground, willing myself to jump. I'm sure now that I would never have done so: I'm not really suicidal by temperament, and I'm a dreadful physical coward. But that essay was my means of arguing myself out of that state. Writing it may not have saved my life, but it helped me survive psychologically. It was one essay I *had* to write.

Some Notes on the Additional Essays

The two articles I have asked to have reprinted in this new edition of *Personal Views* originally appeared in *CineAction!* magazine, of which I am one of the editors. Both are now out of print. "Creativity and Evaluation" belongs clearly with the concerns of this book, perhaps making them more explicit. As for the article on the Lewton/Tourneur masterpiece (I don't think that is too strong a word) *I Walked with a Zombie,* it constituted my response to the semiotics movement, at the point where Roland Barthes (in particular *S/Z*) was the plat du jour: I wanted to demonstrate that I could do it too (in my own slightly deviant way). My motivation was perhaps somewhat complex: I didn't intend it as a joke, exactly, but neither did I have the least intention of continuing to write in that manner, to be "taken over."

Were I asked what I thought about its production, I might have said, in the words of Howard Hawks and his filmmaking, "I had fun." I suppose I wanted to prove something to myself at a time when my self-confidence was at its lowest. It cheats, of course: I removed one of Barthes's "five codes" altogether and modified (or rewrote) one of the others to suit my own purposes. It had results way beyond my expectations: previously hostile semioticians wrote to me from England congratulating me and welcoming me into the club. And I *did* learn from it as an exercise. *S/Z* still stands as an important work, and the kind of discipline imposed by its five codes can still serve as a valuable method of analysis. It is easy to see, however, that one cannot devote one's life to analyzing films or novels or poems in that laborious manner in print. The method of *S/Z* is for the critic's preliminary work, a means of exploring in minute detail the novel/film/etc. that the critic will eventually evaluate.

It was my admirable and creative editor, Barry Grant, who suggested the inclusion of "Responsibilites of a Gay Film Critic" as a relevant third reprint, a proposal to which I happily agreed. It originated as a lecture in London, England's National Film Theatre.

1
Big Game:
Confessions of an Unreconstructed Humanist

> But as to commitment in a general sense. . . . You know, I
> can't believe in the general ideas, really I can't believe in them
> at all. I try too hard to respect human personality not to feel
> that, at bottom, there must be a grain of truth in every idea. I
> can even believe that all the ideas are true in themselves, and
> that it's the application of them which gives them value or
> not in particular circumstances. . . . No, I don't believe there
> are such things as absolute truths; but I do believe in absolute
> human qualities—generosity, for instance.
>
> JEAN RENOIR

I have been often challenged, by friends and enemies alike, to attempt a formulation of my critical position; I have hitherto refrained from such an undertaking. It seemed to me at first that I *had* no position: an absurd assumption, of course, for even critical statement must derive from *some* position, however implicit or unconscious. But any attempt at formulation I made struck me as self-evident, hence not worth stating. If formulation now seems possible, even indispensable, this is because its self-evidence, in the light (or obscurity) of recent developments in film criticism, can no longer be assumed: what a mere five years ago would have struck me as embarrassingly obvious now demands to be passionately affirmed.

I am a critic, not a theorist. I believe that criticism and theory are two different disciplines, partly overlapping, each capable of drawing sustenance from the other, but also partly incompatible. The theorist erects systems, the critic explores works. For the theorist, questions of value will be determined by reference to a previously elaborated system; for the critic, a sense of values arises from placing this experience beside that experience in an endless and flexible empiricism. To the theorist, personal response to a given work will be an irrelevance, even an obstruction; for the critic—while he will be aware that it must be continually probed, questioned, tested—personal response is central to his activity. The critic is much closer to the artist than the theorist is. Between the artist's exploration of experience and the critic's exploration of art there is (or should be) a great deal in common, but between the processes of artistic creation and the intellectual constructs of theory there is an unbridgeable gulf. Art is concrete, and the product of the emotions and the instincts as well as the intellect; theory is abstract, and demands by its very nature the most rigorous and fully conscious intellectual control. The critic is continually in the debt of the theorist, whether he is aware of this or not; if he is not conscious of the theoretical influences and assumptions underlying his work, then he is at their mercy. He should be prepared to open himself to and learn from any theories currently available, but in the spirit of Renoir's remarks about "general ideas" that stand as epigraph to this book: they probably all contain some measure of validity, the validity depending on the particular application. The reader is forewarned, then, that this statement of position will not attempt to masquerade as a theory of film; it will merely be an attempt to rationalize some of the impulses and assumptions behind my work.

I start from my own experience of art, and my sense of its importance in my own life. "Only culture can purify," Pasolini said of the bourgeoisie. It was through the arts, and through education—that education of the emotions and the intellect together, of the whole individual character, that only the arts can offer—that I discovered worlds outside the narrowly circumscribed, unaware world of my immediate environment. Through the arts, I made contact with minds and sensibilities finer than my own; with experiences far beyond my own experience; with apprehensions of existence determined by cultural circumstances very different from those within which I lived. If one could cleanse the word "education" of its association with schoolrooms, enforced learning, pedantry and boredom, and associate it with sensations of delight and discovery by no means incompatible with a frequent sense of profound disturbance and challenge, then I would describe my view of the arts as above all educational. The word, even thus purified, is ultimately misleading in that it evokes a predominantly conscious and intellectual mode of apprehension; but it is difficult to find a substitute.

I am repeatedly confronted with varyingly absurd parodies of my position, in which the terms "Leavisite," "puritanical" and "moralistic" recur rather monotonously. An extended example (not entirely hostile) will be found in an article on Raymond Durgnat by Jonathan Rosenbaum, published in *Film Comment* (May–June 1973), in which Rosenbaum likens me to a Big Game Hunter "basically out for trophies to possess, stuff and hang on [my] walls." A friend (who ought, I think, to have known better—he professes to have read me thoroughly) asked, "Do you believe that works of art teach you how to live?" Like most parodies, this bears a recognizable relation to what I actually *do* believe; in fact, it performs neatly enough parody's usual function of reducing an idea to a formulation so crude that it appears silly. No, I don't believe I learn "how to live" by looking at the "Virgin of the Rocks," reading Donne's Elegies or listening to *Das Lied von der Erde:* if I did, I would exist in a state of acute and chronic confusion. On the other hand, I have been deeply affected by all of these, and presume them to have had some oblique, scarcely definable but potent influence on the development of my sensibility, on my way of thinking, feeling, perceiving, reacting; they have certainly extended and deepened my sense of the possibilities of human experience. Many works I greatly admire (*King Lear,* Schubert's *Winterreise,* Blake's *Songs of Experience,* Bergman's *Persona*), far from "teaching me how to live"—with the overtones of moral edification the phrase suggests—have the primary effect of undermining any certainties I possess. And works that try to "teach me how to live," in some explicit, categorical manner (*Paradise Lost,* for example, or the plays of Claudel, or *Triumph of the Will,* or *Vent d'Est*), I tend to distrust, seeking ways to distance myself from their insistent persuasions.

The sort of "education" I have in mind involves, as an ideal, a total openness to the total experience the work offers: an ideal certainly unattainable, but the function of an ideal is to provide a means of measuring degrees of success and failure. One reason for the unattainability takes us right to the heart of the critical dilemma: the intense personal involvement in the work which is inseparable from any genuine response will inevitably make our "reading" to some degree biased and partial. I see no way of eliminating this problem from criticism, though the chief function for the critic of the tools provided by the theorists is to discipline and counterbalance this personal/subjective element: any theory of art, any scholarship, any historical or cultural research, any analytical procedure, that can help us see the work as it is and ensure that we are responding to something that is there and not something we have invented, is obviously to be welcomed.

From my view of the *usefulness* (and usability) of art, as affecting, influencing, developing, deepening, enriching, refining the human sensibility, I draw three conclusions about criticism. One: though criticism must necessarily express itself as intellectual formulation, and must strive always towards objectivity, valid criticism must never lose touch with the critic's whole response, in which instinctual and emotional elements play at least as important a role as intellectual. Two: a personal element will always have a determining effect in critical discourse; the suppression of such an element is neither possible nor desirable, and its *apparent* absence should always be regarded with distrust. Three: the true end of criticism is evaluation, the evaluation of the total experience the work is felt by the critic to offer; experience derived, that is, from what the work is rather than from what it *says*, structure, style, method all playing their roles. Such evaluation, because of the personal (hence ideological) bias involved, must always be tentative, relative and provisional.

All criticism is situated between two poles: at one extreme, total subjectivity, which can say little beyond "I like this because I like it"; at the other, the notion of a completely depersonalized, "scientific" objectivity. The former can give rise only to inarticulate exclamations of pleasure or pain; the latter tends to reduce the arts to a heap of data to be sifted and computerized, and can only result in the dehumanization of criticism, of art, and ultimately of life. The critic, it seems to me, needs to keep himself constantly aware of the two poles; valid criticism develops out of the tension between them. I would offer as exemplary one of my favourite works of film criticism in English, Jim Kitses's *Horizons West*. The book grew out of the extremely fertile soil of the old British Film Institute Education Department, at a time when Kitses, Alan Lovell and Peter Wollen were all working in it and Paddy Whannel and Peter Harcourt were still present as influences; its coherence is partly determined by the particular disciplines one associates with that group, and with what one might loosely term "British structuralism." Yet Kitses's individual voice is audible throughout, and every judgement has the force of personal conviction, the urgency of a human being intensely involved with his material. It is a work both passionate and disciplined; to argue with it—and there seems to me quite a lot to argue with—is to engage with another mind, another psyche, in a fully human way.

This is perhaps the place to raise the vexed issue of the role of moral values in criticism. My acceptance of the Renoir quotation will have suggested, among other things, that I find Keats's concept of "negative capability"—which implies the rejection of specific commitments in favour of a general openness to experience—however arguable its advantages to the artist, indispensable to the critic. At the same time it is obvious enough that, with evaluation as the professed aim of criticism, this "negative capability" must be in some ways illusory. Even if one rejects all organized systems of dogma (Catholicism, Marxism, etc.) as too restrictive for the critic, the very act of judging implies criteria; there is the danger that the critic will place himself, as our Marxist friends would have it, at the mercy of the prevailing ideology. The safeguard seems to me to be not a specific commitment but a striving for awareness: one is freed from the tyranny of an ideology not by rejecting but by understanding it.

I believe I am widely regarded as some kind of a moralist, and I suppose I must, somewhat warily, accept the description: to refuse it would be inconsistent with my view of art and criticism, for if the ideal criticism arises out of a total involvement of the critic in the total experience of the work—the functioning of the whole human being in response to the work's total articulation—then there is clearly no way in which the critic's moral sense, and his sense of the moral values embodied in the work, can be left aside. Again, however, I find myself frequently confronted with parody—the notion that I judge all films rigidly from a fixed set of moral values. Leaving aside the fact that I live my life in a chronic state of uncertainty on most issues, I might ask just what these values are supposed to be. An allegedly rigid set of values that enables me to accept and admire both Pope and Keats, Mahler and Stravinsky, Bergman and Hawks, *The World of Apu* and *Tout Va Bien,* would seem rather difficult to define with any precision.

Certain things *can* be said positively. Like Renoir, I believe in certain absolute human qualities—"generosity, for instance";

while not uncritical of Renoir's films I would like to associate myself with the spirit of tolerance they embody, with their sense that the only enemy is anything that smacks of totalitarianism. I believe in the value of personal affection, and that people should try to understand one another. I set a high value on creativity, which for me means simply being as fully as possible *alive:* it is consequently the most fundamental of all moral qualities, or the quality from which all morality grows and to which all moral questions must be referred. This aliveness finds concrete embodiment in art, and its expression is art's ultimate purpose and justification, underlying all the many uses to which art over the centuries has been put, all the functions it has fulfilled, from the cave paintings to *Tout Va Bien;* but it is by no means restricted to art. It can be manifested in the most humdrum daily activities when we feel imaginatively, emotionally or spontaneously caught up in them, so that performing them (however laborious, and whatever degree of conscious care and attention the execution entails) becomes a source of satisfaction. Creativity is also closely associated, in some of its aspects, with the sense of communication, one's living relationship with other people. It is obviously deeply rooted in sexuality, which is why all art—indeed, all meaningful activity—is capable of sexual interpretation.

Beyond this, I believe in openness to new experiences and new ideas, balanced by an enquiring, non-destructive scepticism. I value intelligence above stupidity (other things being equal: there are of course many stupid people who are much nicer and much better company than many intelligent ones), sensitivity above insentience, tenderness above brutalism, compassion above cruelty and vindictiveness; though it is not impossible to imagine circumstances in which sensitivity, tenderness and compassion might be validly regarded as liabilities rather than assets. If all this amounts to a "fixed set of values," then I must plead guilty; I am aware that it gives my criticism a certain emphasis. I value the convincing expression of such values in art, though without regarding this as either prescriptive or exclusive, as the sole, or even as the chief, purpose of art. This is, however, what is meant by refusing to separate art from morality: a separation that could only result in a repression of natural response and the impoverishment of critical discourse.

I can exemplify the kind of judgements to which such a position leads by brief reference to two films that were much compared on their initial release: *Straw Dogs* and *A Clockwork Orange*. I shall save myself the detailed stylistic analysis that alone can validate a critical judgement by referring the reader to Charles Barr's brilliant article on the films in the issue of *Screen* for Summer 1972. I would say of *A Clockwork Orange* that a film made exclusively out of hatred and contempt can only be hateful and contemptible: that is a moral judgement, but it is inseparable from the aesthetic one, that the much-praised "visual brilliance" of Kubrick's film is in reality a matter of a self-conscious and crudely self-assertive deployment of movie technology, whose function is to assert the director's superiority to the despised and detested humanity before the camera and (by implication) before the screen. Peckinpah, on the other hand, though his films are frequently vitiated by that perverse attachment to brutalism that makes the presentation of Rudy Butler in *The Getaway* (for example) so disturbingly equivocal, is saved by the fact that his films neither express nor induce a complacent superiority to his characters.

The point at issue here is not whether this particular judgement is valid, but whether this *kind* of judgement is relevant. Granted my view of the function of art, the relevance appears unchallengeable. The suggestion is not that the critic should set himself up as a moralist delivering dicta on How To Live *de haut en bas,* but that he is a human being engaged in a fully human activity, inviting the disagreement and debate that might lead to a modification of his viewpoint. The question of values—eternal in its essence, continually shifting and changing in its emphases and particular application—is necessarily as central to criticism as it is to art, though in criticism as in art it can often remain implicit.

With the charge that I apply to art a fixed set of moral values often goes the rider that these are underwritten by a fixed set of aesthetic ones. The idea has been succinctly and conveniently formulated, in a passage not directed explicitly at me, but in which I believe I am correct in feeling myself included: "Certain criteria, such as coherence, organic wholeness, complexity, subtlety, truth to life, are being put forward as self-evident requirements for a successful work of art; whereas such criteria are, I think, expressions of a certain ideology."[1] One can dismiss the last clause (which it appears nowadays *de rigueur* to trot out somewhere in every piece of critical writing) as indeed self-evident: is it possible to imagine *any* discourse that is not the expression of one ideology or another? That apart, I would want to say, firstly, that in my view *all* criteria are relative and provisional. The greatest of all critical (and perhaps human) virtues is flexibility; a criterion, like a "general idea," is given validity by the particular application. I might, for example, as a means of expressing my contempt for the novels and opinions of Kingsley Amis, wish to invoke positive criteria such as "adult" and "responsible," but this would not, for me, automatically disqualify all works to which such epithets could not be applied. (On the other hand, I cannot imagine myself or anyone else *praising* a work for being infantile and irresponsible.)

With that proviso, I would not be ashamed to be associated with most of the criteria under attack. "True to life" is a concept

---

1. Since writing this I have discovered that the passage quoted was excised from the article in question prior to publication. I take this as an expression of the author's own doubts about its validity. I use it here, however, not to "get at" anyone individually, but for its representativeness, which will, I think, be conceded by anyone familiar with contemporary film criticism.

I have difficulty with—I don't really know what is meant by it and suspect the writer didn't either. In its most literal sense, that of the supposedly faithful "naturalistic" reproduction of behaviour, it has never been used as a criterion by me or, I think, by any of the critics connected with *Movie:* we all know that such true-to-lifeness is illusory anyway, and have never shown much interest in those films that have been supposed, at one time or another, to manifest it (*Bicycle Thieves, Shadows, Room at the Top*). But, if one doesn't take it literally, the phrase can mean anything: *Snow White and the Seven Dwarfs* might be considered true to life because it deals with archetypal relationships; a Norman McLaren abstract cartoon might be considered true to life because its lines, patterns and movements correspond to those observable in natural or scientific phenomena. The writer's application of the term to "works of art" in general is completely baffling. Among the works of art produced during the present century that I find supremely successful are the Schönberg string quartets, Stravinsky's major ballets from *Les Noces* to *Agon,* and the analytical cubist portraits of Picasso; I would be hard put to it to define their success by applying the criterion of "truth to life." I suspect that the writer really means that such a criterion has been applied to traditionalist fiction and to the narrative film—which at least makes some sense, but completely undercuts the suggestion of the criterion's absoluteness. Even within this limited field, one has to substitute some such phrase as "narrative plausibility"—whereupon one will swiftly recognize that the substitute isn't really synonymous. Our sense of plausibility in a movie is determined far more by established conventions than by direct reference to "life." A film both draws on the conventions available—the common coinage of the tradition within which it operates—and establishes within itself how it is to be read; it sets up certain expectations which (in a narrative film) are closely bound up with plausibility—expectations which the artist is then at liberty to fulfill or surprise us by undercutting, the latter alternative being effective only within the limits determined by the individual case, the style, tone, method of the work in question. If Bergman had elected to end *The Silence* with Ester and Anna marrying their respective waiters and, as they walked together up the aisle, bursting into a refrain of "We're just two little girls from Little Rock"—and if this were presented "straight" as a successful resolution of their problems, without irony and without any shift to a different narrative mode—we might, I think, wish to protest that Bergman had violated the "reality" created by the rest of the film. On the other hand, the incident (judged by itself) would be scarcely more remote from most people's experience of the "sort of things that happen" than many events in the film: how many of us have been confronted by a troupe of intoxicated transvestite dwarfs during a nervous breakdown/consumptive collapse in a hotel corridor in the middle of the night?

"Truth to life" apart, one can suggest the relative validity of these alleged criteria by juxtaposing them with their opposites. The opposite of "complex" is not "simple" but "simple-minded" (complexity and simplicity are far from incompatible: think of Mozart, or of innumerable folk-songs and ballads, or even of Beatrix Potter: *Tom Kitten* and *The Tale of Mrs. Tittlemouse*, easily accessible to five-year-olds, exhibit marked complexity of attitude). The opposite of "subtle" is "crude" or "obvious." Certain kinds of crudeness (where "crude" becomes almost a synonym for "forceful") are far from disqualifying: I think of the westerns of Anthony Mann, where crudeness co-exists with considerable complexity. But on the whole, while no one will be surprised to find works praised for complexity and subtlety, I think most would be surprised to find them praised for being simple-minded and obvious.

The real crux appears to be "coherence," by which I understand the internal relations that give a work its structure. (The adjective "organic" I have used to convey a particularly intensive coherence, when the various aspects of a work seem scarcely separable from each other.) All art must strive towards coherence, which is simply another term for significant articulation. There are a number of issues here. The critic will, I suppose, applaud the achievement of coherence in direct ratio to his sense of the work's complexity of inner conflicts and stresses; he will not be particularly impressed by the coherence of "Mary Had a Little Lamb," but may be by the coherence of Mahler's ninth symphony. The notion of coherence needs to be carefully dissociated from any nonsense about artistic "inevitability"—the mystical notion that every detail in a given work had to be that and no other. The artist is at all times confronted with choices, within definable limits: some alternatives may be demonstrably better than others (as we can see, for example, by following the evolution of Yeats's *Sailing to Byzantium* through all its rough drafts), but there is no one unarguably right and only solution: Beethoven composed two very different finales for his B flat major quartet and four overtures for *Fidelio;* the endings of Sjöström's *The Wind* and Murnau's *Sunrise* are different from those originally envisaged, but both seem perfectly satisfying.

The notion of coherence is only meaningful in conjunction with concepts like "complexity," "density," "inner tensions"; it can never be an absolute criterion. I can illustrate this sufficiently by reference to two works—one novel, one film—that I value very highly despite the fact that they fail to achieve complete coherence. Lawrence's *The Rainbow* is, for me, certainly among the half-dozen greatest novels in the English language; yet the very ambitiousness of the undertaking—the intensive exploration of areas of experience previously untouched in literature—entails problems of articulacy and organization that Lawrence doesn't always solve. I am thinking particularly of the development of the Will/Anna relationship in chapters six and seven. The extremely long chapter six ("Anna Victrix"), with its passages of opaque and repetitious writing where one feels

Lawrence struggling to express emotional states that defy verbalization, is the point where uncommitted readers frequently give up in exasperation. The following chapter ("The Cathedral") is among the book's finest passages, but it poses a curious structural problem. It describes an incident in the lives of Will and Anna which Lawrence clearly means us to see as crucial to their subsequent relationship; chronologically, it belongs somewhere in the "Anna Victrix" chapter (it occurs during Anna's pregnancy), but it is impossible to say confidently *where:* the developments somewhat obscurely described in chapter six nowhere take into account an incident whose effect is registered as decisive. My own theory is that the "Cathedral" scene once (the book is said to have undergone seven re-writings) formed part of chapter six but assumed such importance that Lawrence detached it, developing it into a separate chapter but failing to take stock of the problem of organization this entailed.

The partial incoherence of Murnau's *Sunrise* is more complicated, as it appears to derive from more than one source. The inclusion of some of the comic business of the middle section—the runaway pig, the drunken waiter, the slipping dress-strap—may have been "encouraged" by the studio to lighten the film for American audiences. The narrative accommodates these incidents easily enough, and they are tolerably amusing, but their thematic relevance is vague and tenuous, and the texture of the film consequently thins, the sense of a rich and significant interrelatedness diminishes. The film's other main problem is related to this, but seems also rooted in the complexities of Murnau's personal psychology. It is difficult to see any significant relationship between the "Woman of the City" and the city itself, as presented later in the film; the figure developed through Murnau's imagery seems more closely related to Nosferatu, a Woman of the Night or a Woman of the Marshes, a scarcely explicable force, more psychic emanation than character.

I don't see how incoherence can possibly ever be regarded as an asset; it follows, therefore, that I accept the notion of coherence as a valid criterion. What I would stress is its relativity: I value *The Rainbow* and *Sunrise* above thousands of perfectly coherent works of less density and power. But the work of any major artist bears testimony to the thesis that art strives towards coherence. Consider, among many possible examples, the striking case of Godard. *Pierrot le Fou,* the culmination of his early phase, is a film that teeters on the brink of chaos, its compositional principles being barely adequate in strength or definition to hold together the complex impulses at work. Since then, Godard's whole career, aesthetically considered, can be seen as a single-minded search for the unifying principle he has found in revolutionary politics: a quest leading to the achievement of perfectly coherent works like *La Chinoise, Vent d'Est* and *Tout Va Bien,* of which every aspect and every detail can be clearly accounted for in relation to their central concerns. This achievement of coherence, however, does not necessarily make these films superior to *Pierrot,* which many will continue to regard as Godard's richest film. Clearly, the unity of *Vent d'Est* is bought with the elimination of many of the impulses that animated *Pierrot.*

I can define my own critical position more precisely by juxtaposing it with that of a critic whose work I greatly admire and have benefited from, and with whom my name is occasionally linked through our common association with *Movie:* Victor Perkins, whose *Film as Film* (Penguin Books, 1970) seems to me among the most valuable books on the cinema so far written. Though I sometimes disagree with him over details of evaluation, I find Perkins's argument—beautifully developed with meticulous logic—virtually impregnable. It is only when I stand back from it and contemplate the judgements (explicit and implicit) that have resulted from the application of Perkins's criteria of excellence that I experience dissatisfaction. If I then return to the text, I find it difficult to pinpoint the sources of this dissatisfaction convincingly: every objection I want to raise is countered somewhere in the book, or covered by the disclaimer to the effect that the theory offered is not meant to be all-embracing. This is, of course, fair enough: it is characteristic of Perkins's "classical" modesty that he should set himself limited objectives, the modesty itself being a quality that commands respect. (It is also, I think, a quality to which as a critic he is attracted, hence intricately bound up with his criteria of excellence.)

As I cannot fault Perkins's argument, yet remain dissatisfied, I am forced to talk more vaguely about "tendencies" in order to define my own divergence from him. I am also forced to conclude that a theory, however objective and rational in appearance and presentation, is ultimately determined by the temperament of the theorist. The terms "Classical" and "Romantic" have a limited usefulness in critical discourse. To treat them as mutually exclusive categories has always proved fruitless and misleading, but (beyond their obvious local application to specific periods) they can be more profitably used to describe dominant tendencies and to define possible poles. The Classical tendency is towards order, discipline, formal play, dependence on conventions and tradition, objectivity; the Romantic tendency is towards self-expression, freedom, originality, iconoclasm, subjectivity. In a "pure" form, either becomes valueless. The polar extreme of Classicism can perhaps be typified by those endless jottings of conscientious heroic couplets that became so easy in the eighteenth century. The Romantic pole can be represented by automatic writing and the "doin' my own thing" school of Underground cinema in which spontaneous self-expression becomes an absolute end, giving rise to work that might conceivably be of interest to the psychoanalyst but is quite outside the interest or jurisdiction of any responsible critic. It is obvious that the greatest art transcends either category: arguments as to whether Shakespeare and Donne are to be considered "Romantic" or "Classical" are the last word in academic futility. Beside André Gide's aphorism that "Classicism is beautiful by virtue of its subjugated Romanticism," one needs to set the corollary that Romanticism is meaningful in so far as it submits to "Classical" disciplines: The Prelude, the "Nightingale" Ode, the "Songs of Experience," are scarcely specimens of untrammeled self-expression.

Within the context I have suggested it seems appropriate to describe Perkins as a Classicist: a description confirmed by his gravitation to the classical Hollywood cinema. The area within which his theory *does* claim validity is the fictional narrative film; he *could*—he has said so himself—have drawn his examples from Renoir and Mizoguchi. But he doesn't, he draws them from Preminger, Hitchcock, Nicholas Ray, Richard Brooks. I make the point here, not to deduce anything from it at this stage, but in order to take it up again later. For the moment, I shall content myself with expressing the personal conviction that the best films of Renoir and Mizoguchi are finer than almost all the works from which Perkins draws his examples, adding that he would very likely agree with me and say, "But that is not the point."

I find the precise evaluative status of many of Perkins's examples rather difficult to determine. He uses very specific, local comparisons (particular sequences, isolated effects) in order to establish critical preferences which tend in the mind of the reader (whether this was intended or not—I find the effect somewhat equivocal) to spill over into whole films. A passage on pages 84–86, in which a colour effect from *The Red Desert* is sandwiched between contrasting effects from *Bigger Than Life* and *Elmer Gantry* greatly to Antonioni's disadvantage, is worth examining in some detail as fairly representative of the book's intermittent weaknesses. Various problems coincide here. Firstly, there is the sense that the responses Perkins formulates are much more subjective, less textually demonstrable, than he realizes; secondly, there is the possible spilling over I referred to above, the uncertainty as to whether we are being invited simply to prefer effect A to effect B (admittedly, all that Perkins can actually be pinned down on), or whether the effects are to be understood as representative, so that we are really being invited to prefer *Bigger Than Life* to *The Red Desert* and Nicholas Ray to Antonioni; thirdly, an uneasy sense that the comparison offered is in itself unjust and unrealistic, that lurking behind the specific differences described there are differences between the *kinds* of art involved so basic as to make Perkins's deductions untenable.

> As [the protagonist of *Bigger Than Life*] walks away from the school building with its background of respectable greys and browns, the image dissolves into a general view of the cab-park photographed so that the screen is virtually covered with the garish yellow of the taxi-ranks. The transition thus handled gains an emotional colouring which conveys not only the physical strain under which the man lives, but also his *déclassé* feeling of shame in his secondary occupation. (pp. 84–85)

This complex significance seems to depend almost exclusively on our responding to the yellow cabs as "garish": substitute "bright and cheerful" and the significance vanishes, the transition then conveying (perhaps) a sense of release that is soon to be ironically contradicted, but no "physical strain," let alone a "*déclassé* feeling of shame."

I have a similar problem with the remarks on *The Red Desert*:

> Towards the end of the film [Giuliana] is made love to while on the verge of complete mental collapse.

And from shot to shot the bedpost becomes an ever more threateningly glaring red. We observe that colour is being used to create an effect. Intellectually we can identify the effect required. But of the effect itself we feel no symptom. We are so busy *noticing* that we respond rather to our awareness of the device than to the state of mind it sets out to evoke. (p. 85)

I had better admit, somewhat shamefacedly, that during three viewings of the film I have never become aware of the effect Perkins describes. This may be a reflection on my capacity for observation; I prefer to believe that it is due rather to the fact that the effect works for me precisely in the way Perkins says it does not, and that he is "so busy *noticing*" because he is already quite out of temper with the film. Certainly, I have always found the scene in question emotionally very powerful and disturbing.

But I think Perkins's conclusion that the *Bigger Than Life* effect is acceptable because achieved without destroying credibility, while *The Red Desert* effect represents an unwarranted intrusion of the director, can be challenged on securer grounds than differences of subjective reaction. All intelligible art (as Hans Keller has suggested in his brilliant musical analyses) depends on the creative use of conventions, on the tension between (in Keller's terminology) "background" (the conventional formulae with which the audience can be presumed to be familiar) and "foreground" (what the individual artist actually does, which is likely to involve the cheating of the expectations set up, either by contradicting or surpassing them). The classical Hollywood cinema, with its strong generic structures and accepted stylistic procedures, can be very fruitfully analysed along these lines. Artists outside such traditional disciplines, however, may find the freedom to make bolder jumps, to which audiences may take longer to adapt. Antonioni's procedures in *The Red Desert* can be examined in this light. The meaning and total effect of the film are very closely tied to the subjective experiences of its central character, Giuliana (Monica Vitti). The cinema has developed its own conventions for expressing a subjective viewpoint, the commonest of which is to follow a close-up of the character's face with a shot of what he/she is supposed to be seeing; the convention permits any distortion in the latter image, whose function is the expression of a state of mind—a blurring of the image to suggest the idea of fainting is an obvious example. In *Marnie,* Hitchcock (not without precedents, including moments in his own work) extends the possibilities of this convention by means of compression: when Marnie sees the colour red, Hitchcock gives us a close-up of her face and suffuses the image with red simultaneously: we understand without difficulty that the red effect is how Marnie herself is supposed to be seeing the world at that moment. In *The Red Desert* Antonioni (with the far-from-unmixed advantages of the "art-house" director) goes further in this compression. He dispenses altogether with the business of alerting us to the subjective nature of the image by means of "conventional" signs (close-ups, shots from the character's viewpoint), and simply incorporates the heroine's subjective view in the image, often showing her in medium- or long-shot at the same time: hence the grey fruit and vegetables on the street-stall, the white rubber-plants in the hotel lobby, the reddening bed-posts.

The circumstances that encourage such formal boldness simultaneously encourage the personal expression and assertion that the classical Hollywood cinema tended to suppress. It would be simplistic to characterize the European "art" cinema as Romantic, but in certain respects it is in the Romantic tradition. It was in the Romantic period that the poet's consciousness became the explicit centre of the poem. One of the crucial differences between the classical Hollywood cinema and the European "art" cinema lies in the different status of the director, hence in the different expectations brought to the films by spectators. Audiences were expected to go to *The Red Desert* because it was an Antonioni film; they were not expected to go to *Elmer Gantry* because it was directed by Richard Brooks. My sense that one cannot with justice compare the colour effects in these films as Perkins does is closely connected with this difference: underlying it is a totally different concept of art. One might point out (Perkins's "criteria of excellence" being in question) that the examples he gives from Ray and Brooks are virtually, for practical purposes, interchangeable: there seems no particular reason why the transition from grey buildings to yellow taxi-cabs should be associated with Nicholas Ray except that he happened to think of it; and the use of colour in *Elmer Gantry* that Perkins so sensitively analyses, while certainly an example of directorial skill, tells us nothing very personal about Richard Brooks. On the other hand, throughout *The Red Desert* we are very much aware of Antonioni: it is almost as if *his* consciousness rather than Giuliana's were the centre of the film (and the two, though one senses a relationship, are obviously not to be identified). The grey potatoes, the white rubber-plants, the red bed-posts, while perfectly "plausible" in relation to the neurotic consciousness of Giuliana, are also images in a visual poem by Antonioni, a very conscious artist who expects his audience to be aware of him and builds on that expectation.

This is not an attempt to reverse Perkins's (implicit?) judgement. I do not wish to argue that *The Red Desert* (a work for which my enthusiasm is not exactly unqualified) is a finer work than *Elmer Gantry,* let alone *Bigger Than Life;* nor to suggest that Brooks and Ray lack personal styles. My purpose is not to attack Perkins's position but to complement it. Beside (not against) the Classical values of skill, intelligence, discipline, which get such thorough (if largely implicit) endorsement in his book, I would want to set the Romantic values of passion, intensity, personal expression. It seems further relevant to note here areas of cinema to which I feel generally more sympathetic than Perkins appears to be. (I don't want to suggest that he, as a theorist, rejects these areas; simply that by temperament and inclination he does not appear spontaneously drawn to them.) One of these areas is, I have already intimated, the European "art-house" movie. The degree of admiration I feel for Bergman, Antonioni, Fellini, Godard and Chabrol varies greatly from director to director, but I am reasonably confident that in each case it is higher than Perkins's. The other area is that of the American cinema of the last decade, since the general collapse of the studio/genre system. There is of course a connection: the American cinema has of late moved much closer to the European model, with far more emphasis on the director-as-author, a growing tendency to encourage overt personal expression. I value *Bonnie and Clyde* and *Alice's Restaurant, The Ballad of Cable Hogue* and *Junior Bonner, McCabe and Mrs. Miller* and *The Long Goodbye, Klute* and *American Graffiti,* as highly as I value the films Perkins treats as exemplary. His valuation of them is not on record; there is no reason to assume hostility or indifference. They embody, however—while remaining in many respects strongly traditional, intelligible in relation to the Hollywood cinema of the past—artistic impulses which get little emphasis in *Film as Film.*

I choose two examples—one European, one recent American—with which to clarify the difference of position I am trying to define. In both cases, the effect achieved seems to me to lie just outside the limits of acceptability Perkins's book (with its insistence on the subjugation of the director's personal expression to the action) so skillfully and persuasively defines. There is a scene fairly early in Bergman's *Shame* where husband and wife, formerly violinists in the Stockholm Philharmonic, have dinner in the open air and (in the shadow of war) talk about their decision to revive their music-making (and, by implication, their relationship). The substance of the scene is given in a single, mostly static, take, the camera fixed on Liv Ullmann's face. After some minutes without a cut or a camera movement, the husband (Max von Sydow) speaks of his ability to change himself, saying, "I'm not a determinist." On the word "determinist" the camera suddenly tracks in to frame Liv Ullmann more tightly as an expression of unease appears on her face—she does not understand the word but is troubled by it. In the context of the film, it is impossible not to read this camera movement as a directorial nudge, an intrusion of the artist into the action: Bergman is alerting us to a central concern of the film. The track-in does other things too, which one may feel are at least equally important and which are anyway not really separable from this: it shows us Liv Ullmann's expression more clearly, underlining not merely the "determinist" theme but her own disturbance; and, the secure mood of the dinner having been established by the static camera, the sudden, unexpected movement works subjectively, communicating her unease to the audience by direct means. It seems to me a marvelously expressive moment; I feel no resentment at being made aware of Bergman's presence at that point. One could put it even more positively: our consciousness during the film of a directorial presence is an important factor in distancing us from an action we need above all to view with critical detachment if we are not merely to succumb to the overwhelming despair which it is *part* of the film's impulse to communicate.

My second example is from *The Long Goodbye*. The zoom lens has been central to the development of the American cinema since the early sixties; Altman is one of the few directors to use it for its expressive possibilities, not just for convenience. In one scene Philip Marlowe (Elliott Gould) and Eileen Wade (Nina van Pallandt) talk at night before a window overlooking the Pacific coastline. When the shot begins, they are in sharp focus and fill most of the screen; the space between them is a blur, but we are vaguely aware of the beach and the waves, and perhaps of a sense of a small distant movement so dim and indecipherable that we may not register it as a significant component of the image. As the dialogue continues, the focus begins to change; the foreground figures blur—as the zoom-in progresses, they will disappear from the frame altogether, though their voices continue—and, simultaneously, the indistinct movement takes shape and meaning: it is Eileen's husband, the man Marlowe was hired to save, walking out into the sea to drown himself. There is no way of tying this effect to the consciousness of either of the characters on whom the shot originally focused our attention: indeed, its whole point is that they are entirely unaware of the event taking place outside, and remain so until it is too late to intervene effectively.

We cannot but be aware here of an artist directing our attention. I am not entirely confident that such an effect lies outside the range of acceptance Perkins offers: it is distinguishable from the effects Hitchcock achieves in *Rope* only in the degree of its obtrusiveness. It might be argued, however, that the zoom lens—in the hands of a director prepared creatively to exploit its properties rather than try to conceal them—is itself an anti-Perkins device: the spatial distortions inseparable from its use inevitably attract attention to the technique much more than a "classical" camera movement. Underlying this difference in effect is the changing relationship between the director and his audience.

I want to return here to the point I threw out earlier, that Perkins could have drawn his examples from Renoir and Mizoguchi but did not. My intention was certainly not to suggest that these are in any sense to be considered "Romantic" artists in contrast to the "Classical" cinema of Hollywood. But they were both able to evolve a personal style so complete and expressive that it seems in itself to embody a view of existence. To some extent the same might be said of Hitchcock, Hawks, Ray. But try to define the world-view of each of these directors without reference to a single actual film, drawing exclusively on the habitual stylistic procedures of framing, composition, camera-placement and movement: you will find yourself nearer satisfaction with Mizoguchi and Renoir than with the Hollywood figures. The case of Hitchcock (the Hollywood director with the most pronounced and instantly identifiable personal style) is clouded by one's sense that his style is determined as much by his preoccupation with manipulating audiences as by a definable "view of life" (though in the last resort the two cannot be separated); with most Hollywood directors, the urge to move into *thematic* analysis would be felt quite early on.

Personal style is scarcely a phenomenon to which Perkins is insensitive. Again, our difference is one of emphasis rather than a disagreement. I do not regard (I had better hasten to say) the achievement of a fully evolved personal style as in itself a criterion of greatness, nor even as an indispensable prerequisite, but the essays on individual films and directors in this book will testify, I think, to the importance I attach to it: an importance that would frequently give it precedence over the virtues of "credibility" and skill that get so much emphasis in *Film as Film*. I shall illustrate this briefly here by means of a comparison which may appear at first sight more unjust and arbitrary than Perkins's *Red Desert/Elmer Gantry* opposition; but my purpose is not quite the same as his. McCarey's *Make Way for Tomorrow* and Ozu's *Tokyo Story* are two films about the desolateness of old age; their backgrounds (Hollywood, 1937; Japan, 1953) are of course completely different. I greatly admire both films: in some ways, McCarey's is the more remarkable achievement, given the film's context and the difficulty he had in setting it up. Yet I would want to establish a judgement that Ozu's is the greater work. Perkins would probably agree, and might be able to argue this preference within the terms his book lays down. I would myself want to argue it in terms that seem to me to lie outside the scope of *Film as Film:* I would argue that, while

McCarey's film moves me much more immediately and gains in stature on every viewing, Ozu's style gives *Tokyo Story* a dimension that *Make Way for Tomorrow* lacks. I would be hard put to it to describe the visual style of McCarey's film in terms other than general ("classical Hollywood") or negative (words like "reticence," "taste," "discretion" come to mind); his presentation of the action is (arguably at least) faultless, he has clearly achieved an extraordinarily sensitive *rapport* with his actors, and, despite the director's "invisibility," his personal involvement is not in question. The extra dimension of *Tokyo Story* is not easy to define briefly, but it seems to me that Ozu's style (the characteristics of which I shall not detail here) places the action in a perspective for which McCarey has no equivalent. (Obviously, the difference I am indicating is not only "personal," and to account for it satisfactorily one would have to examine the cultural backgrounds and specific "conditions of production" of the two films; but I am not concerned here to explain the difference.) It is not enough to say that Ozu's style establishes a contemplative distance; it also makes possible (through an action as meticulously realized as McCarey's) a force of generalization or of generalizing implication, a carefully pondered view of human existence. Its presence implies a higher level of consciousness, leaving the artist less at the mercy of the prevailing ideology; in terms of audience response, though neither film offers an alternative to the society presented, Ozu's film instills, even as it expresses, a higher awareness of the issues. If I were challenged to produce a single word to describe the extra dimension, the word would be "metaphysical."

The reader will not, I hope, be able to take from the foregoing any sense that my position can be summed up in a word or a phrase. Lawrence's "Never trust the artist—trust the tale" can perhaps be applied to the critic as well: I would like to be judged by what I do, not by what I say I do. If there is a sense in which I hunt "Big Game," this is not for trophies to stuff and hang on my walls: the analogy hideously brutalizes the relationship I seek with works of art. My interests in the cinema are wide and various (it is not in the expectation of masterpieces that I have sat through several dozen British horror movies during the past few years), but my central emphasis on evaluation inevitably leads me to those works that seem to me to offer the richest experiences. If I insist that a work of art affects and influences the individual sensibility, this commits me neither to a demand for moral lessons nor to a rejection of everything that is not conventionally "wholesome" (I tend to distrust both). If I admire Dr. Leavis, this doesn't make me a "Leavisite" (the term "Leavisian" is marginally more acceptable, implying the acknowledgment of an influence rather than blind discipleship). If I believe in art as, in a deep and complex way, educational, this does not mean that I go to a movie in order to "learn how to live" (picking up a few useful tips from Ozu, perhaps, and one or two from Bertolucci). I. A. Richards saw literature as our "storehouse of recorded values." I see the arts as our storehouse of recorded experience—experience as rich and diverse as the potentialities of life itself, opening new worlds or refining and deepening our perception of our own. A Marxist acquaintance characterized me as an "unreconstructed humanist"; if I have to have a label, it is as good a one as any.

2

In Defence of Art:
On Current Tendencies in Film Criticism

> And what rough beast, its hour come round at last,
> Slouches towards Bethlehem to be born?
>> W. B. YEATS, *The Second Coming*

I have never felt myself a part of any critical establishment, sub-establishment or anti-establishment; I have tried to be myself, and to go my own way. Yet I always seemed to get on easily enough with my fellows in different camps—despite my intermittent tendency to insult some of them in print. Then I went to Canada for three years, and when I came back, everything had subtly changed, to an extent that I have only gradually begun to measure. Everyone had read books I had never heard of, in disciplines I scarcely knew existed; everyone was talking about semiology, and about "bourgeois ideology"; everyone gradually became revealed as (more or less) a Marxist. I have never felt exactly taken to the heart (or hearts—it has undergone several transplants) of the English critical fraternity, but I have never felt so little welcome, so alien and alienated, or so "*vieux jeu,*" as I have since my return. If I sound at times like Kevin McCarthy in the later stages of *Invasion of the Body Snatchers,* the reader's forgiveness is asked in advance: it does seem to me sometimes as if, every time I turn around, another of my acquaintances has become a "pod."

"Everyone" is of course a somewhat absurd exaggeration: the Marxist-semiologists (not all of them are necessarily Marxists, and not all are committed to semiology, but the generic title is difficult to avoid) form, after all, quite a small group. They are, however, by far the most active, the most assertive, the most dogmatic, the most impressive and the most organized group currently operating; and the development of British film criticism in the past decades has been largely a matter of small groups overlapping, displacing, superseding one another, each centred on a magazine: the *Sequence* group, the *Movie* group, the *Monogram* group, the *Screen* group. What is so impressive, and so daunting, about the last is the impression it gives of impregnable organization; the sense of certitude it exudes, as though opposition were superfluous—outmoded, as it were, by definition; the strength it draws from resting upon a formidable body of doctrine, a fully articulated ideological substructure, as well as upon a science with its own elaborated vocabulary and its own extensive bibliography. All must feel intimidated, as they never were by *Movie* or *Monogram;* the commonest reactions seem to be to submit humbly, or to try, uneasily, to laugh it all off; neither strikes me as healthy.

The problems of grappling with it all are, however, immense; to do so adequately would require an intimacy with both the ideology and the science that I do not possess. What follows will scarcely worry the exponents and champions of the new criticism, who will not regard it as an effective challenge. I offer, at most, a series of skirmishes, not a major battle; my aim is to voice doubts, questions and anxieties rather than to demolish. I do not believe, however, that I am concerned merely with the peripheral: on the contrary, the tendencies and implications that most worry me are so deeply embedded in the process we are experiencing as seldom to rise to the surface in the form of explicit admission. My attitude to the movement as a whole, and to any of its major components (Marxism, semiology, the recent work of Godard, the investigation of the Hollywood cinema, the deconstruction of Realism), is far from simple. I hope the series of probes that follows—deliberately discontinuous, allowing me opportunities for digression, qualification, approach from different angles—will be found ultimately to have its own unity as the expression of a complex but not incoherent position.

1. Lines of Advance

First, lest the dilettantes of film criticism feel tempted to draw any comfort or support from my work, I want to dissociate myself decisively from those whose attitude to *Screen* (and I use the magazine here as a convenient short-hand to indicate the whole movement for which, among English-speaking peoples, it has become chief spokesman: much of the initiative is derived from *Cahiers du Cinéma*) is expressed in facile ridicule. I may join them in finding its language frequently impenetrable, but (while reserving the right to trace a relationship between that language and the aspects I find most sinister) I feel that the problem is as much ours as the writers': every new discipline creates its own vocabulary and idiom.

Most that is interesting and valuable in current film criticism has developed out of the semiological/structuralist/Marxist school. I don't see this as proof of the absolute or exclusive "rightness" of that school; simply as yet another demonstration that any concerted movement involving a number of gifted and intelligent people in a living interchange and development of ideas will, whether in art or criticism, inevitably produce good work. The laboriousness of current semiological analysis—I have in mind as example Raymond Bellour's analysis of twelve shots from *The Big Sleep* in *Théories—Lectures* (translated in *Screen*, Winter 1974/75) whose interest, we are told, lies in their "relative poverty"—should not be surprising, nor its apparent mistaking of means for ends: it is as if an English teacher suddenly discovered clause analysis and was so excited by it that it seemed, for a time, the *only* way to talk about a Shakespeare sonnet. We urgently need a syntax of film which we can draw on freely—as an occasional recourse to clause analysis may miraculously clarify a passage in Shakespeare—and semiology (when the excitement has settled down) may turn out to have supplied one.

A number of specific (and interrelated) lines of enquiry in current criticism seem to me particularly important and rewarding:

a. The whole investigation into the ideological substructure of art, which has already provided its revelations. Of course we should be aware of the implicit ideology supporting and structuring a given work: nothing should be merely taken for granted or left unquestioned.

b. The investigation into the narrative conventions of the American classical cinema and their ideological determination, the reasons why certain plot-structures recur insistently while others appear freakish or inadmissible.

c. The ways in which ideological structure may be cracked or subverted in individual cases, and by what means (the celebrated *Cahiers* text on *Young Mr. Lincoln* can stand as *locus classicus*).

d. The enquiry into Realism, and the exposure of the artifice that underlies it, the strategies and conventions through which "Realism" seeks to impose itself as "reality."

e. The attempts at offering detailed "readings" of particular films that, while acknowledging the evidence of directorial authorship, go beyond the tracing of personal themes to reveal the multiple determinants that may contribute to the finished product.

All of these developments have had their effect (as a stimulus, and not merely a negative one) on my own recent work. Together, underpinned as they are by Marxist doctrine and the discipline of semiology, they constitute so formidable a critical front that the problem is how to assimilate them without getting assimilated by them (a fate that has, I'm afraid, overtaken a lot of people recently); how to learn from them without losing one's personal voice and individual integrity. I do not, myself, find them necessarily incompatible with the view of art and its function that I have previously expressed; indeed, I would assert that their validity largely depends on their compatibility. Without some such sanction—should they come to be generally accepted, that is, as ends in themselves—there is a danger of their becoming destructive of art itself.

2. Against "Impressionistic" Criticism

Semiology is commonly proposed as the answer to "impressionistic" criticism. No one who has tried to write on film with any precision will doubt for a moment the need for analytical tools that can help guard against vagueness and lapses of memory and render the sort of useless disordered casual jottings that frequently pass for perceptive criticism impossible.

One could illustrate what is meant by "impressionism" in this context, and so give force to these assertions, from a superabundance of sources (including much of my own past work). I choose Manny Farber's *Negative Space* partly because the book is (I believe) highly regarded in some quarters, partly because of its general air of confidence and the apparent precision of many of Farber's observations. For striking examples one need look no further than the introduction.

Here is Farber on *Touch of Evil:* "A deaf-mute grocery clerk squints in the foreground, while Charlton Heston, on the phone, embarrassed over his wife's eroticism from a motel bed, tries to suggest nonchalance to the store owner." One wonders for a moment whether Farber has seen a print containing a scene generally cut; but his account bears just enough resemblance to a familiar scene to make this improbable. Farber seems to think there are two people in the little general store with Heston, a deaf-mute clerk and the store owner; there is in fact only one, and Heston would have difficulty in suggesting "nonchalance" to her (unless with his voice): she is blind, not deaf-mute. Farber continues, again with an air of confident precision: "A five-minute street panorama develops logically behind the credits, without one cut, just to arrive at a spectacular reverse zoom away from a bombed Cadillac." Pedantic, perhaps, to point out that the opening shot lasts three minutes twenty-five seconds and that "panorama" is somewhat misleading as it suggests a panning shot; less pedantic to point out that, just after the explosion is heard off-screen, Welles *cuts* to a shot of the blazing car (it would have been difficult to do otherwise without actually blowing up two actors) on which he then zooms *in*.

A few pages later we find Farber summing up the "resonance" of *Weekend* thus: "These hopped-up nuts wandering in an Everglades, drumming along the Mohawk, something about *Light in August*, a funny section where Anne Wiazemsky is just sitting in grass, thumb in mouth, reading a book." The term "impressionistic" has particular felicity applied to writing like this: the sentence evokes a generalized impression of Godard movies with which the casual reader (and viewer) is assumed to be satisfied. There *were* funny scenes in *Weekend* (though whether Farber means funny-peculiar or funny ha-ha I'm not sure); there was a shot in which Anne Wiazemsky sat by a lake reading a book, though it is difficult to see what Farber found funny about it. She was, in fact, smoking a cigarette, but perhaps she was also sucking her thumb in another movie, or perhaps that was Anna Karenina somewhere else, or perhaps Farber (having discussed *The Big Sleep* a few pages earlier) was confusing her with Carmen Sternwood; and Godard said somewhere that *Made in USA* was a remake of *The Big Sleep*, so it all sort of links up, so what the hell? The whole chapter, with its extraordinary associational processes, comes very close at times to stream-of-consciousness, and is worth looking up as an example of what you can get away with, with a bit of swagger. Such "impressionism" says as much about Farber's assumptions about his readers as it does about his own perceptions and his way of experiencing films. It is assumed that they will not know the films very well either, but will not feel this as much of a handicap in attending to discussions of them so vague as to be unchallengeable.

Faced with writing like Farber's, one's sympathy for semiology certainly increases. The trouble is that the claims made for it as the alternative to this kind of thing rest on a use of the word "impressionistic" to cover pretty well everything from *Sight and Sound*'s "guide to current releases" to V. F. Perkins's *Film as Film*: if it is not semiological then it is "impressionistic." The term becomes a means of vilifying everything indiscriminately by blurring all distinctions. Peter Harcourt's studies of six European directors, in his book of that name, are (though also prone to descriptive errors) in a different class from Farber's "impressions," offering the precise and cogent articulation of responses to central features of the directors' work; the analyses in Perkins's book gain their validity from their meticulous precision; the term "impressionistic" cannot possibly do justice to either. Both books demonstrate that it is possible to present precisely defined and arguable propositions about films and still write what the general reader can recognize as the English language. One can imagine readers of weekly "journalist" criticism learning to master Harcourt and Perkins (and learning, as a corollary, to reject most of the journalism); they could not master a great proportion of recent issues of *Screen* without substantially re-educating themselves. This may be—as most *Screen* editors and writers would claim—because Harcourt and Perkins both write "within the prevailing ideology." The implication—that one cannot make oneself generally intelligible without thereby becoming "bourgeois"—is an alarming one, and relates interestingly to Godard's present quandary as a film-maker. I am less pessimistic (perhaps because I am a bourgeois myself): it seems to me that semiologically-orientated criticism may in time, after its necessary period of intensive consolidation, learn to move (to pursue the Godardian parallel) from a *Vent d'Est* phase to a *Tout Va Bien* phase. Meanwhile, my quarrel is less with what it is actually doing than with its arrogant self-assertion: the common assumption that any alternative is now discredited and made obsolete by its example.

3. Mizoguchi Replies to George Steiner

Two basic objections to the view of the function of art put forward in my opening essay need to be confronted. They can be summed up crudely as (a) it doesn't work and (b) it isn't valid. The former has been put with considerable show of efficacy by George Steiner, in *Language and Silence* (he is talking about literature but the point applies, I think, to the arts generally):

> The simple yet appalling fact is that we have very little solid evidence that literary studies do very much to enrich or stabilize moral perception, that they *humanize*. We have little proof that a tradition of literary studies in fact makes a man more humane. What is worse—a certain body of evidence points the other way. When barbarism came to twentieth-century Europe, the arts faculties in more than one university offered very little moral resistance, and this is not a trivial or local accident. In a disturbing number of cases the literary imagination gave servile or ecstatic welcome to political bestiality. That bestiality was at times enforced and refined by individuals educated in the culture of traditional humanism. (p. 83, Pelican edition)

It is common knowledge (or common myth, which is often

truer than knowledge) that concentration camp commandants would come home after work in the evenings and play Schubert exquisitely on the piano. But this seems to me an incitement, not to despair or to the surrender of my position, but to greater awareness, more rigorous definition, more militant commitment. Let us admit at once that art and the study of art offer no instant solution to human problems, no instant exorcism of human evil, no instant strengthening of human goodness; that it is naive in the extreme to argue that contact with the arts in itself refines, ennobles or humanizes. The simplest answer to the objection is that the commandants probably had not studied under Dr. Leavis. In case that sounds frivolous to some and downright silly to others (I should not, certainly, wish it to be understood too literally!), let me expand. We all know that an alleged interest in art can be cultivated in many forms, at many different levels of respectability: as a sort of snobbish social or intellectual one-upmanship; as the development of "correct" taste or connoisseurship; as the accumulation of knowledge—what is commonly meant by "scholarship." Taken together, these forms can be claimed to represent the dominant tradition of our culture, the "establishment" view of art from the university milieu that has always found Leavis such an embarrassment, down to the Sunday colour supplements. What all these forms of interest have in common is the treatment of art as something out there, external to the individual, to the values by which he lives (as opposed to the values to which he pays lip service), the way he thinks and feels from moment to moment in his daily life, in his social activities, his work, his personal relationships. "Appreciation" (such as is often taught in schools) is a term that comes to mind: one learns to "appreciate"—at a certain distance. One learns to say the right things and even, up to a point, mean them—one can even teach oneself to feel the right feelings. The distinction between "appreciation" and critical evaluation is crucial. Art remains a leisure-time activity, something one comes home to whether from the concentration camp, the factory, the office, the university lecture theatre. When I was at Cambridge reading English this was an attitude that all the lectures tended to encourage and endorse, except those of Leavis and A. P. Rossiter; and an attitude gratefully accepted by the majority of students.

The most sophisticated and insidious form of this externalizing of art is to aestheticize it—to purge it of all its moral, social and ideological perplexities. Leni Riefenstahl offers a frightening example, which relates very closely to George Steiner's objections and illustrates simultaneously the sort of aesthetic position to which Leavis is so strongly and committedly opposed. According to her present testimony, when she made *Triumph of the Will* she was interested solely in her "art," and was quite ignorant of the socio-political implications of what she was filming: she was the "innocent" but dedicated artist, feeling a responsibility to nothing but her "art" (equated roughly with abstract aesthetic beauty). We may believe her or not: all that is necessary for the present argument is to establish the terrible possibility of the unaware artist, placing himself unwittingly at the service of some enormity, and the unaware "appreciator" who passively reflects his attitude to art.

The answer to George Steiner (and to Leni Riefenstahl) is also implicitly given in *Sansho Dayu* (itself a supremely great work of art, which is part of the point). Sansho keeps his slaves in abject misery, branding them with red-hot irons if they try to escape. His estate is not altogether unlike a concentration camp: the film, made less than a decade after World War II, opens with an ironic foreword locating the legend it recounts in an age "before man awakened from barbarism." In one scene, Sansho entertains an emissary from the Minister of Justice (on whose behalf he runs the estate) with a display of high culture in the form of traditional song and dance. The performance is largely ignored: Sansho is intent on watching its effect on the emissary, the emissary is more interested in the chest of jewels with which he has been presented, Taro (Sansho's son) turns aside in disgust. The music continues through the following scene in which Taro talks to the two slave-children (the film's central figures) prior to his departure, outraged by his father's brutish insensitivity to the suffering around him.

The comment on a particular use (or abuse) of art is plain enough. But Mizoguchi's answer to Steiner is not that one scene, but the whole film, which, though made within one of the world's largest commercial film industries, is itself a work of high art. Its leading theme is the necessity for preserving one's humanity, one's capacity for human feeling and human commitment, even in the most brutalizing and seemingly hopeless circumstances. The film, rich in disasters, reveals as the only absolute disaster the loss of that humanity, as typified, temporarily, in the protagonist Zushio's submission to a "realistic" attitude to his situation—his acceptance of the need to brutalize himself and adjust to the condition of the earthly hell in which the slaves exist. That theme, and the values that make its expression valid and convincing, are realized in the art of the film, through its structure and its style, the constant tension and balance set up between involvement and contemplation. Thus the film embodies the concept of humanity that it upholds, implying an attitude to art and a sense of its function very different from Sansho's.

4. Schubert Replies to Colin McArthur

The second objection—that my conception of the function of art is invalid—takes us nearer the heart of the current film critical debate. The clearest brief statement of it I have found is in a review of Peter Harcourt's *Six European Directors* by Colin McArthur, which appeared in *Tribune* (5.7.74). It is significant (and symptomatic), I think, that, while granting the book a certain intelligence, McArthur nowhere attempts to grapple with its arguments: he simply rejects its position on ideological grounds, the intelligence being, apparently, neither here nor there. That quality is no longer a relevant concern is an assumption one encounters in many forms nowadays: at its base seems to be a sense that the notion of "quality" is itself "bourgeois." After placing Harcourt's book within a "liberal/bourgeois/romantic view of the world utterly at odds with the materialist view," Mr. McArthur writes:

> Mr. Harcourt's romantic commitment to the personal response of the critic is paralleled by his ultimate commitment to the notion of personal artistry . . . the materialist critic would offer an alternative model of the critical activity. Naturally, he would pay scant heed to his own (or anyone else's) personal response to a film since, from the materialist perspective, "personal" responses are not personal at all but are culturally and class-determined.

The surprising thing about that last remark is the triumphant way McArthur brings it out, playing it like a trump card, as if he had just discovered it. But has anyone ever doubted that our responses are conditioned by our upbringing, background, environment, by a vast intricate network of influences consciously or unconsciously assimilated? Could it conceivably be otherwise? And how does this suddenly make them not personal? If I sit next to someone from roughly the same cultural background as myself watching *Tokyo Story, Rio Bravo* or *Diamonds Are Forever*, am I to assume that our responses are identical—that there is no personal "I" and "he" who might be relating to the film in radically different ways? Or is the assumption (which I find profoundly sinister) rather that the personal "I" and "he" no longer matter, are irrelevant to what life and art are really about and

·had better be discounted or obliterated?

There are a number of objections to be made to McArthur's objection, though the critical (and ideological) position it implies is today very common among the "intellectuals" of film criticism. First, his position seems to depend on an extremely simplified and crude notion of the term "response": he appears to conceive personal response as a subjective and mindless emotional gush, not as the delicate and complex intercourse between emotion and intellect that I have always taken it to be. Second, McArthur's position frighteningly implies, logically, a rejection of feeling itself. For if our responses to art are to be dismissed as "culturally and class-determined," then surely our responses to other people, and to situations in life, must be so too? The only solution would be a willed inhibition of all emotion as we ruthlessly deconstruct ourselves, our friends and our relationships.

I am reminded of a brief passage (two shots) in Godard's *Vladimir and Rosa* which I also find somewhat chilling. We are shown Juliet Berto as activist and militant (a close shot of her in a tense, defiant pose), then a shot typifying the way she lives. Meanwhile, the voice-over commentary informs us sternly that she has not yet found the way to relate the two images—the public, activist life, the private, daily life. One might expect from this description that the second shot would show her sitting before the fire with her bourgeois parents darning the family stockings. Not at all: we see her relaxing with some fellow students in what looks like a communal home. Now what, one may ask, does Godard want the poor girl to do? Can she not sit and chat with her friends? Must life be one long conscious (and self-conscious) deconstruction? There is, of course, a real quandary here, to which one cannot but be sympathetic: to revolutionize the whole of society must be to revolutionize every aspect of one's own life. Yet the damage this must inevitably do to the human personality scarcely bears thinking of. Yeats's lines on fanatics come aptly to mind—they haunt me continually when

I watch recent Godard:

> Hearts with one purpose alone
> Through winter and summer seem
> Enchanted to a stone
> To trouble the living stream.

I have been told, on very good authority, that I am an "anti-intellectual," because my work consistently implies a refusal to separate my emotional life from my intellectual life. Such a separation, in my view, can only be, ultimately, to the detriment and impoverishment of both.

There is a third, related objection to the position implicit in McArthur's review (and, I believe, in the pages of *Screen*): it appears to lack any sense of the function of art. The review continues: "He (the materialist critic) would be concerned with the cinema as a social process and with producing knowledge about that process, which implies knowing equally about socio-economic structures and aesthetic structures and posing relationships between them."

Let me say at once that the posing of relationships between socio-economic structures and aesthetic structures seems to me an admirable and potentially very rewarding critical pursuit. Also, there could be no possible objection to anyone's examining the cinema as a social process. This cannot, however, logically be considered a *substitute* for the traditional relationship between art and criticism. The fact remains that artists don't create works of art in order to provide sociologists with data. Works of art, like everything else, *become* potential sociological data, and it is perfectly valid to explore their significance from that point of view. But without a sense of the creative process on the one hand and the experience of art on the other—in other words, of personal artistry and personal response—the critic cannot talk about art as art: he is denying it its original, central and defining function. Ultimately, an exclusive approach that in effect reduces the arts to a heap of data can only be destructive of art.

A work of art affects our emotions, fascinates our mind, becomes a part of our consciousness and of our unconscious—a part of our *selves*. Repeatedly, through life, I have found myself living with a particular work, or the works of a particular artist, over a period of time, with the greatest intensity and growing intimacy: at present it's Schubert's *Winterreise,* which I have recently discovered. It's not just that I want repeatedly to listen to it—it's part of my breakfast every morning, it runs through my dreams at night, it's with me while I do the cooking or fiddle about the garden. Gradually, I feel it becoming a part of me, and the obsession begins to diminish. From there on, I need to experience it less, because it's absorbed into my life, it's in my bloodstream.

This kind of assimilation—of which I've given an extreme example, for we are not capable of "living" every work of art we encounter at such a pitch of intensity—seems to me fundamental to any understanding of what art is and what art is *for.* The process of absorption I have described is clearly not only—perhaps not primarily—a process of conscious understanding and of intellectual exploration: it is a process engaging the emotions and instincts as much as the mind. It becomes impossible without some degree of trust: trust of our own response, trust of the artist and the work. It is easy to see that, from the Marxist viewpoint, this trust is itself an aspect of bourgeois ideology, or, rather, the means whereby that ideology can perpetuate itself. Yet if we deny it, it seems to me that we deny our own humanity and deny art (as Godard, indeed, has done or at least tried to do).

At the same time, such trust has to be counterbalanced by its opposite, by the achievement of critical distance, by questions of choice and value. The process by which we *decide* what works of art we will live with, what we shall allow to affect, influence and modify our sensibilities, is obviously a complex one. When the decision becomes exclusively one of the intellect and the will—when it is determined, that is, by a rigidly held body of dogma allegiance to which demands that our spontaneous responses be suppressed—then we do both ourselves and art an injury.

5. Totalitarian Tendencies in the Cinema

> Within the revolution, anything;
> against the revolution, nothing.
> FIDEL CASTRO, *Words to the Intellectuals*

Let us juxtapose, for a moment, *Battleship Potemkin, Triumph of the Will* and *Vent d'Est:* three films quite distinct from each other in period, cultural background, political ideology, form and style. They have one thing in common: none of them permits the spectator, within the work, an alternative view to the one promulgated by the film-maker. Eisenstein (for better or for worse—the point is arguable) does not allow us to think, "The ship's officers are human beings too"; Riefenstahl does not let us think, "Hitler may be a real bastard." The case of *Vent d'Est* is slightly more complicated (much has been made, notably by Peter Wollen in his article "Counter Cinema" in *Afterimage No.4,* of its formal "aperture"). But, while his film expresses some uncertainty as to the most effective methods for revolutionaries (or revolutionary film-makers) to adopt, Godard nowhere allows us to question the desirability of revolution.

Against these films set Pontecorvo's *Battle of Algiers* (a film the "politicized" tend to lump indiscriminately with the works of Costa-Garvas—another manifestation of their indifference to quality). The main inclination of the film's sympathies is abundantly clear. Yet Pontecorvo is able to present the commander of the paratroopers as an intelligent human being capable of presenting a rational defence of his position; the film's argument allows that, while that position is regarded as "wrong," it has something to be said for it, it can be rationally defended. Pontecorvo's film also confronts the issue of the morality of placing bombs in public places where "innocent" people will be killed and injured, and here it offers opportunities for direct comparison with *Vent d'Est. Battle of Algiers* presents the argument that the terrorist acts were necessary, though terrible: we are encouraged to respond to the terribleness, to ponder the consequences seriously. Godard's film, after offering some instruction in the manufacture of bombs, simply tells us (in a voice-over commentary accompanying some typically "anonymous" images) that any objections we may raise to the placing of bombs in supermarkets are examples of liberal humanitarianism which is one of the disguises or subterfuges of capitalist ideology: any qualms we may feel about the indiscriminate massacre of shoppers are brutally squashed by the method of making us feel ashamed of them. The issues Pontecorvo's film raises could be discussed from different positions by people of different political persuasions, drawing on and developing arguments implicit within it; the propositions offered by *Vent d'Est* could only be discussed by committed revolutionaries. To discuss the film's overall position one would have to move outside it, and in effect argue against it: there is no foothold within it for anyone less than totally committed to its premise. It is one of the most extreme examples of "elitist" art in my experience. It seems fair to describe *Battle of Algiers* as a democratic film, and "open"; the other three as, in their different ways, totalitarian, and "closed."

A more flagrant example of cinematic totalitarianism is offered by *Pravda,* the Godard-Gorin political documentary on Czechoslovakia. The voices of the two commentators (who call themselves "Vladimir" and "Rosa") warn us near the beginning that if we do not understand Czech we had better learn quickly.

Subsequently, we listen at length to an (unsubtitled) Czech factory worker; we are then told that if we do not understand it does not matter after all—the worker talks like Henry Ford. The same tactics are repeated later (slightly varied) with farm workers. So much for the presentation of evidence. And so much for respect for the human individual, be it the workers (who are denied their own viewpoints) or the viewers (who are denied the right to judge for themselves). All particularities are annihilated in favour of the crudest ideological generalization. One might be tempted to call such tactics "Fascist" if they were not merely silly. They raise, acutely, the recurrent problem in Godard, the problem of tone, or degree of seriousness. One feels at times that he and his associates are playing at revolution, very dangerously, like a gang of kids left in a room with matches and explosives.

One rider must be added here: the preceding argument does not necessarily mean that I value *Battle of Algiers* above *Vent d'Est:* simply that I find it ideologically more acceptable. Such conscious ideological concerns must enter into that bewilderingly complex process we call evaluation (and unconscious ones cannot, by definition, be kept out); but they represent only one strand among many. It is a process, in any case, that should never be supposed to have reached the stage of the "definitive" towards which it must perpetually strive.

6. Totalitarian Tendencies in Criticism

The attitude to democratic critical debate revealed generally in *Screen* significantly parallels the attitude of *Pravda* and *Vent d'Est.* ("Within the revolution, anything; against the revolution, nothing.") Before taking up the issue in general terms, I want to examine one or two local details. I do not intend that they be taken as representative of *Screen* as a whole, but I feel that, in their relatively trivial way, they are symptomatic. I offer two examples from an editorial, two from an article.

In the autumn of 1972 the editor of *Screen* undertook the task of introducing two critical articles, the *Cahiers* text on *Young Mr. Lincoln,* and John Smith's article on certain of Hitchcock's British films. This is how he dealt with an essay he (or the editorial board) had selected for publication: "John Smith relates to an older and I think incorrect aesthetic position but one nevertheless in the mainstream of British film criticism. . . . Both formalism . . . and semiology have revealed the essential realist and hence ideological impulse involved in this species of romantic aesthetics and at the same time, in work on the sign systems of art, have theoretically demonstrated the untenability of that aesthetics." In other words, if you can't speak Czech it doesn't matter. It happens from time to time that an editor finds it necessary to dissociate himself from positions he has none the less found interesting enough to represent. Bazin did it in *Cahiers* in a way I find exemplary, in that it constituted a challenge to his own "*jeunes* Turcs" to consolidate and define their position more convincingly. He did not, however, emasculate articles in advance, warning his readers, in effect, not to take them seriously.

There is a very curious moment earlier in the same editorial—the writer here being involved in a parallel manoeuvre to justify the *Cahiers* text, in the form of an advance explanation:

> The ideology of Ford's film which the *Cahiers* writers describe variously as "the Apology of the Word" (natural law and the truth of nature inscribed in Blackstone and in the Farmers' Almanac), the valorisation of the complex Law of Nature/Woman, the repression of violence by the Law, and the suppression of history by the myth, are disrupted by the

> film's signifiers. For example the violence repressed by the Law and the Word is reinstated by the violence of that repression (Lincoln's castrating look, the murder, the lynching).

The writer's somewhat feverish haste is suggested by the faulty syntax ("The ideology . . . are . . ."); his example (the only one offered) of "disruption by the film's signifiers" comes perilously near the meaningless. "The murder" and "the lynching" cannot possibly be put forward as examples of the violence with which violence in the film is *repressed:* the lynching *is* the violence that is repressed; the murder (which Lincoln does not witness) by no stretch of the imagination represents the repression of violence "by the Law and the Word." One is left, then, with "Lincoln's castrating look"; whether "violence" (as opposed to some such term as "moral force") is really the right word seems open to argument: both here and in the *Cahiers* article itself, the equation of moral force with *physical* violence is somewhat dubious. The lapse in the editorial, however, strikes me as the kind of sleight-of-hand (no doubt unconscious) that goes with a general sense of the end justifying the means: as long as the *Cahiers* article and its aesthetic position are validated it does not much matter how.

My second pair of examples comes from an article *Politics and Production* by Christopher Williams, published in the issue of *Screen* for Winter 1971/72. In the first paragraph, after attacking "the diachronic version of Film History," Williams tells us that "it took history itself, in the shape of the French revolution of May 1968, to force a necessary re-evaluation of the whole concept of political cinema: a re-evaluation that is only just beginning." He then proceeds to offer us a remarkable piece of film history of his own. I must quote at some length, or I risk being charged with misrepresentation:

In the aftermath of the revolution, *Cahiers du Cinéma* began to re-publish a wide selection of original Russian material; *Cinéthique* attempted a meditative praxis in the whole area of political cinema. These moves had their echoes in other cultures. At the same time, about 80% (at a frivolous estimate) of young film-makers became "revolutionaries" of one sort or another. This ferment was so disparate and various that it can't possibly qualify for description as a "movement," running as it does the whole gamut from Warholian voyeurism through re-vamped social-concern "realism" to agitational propaganda and sheer abstraction.

The sense is not, perhaps, free of syntactical ambiguity (often an unconscious method for performing sleight-of-hand, asserting what one wishes to assert but does not really believe): it is not entirely clear whether the fact that "about 80% (at a frivolous estimate) of young film-makers became 'revolutionaries'" is meant as an example of the "echoes" of "these moves" "in other cultures" (if it is not, then the examples are left to our imagination). What is unambiguous is that this happened "at the same time," which can only mean "in the aftermath of the revolution." In other words, the American underground (including, explicitly, Warhol) and *Cinéma-Vérité* (including, implicitly, Rouch and Leacock—Williams goes on to talk about "true-confession, talking straight into camera documentary") happened after the events of May 1968 and perhaps developed directly or indirectly out of them. Either the piece is just very clumsy or we hover here on the verge of Orwellian "doublethink."

As the second example from Williams's article concerns myself, I shall be accused of personal animus; I am certainly ready to confess to irritation. It seems to me, however, a good example of a certain way of dealing with any critical opposition.

Williams is discussing *Weekend.* He remarks: "The film is built around the question of culture, which is what allowed Robin Wood to claim Godard as a belated, tragically-despairing adherent to Leavis and the Great Tradition (*New Left Review* 39)." Whether "built around the question of culture" is a satisfactory description of *Weekend* I shall not argue here; whether my article in *New Left Review* can be fairly described as "claiming Godard as a belated, tragically-despairing adherent to Leavis and the Great Tradition" is best left to readers to decide. However, the fact that *Weekend* "is built around the question of culture" could not possibly have allowed me to claim Godard as that or anything else in an article written three years before *Weekend* came out.

As Williams must have known, I wrote my article at about the time of *Masculin-Féminin;* as he might have deduced from its total lack of reference to that film, I had not been able to see it when I wrote. The article discusses Godard, then, up to and including *Pierrot le Fou,* but that does not prevent Williams from presenting it to his readers as if it dealt with *Weekend.* He must also have been aware, I think, that I wrote a much later article specifically about *Weekend* (first published in *Movie,* reprinted, slightly cut, in *The Films of Jean-Luc Godard*) which drastically qualifies the position represented by the earlier piece; bur he sees no reason to refer to this or to acknowledge its existence. It raises questions about Godard that I think still have not been satisfactorily answered, by Williams or anyone else.

It is fair to mention that the editorship of *Screen* has changed since these examples appeared, and to repeat that they are not adduced here to discredit that magazine as a whole. Nor, of course, are such tactics by any means restricted to the new critical school. I feel, however, that wherever they appear they should be exposed, and the exposure put on record.

7. *Screen*'s Dirty Words

Such minute particularities as those I have just examined, however, are mere gnat-bites in the context of the general attack on
traditional aesthetics of which *Screen* has placed itself in the
front line. The attack is characterized by the emergence of a
whole new vocabulary of "dirty words"—terms which scarcely
need to be defined or examined, but can be relied upon, apparently, to elicit an instant stock response from readers. My own
readers can test their positions, perhaps, by asking themselves at
what point in the following list they begin to feel surprise that
the words should be automatically accepted as terms of abuse:
bourgeois ideology, liberal, humanist, élitist, Romantic aesthetics, genius, personal artistry, expressivity, creativity. Again, my
aim here is not to attack the positive achievements of *Screen* and
the movement it represents, but to raise questions about what
is being recklessly swept away and about the implications—for
art, for society, for life—of its hypothetical annihilation. My
own reaction to these terms is not simple, as I hope the following annotations will suggest.

"Bourgeois Ideology"

For most of us, the term "bourgeois" evokes suburban streets,
privet hedges, a narrow moral code, values based on material
possession: none of us wants to be thought "bourgeois." In
Marxist criticism, the term inevitably retains these overtones
but, by a process of insidious synecdoche, comes to cover a great
deal more. Hence its usefulness as a means of effecting recoil
over a remarkably wide front. The position of *Vent d'Est*, for
example, comes to appear impregnable. As the term "bourgeois
ideology" can be made virtually all-inclusive, covering everything outside Marxist-Maoist doctrine, any objections to the
film can be easily "exposed" as its product or its means of self-
defence. The instincts (except the instinct to destructive action)

and the emotions (except that of anger) appear to be a part of "bourgeois ideology." Impulses of love, generosity and tolerance, all readiness to listen to other points of view, everything we have learnt to call, in the finest sense, "human," all these are aspects of "bourgeois ideology" and its means of perpetuating itself. I do not think we should allow ourselves to be intimidated by this; whenever we encounter the term "bourgeois ideology" in art or criticism it is necessary to determine carefully exactly what it indicates. To off-set the emotive overtones, one might mentally substitute the word "traditional" for "bourgeois."

"Élitist"

Another word with (in any democratic tradition) emotive overtones that tend to get in the way of what it is actually being made to stand for: it implies snobbery and exclusivity. When confronted with generalized denunciations of the "élitist" view of art, one must begin by asking for a definition of the "élite" in question—what constitutes it, what are the conditions for membership? The answer appears to be "education": "élitist" art is art you have to *learn* to appreciate. But the emphasis, surely, must always be on *self*-education, or, at the very least, on active cooperation between pupil and teacher. No merely passive (let alone hostile) pupil can be made to learn to understand and evaluate works of art. Our "élite," then, consists of people who either spontaneously want, or deliberately choose to want, to educate themselves. (I am not, of course, talking about those who "cultivate" the arts as some kind of social performance, for cocktail party repartee; I presume the argument is not about *them.*) It is a closed "élite" only in so far as social ("bourgeois") pressures encourage philistinism: it is not a club with exclusive conditions of membership. I have spent fifteen years educating myself to respond to and feel at home with the Schönberg quartets, a process at first painfully frustrating, ultimately deeply rewarding. I can now "hear" the third quartet (reputedly the most difficult) almost as naturally as I "hear" the Beethoven third symphony. This places me among a very small minority, but I am not aware of any self-congratulatory feelings of superiority. I am not particularly musical, have had no training and quite fail to grasp the technical intricacies of twelve-tone composition; the experience I get from Schönberg seems to me to be open to anyone who wants it. If I feel no pride because I enjoy allegedly "élitist" art, I also feel no guilt.

It does seem to me, however, that the development of any full response to significant art demands effort, discipline and patience. There *are* great works of art—plenty of them—which have been enjoyed readily by the general public, but a condition of this enjoyment seems to be that they are not perceived as art. One is glad that *My Darling Clementine* and *Rio Bravo* were commercial successes, but do not let us kid ourselves— the audiences who enjoyed them made no significant distinction between them and *Gunfight at the OK Corral* and *High Noon* (unless, in the case of the last, they felt they were seeing something more serious and important, with a message). The (Marxist) editors of *Cahiers du Cinéma* have demonstrated very convincingly that *Young Mr. Lincoln* is every bit as "difficult" a film as *Persona* or *Pierrot le Fou.* If the term "élitist" is defined as "anything that cannot be fully appreciated by anyone, irrespective of background, training and education," then all art is élitist. As soon as one allows for the desirability of discrimination, then élitism creeps in. What, for that matter, could be more élitist than Godard's politicized movies on the one hand and semiological discourse on the other? Of the former, Christopher Williams writes (in the *Screen* article cited earlier): "The (Dziga Vertov) group itself stresses that the films are not intended for large audiences, but for small groups conscious of ideological questions." You cannot get more élitist than that.

The paradox that it is those very critics who talk contemptuously about "élitist" art and "élitist" positions who also champion the most élitist of all art, can be explained but not very satisfactorily resolved. Avant-garde art (*any* avant-garde art, one infers from the remarkable extra chapter Peter Wollen added for the second edition of *Signs and Meaning in the Cinema*) is valuable because it is "progressive": the work of Godard/Gorin is of course the centre of attraction, but even when the art is not specifically revolutionary in the political sense, its tendency is to undermine and destroy "bourgeois" forms and "bourgeois" assumptions. The avant-garde, in other words, is admirable only in the bourgeois context, as a means to an end: when the revolution comes and a Marxist society establishes itself, it will automatically become redundant. *Vent d'Est*, it is worth pointing out, although it was very difficult to make within the bourgeois-capitalist context, would be *impossible* to make outside it: its method, style, peculiar qualities, are all directly dependent on the difficulties. So what sort of art will be able to exist in our coming Marxist utopia?—what is the alternative to the "élitist" art that is being discredited? I find myself unable to supply any answer, but do not wish to imply that there necessarily is not one (I may be too much determined by and enclosed in traditional ideology to be capable of imagining it). It cannot, obviously, be anything that suggests the traditional ("bourgeois") aesthetic, which will be anathema, and it cannot be anything avant-garde, which will be redundant: the problem with all utopias is that once you have got there, there is nothing to be "progressive" about any more.

In the same light, I think the interest of Marxist critics in traditional art needs to be examined, and fundamental questions asked. The most interesting and stimulating Marxist criticism is clearly that in which the impulse is not to denounce and reject but to salvage. Lurking in the background of the *Cahiers* text on *Young Mr. Lincoln*—and necessarily suppressed, but implicit in the article's own gaps and dislocations—one senses the quandary of critics who grew up loving Ford's movies, became converted to Marxism after the events of May 1968, and were faced with the task of re-structuring their own past allegiances. (It is striking that the change in ideology has not been accompanied by any significant change in the works and directors admired: the pantheon is the same, but the gods have to be reinterpreted.) The solution of the *Cahiers* editors is highly intelligent and sophisticated. The film is examined, and implicitly admired, for precisely those features which would appear flaws or failures of realization from a traditional viewpoint: "gaps," "dislocations," inner contradictions that disrupt and subvert the film's ostensible (conscious) purposes, and that finally present Lincoln as a "monster." I am not at all sure what is left of *Young Mr. Lincoln* as a work of art after the *Cahiers* team have done with it; nor is it clear to me that *they* are sure.

This has taken us some distance from my initial defence of the "élitist" position (which is partly a defence of it against the term "élitist"), but I hope it is still within sight. Before passing on, let me return to it with an obvious, but I hope provocative, question: can anyone capable of genuinely appreciating and assimilating Mozart and Mizoguchi possibly say that he is not, in that respect, immeasurably better off than someone whose cultural horizon is limited to bingo and *The Black and White Minstrel Show*? The assimilation will not necessarily make him a better person (a common, and obviously fallacious, assumption), but it will open to him possibilities that are closed to his less fortunate fellow humans. If that is what is meant by an "élite," then I for one shall not willingly sacrifice my membership of it in the name of some perverse and destructive egalitarianism: to put it succinctly, nothing is ever going to come between me and *The Magic Flute*. It is not, however, an élite from which I would wish anyone to feel excluded: on the contrary, I would like to share my advantages with as many others as possible. That is why I am a teacher.

What is actually under attack here turns out always, on inspection, to be some absurd parody-concept that no one today could possibly wish to defend, and which would have looked excessive even at the height of the Romantic movement: the notion that works of art are produced by some process of immaculate conception out of the creativity of an isolated individual genius. But the opposite notion, that denies the concept of personal creativity and individual genius any validity whatever, is no less absurd: do these critics really suppose that Ford's or Hawks's films would somehow have come into being by accident if Ford and Hawks had never existed?—or that some readily interchangeable substitute would have been "produced" ("productivity" being, apparently, the alternative to "creativity")? There is no substitute for an individual work of art, just as there is no substitute, no possible replacement, for an individual human being.

Fra Filippo Lippi's beautiful "Annunciation," that hangs in London's National Gallery, reproduces emblematically a traditional Christian myth, and in doing so draws on an intricate system of aesthetic and iconographical codes and conventions that determine not only the placing and treatment of the figures but govern every detail of the painting down to the execution of the smallest leaf. Yet I see no way of accounting for the totality of the picture's effect but in terms of the individual sensibility and skill (the latter inseparable from the former, as its means of expression) of a particular painter. The painting is structured on an exquisite system of balances and contrasts. The heads of the two female figures, both haloed, are roughly equidistant from the centre of the frame, but the Angel's is very slightly higher than the Virgin's; behind the Angel are slim, young tree-trunks, behind the Virgin a wall (right) and the bed of childbirth (background). The Virgin holds up the folds of her robe with her right hand, the Angel with her left. Beneath the Angel are flowers and foliage, beneath the Virgin tiles; the former appear uncrushed, so that the Angel seems weightless, whereas in the depiction of the Virgin there is a heaviness, a pulling earthwards. Immediately behind the Virgin a gold robe, also seeming to pull downwards, is draped over the back of a chair; it is balanced almost symmetrically by the Angel's wings, composed of peacock feathers like small arrows pointing upwards. Near the base, just left of centre, is a lily, forming the bottom point of a near-parallelogram of which the other three points are another lily held as emblem of purity by the Angel, the hand from Heaven pointing down, and the dove representing the Holy Spirit. Cutting across this parallelogram is the pattern of looks: the eyes of Angel and Virgin both on the dove, which impregnates the womb. The notes supplied by the Gallery speak of the influence of Masaccio, and tell us that the picture was commissioned by the Medici family, whose device of three feathers and a ring is incorporated in the composition.

I choose deliberately here an example from a field of which I am largely ignorant. I know little about painting, less about the background to this particular painting, nothing about Lippi as man or artist. Yet I feel confident that this picture, "determined" on all levels and in every detail by the prevailing ideology, by a structure of thought and belief, by an elaborated system of signs and conventions, by the circumstances of its production, is the creation of an individual sensibility. Virtually all the same constituents—the central division, the Angel's wings (peacock feathers), the Virgin's drape suspended behind her, the dove, the herbage, the lily—are present in another "Annunciation," by "a follower of Fra Angelico," that hangs in the same room, probably painted slightly earlier. The effect is very different: to my untutored eyes much clumsier, lacking the extraordinary delicacy and refinement, the precisions of balance, of symmetry and asymmetry, of the Lippi. I have no wish to denigrate scholarship; I am sure that my response to this painting could be refined and deepened through a more meticulous knowledge of the conventions within which the artist worked. Yet I dare assert that both the picture's "conventionality" and its unique quality can be part-deduced, part-intuited by simply studying it in the context the National Gallery provides. And I would make equivalent assertions about a Haydn symphony, or about *Rio Bravo*.

The digression into which I have allowed myself to wander is only apparent. The crux of this whole critical/ideological question is clearly the question of individuality—whether it exists, and what value should be placed on it; the debate about personal creativity versus determinism is inseparable from the debate about personal response versus scientific knowledge. The animus repeatedly expressed in recent criticism against the notion of individual creativity has as its necessary corollary the whole massive, formidably organized search for a scientific-objective criticism, the purpose of which is to do away with the individual voice altogether: it is in this light that the language, the vocabulary, the tactics of *Screen* have their real significance. This is scarcely the place for political debate (and I am scarcely a political thinker), but it is directly relevant to all my work as critic and teacher that I set supreme value on the quality—and individuality—of the individual life, cannot contemplate favourably any form of social organization that does not have the preservation and development of individuality as its end, and regard the function and meaning of art as *essentially* related to that concept. Life in a society from which belief in personal creativity was banished would necessarily be incapable of transcending the drabbest mediocrity; art would die in it, and with it all that which in the individual life corresponds or responds to art.

Let us be quite clear about this. Without personal creativity (both the concept and the fact) there can be no art. There may be something else—a sort of game played with counters or computers—for which some other name would have to be found.

Meanwhile, we have art to reckon with, and artists, in all their complexity and humanity. A last example: it is doubtless possible to explain, without reference to the respective individual talents (or "genius") of Kurosawa, Ozu and Mizoguchi, how *Living, Tokyo Story* and *Sansho Dayu* (three films centrally concerned with the relationships between parents and children) all came to be made in Japan within a few years of each other. The reasons—cultural, social, political, ideological, economic—might be of limited usefulness in helping us to understand the films; to claim for them more than that is—art being in question—to mistake the peripheral for the central. Perhaps a study of socio-political-economic determinants might also explain why the dominant technical device for transitions in *Living* (and other Kurosawa films) is the wipe, in *Sansho* (and other films by Mizoguchi) the dissolve, and why both are totally absent from *Tokyo Story* (and other late Ozu films). I hope it is not too great an ellipse for me to jump from that observation to the opinion that to shift from the verb "create" to the verb "produce" is perversely to belittle and trivialize not only art but life.

I have come to feel, during the past few years, that *Sansho Dayu* and *Tokyo Story* may (I am careful to acknowledge a continuing uncertainty, which has several sources) be superior to any American film I know; superior even to *Vertigo*, to *Rio Bravo*, to *Letter from an Unknown Woman*: superior in a greater maturity of vision, and in the completeness and conscious authority with which that vision is realized. But I do not base this intimation of value on any simple assumption that Mizoguchi and Ozu were somehow mystically blessed with greater powers of personal creativity than Hitchcock, Hawks and Ophuls (just as I do not assume that the reason Mahler's symphonies are rather different from Haydn's is simply a matter of personal temperament). An attempt to account convincingly for the superiority (which is not the same as demonstrating it—that could only be done by examining the films themselves) would clearly involve a very thorough investigation of working conditions, the expectations brought by Japanese audiences, the conventions and traditions available to the artists, the general background and history of Japanese culture, the socio-economic-political circumstances of contemporary Japan. I would, at the same time, envisage no possible way of explaining the films' greatness without reference to such concepts as "genius" and "personal creativity": I would see no possibility of supposing that the films could somehow have come into being without the presence at their heart of individual creative genius.

8. The Myth of "Modernism"

The questions raised by the emphasis on avant-garde, "progressive" art can be pursued further via an examination of the conclusion to the second edition of *Signs and Meaning in the Cinema*. Let me preface this by remarking that, applied to works of art, terms such as "progressive" and "reactionary" have no evaluative status: they are purely descriptive. They may, however, take on a relative or transitory evaluative force in accordance with shifts and changes in society. One might argue, for instance, that in a period of revolution "reactionary" art assumes potential importance in that it embodies concepts and values that are threatened with obliteration and which might have something to be said for them.

There are two important documents by Peter Wollen on "modernist" cinema, the other being his essay on *Vent d'Est* in *Afterimage 4*. I find them very different in quality: the *Afterimage* article, which I take to be the later in composition, is incomparably the finer, reasonable, disciplined and illuminating—I find its position almost wholly acceptable. It is a pity that the *Signs and Meaning* additional chapter, because it has the comparative permanence of book form, is likely to be far more widely circulated. I am compelled to say that Wollen's account of the difference between our "reading" of "modernist" works and the traditional ways in which art has been read, seems to me compounded of confusions, distortions and self-delusions in roughly equal measure: an extraordinary piece of frenzied mystification. In traditional aesthetics, apparently, the mind was "an empty treasure-house waiting to receive its treasure," but the modernists force us to do some work: instead of meaning being communicated it is now "produced," as the result of this dialogue. Wollen creates continual problems for the reader (but a compensating convenience for himself) by never allowing us any very precise idea as to what he is talking about—which works, which critics. But we can safely assume, I take it, that he would accept *Vent d'Est* (one of the few actual works he specifies) as a representative example of "modernism." We might conceivably read this film in the way Wollen appears to suggest—as a sort of uncoordinated rag-bag of bits and pieces—until we have mastered the principles on which it is built. When we *have* mastered those principles, however, the film is no more difficult to read than *Middlemarch.* Correction: it is much *easier* to read, George Eliot's novel making far greater demands on the reader's intelligence and concentration. When I read *Middlemarch,* I enter into a continuous dialogue with it, and that is the only way to read it; the mind that is "an empty treasure-house waiting to receive its treasure" is fated to remain empty, for there is no work of art of any significance that can be adequately received by being passively absorbed. "Modernism," according to Wollen, "produces works which are no longer centripetal, held together by their own centres, but centrifugal, throwing the reader out of the work to other works." What works actually perform this function is not revealed: presumably *Vent d'Est* can again be taken as an example. The "gaps" and "dislocations" that critics now seek in traditional texts are presumably raised by "modernists" to the status of a conscious artistic principle. There are serious problems here. Obviously, any bad, incompetent work is so because of its failures—its gaps and dislocations. One could argue that an inept mystery story in which the solution is inadvertently made obvious from the beginning deconstructs itself, gives the reader critical distance, enables him to inspect the ideological structure, etc. . . . Gaps and dislocations only become of positive interest when they are felt to have constructive meaning, to be significant—when they become, that is, an aspect of the film's coherence. This seems to me the case with *Vent d'Est*. Like any work of art of any value, Godard's film challenges me to look at my assumption about life, to question my own values; it does not "throw me out of (itself) to other works," except in the absolutely traditional sense that I am compelled to place my experience of it beside other experiences.

The reluctance to specify makes it equally difficult to pin down the distortions in Wollen's account of traditional aesthetics:

> Non-realist aesthetics . . . are accused of reducing or dehydrating the richness of reality; by seeking to make the cinema into a conventional medium they are robbing it of its potential as an alternative world, better, purer, truer and so on. In fact, this aesthetic rests on a monstrous delusion: the idea that truth resides in the real world and can be picked out by a camera. Obviously, if this were the case, everybody would have access to the truth, since everybody lives all their life in the real world. The realism claim rests on a sleight-of-hand: the identification of authentic experience with truth.

Just as it is impossible to identify these "centrifugal" modernist works, so is it impossible to grasp exactly whom Wollen is talking about here: who is supposed to hold this incredibly naive and silly position? Simply to place (say) Hawks's films beside Bergman's is to realize that they can't *both* be presenting an absolute, objective "truth"; to add a third term to the comparison would be to suggest that neither does. Simply to speak of an artist's "view of life" is implicitly to recognize that he is not imparting "truth" in Wollen's sense. "Authentic experience" is obviously one of the things the critic is concerned to identify and evaluate—with all the complexities and qualifications that will involve. But who identifies it with "truth"?

These arguments are elaborated to justify a commitment to an avant-garde that appears barely to exist: apart from recent Godard, no one is allowed in it without reservations. The commitment, none the less, is extraordinarily intense: "it is necessary to take a stand on this question and to take most seriously directors like Godard himself, Makavejev, Straub, Marker, Rocha, some underground directors. . ." There is a very curious passage about the potential "destructiveness" of texts: "*Ulysses* or *Finnegans Wake* are destructive of the nineteenth-century novel," but destructive in what sense is not clear: obviously they have made it difficult to write nineteenth-century novels, but one hardly needs to be told that, and one suspects that Wollen means it has also made it irrelevant to read them. I find the whole paragraph (pages 171–72) extremely confused and confusing. One can give most of the statements, considered separately, a guarded assent, but the overall argument remains partly unintelligible. The passage culminates in this: "A valuable work, a powerful work at least, is one which challenges codes, overthrows established ways of reading or looking, not simply to establish new ones, but to compel an unending dialogue, not at random but productively." I am not clear as to the exact distinction implied by that "at least" between "powerful" works and "valuable" ones: I suppose a powerful work might not necessarily also be valuable, but value seems implied by the rest of the sentence. It is obviously true that a great artist—an artist, that is, who achieves, through pertinacity, integrity, discipline, dedication and personal genius, a truly individual voice—modifies our sense of all that has gone before, forcing us to readjust; and obvious too that the history of art is a history of continuous transformation and development. But many of the greatest artists have been as much consolidators as innovators. Bach and Haydn, for example, scarcely "overthrew established ways" of listening: they built on the formal procedures and established idioms with which their audiences were familiar, developing and extending their possibilities. There may be ways in which the B Minor Mass (which I take it would be generally accepted as both "valuable" *and* "powerful") "challenges codes," but any account of it that saw its significance exclusively or even primarily in such terms would surely be extremely partial. It becomes difficult to separate Wollen's arguments decisively from the most naive belief in progress, from a sense that only art that can be unequivocally associated with "progress" is valuable, and finally from a desperate commitment to the latest thing, irrespective of quality. Welles, for example, has come to look "hopelessly old-fashioned and dated," apparently because it can now be seen that he was only an innovator within a certain context (true, I would have thought, of most innovators). Wollen actually lets himself get carried (there is a general sense of someone not really in control of his ideas) to the point where he finds it necessary to warn us that Hollywood should not be "dismissed out of hand as 'unwatchable'" (whom can he be warning of this except himself?). Works that challenge existing codes may make those codes unusable, but they are not destructive of previous works that employed those codes: no one could or would wish to write a *Middlemarch* today, but *Middlemarch* is not thereby invalidated. What is destructive is a view of art that insists that its only real interest lies in its destruction of the past, and that sees the critic's first priority as a frantic quest for the latest thing.

One of the greatest "progressive" artists of the present century saw things rather differently: "His lessons were very interesting. He never said a word about the twelve-tone system. Not a word. He looked through what I had written, he corrected it in a very wise manner, and we analysed Bach motets" (the late Dr. Otto Klemperer on Schönberg).

9. In Defence of *Vent d'Est*

Part of the problem raised by Godard's recent work can be suggested by the question, "Whom are the films for?" The obvious answer, supplied by Godard and Gorin themselves, is for a small educated Marxist élite. With this goes the implication that the films are almost instantly disposable: revolutionary tools made for a specific local purpose, redundant as soon as that purpose has been served.

Related to this is the question, "Whom am I writing *this* for?" Not, certainly, the Marxist élite equipped to welcome *Vent d'Est* without pain, or bewilderment, or confusion. Nor, really, those who profess to find the films merely "boring"—unless they are prepared to re-think them (or, rather, *think* them, for their reaction suggests an abeyance, or even a deliberate withdrawal, of thought). Perhaps the prime audience anyone writes for consists of people who reflect the writer's own degree of uncertainty. The question that most interests me (and about which I am very uncertain) is, how does a critic who is not a Marxist, or a Marxist-Leninist, or a Maoist, cope with recent Godard honestly?—and how does he do critical justice to an artist who has renounced art (short of renouncing *him*)? The Marxist answer will be, presumably, that of course he cannot, as bourgeois ideology is an edifice of lies and anyone who is not a Marxist is a bourgeois (including the workers, who would far rather see *Bonnie and Clyde* than *Vent d'Est*). Those of us who are sensitive to the enormities of capitalism, yet fail to find Marxism an acceptable alternative, may feel that the problem is not so simple. One is helped and encouraged by one's intermittent recognition (despite appearances to the contrary) that Godard doesn't always find problems simple either. His early work, up to *Pierrot le Fou* and a bit beyond, can be seen in terms of, above all, an effort to define and hold in balance his uncertainties: "Je ne sais pas," opening line of *Le Mépris* and *Une Femme Mariée*, is an appropriate motto. And, although the bounds of his uncertainty are now more securely fixed, more narrowly defined, a decent tentativeness, a refusal either to assert or to bully (qualities temporarily submerged in the tense repressiveness of *Vent d'Est*), resurface in *Tout Va Bien*. People *in* his films assert all the time, but that is clearly not the same thing: except when Vladimir and Rosa supervene, it is difficult to think of a single statement (beyond that of uncertainty, perhaps) delivered in a Godard film that can be unequivocally construed as "Author's Message": the statements are set side by side as so many pieces of evidence for our serious consideration, Godard's point of view being defined only in terms of the areas of interest implied by the selection.

The paradox of the "artist who has renounced art" is central to the critic's problem. There is a sense in which any film is a work of art and cannot *not* be, since some organizing principle must be in operation. Yet there are a great many films (e.g., newsreels) where what one must call (recognizing that the term begs certain questions) the "aesthetic" response is scarcely appropriate, or not appropriate as prime consideration, as the central focus for discussing our experience. The "aesthetic response" is not, for me, something separable from our whole response as human beings: indeed, its nature is defined by this wholeness. But it also represents the critic's way of attempting to achieve a *relative* impartiality, to see and evaluate the work apart from shared or disputed particularities of dogma or creed. The opposition between "work of art" and "revolutionary tool" may seem at first glance illusory, but I find it inevitable. Revolutionary tools and works of art are subject to completely different evaluative systems, because they invite a different sort of response. The former invite to direct action (and invitations to direct action form a significant part of *Vent d'Est*'s raw material); the latter does not ask us to *do* anything, the response it aspires to elicit being altogether more complex. A work of art may affect our lives deeply and permanently, but it takes other forms of discourse—reasoned argument, slogans, direct exhortation—to send us out into the streets. As soon as we respond to a work as an organic (or at least organized) whole—respond to what it *is* rather than what it *says*—then formal questions of structure, order, balance, assert their pre-eminence, and the possibility of effective exhortation accordingly recedes. Such a distinction does not emasculate art; rather, it insists upon its much greater, less ephemeral (if also less precisely directed) potency.

The prime purpose (explicit in statement, implicit in formal procedures) of Godard's "politicized" cinema is not to create "complete" works of art for the aesthetic (moral, emotional) satisfaction of the beholder, but to stimulate or provoke to revolutionary activity.[2] Godard's radicalism has led him repeatedly to demand and announce a "return to zero": the revolution is not against certain incidental injustices of capitalism, but against the whole development of Western culture over (at least) the last two thousand years. What Godard's attitude now is to the art of the past is not entirely clear to me; it was always somewhat

2. The reader will understand that, throughout this essay, the term "Godard" stands for "Godard/Gorin," or for the whole "Dziga Vertov group," whenever the recent films are under discussion. The problem is a delicate one: one wants to place the films within Godard's development, while not altogether losing sight of the possible importance of his collaborators.

A soldier in *Les Carabiniers* reacts to the Rembrandt self-portrait.

equivocal. The early films swarm with "artistic" references, like fragments Godard wished to shore against his ruin, or emblems of allegiances by means of which he would establish an identity. Yet it was never certain just how deep a commitment this magpie agglomeration represented: one might doubt whether it meant to Godard, for example, what Bach evidently means to Bergman. The references were always external and explicit: the Bach fugue picked out on the piano in *Wild Strawberries* points us to the structural principle of the entire film; Haydn in *Le Petit Soldat* is just a record on the gramophone. Retrospectively, it is easy to see that Godard was already, at least in negative terms, prepared for the step into Marxist politicization: he had already formed the habit of regarding the arts as so much material to be pillaged intellectually rather than as offering enriching experiences to be assimilated into one's inner emotional-intuitive life, and it is much easier to pass to a strictly ideological analysis from the former attitude than from the latter. The apparent rejection of art in Godard's recent films could be felt to have been implicit already in *Les Carabiniers,* where the soldiers react briefly to a Rembrandt self-portrait and a Madonna-and-child but remain permanently or deeply affected by neither: the point of the scene was the *uselessness* of art in relation to society at large, a sort of visual epitome of the view of George Steiner discussed earlier. From *Masculin-Féminin* onwards, artistic references give place increasingly to political references; after *Weekend* they virtually disappear from his work or (like the western in *Vent d'Est*) are referred to with a view to ideological exposure and denunciation.

What, then, is the status of these films, and how does the non-Marxist (but not unsympathetic) critic handle them? One might add another question which may at first sight seem irrelevant to films so determinedly and insistently contemporary in their concern, in their range of subject-matter, in their provocation to action here and now, but which is central to this issue: What will they look like ten, twenty, a hundred years from now? How shall we handle them then? Discard them, as outmoded instruments that have served their purpose? Preserve them as historical documents? View them as perverse curiosities, or as the tentative, primitive beginnings of a new direction not only for art but for civilization? Or see them, shorn of their contemporaneity, as the works of art they perhaps already are? A precedent might usefully be cited here: an artist whose aims, though not identical with Godard's, were not dissimilar; whose work represented a comparable challenge to traditional aesthetics; and to whom Godard himself repeatedly refers, in films and interviews. In *Tout Va Bien* he has Yves Montand (as ex-New Wave film-maker) say, "I've discovered things that Brecht was into forty years ago." The remark is made in connection with Montand's abandonment of a cherished project to film a David Goodis novel. Goodis wrote the book on which *Tirez sur le*

Pianiste was based, and Godard uses his name for a character in *Made in USA:* Montand's abandoned project, then, is a convenient synthetic reference-point for the pre-1968 New Wave (including Godard's own films), with its critical championship of and obsessive *hommage* to the Hollywood cinema. Its replacement by "things that Brecht was into forty years ago" epitomizes the replacement of tradition by revolution. Yet Brecht is now himself a generally accepted and respected part of tradition: his plays are produced by such bourgeois-capitalist organizations as the Royal Shakespeare Company without any sense of incongruity. Walter Benjamin saw Brecht as rendering the traditional theatre, and such bourgeois forms as opera, obsolete, and as intrinsically opposed to them; yet one can now pass from, say, *Don Giovanni* to *The Caucasian Chalk Circle* quite easily and naturally, with no sense of irreconcilable experiences.

This phenomenon is susceptible of various explanations. The two most obvious are that time has revealed the permanent artistic value of Brecht's work, its human qualities, its power to move audiences to tears and laughter independently of any political stance or message; and that the conversion of Brecht's plays into standard classics is merely another example of how the bourgeois ideology renders revolutionary writers safe by a process of gradual assimilation and betrayal. The two are not of course incompatible: one could easily find both true simultaneously, or see the first as merely a bourgeois rationalization of the process described in the second. Both, even in combination, are unacceptable without two important corollaries. Firstly, we may now, having accepted Brecht and apparently rendered him safe for bourgeois consumption, be unconsciously assimilating his socio-political attitudes; absorbed into general "culture," he may have become a more potent, more pervasive (if less direct) force than he was when his plays addressed minority groups, a part of an historical process operating in multitudinous ways in multitudinous contexts preparing the world imperceptibly for a new social order. Secondly, if tradition has changed Brecht by assimilating him, Brecht has changed tradition. Only the most intractably "bourgeois" (in the narrower sense) areas of the theatre have been unaffected by him; it is now not only possible but easy to imagine a "Brechtian" production of *Don Giovanni* (any Mozart opera would respond to such treatment admirably), which is partly why we can pass from it to *The Caucasian Chalk Circle* without loss of equanimity.

Something of the same process may come to pass with Godard; in some respects it has already begun. I find it difficult to imagine that *Pravda, British Sounds* and *Vent d'Est* (and the second, at least, was made for audiences beyond an intellectual élite) will ever prove as assimilable into the mainstream of tradition as *The Caucasian Chalk Circle* and *Der Dreigroschenoper,* but *Tout Va Bien* may: it is a film one can learn to enjoy. On the other hand, just as Brechtian practice has had pervasive effects on stage production, so Godardian practice has on the cinema: though Altman need never have seen a Godard movie, certain aspects of *The Long Goodbye* (the way the theme music is used, for example) which are not at all like Godard, would probably be impossible without the fact of Godard somewhere in the distant background.

The interest of *Vent d'Est* (outside its intellectual élite) is not easy to define. Its aesthetic, obviously, is inseparable from its revolutionary politics; yet as soon as one realizes it *has* an aesthetic, and a perfectly coherent one, it becomes possible to accept the film without necessarily accepting its socio-political position. It becomes, in fact, to adopt a Godardian title, "un film comme les autres." The more I see it, and the more I ponder it, the more clearly does this revolutionary tool reveal itself as a work of art.

A brief examination of a couple of sequences from the film may make my point clearer. Near the beginning, we see two of the actors being made up: the girl who (in the continually undercut but still present "fiction" of the film) will stand as a representative of bourgeois repressiveness, and the man who will appear as the Indian. The fact that we see the make-up being applied establishes the status of the actors in the film: they will not "act" but "represent" (in the sense in which a mark on a map might be agreed to represent a town), and this rejection of illusionism, freeing Godard from the constraints of narrative plausibility, will allow him to put them to many different uses. The possible complexity of effect arising from a combining of some of those uses is adequately suggested by the detail of the make-up sequence itself. Two distinctions are made between the two players: one, the girl is being made up "realistically": when her make-up is completed, she will look like the heroine of a western ("Southern Belle" variety). The man's make-up is strikingly (and increasingly) non-naturalistic: great streaks and smears of greasepaint are applied to his face so grotesquely that he ceases to look like anyone's idea of an Indian (real or cinematic). Two, the man is applying his own make-up; the girl is being made up by an off-screen assistant. These differences (which are exclusively visual, nothing in the commentary—which is concerned with a history of revolutionary cinema—drawing our attention to them) permit Godard here a poetic synthesis of related ideas central to the film: the opposition of "bourgeois" (representational, "realist," illusionist) cinema and "revolutionary" (anti-illusionist) cinema; the notion that bourgeois ideology can count on support and depends on pretence or subterfuge, while the revolutionary must do everything for himself and rejects pretence; class exploitation (the make-up man as the "Southern Belle's" servant). The commentary (characteristically of the film as a whole) is at once autonomous and related: it satisfyingly counterpoints the images without explaining them. An account of the setbacks and victories of revolutionary cinema accompanies the concrete embodiments of the two ideologically (hence methodologically) opposed cinemas in the image. It is also important that one cannot understand the images without *consciously* working out the ideas they imply: a further, and necessary, characteristic of revolutionary cinema, as opposed to the emotional involvement encouraged by the bourgeois cinema.

Later, we see the Indian (and two other prisoners—the chained couple of the film's opening) led through the countryside by a cavalryman, a Union Delegate acting as intermediary: one of the passages in the film where commentary gives place to dialogue. The cavalryman oppresses and maltreats the Indian, while the latter's cries of "Down with the ruling class! Power to the working class!" are "translated" by the Union Delegate into a plea for "better working conditions and more pay." Again text and picture combine to produce a complex poetic image of oppression on many levels. The dialogue connects class oppression with Fascist tyranny (the Indian is being taken to a "concentration camp"); the image adds to this, as another facet, the subjugation of the Indians in America; the presence of the constrained couple adds a suggestion of sexual repressiveness; Godard's anti-illusionist method (the setting is an anonymous bit of very un-"western" countryside) reminds us that we are not watching a western but a film that *makes reference to* westerns, encouraging us to reflect that the western itself has been a vehicle for the imposition of American bourgeois ideology (a point taken up explicitly later in the film).

Obviously, if one responds positively to *Vent d'Est* (and it is not without its arid stretches) one will be affected and influenced by its attitudes: that could be said of any work of art. What its champions insist on, however, is its anti-traditional nature, its demand for (if not actual creation of) a new aesthetic that will effectively destroy the old. On a superficial level this is obvious enough—certainly, one cannot sit back and enjoy the narrative. On a deeper level, *Vent d'Est* seems to prove that it is impossible for a work of art to avoid satisfying the fundamental criteria denounced as "bourgeois" short of degenerating into a nonsense. As soon as it becomes possible to respond aesthetically to *Vent d'Est*—to take pleasure in its organization of complexities, its internal relationships, its *coherence*—the film automatically takes its place beside the works of the past, and one is no more *forced* to accept or reject its viewpoint than one is forced to accept or reject the values and world-view of Jane Austen. Its complex of attitudes, that is to say, becomes one of many by which one can choose to be indirectly affected, can regard as an "authentic" experience to place beside one's own. One can respond to the *St. Matthew Passion* without having to be a Christian or feeling oneself threatened with instant conversion; one can respond to *Vent d'Est*—even, in certain ways, be moved by it—without being, or feeling that one must become, a Marxist.

10. Against Conclusions

At the end of *Tout Va Bien* (or, "I'm All Right, Jacques"), the two central figures (Yves Montand and Jane Fonda) have evolved to the point where they realize that they must learn to "live historically"; to define themselves and their role in relation to the movement of society and the progress of history; to reconcile and make coherent private and public life, personal relationship and social function, sex and politics. Through its open-ended structure, through a method and style that continuously invite the spectator's active participation, the film clearly constitutes a challenge to its spectators analogous to the challenge confronted by its protagonists. The confluence of the recent cinematic and critical developments I have been examining makes it impossible for any critic today to evade that challenge unless he is willing to resign himself to life on a private island (not to mention the wider social-political-cultural context within which those developments have their meaning). That I feel my own role both precarious and difficult to define will perhaps by now be sufficiently clear. My relationship to the trends I have been considering is not one of simple antagonism: my attitude to anything that challenged the prevailing critical establishment could never be that.

A regular attendant at a series of lectures I gave reported to me that my favourite word was clearly "ambivalent"; when I told this in turn to a close friend he said, No, my favourite word is "um." I have a feeling that both are becoming supplanted by the word "tensions": it points to a concept which is fundamental to my sense of life, art and criticism. Man himself appears a system of tensions—between angel and devil, superego and id, reason and instinct, intellect and emotion. The structural oppositions on which we, like works of art, are built, are probably not reconcilable but can be held in balance: what we mean, surely, by talking about a "balanced" person. I earlier described valid criticism as developing out of a tension between subjective and objective poles, and personal response as an intercourse between emotion and intellect. I think our relationship with works of art can be defined in similar terms. There is, on the one hand, the process of assimilation, of emotional and intellectual absorption, without which art has no purpose. Against this must be set our sense of the work's "otherness," our awareness of modes of thinking and feeling quite different from our own, whose difference we should respect without wishing to change it. What I am describing is something very like an ideal personal relationship, and I think the analogy has partial validity. We do not, ideally, demand that our friends be mere reflections of ourselves; we try to understand and accept them as they are. The more we know about them the better: there is no value in friendship built on illusion or on a lack of understanding of what the other person really is. But as soon as the essential spark of response dies, it is no longer proper to speak of friendship. Similarly with art and criticism: the work that is coldly inspected *only* for its ideological assumptions or its possible contributions to knowledge has become a corpse on the dissecting table, and we are no longer critics but anatomists: the *aliveness* of the work is lost to us. As with people, the relationship is a living one or it is nothing—if we are concerned with art as art, not art as data.

The necessary end of criticism is evaluation; but evaluation must always remain an open-ended process. The process itself is characterized by a tension between our sense that a work of art is unique and incomparable, and the necessity of continual comparison, the setting of this experience beside that. It is a process that implies a sense of the multiplicity of life and a ready acceptance of that multiplicity. It is closely bound up with the concept of ideal democracy. Democracy is not only a means of socio-political organization, it is also a state of mind, the leading characteristic of which is an openness to heterogeneous and possibly contradictory experiences and a guarded willingness to be influenced by them.

According to widespread assumption I seem to be cast for the Leavis role in British film criticism (which is rather like casting Mickey Rooney as Tarzan). I am worried by this—to a degree that has made it difficult to write this book—on two counts. First, I am afraid that my own inadequacies, indecisions, uncertainties, may be used to discredit the Leavis position. Second, I feel that the "Leavis position," in its pure and integral form (with which I seem to be associated in people's minds, though my actual writings scarcely support this), is no longer tenable: the disintegration of civilization—of Western civilization as we know it—has gone too far, the collapse of standards has become too absolute, the possibility that the only *realistic* alternative to total breakdown may be some form of Marxist society forces itself too powerfully on the consciousness. Yet if the choice really proves to be between the "mere anarchy" Yeats saw as "loosed upon the world" and the "rough beast" whose birth the anarchy makes possible, then it is at least arguable that the only decent response is to withdraw into despair. Despair—at least in the public realm—is for me (and, I imagine, many others) a permanent temptation, the desire to retreat into a private world very strong. I am saved from it less by any optimism than by a certainty that personal happiness, if it is purely personal, cannot exist—that happiness depends always on a sense of function.

This is why the ending of *Tout Va Bien,* with its challenge to "live historically," to define a function for oneself that unifies the personal and the public, has come to mean so much to me. And I may remark in passing here—though it is but cold comfort—that I have come to wonder whether Godard and I are really so far apart as I had supposed and as the political dogma and rhetoric of his recent films insistently asserts. In the factory scenes and workers' monologues/interrogations, despair rises dangerously near the surface: the speakers argue themselves towards silence, towards a recognition that the fundamental issue is not being faced. Godard, with his probing honesty, is driven to the point where it becomes evident that the real object of protest is not capitalism or the class system but the technological society itself—that, whatever the social arrangement, the great mass of humanity will still be committed to the routine performance of boring jobs in which they can feel no human or creative involvement. And Godard, of course, knows that no alternative to the technological society any longer exists—that there can now be no turning back. One would like to know why, since *Tout Va Bien,* he has himself been silent.

It is necessary, at this point, to develop further the statement that I find Dr. Leavis's position, in its pure form, no longer tenable. The ways in which my own differs from it seem to me pretty obvious, but—to judge from remarks about my own work both in and out of print—they are not obvious to everyone, and had better be made explicit. Leavis is a great critic, and a great man: although a critic, one of the great *creative* minds of the century—the remark will not appear paradoxical to those familiar with Leavis's own use of the word "creative" in the indispensable *Nor Shall My Sword*. It is not a matter (as is sometimes given out) of his telling us which books to read and which not to, "prescribing" this and "proscribing" that; it is not simply a matter of "literary values." For many students and readers (myself among them—though I never, to my now deep regret, made contact with him beyond the lecture theatre) he has given life value, or revealed its potential value. I, on the other hand, am not an original thinker, and I have never achieved the purity and integrity that Leavis so impressively represents. That the point needs to be made at all testifies only to the injustice that is commonly done Leavis, by distortion or simplification. Like the work of a great artist, Leavis's writing cannot be reduced or paraphrased; yet it is through paraphrase (usually amounting to parody) that it seems most current—certainly in film circles. As for the force and cogency of Leavis's arguments where, indeed, are the snows of yesteryear? Yet it is distressing that acknowledgment of that cogency remains largely tacit: the figures Leavis demolishes are quietly dropped, but the "culture" they represent stubbornly continues.

My own inferiority is perhaps sufficiently recognized in the term "disciple" which is commonly applied to me. Yet it is not a term I like—not with the connotations it commonly carries: uncritical follower, one who "spreads the word" of the Master. I see my work—for all its manifest inadequacies—as developing out of Leavis's; and it is *development* that seems to me crucial. For Leavis is not a dead end, as the Marxist/semiological school appears to imply (largely by ignoring him): a line of descent *must* be preserved. His essential concerns are not outmoded and have never been discredited: how could they be, given that the central concern is with life, the value of life, the quality of life? Though this is not noticeably a concern of the Marxist/semiologists, bent on making of criticism a "science": for them, it is merely "within the ideology," along with the individual creativity from which it is inseparable.

But "development" suggests change and transformation, and brings me to those areas where "discipleship" becomes something different; to my "Yes, but . . ." to the "This is so, isn't it?" that Leavis proposes. I take my stand on fundamental Leavisian principles. Like Leavis, I believe that "'Life' is a necessary word"; like him, I can think of nowhere but in individual lives that "social hope" could be located; like him, I find all questions of artistic quality inseparable from a concern with the quality of life—both individual lives and the life of the culture within which they develop. And, as a university lecturer, I endorse unreservedly Leavis's view of the university's function as "a creative centre of civilization," with the full force he gives to the word "creative." Leavis's indispensability can be summed up by saying that he stands for all those aspects and potentials of critical discourse that *Screen* appears bent on suppressing. (My choice of word is deliberate: it is not simply that Leavis's concerns are ignored—one of the efforts of the critical language that the Marxist/semiologists are seeking to impose is to make discussion of them impossible.) My view of art and its function has been sufficiently defined for further recapitulation to be unnecessary: the reader will be aware, at least, of broad areas of common ground I share with (or have inherited from) Leavis. At the same time, while insisting on the necessary centrality and dominance of questions of value and quality, I feel there are perfectly valid interests in art which Leavis's approach (while it does not preclude them) does not actively favour: an interest, for example, in the way in which the development of popular genres reflects the essential movement of the society that produces them: an interest that would involve the exploration of areas and levels that the Leavisian concern with value tends to reject wholesale.

There is, perhaps, no point where I can disagree with Leavis cleanly and completely; to dissociate myself from certain aspects of his thought is consequently a delicate operation. One such aspect, however, is that suggested by the term "permissiveness": I always feel uneasy at those points where Leavis uses it, because I think he treats the issue it indicates too simply. For Leavis, it seems to mean simply "mindless promiscuity," and a trivializing of sexual relationships. One can hardly doubt that the move towards "permissiveness" in our society carries these dangers, but it cannot simply be equated with them. As a homosexual (for the sake of honesty my personal interest in the issue must be made clear), I am profoundly grateful that my adult life is being lived now rather than fifty years ago—when I could scarcely have written these words or found a publisher willing to print them. The failure of creativity that Leavis diagnoses in E. M. Forster (see the last essay of *Nor Shall My Sword*) cannot be explained simply in terms of "coteries": one can trace throughout Forster's work the blocking of creative energies by a self-imposed (but socially determined) censorship. That I am able to live happily and openly with another man, without fear of public harassment and without the least sense of social ostracism, is a phenomenon that I take to be inseparable from the development of "permissiveness." (Society still has a long way to go: I am well aware that my own relative freedom is dependent upon the circles in which, as university lecturer and film critic, I move.) I offer it here as one small concrete example of potentialities for life that the relaxing of social taboos has made possible.

More widely, those potentials must be seen in relation to the way in which the traditional notion of marriage-and-family has relaxed its ideological grip. In a truly healthy society—or so it seems to me—marriage-and-family would be regarded as one of several possible options; a society that insists upon it as the one true norm and a society that regards it as outmoded and ridiculous should be equally unacceptable. Deliberately childless marriage, celibacy, impermanent unions, homosexual union, would be other options accepted by society and open to its members; so, if they ever proved workable, would more complicated setups from the *ménage à trois* to the commune (which might itself contain all the various possibilities within it). I do not see that an emphasis on the individual and social need for responsibility in life and in relationships is incompatible with such an ideal. Where Leavis's tendency is to discriminate *against* "permissiveness," mine is to discriminate *within* it.

The other area where I find it necessary to dissociate myself from Leavis is, inevitably, the cinema; though the implications go far beyond a fondness for films. About the cinema, Leavis is silent; for me, it has become the central focus for creativity in the twentieth century, taking over from the novel as the novel took over from poetry in the nineteenth. There seem to me three main reasons why Leavis should find it convenient to ignore (or should choose to remain unaware of) the achievements of film, and between them they cover the cinema fairly comprehensively.

First, he would be forced to redefine—and in far more complex terms—his attitude to twentieth-century popular culture. There are immense differences between the Elizabethan drama and the Hollywood cinema (and they are mostly to Hollywood's disadvantage); if the cinema has produced its Shakespeare, it is not within the English-speaking world. Yet, if one is looking for something one might reasonably call "Shakespearean" art (in the sense in which Leavis sees Dickens as its last representative), one would do better to explore *The Searchers, Rio Bravo* and *Vertigo,* than to await the emergence of a new popular novelist, dramatist or poet.

Secondly, the fact that film represents a movement away from language to images—a dislodging of language as the prime means of creative communication—would constitute a serious obstacle to Leavis's acceptance of it as the central art form of our time. That dislodgement clearly has far-reaching consequences for civilization, because it separates art-expression from our normal primary means of communication (we cannot talk to one another in images). Yet the cinema has established itself—beyond dispute, I think—as a medium for total human expression as complex and comprehensive as the drama or the novel. I would not want to argue that the English School to which Leavis ascribes "a central function" in the university should be superseded by a School of Film; I would certainly wish the two to exist in close and fruitful partnership—a partnership in which the junior member would gradually rise to a level of equality. The presence of such a School of Film would enormously facilitate the work of liaison to which Leavis (rightly, of course) attaches such importance—film relating naturally, by virtue of its hybrid characteristics, to so many seemingly disparate disciplines.

Third, if Leavis came to acknowledge the importance of film, he would be forced to modify his position vis-à-vis national culture, and his emphasis on continuity within a peculiarly British tradition. Claims for the universality of film have perhaps been exaggerated, and problems of trans-cultural understanding correspondingly played down. Paul Willemen clarifies the issue admirably in a useful article in *Screen* (Winter 1974/75, p. 66):

> The film maker cannot but organize the text in function of his own internal speech. If the director is Japanese, the Japanese language will be present in that film, even if it is utterly silent and without any intertitles. . . . On the other hand, the reader cannot but have recourse to his own, necessarily limited, knowledge of languages to activate the signifying structures of the text. It should be stressed that this does not mean that it is impossible to read a text which was composed within the domain of another

language, as the code of internal speech is only one of the many codes at work in the text, the vast majority of which are cross-cultural. But this presence of internal speech, tied to a specific verbal language, nevertheless deals a serious blow to any notion of the cinema as some "universal" language.

Despite the doubts this raises, it is obvious enough that a foreign film can communicate on the visual (and, dialogue apart, auditory) level without the intermediary of a translator: we *see* Mizoguchi's images; we don't read Tolstoy's words. Hence an interest in film (especially as, if he is British and centrally concerned with value, the critic will find little to sustain him within the cinema of his own national tradition) is likely to take in, and even be centred on, such figures as Renoir, Godard, Chabrol, Bergman, Satyajit Ray, Ozu, Mizoguchi, and this will inevitably threaten one's sense of the integrity of a national culture. The film critic tends necessarily towards the international and cosmopolitan; my own proclivities here are doubtless influenced by the fact that music, rather than literature, has always been for me the most personally important of the arts.

It will be recognized that these are not simply local differences: they inevitably affect, directly or indirectly, every area of my own work, and I cannot but suspect that, from Leavis's point of view, they are sufficient to place me in the enemy camp, as an agent of dissolution. But, like a great artist, a great critic does not have to be fully agreed with to be accepted as a major force in one's life and values. Leavis is one of the great *radical* minds of the twentieth century: by which I mean that he confronts one, everywhere, with the essential issues about art, civilization and life. As I write this, I am planning my university course for next year; and its basis, I know, must be a confrontation of Leavis and Godard. *Nor Shall My Sword* will be an obligatory text, and *Tout Va Bien* an obligatory film. What will arise from this vital tension is not yet clear to me; what is clear is that therein lies a challenge that makes most of the current fuss about critical positions seem merely trivial. The challenge lies, essentially, in the necessity for attending to both voices without facilely rejecting the one or the other: in placing oneself at the centre of a fruitful dialectic that will have as its unifying focus a sense of human needs.

I have no wish to set myself up as the enemy of social revolution. Capitalism, with its combination of injustice and inefficiency, could only seem desirable as the least of possible evils. Besides, the capitalist system is obviously entering the phase of final disintegration. I believe that revolution may come, and there are many compelling reasons for welcoming it. I see my own role, however (because determined, no doubt, by the "dominant ideology"—by the complex cultural tradition that has produced me, and to which I am in many ways unrepentantly grateful to belong—I am what I am), as existing outside the revolution; my work as an attempt to uphold values widely regarded as irrelevant or retrograde but which, nevertheless, seem to me still worth preserving, if they can be preserved. Perhaps the revolution, when it comes, will sweep them away, together with everything that I understand by the term "art": those who have really exposed themselves to Godard's recent films (for example) will not, I hope, regard this as mere hysteria. On the other hand, revolutions are seldom so absolute and so permanent, and our Marxists may not find it so easy to impose, universally, a single way of looking at the world, especially where other highly developed cultural traditions are still strong.

I believe in art, in democracy, and in the value of the individual life: the three going, for me, indissolubly together.

3
Levin and the Jam
Realism and Ideology

The concept of Realism has been tackled (and attacked) of late with formidable theoretical elaboration; all that seems lacking is common sense, which I shall endeavour to supply. Fundamentally, any attack on Realism must be an attack on narrative itself. The essential features of Realism (and the audience's experience of it) are the tendency to become interested in characters as if they were real people (the "as if" a matter of the willing suspension of disbelief, and allowing for considerable latitude in terms of degree); the tendency, therefore, to care about the characters and what happens to them; the tendency, therefore, to become emotionally involved, to participate, to identify. All narrative art plays on these closely related tendencies: however many placards Brecht displays, however often he reminds us that we are in a theatre watching actors, the *effectiveness* of his art depends on our interest in the characters and on our emotional involvement—on the way feelings of sympathy and recoil, affection and anger, are aroused and developed. When Godard, with *Tout Va Bien,* returned to a cinema intended for public (as opposed to sectarian) interest, he inevitably returned to narrative: the characterization in *Tout Va Bien* may be tenuous, and our awareness of Montand and Fonda as themselves constant, but the film none the less refers us to the imagined predicaments of a fictitious couple—predicaments with which we are clearly meant to become involved, to which we are invited to relate on a personal level. And one would have to be pretty fanatical to see *Tout Va Bien* as a step down from *Vent d'Est.*

The earliest surviving works of art—the Palaeolithic cave

paintings—are representational, "Realist" (to the point of skilful foreshortening), and arguably narrative (they show not merely animals but men hunting animals). From there on until the present century, every great period of art has been characterized by the same tendencies, from Homer through Chaucer to Lawrence. The *precise* function of art varies from society to society, from age to age (we do not know exactly why the cave-paintings were made or what social role they fulfilled); the desire to represent reality (in however stylized a manner), to tell stories, to engage the spectator's emotions and sympathies, is constant. It is also constant in folk-song and legend. We are told that Realism is the method whereby bourgeois society reassures itself by re-creating a known reality and placing the spectator in a position of dominance and privileged knowledge; the only possible conclusion seems to be that all societies have always been bourgeois, that Palaeolithic man was the first bourgeois, that "popular" and "folk" culture is irredeemably bourgeois. That man has always striven to deal with reality by understanding and mastering it, and that representational or narrative art (given various inflections by cultural determinants in different ages and societies) has been one of his ways of making that attempt, appears a somewhat more acceptable general proposition.

The reason why representational or narrative art has been dominant in all ages is simple: it makes possible a human richness—an appeal from human beings, to human beings, about human beings—that abstract art or art that denies us all emotional involvement and satisfaction cannot (for all their potential interest) possibly encompass. This is not to reject abstract painting on the one hand or *Vent d'Est* on the other: they have their contributions to make, and the nature of those contributions depends on certain deprivations. It is, however, to resist any suggestion that the displacement of narrative or representation by such ventures would be beneficial: the loss would be incalculable.

The growing dominance of the novel among art forms in the nineteenth century represented also the triumph of Realism: the culmination of a process traceable back to the Renaissance (at least), which led in the visual arts to the invention of photography and the cinematograph. The narrative film—owing as much to the development of the novel as to the invention of the camera—provides, then, a remarkable synthesis of the manifold strivings towards Realism in the arts: small wonder that it has established itself as by far the richest and most prolific form of our own century.

It is in the nature of culminations, however, to carry within them the seeds of their own death. Film, most "realistic" of art forms through its photographic representationalism, and notoriously the purveyor of illusory experiences, is also, because of its complicated mechanics, the easiest of art forms to deconstruct. The situation could be suggested through a series of paradoxes; the chief stimulus behind the major technical innovations—sound, colour, wide screen, etc.—seems to have been the urge to perfect the illusion of reality, yet each innovation has offered further possibilities for deliberately artificial (hence anti-Realist) effects; the film-maker most dedicated to the creation of illusions to which the spectator is encouraged to surrender (Hitchcock) is arguably also the one whose artifice is the easiest to penetrate and whose devices are the easiest to become aware of. Even the phenomenon usually regarded as most conducive to fantasy indulgence, the "star," acts on one level as a limitation on cinematic illusion, for even the most unsophisticated of movie-goers, who may be quite unconscious of cameras, of directorial decisions, or of ideological determinants, knows perfectly well that that is not a real cowboy up there on the screen but Jimmy Stewart on a horse again.

Despite appearances and assumptions to the contrary, it seems to me probable that the cinema has never offered quite as engrossing an illusion of "reality" as the novel. Such an illusion depends partly on our imaginative participation, and even the most vividly realized of Realist novels necessarily allows us greater freedom to "picture for ourselves" than a film, where "reality" is created for us, visibly and externally. In taking up the current critical preoccupation with Realism—and particularly with Realism as a means of purveying and enforcing an ideology on unconscious levels—I want to turn progressively from the cinema to the nineteenth century novel, and finally to *Anna Karenina*, "*the* European novel . . . the great novel of modern—of our—civilisation" (F. R. Leavis). The cinema cannot, I think, yet show a comparable achievement; Tolstoy's triumph is the culminating triumph of Realism, in the period immediately before the cinema carried Realist tendencies to their conclusion and beyond; and the book's authoritativeness, the overwhelming scope and success of Tolstoy's venture, makes of it one of the most intimidating of all works to challenge.

"Realism" is a concept generally taken for granted and in fact very difficult to define satisfactorily. The commonest notion of it would probably be "the plausible reproduction of reality as we know it." Such an assumption leads to absurdities of varying degrees of sophistication from (within my own experience) "I've never met anyone like Heathcliff, so *Wuthering Heights* can't be a very good novel," to the remark of a distinguished film educationalist that he disliked *North by Northwest* because he could not stand "that cocktaily sort of people." The criterion by which Realism is assessed is our own experience of life, beside which we place the work in a straight "one to one" relationship; its value is determined by how recognizable we find its characters or by how we would like those characters if we had to live with them. Such a criterion is detrimental in two ways. Most simply, our own experience of life may be limited (there may be Heathcliffs outside it), and our capacity for sympathy deficient. More importantly, a novel or film defines—through method, presentation, style, structure—how we are to read it; defines, that is, its own "reality." Hence "Realism" is relative, not absolute, and can only be judged by reference to the work's internal relationships.

A more acceptable notion of Realism sees it not in terms of the faithful reproduction of an "absolute" objective reality (such a reproduction could never exist, as a moment's serious reflection makes obvious), but as a particular artistic method or strategy. This is not to suggest that the problem is a simple one, or capable of some formulaic solution. It seems to me impossible to experience a work of narrative fiction (whether or not it falls within anyone's definition of Realism) without a degree of imaginative involvement with the characters: indeed, to undertake the writing of a novel or the direction of a fictional film is to invite such participation and to explore its experiential possibilities, be it positively or negatively, by realizing expectations or denying them fulfilment. It is in the question of degree that the relativity of Realism becomes clear: the precise nature of our involvement, its kind and its intensity, will differ appreciably from work to work, each writer or director determining our relationship to his characters through method and style.

The Realist novel, and its most important legacy, Realist cinema, are so central to our culture that we have become indoctrinated to take Realism for granted as an inevitable criterion. One has to set Realist fiction beside other narrative modes—Greek tragedy, say, or the Morality Play, or the *nouveau roman,* or the anti-illusionist cinema of Godard—to realize the relative nature of such a criterion. Greek audiences related in some sense, presumably, to the characters and action of the *Agamemnon,* but they were not invited to suppose that what they were watching was "really" happening or was presented as it actually happened. It is just such an illusion that the Realist novelist or film-maker strives to create. It follows that an alternative term for "Realism" is a word that might at first appear its opposite: Illusionism. It also follows that the opposite of a "Realist" novel is not a novel that is psychologically implausible but a novel that keeps reminding us that it is a novel—which undermines, that is, our illusion of reality and hence allows us a more distanced and critical view of the characters, the narrative and the moral values or ideological assumptions the narrative carries. All nineteenth-century novels are, broadly speaking, Realist, in that they present narratives we are meant to consider plausible (within the context of the "reality" the book defines) and characters we are expected to take an interest in; but they are Realist to very differing degrees. In reading one of the later James novels, for example—*What Maisie Knew, The Awkward Age*—we are so aware of style and structure, of literary strategy and authorial artifice, that the illusion of imaginatively participating in "real life," though certainly not absent, is continually counterbalanced: we *cannot* read *Maisie* simply by submitting to a narrative flow and allowing ourselves to be carried along. James forces us—every one of his stylistic mannerisms is dedicated to it—into analytical awareness. *Anna Karenina,* on the other hand, is clearly by my definition the Realist novel *par excellence,* with only the most minimal sense of an author mediating between us and the "reality" presented; though, paradoxically, the greater the awareness brought to it the greater the book appears.

One of the greatest potential strengths of Realism is the freedom it allows the artist's impulses. Central to all artistic creation is the tension between spontaneous-intuitive impulse and conscious, shaping control. In Realist art, just as we are caught up in an imagined narrative flow, so to varying degrees and on differing levels is the artist: we often hear—and from artists themselves—of characters "taking over," as if for the artist too they had an independent, "real" existence, and this is a way of describing concretely the sense that his conscious control and watchfulness have been partially relaxed, that he has allowed himself to be led in directions not consciously planned. The phenomenon is obviously not restricted to Realist novels and films, but the habits of Realism may be felt to encourage it. This is especially true in the case of "popular" artists like Dickens or Hitchcock, with their advantages of freedom from intellectual self-consciousness.

Scarcely Realist at all in the familiar sense of offering a faithful reproduction of "reality," Dickens and Hitchcock belong pre-eminently to Realism (or Illusionism) as I have defined it. Both are highly conscious artists on certain levels: Dickens's later novels reveal profoundly satisfying structures that completely transcend linear narrative, and it is well known how meticulously Hitchcock plans his films. Yet the richness of their respective work seems at least partly attributable to that freedom from consciousness on other levels which is intimately bound up with their view of themselves as entertainers—the freedom to follow the promptings of the unconscious without too much probing and questioning. One may feel, in many areas of their work, some uncertainty as to what degree, or what kind, of awareness underlies artistic decisions or pieces of invention. In the pre-Freudian days of *Great Expectations,* for example, one might presumably interpret the remarkable insights into sexual pathology in Dickens's depiction of the married life of the Joe Gargerys as intuitive—centred as they are on the phallic symbolism of poker and cane. As Joe tells Pip about his childhood (pages 76–80, Penguin edition), he moves the poker obsessively "between the lower bars" of the grate, "without which I doubt whether he could have proceeded in his demonstration," as Pip remarks. Joe explains how his father "hammered away" at his mother, and unconsciously accounts for his own impotence. It is a childless marriage; Joe's own childlike qualities (he repeatedly associates himself with the pre-sexual Pip as an equal) are continually emphasized; he has rendered himself impotent and married a woman who punishes him and mercilessly suppresses any possibility of rebellion in him ("for fear as I might rise" is the revealing phrase he uses), as compensation for his mother's sufferings. Joe's handling of the poker (obsessive but ineffectual) is referred to eight times within four pages; at one point, Joe rubs his eyes with the "round knob" on its top, an image strongly suggestive of masturbation. The unconscious symbolism is so strong as to keep forcing itself on Dickens's (and the reader's) attention. On the other hand, we have Mrs. Joe's "rampages" of uncontrolled violence, in which she frenziedly wields the "wax-ended piece of cane," Tickler. Cane and poker seem closely linked in Dickens's associative processes: they are introduced into the action almost simultaneously (page 40). Sexual frustration has seldom been so vividly rendered, the pattern being completed by Mrs. Joe's curious and unexplained (on a rational level) love of Orlick, the dangerous, "potent" male who finally strikes her down.

Orlick himself is a fascinating invention. Virtually unexplained in the book as a "character," he is introduced parallel with Pip (both work in Joe's forge), and presented as continually lurking in the shadows. His role strongly suggests that he is Pip's suppressed, "darker" self: his two criminal acts are committed against just the two characters Pip has most reason to resent and to want revenge on, Mrs. Joe and Pumblechook; the instrument with which he strikes down Mrs. Joe is the convict's fetter, the emblem of Pip's own criminality (or, at least, his link with the criminal world, itself presented in the book as a dark underside of Victorian society). At one of the novel's climaxes, Orlick all but overcomes Pip in a dark mill, before being in turn overcome by Pip's "higher" *alter ego* Herbert Pocket (representative of the qualities of the "true gentleman" to which Pip aspires). Orlick's structural significance seems so plain that one is left wondering just how Dickens explained it to himself: to suppose full consciousness of the character's psychological meaning would be unhistorical, yet it is difficult to believe that Dickens was aware of no more than the working out of "plot."

Similarly, one might query the degree of consciousness operating in many Hitchcock movies. The sexual significance of the "key" imagery in *Notorious,* for example—the key Alicia (Ingrid Bergman) steals from her husband (Claude Rains) to give to her lover (Cary Grant). Hitchcock, of course, far from being pre-Freudian, had already made very ostentatious use of Freud in *Spellbound.* Yet the treatment of the key in *Notorious* is very different: completely integrated in the narrative, hence unobtrusive, free from *Spellbound*'s self-conscious insistence, not *demanding* the sexual interpretation. One might even argue that the more conscious Hitchcock is on one level, the freer he becomes on others—as if he needed to be distracted from the deeper implications of his own films. Much of the fascination of *Psycho*—most meticulously calculated of all his films, and calculated, according to Hitchcock's own account, almost exclusively in terms of audience response—obviously derives from its appeal to deep and potent drives only partly accessible to conscious analysis. By what creative process, for example, did Hitchcock (or the film "taking over" from Hitchcock) arrive at the pervasive "eye" imagery and its ultimate extension to the eye of the spectator ("the cruel eyes staring" at Norman in the cell)? Its deliberateness on one level is obvious; but its "meaning"? The question for the critic is less, How did Hitchcock think about its meaning? than, How does one *talk* about it?—"meaning" here being a matter, not of precise or definable symbolism but of complex poetic resonance and suggestion.

The question of what is conscious or not in an artist's work is not really very interesting. What I want to establish here is the expressive potency of the unconscious in much Realist art, and the importance of the artist's readiness to surrender, provisionally at least, to impulse; and, in addition, the necessary connection between this readiness and the involvement of the reader in a narrative flow. There seems to me a direct ratio between the writer's degree of awareness of what he is doing and the degree to which the reader/viewer is encouraged to be aware, distanced, critical. To pass from Dickens's novels to James's is to experience a sense of simultaneous gain and loss. The gain is in clarity of line, precision of effect, immediate sense of relevance; the loss is in richness of resonance.

The challenge to the Realist aesthetic represented by recent film criticism is necessary and admirable; yet here too there is inevitably loss as well as gain. The attack on Realist art is aimed at what is inseparable from certain of its greatest strengths, the fact that it is ideologically unaware. The relative lack of conscious awareness, or its possible intermittent abeyance, accounts for the tension that markedly characterizes many Realist works (though it seems to be to some degree inherent in the artistic process itself): the powerful, often unresolved conflict between subversive and conservative elements. Art grows most frequently out of disturbance, often psychological disturbance, out of those conflicts which, according to Hans Keller's dictum, in a creative person produce art and in an uncreative person neurosis; hence out of a striving for development, progress, change. Yet the artist who submits to the flow of what the Romantics called inspiration is automatically at the mercy of the ideology within which he has developed and which he has absorbed into his being. *Anna Karenina* offers perhaps the most magnificent and extended example of this tension in the whole of literature; but again one can turn to *Great Expectations* for simpler illustration. Dickens masterfully uses the apparently cumbersome machinery of the Victorian melodramatic plot (both here and in *Bleak House*) to build an impressive symbolic structure at the centre of which is Chancery and the Law (*Bleak House*), Newgate and the Law (*Great Expectations*). Both structures become representations of Victorian capitalist society—a society built on money-values, privilege, exploitation and an unpardonable complacency—a society revealed as fundamentally criminal. One of the culminating points of *Great Expectations* (and a superb example of novelistic *mise-en-scène*) is Magwitch's trial, with its pervading theatrical imagery: society complacently confronts its scapegoats (the prisoners in the dock) like an audience at a play; the division is denied by the beam of sunlight that unites audience and spectacle, and by Pip's gesture of holding Magwitch's hand across the partition. This moment, and the whole edifice of which it is the culmination, realize an intense poetic vision of extraordinary cogency and radical insight, profoundly subversive. Yet Dickens, a middle-class writer writing for a middle-class audience, is finally too imprisoned in the traditional bourgeois ideology to offer an effective alternative: to do so, he would have had to cease to be Dickens and become Karl Marx. Pip's salvation takes the accepted middle-class form of hard work and paying one's debts—within the society that the book's more visionary aspects have denounced.

Hitchcock—another profoundly subversive middle-class artist—again provides a parallel. *Psycho* is scarcely a work of overt social criticism, but the picture it offers of a society poisoned and perverted at its very base (the family) is not exactly calculated to induce optimism or complacency. Yet Hitchcock's art, like Dickens's, exists inextricably within the ideology it subverts: the only "positives" the film offers are curiously like Dickens's: hard work to pay off debts, with Marion "licking the stamps" in the back room of Sam's seed shop.

The richness of the work of Dickens and Hitchcock goes with their ideological helplessness: the stance outside their respective societies which alone would make possible a conscious ideological restructuring would automatically make *im*possible the richness, dependent as it is upon their role as entertainers within society, and upon a certain degree of trust of intuitive-emotional impulse. In art, one might argue, ideological awareness is bought at a terrible price. Admirable in some respects as one may find Godard's recent "politicized" films—admirable in their rigour and astringency—one cannot but be aware of their relative thinness of texture, a thinness resulting from the necessity for total vigilance, every impulse, every idea, being ideologically scrutinized and "vetted" before it can pass the censorship. The anti-Realist rigour of *Vent d' Est* is—and must be—above all a refusal to trust oneself, a refusal to make that surrender that Dickens and Hitchcock have made so freely. It is also, of course, a refusal of the very concept of "entertainment," a refusal to allow the audience to enjoy the film on any level but that of conscious cerebration.

No artist has ever carried Realism further than Tolstoy. Much of his art is dedicated to creating the illusion that his characters are "real people." It is not only that we feel that we "know" Anna, Vronsky, Levin, Karenin, more intimately and thoroughly than any other characters in fiction; it is also that the suggestion is continually offered that we do not—and cannot—know *all* about them, that there are areas of mystery that will always be unexplained, which are concealed both from the reader and from the characters themselves. One might point to Anna's and Vronsky's dreams: richly suggestive and haunting, their elements can be interpreted up to a point, but there is always the sense that total understanding is elusive. The dreams are merely the most obvious examples of a strategy discernible on almost every page, in the repeated hints of motivation too complexly determined to be completely explained. This is closely bound up, of course, with the strong "determinist" tendencies of the book—the sense that the characters are impelled by forces they do not completely understand and consequently have inadequate control over. But its effect is everywhere to intensify our illusion of the characters' "reality."

Essential to the completeness of that illusion is the "invisibility" of the author. No novel is more completely dramatized than *Anna*: everything is conveyed through the presentation of action and dialogue or through the rendering of a character's inner life; nowhere does Tolstoy intervene with authorial comment. With this goes the "moral neutrality," the *appearance* of which he strove consistently to maintain, his professed aim being that the reader should never be able to tell what side the author was on. The point can be reinforced by comparison with the English novelist generally regarded as closest to Tolstoy yet in fact far removed from him in method: George Eliot. It is now possible to regard those aspects of George Eliot's writing that became in the twentieth century and in the wake of Henry James so unfashionable—the insistent presence of the author, offering explicit moral commentary, telling us how to regard the characters, what our attitude towards their actions should be—in a more favourable light: they have the effect of setting us at a critical distance from the narrative, reminding us that we are reading a novel, and presenting a defined point of view with which we can argue. It is much easier to argue with George Eliot than with Tolstoy, not because we feel she is more often wrong, but simply because she is always *there*.

"Realism" as complete as Tolstoy's testifies to the artist's total imaginative command of the life he creates. It is also his way of carrying us irresistibly to conclusions without our ever becoming conscious of the means by which we are carried—conscious, that is, of the work as an artificial construct, product of a particular artist governed ultimately by a particular ideology the workings of which he, in his turn, will not be entirely aware. The ideology presented by the book—an ideology central to the movement of European civilization and fully justifying Leavis's claim that *Anna* is "*the* European novel"—is so rich and complex, so intricate in its inter-relationships and interacting qualifications, that an attempt to disentangle a leading thread risks dangerous simplification. Nevertheless, one must learn to resist Tolstoy's persistently offered temptations to accept the progress of the novel as "truth" or "reality." Awareness of essential structure should bring with it awareness of Tolstoy's strategies and clarify the structure of ideas and values which the Realism communicates by imposing itself as "reality."

The book is built on the opposite movements (kept parallel throughout the novel) towards disintegration (Anna/Vronsky) and the achievement of wholeness (Levin). "Wholeness" is conceived in terms of identity or the sense of belonging. Anna and Vronsky forfeit everything that had previously defined them: his career as army officer, the approbation of his mother and brother, comradeship with his peers; Anna's position in society and the respect which, while the acknowledgment of her personal qualities, is also inseparable from that position; and her role as wife and mother. Their subsequent development takes the form of assuming a succession of roles like costumes that never quite fit, in an increasingly desperate search for a sense of belonging. Tolstoy is concerned to demonstrate the insufficiency of passion (however genuine and reciprocal) in a vacuum, the sense that human needs cannot be satisfied solely by another person: one may recall that Levin, in the parallel story, continues to contemplate suicide *after* his marriage to Kitty and the birth of their first child, having still no sense of meaning in life.

Against the final disintegration of Anna and Vronsky (her suicide, his departure for a war in which he hopes to get killed) is set Levin's discovery of "faith": faith being conceived in terms of a total and unquestioning submission to traditional ideology, the ideology indoctrinated from birth:

> Whence comes the joyful knowledge I have in common with the peasant, that alone gives me peace of mind? Where did I get it? . . .
>
> Yes, what I know, I know not by my reason but because it has been given to me, revealed to me, and I know it with my heart, by my faith in the chief things which the Church proclaims. . . .

At the back of every article of faith of the Church could be put belief in serving truth rather than one's personal needs. And each of these dogmas not only did not violate that creed but was essential for the fulfilment of the greatest of miracles, continually manifest upon earth—the miracle that made it possible for the world with its millions of individual human beings, sages and simpletons, children and old men, everyone, peasants, Lvov, Kitty, beggars and kings, to comprehend with certainty one and the same truth and live that life of the spirit, the only life that is worth living and which alone we prize. (pp. 834–35, Penguin translation)

Psychologically, in the context of Levin's character and its development, this is an entirely plausible and satisfying conclusion. Yet this is the essence of "Realist" strategy: to impose a general ideology through the psychological plausibility of a particular case.

Tolstoy employs various tactics to enforce the "inevitability" of his conclusion, notable among them the treatment of "reason"—in the sense of objective, dispassionate enquiry. "Reason" is consistently denigrated throughout the book, most obviously through the attitudes of Levin (the character with whom, most readers will agree, the "appearance" of moral neutrality is most easily penetrated and Tolstoy's bias most discernible). Levin is of course an "intellectual," but he uses his intellectual powers primarily to reject as useless ideas not immediately relevant to his situation. He also sees little use in "progress," be this in the form of railroads or education, or in local politics. Characters in the book who place high value on "reason," or on ideas for their own sake (notably Koznyshev, Levin's half-brother) are regarded (by Levin, hence by Tolstoy) with distrust or are lightly ridiculed: they are wanting in that "rootedness" in which Levin eventually discovers the true value of existence. This attitude spills over into the "Anna" story, Tolstoy subtly undermining any willingness we might have to take Vronsky seriously as a "progressive" agriculturalist; even his building of a hospital is presented as suspect and perhaps not really useful. Most revealing of all, however, is the passage that immediately precedes the lines I quoted (Book 8, chapter 13), in which, in a most curious analogy, the use of "reason" is compared to Dolly's children's attempt to make raspberry jam over lighted candles, a comparison whose function is to render the objective use of intellect trivial and absurd. Tolstoy clearly wishes us to see Levin's finding of "faith" as the discovery of eternal truths. One can see it, instead, as a total submission to indoctrinated ideology: a deeply conservative and reactionary attitude against which *only* the free play of reason could be a safeguard or provide a counterbalance.

The most interesting question is, How does this affect our reading of the "Anna" story?—for the book is the supreme example in all literature of that inter-relatedness that Lawrence saw as the greatest quality and justification of fiction. The "inter-relatedness" certainly causes problems which Tolstoy never really resolves, for all the appearance of triumphant resolution: that "belief in serving truth rather than one's personal needs," so convincing as the outcome of Levin's experiences and self-searchings, becomes nothing short of callous when applied to Anna. Do we read the "Anna" story as the inevitable tragedy of those who affront the immutable laws ("truth" conceived as something absolute, permanent and accessible to intuition) of God and Nature (including their own natures)? Or the tragedy of two people unable to distance themselves sufficiently from the prevailing ideology? Tolstoy presents it (with the methodological aid of a psychological Realism unparalleled in narrative fiction for its richness and density) as the former; we may prefer to see it as the latter. This would involve the recognition that Tolstoy, like Levin, was ultimately trapped in that ideology himself.

It is revealing to put here a question of the sort that should never be asked about the characters of fiction: what would happen to Anna and Vronsky today?—would they still be destroyed? If one can hold at bay for a moment one's awareness of the absurdity of such questions (treating characters who exist only in a specific fictional context as if they were real people), one may answer, perhaps, that, while one cannot be dogmatic, they would certainly stand a much better chance. Their friends would all rally round and share boxes at the opera with them, there would be no question of social ostracizing, and Seriozha could visit at weekends. I mean by this slightly frivolous suggestion to cast some doubt on the absolute validity of Tolstoy's assumption that they have offended against eternal, immutable laws. They have clearly, on the other hand, offended against much more than mere "society": Lawrence's objections to the book strike me as quite simplistic and personally biased. The offence might be seen as one against very deeply rooted *ideological* assumptions of a kind easily mistaken for instinct or eternal truth—the identical assumptions to which Levin finally submits: central Christian values, marriage and family, transmitted (hence time-sanctioned) beliefs. The couple's only possible salvation from disaster would lie in an ability to distance themselves from the accepted ideology, which could be done only through intellectual detachment and dispassionate analysis. The impossibility for Anna (as a marvellously conceived and realized character) of achieving such a distance is rendered by Tolstoy with overwhelming intensity in the sequences of her last, helpless journeys and her suicide: again, the "Realism" is psychologically unimpeachable. At the same time, we have seen how Tolstoy treats intellectual detachment elsewhere in the novel, and how Levin has deliberately to annihilate it from his own make-up in order to submit to traditional authority.

"Reason" turns up, very revealingly, at two crucial points in the "Anna" story. Anna uses it to defend contraception, "What was my reason given me for, if I am not to use it to avoid bringing unhappy beings into the world?" (page 669). We must, I think, accept that Tolstoy is solidly behind Dolly in her horrified reaction to this, wretched as Dolly's situation (as child-bearer to a man who has lost all sexual interest in her) is presented as being: Tolstoy's attitude is confirmed by another "key" example of inter-relatedness, the birth of Levin's and Kitty's son, "the greatest event in a woman's life" (page 740), which "answers" the discussion of contraception, contrasting the beauty of Kitty's motherhood with Anna's mockery of pregnancy, "She curved her white arms in front of her stomach" (page 669). The second crucial reference comes just before Anna's death. She hears a woman on the train remark to her husband, "Reason has been given to man to enable him to escape from his troubles" (page 799). It is possible to read the irony of this in a way Tolstoy can hardly have intended: he presents it as mockery of Anna's hopeless position, we may see it as pointing to a lost possibility of salvation. In either case it is of no use to Anna, who at that stage can interpret "escape" only in terms of death. Levin's finding of faith also has its significant anticipation in the moment of Anna's suicide: just before she drops under the train, she automatically crosses herself (page 801), a gesture she has mentally ridiculed a little earlier (page 799); and, just as Levin's revelation is of a faith rooted in his childhood inheritance, so here "The familiar gesture brought back a whole series of memories of when she was a girl, and of her childhood, and suddenly the darkness that had enveloped everything for her lifted." It is not the surrender to sexual passion that Tolstoy's novel implicitly denounces, but the use of "reason" to provide ideological awareness and distance—the only possible way in which the "inevitability" of Anna's tragedy might have been countered. One is led again, in other words, while venerating Tolstoy's art, to question

the ideological assumptions that his Realism imposes as absolute truth.

It was after writing *Anna Karenina* that Tolstoy renounced
art altogether, and the rejection, interestingly, took the specific
form of a contemptuous dismissal of fictions about adulterous
relationships between officers and ladies. The experience of
writing the novel was obviously a profoundly disturbing and
subversive one. Anna's tragedy is presented with extraordinary
empathy and inwardness, imaginatively "lived," every step of the
way, by its author, and the logical extension of a sympathy for
Anna and her predicament would be a sense of the necessity
for radical social change. It is easy to see, within the reactionary Tolstoy, a precariously suppressed revolutionary struggling
to get out: a revolutionary who, given Tolstoy's incomparable
artistic seriousness and depth, would have insisted on going all
the way. It is part of my point—in relation to the whole question of Realism in literature and film, and the related question
of art and ideology—to insist that this would not have made of
Anna Karenina a greater novel; that artistic value and ideological acceptability are two quite distinct matters—however great
the difficulty many of us may have in keeping them separate yet
in balance. That Anna, who dares to affront society and the "law
of God," is destroyed by the railroad that Levin despises, is at
once the ultimate (if oblique) expression of Tolstoy's dominant
conservatism and a triumph of artistic inter-relatedness: when
Anna, during her last despairing journeyings, remembers her
childhood her first thought is, "There were no railways in those
days" (page 790).

The complex nature of our relationship to works of art needs
stressing here: it is seldom likely to be one of simple, total acceptance. The fact that a book I find increasingly questionable
ideologically continues to affect me as among the half-dozen
greatest works of art in my experience, neither troubles me nor
strikes me as paradoxical. Ultimately, it is only possible to ap-

preciate *Anna Karenina*—to respond to it as a work of art, to follow emotionally as well as intellectually the subtle complexities of its inter-relationships—by voluntarily re-entering the ideology and submitting to it provisionally. The adverbs are crucial: it will be our awareness of the voluntary and provisional nature of our submission that will prevent us from being merely enslaved.

4
The Play of Light and Shade
The Scarlet Empress

> A value-judgement can't, we all know, be demonstratively
> enforced; the critic can only attempt to help other readers
> to an approach by which, freed from inappropriate expec-
> tations and preconceptions and adverted as to the kind of
> thing they have in front of them, they will be able to *take*
> the poem—take it for what it is: the judging goes with the
> taking.
>
> F. R. LEAVIS, *Scrutiny,* 1943

Even the name is ambiguous: Joe Stern, or Josef von Sternberg?
The ambiguity, in any case, is singularly appropriate to a director with insistent aspirations to high art and European culture
destined to struggle to realize those aspirations within the context of the Hollywood cinema: a struggle doomed to eventual
failure, but producing a series of triumphs before the inevitable
defeat.

Von Sternberg's career is marked by an effort to dominate
so extreme as to most eloquently express his terror of losing
control: a dichotomy also manifested in the simultaneous arrogance and vulnerability (the former masking the latter) so characteristic of his autobiography *Fun in a Chinese Laundry.* We
know that he preferred to make his films in studios, where he
could control every detail; that he exercised the most meticulous
control over decor, so that every leaf, every festoon, every bit of
veiling, is there because he meant it to be there: tendencies carried to their ultimate in his last film, *The Saga of Anatahan,* for
which he went out to Japan in the interests of authenticity, and
then built an island—trees, creepers and all—in a film studio.

The obsession with control stretches to all aspects of his films: apparently he not only conducted the *Scarlet Empress* score but composed it, with the help of Mendelssohn, Wagner and, especially, Tchaikovsky. It extends to his attitude to actors, who are "puppets": every detail of Dietrich's performances in the seven films they made together, every gesture, every movement, every expression, was created by von Sternberg—according to von Sternberg.

He has offered various pronouncements that, in their combination of arrogance and concealment, are profoundly typical. For *Morocco* (the first Hollywood film with Dietrich, after he had introduced her to the world in *The Blue Angel*) he purposely chose a "fatuous" subject, so that the spectators would not be distracted from "the play of light and shade." He also said he would like to have his films projected upside down, for the same reason. The motivation prompting such remarks is not difficult to guess. The films were made at a time when (even more than now) for the great mass of the public directors were "invisible" and films were experienced in terms of their stars and their plots; von Sternberg was simply over-compensating, insisting on his own presence as determining force, on the phenomenon of visual style. But the consequences of such pronouncements are potentially dangerous: taken literally, they encourage an assumption that von Sternberg, in the clutches of the Hollywood machine, dwindled into an aesthete, that the films can be dismissed (as they often have been) as over-decorated "aesthetic" nothings: the dread word "camp" is not far away. In fact, the "subjects" of the Dietrich films can be conclusively demonstrated, in every case, to be of the utmost importance—the true "subject" of a film being created by its style rather than existing in opposition to it. The plot-lines might not look very inviting on paper but a story only exists when it is told and becomes a "subject" from the manner of the telling. The plot of *Morocco* concerns a romance between a showgirl and a foreign legionnaire; its subject is the ambiguities of free will and determinism. The "play of light and shade" is not an aesthetic abstraction but an essential factor in the films' total articulation. One feels, too, that von Sternberg was perfectly aware of this: no effect in *The Scarlet Empress* appears inadvertent.

The precise character of a film is necessarily determined partly by the material circumstances of its production. *The Scarlet Empress* belongs—somewhat uneasily—to the genre of historical romance; it is also a vehicle for its star. Its peculiar quality can be attributed to von Sternberg's deliberate acceptance and manipulation of "genre," "star vehicle" and all that those terms imply—the necessity that the film be palatable to mass audiences and that the studio heads (at least) be convinced of its commercial viability. (It was, in the event, a flop, but that does not affect the point.) It is very difficult—impossible perhaps—to distinguish clearly between von Sternberg's highly idiosyncratic personal impulses and what he may have regarded cynically as "commercial" compromise. Would the film have been different if he had made it in complete freedom? It is unlikely that it would have been better. But its central problem and fascination—the question of tone—seems intricately bound up with its ambiguous status as "art" movie and "pop" movie, as much as with von Sternberg's strange personal fusion of anguish and cynicism.

I want to work through the film chronologically (but not exhaustively) offering a series of annotations that will, it is hoped, accumulate and coalesce into a coherent but unschematic "reading." One may start, simply, by noting the appropriateness of the title, "scarlet" here uniting associations with sexuality and blood.

The problem of tone is present from the outset, in the music: popular classics, Tchaikovsky preponderant (fourth Symphony, *Marche Slave,* 1812 Overture) with the occasional use of Mendelssohn (the *Midsummer Night's Dream* Overture) and Wagner (those indispensable Valkyries). Film scores frequently pilfered from the classics in the early years of sound (Ulmer's *The Black Cat* is but one notable example)—continuing, doubtless, the tradition of the piano accompaniment in the silent era. Yet the use in *The Scarlet Empress* seems rather different: more deliberate, more obtrusive, more pervasive, more integral: a major artistic strategy rather than mere "mood-music" accompaniment. Is it the sort of music that Joe Stern (the democratic American) enjoys or the sort that Josef von Sternberg (the European aristocrat) cynically assumes the mass audience will be impressed by? Certainly, it has the function of introducing a popular entertainment we are to find "classy" but not too esoteric. Perhaps the most important thing about the music is that it is at once vaguely authentic (being mostly, though far from exclusively, Russian) and inauthentic (being completely out of period): it suggests a stylization of Russia, a Russia of legend rather than of history.

The point is reinforced by the fairly close juxtaposition of the screenplay credit with the first narrative caption. The credit insists on historical authenticity, claiming Catherine the Great's private diary as authority; the caption immediately evokes fairy-tale or legend—the "little princess" destined to become the "Messalina of the North." It sets the tone for the captions that punctuate the action, like the preambles to new chapters: a combination of legend, popularized history and romance, like the music ambiguously imposing and tongue-in-cheek, depending on the degree of sophistication the spectator brings to them.

This is an appropriate place to deal briefly—glancing ahead—with related problems of dialogue and acting. The question is the same: that of the level of seriousness on which the film is to be taken. There are elements in the tone that (combining with the mythologization of Dietrich developed throughout the series of films and reaching its apotheosis here and in *The Devil Is a Woman,* and with the extravagance of the décor) have lent themselves to a view of the film as glorified camp—a view that inevitably trivializes it. Von Sternberg is careful to prevent our taking the film too seriously as an "authentic" historical reconstruction: on that level, the tone—deliberately banal dialogue laced with glaring colloquialisms such as the Dowager Empress's addressing of the scheming Countess as "Lizzie," the flat, stylized delivery of (especially) John Lodge—is that of a charade rather than of "documentary." But to stop at that level is to miss the intensity and anguish that, after all, it only half conceals: intensity and anguish that have little to do specifically with Russian history and a great deal to do with the obsessions characteristic of von Sternberg's films, whatever their period or locale.

The opening scene confirms the suggestion of fairy-tale by presenting, in the child Sophia Frederica, an archetype of innocence, blonde and angelic, and opposing to it a mother who, bent wholly on material success, removes its toys: the child is to become a queen. Against the mother is set the humane doctor who clearly disapproves of Mama's mercenariness and arranges for the child eloquently to stick out her tongue at her. The simple attitudes thus elicited are swiftly undermined: the humane doctor is also the public hangman, and the angelic child's innocence is already equivocal: nothing is what it appears. "Can I.become a hangman some day?" Sophia Frederica asks the kindly manservant—who responds by reading her a book about hideous tortures and executions. The word "hangman" is important: the doctor is in fact an executioner, leaving to perform an "operation" by removing a head; yet the visual image "hangman" evokes has closer relevance to the intricately interconnected imagery of the film.

From a close-up of the child's face von Sternberg dissolves to the extraordinary fantasy-sequence of horrors, which uses an editing device suggestive of turning the pages of a book: each image flattens as it gives place to the next. The technical devices and the preceding dialogue permit a three-fold implication: one, the images represent the horrors actually perpetrated in the world, past and present—the world into which Sophia Frederica will grow up (the manservant mentions Ivan the Terrible and Peter the Great); two, the fantastic and grotesque nature of the images suggest nightmarish illustrations in a child's storybook; three, the long dissolve from the child's face suggests that what we see exists inside her mind—is her visualization and perhaps partly her fantasy. Several of the images associating torture and nudity carry strong sado-erotic overtones. The executioner clearly enjoys his work, performing it with immense zest. The start of the sequence also offers an extraordinarily vivid prophetic metaphor for what becomes of Sophia Frederica in the course of the film: the opening dissolve associates the child's wondering face with the image of an Iron Maiden from which, when it is opened, there sinks a limp, naked female body—the soul, stifled to death within the protective shell of will-power and brutalization.

The final item in the procession of horrors has the executioner ("hangman") pulling on a bell-rope, followed by the revelation that the clapper is a near-naked man, dangling upside-down by his feet, thrown helplessly from side to side of the bell-mouth. As von Sternberg moved into the sequence by way of a dissolve, so another very long and slow dissolve leads us out: Sophia Frederica, now grown up, is moving joyfully to and fro on a swing. The dissolve superimposes the two images so that the movements coincide: briefly, the human bell-dapper and the girl on the swing become one. The fusion, in the very complexity of its suggestions, is central to the film's meaning. Such a juxtaposition can imply either comparison or contrast, likeness or unlikeness. Our first impression may well be of the contrast between the nocturnal fantasy-horrors and the blithe and carefree girl in the spring light. Yet the fantasy was partly the child's (as the return to Sophia at the end of the torture-sequence confirms), and grew out of her question, "Can I become a hangman some day?": torture and girl are mysteriously connected, and linked to the idea of Destiny. Similarly, we may first wish to contrast the volitional movement of the girl on the swing with the helplessness of the torture-victim; yet their identification by means of the dissolve immediately qualifies this impression: perhaps (the suggestion is) the girl's freedom is only illusory, the man's terrifying helplessness a metaphor for her inability really to control her fate. The fusion of images also has strong sexual overtones: Sophia Frederica swings right into the camera, so that we look up into the darkness inside her skirts, which are rounded like a bell, and this is connected with the half-nude male figure in the real bell-mouth: power, sadism and sexuality are thus closely associated, impotent phallus juxtaposed with flaunted and triumphant vagina. From this point on, swinging objects will recur frequently in the film and bells will ring to announce each stage in Sophia Frederica's rise to power: the dissolve provides a germinal image-cluster from which various outgrowths of related imagery will develop. The peal of triumph will in each case carry strong overtones of irony (the marriage to a madman, the birth of the heir to the throne who is in fact a bastard). And so unforgettable is the image, every time the bells peal out we shall remember the human bell-clapper.

The sequence depicting the arrival of Count Alexei (John Lodge) and culminating in the departure for Russia of Sophia Frederica, introduces a further complex of motifs unified by the underlying notion of imprisonment or suppression. Throughout this part of the film, Sophia Frederica's youthful, spontaneous but undirected energy is everywhere stressed and carries strong positive connotations: she swings vigorously, she runs everywhere, she jumps up and down and claps her hands with childlike excitement. Equally stressed are the curbs imposed on this vitality. On the simplest, most literal level, when Alexei arrives she is locked in her room. The woman's clothing, throughout the film, is at once sexually provocative and cumbersome. The bell-shaped skirts recur and become an aspect of the imagery of entrapment: later, at the Russian court, we shall see Sophia being strapped into a petticoat like a cage, and when Alexei gives her a pendant her tight-fitting dress will allow her nowhere to conceal it. Sophia's impetuous running is forced into a meaningless and constantly interrupted circling, as she rushes round the circle of relatives pausing breathlessly to kiss each hand in futile ritual (an effect underlined in the music, von Sternberg repeatedly interrupting the onrush of Mendelssohn's fairies). The décor is also used to intensify the sense of oppression. The swing itself is in a small space enclosed in lush shrubbery against the constriction of which the girl's energetic movements seem a protest. The camera watches her circling of the relatives in an overhead shot; a chandelier enters the top of the image, dominating it, its weight seeming to bear down on the scene's superficial gaiety. Such effects will be taken up and intensified later when the action moves to the Russian court, the décor altogether heavier, darker, more oppressive, the glittering glass of this chandelier exchanged for a weighty wooden one in a similarly constructed shot. It is as if, as the heroine's desires become stronger and more defined—more explicitly sexual—less able to be dissipated in play, the burden of oppression is correspondingly increased.

Those desires find definition, the undirected animation a goal, in a motif established at the first meeting of Sophia Frederica and Alexei: the exchanged look. One might examine the structure of the whole film in terms of the close-ups of its heroine that mark the decisive stages of its development, from the wondering gaze of the child at the beginning to the triumphant maniacal grimace of the end. But these close-ups acquire their clearest definition of meaning when they become part of a pattern of looks exchanged between her and Alexei. During the scene of their first meeting, von Sternberg accords this motif a privileged status in three ways: by the isolation of full-face close-ups, by the symmetry of certain of the cross-cut images, and by the duration of the shots. In referring to symmetry I have in mind particularly the angle of the heads in the image: in one pair of shots, Sophia Frederica's is tilted to the right, "answered" by Alexei's tilted to the left, like a mirror-reflection; the effect is to suggest not only a relationship but a parallel. The length of the takes—notably, but not only, the long-held final shot of Sophia Frederica as she leaves the room and pauses at the door to look wonderingly at Alexei—serves further to isolate them from their context (both in the decor and in the sequence): it is as if the couple were temporarily lifted from the surrounding action. Yet if we are responding to the action on the "naturalistic" level, we may feel anxiety lest, in the prying and repressive world the film creates, the couple's evident interest in each other be noticed. Such reactions cannot justly be considered irrelevant: however stylized, this is after all a Hollywood narrative film. The conventions of the historical romance immediately suggest that the two are potential lovers, and the link between them is strengthened by the fact that in describing Peter (Sophia's husband-to-be) Alexei describes himself. The spectator's anxiety points to the essential: the sense that the exchanged look cuts across not only the space of the action but the conventions and values of the society depicted—that it represents the challenge to, and potential salvation from, the oppression that weighs on all spontaneous expression throughout the film.

Facial expressions are notoriously difficult to read with confidence and it is dangerous to build interpretations on them, yet here the attempt is unavoidable. The characteristic impassiveness of faces (especially men's faces) in von Sternberg's films—the impassiveness itself representing the repression of emotion—adds to the difficulty. Alexei is presented from the outset as an inveterate and opportunistic seducer (his titles include, appropriately, Master of the Hunt and Lord of the Chamber) and with Sophia Frederica the emphasis is still on girlish inexperience and that equivocal "innocence"; but the intensity conferred upon the exchanged looks by the operation of the cinematic codes noted above insists on a significance beyond—and transcending—such superficial aspects of character. Sophia's look, in which wonderment and yearning are the dominant emotions, seems at once "innocent" (the longing of a sheltered girl for the expected release into a world of fairy-tale) and deeply erotic: the fusion of these connotations is important.

The end of the first "movement" of the film (to which the brief childhood sequence was introduction) is marked by another of the expressive dissolves that punctuate the whole: a technical device as essential to von Sternberg as it is foreign to, say, Ozu, and which almost always carries meaning in his films beyond its basic usage to suggest continuity and the passing of time. Sophia is ready to depart for Russia; as she sits in the coach her kindly and dignified but ineffectual old father delivers a brief homily, a series of conventional moral precepts that should govern her behaviour (she will learn in time to flout all of them in order to adjust to the life into which she is thrust) and make her "worthy of her glorious destiny." As he speaks the last words, von Sternberg dissolves very slowly to a shot of the coach—the whole procession disappearing into an utterly black tunnel. The sexual symbolism is (in relation to Sophia's "glorious destiny") scarcely irrelevant; the dominant effect of a tragic-ironic pessimism is even more important if we are adequately to receive the force of the film.

The transition in the décor noted above, from the relative lightness (in both senses) of Sophia's home to the sombre and oppressive Russian court, has its parallel in the transition from Sophia's mother to the Dowager Empress, two dominating women determined to bend all others to their will, the latter a much more formidable and overpowering version of the former (who, become redundant, is soon despatched home and disappears from the film). Louise Dresser's performance grates on those who come to the film with prior expectations of historical authenticity (or the "conventional" appearance of it); its American-ness and vulgarity, however, give the film an extra dimension. On the one hand, von Sternberg clearly needed the "cover" of historical verisimilitude in order to smuggle past the eyes of the guardians of public morality an intrigue (not to mention his personal predilection for outrageous sexual innuendo) that flagrantly flouts several laws of the Hays Code; on the other hand, he uses Louise Dresser, the archetypal American matriarch, to establish the film's contemporary relevance. The licence seems perfectly permissible within the format of legend, the court of Russia becoming a fairy-tale stylization of the American home, offering, like a dream, the possibility of fusing fantasy and essential psychology.

The second movement of the film culminates in the extraordinary sequences of the wedding and the ensuing banquet. The progress of the film—the progress towards the "glorious destiny"—becomes more clearly defined: each of Sophia's natural responses is frustrated or perverted, her energies channelled into increasingly unnatural drives. On her arrival at the court—the set dominated by the Empress on her huge eagle throne—she is immediately deprived of her real name and subjected to the humiliation of public examination by the doctor. The process begun by the removal of her toys in childhood reaches its first major crisis in her enforced marriage to a malicious and impotent "royal half-wit" (Sam Jaffe) under the gaze of the man to whom she is tied by intense and mutual erotic impulse.

The short scene in which Sophia (now Catherine) is prepared for the wedding develops the imagery of entrapment, counter-pointing and intensifying it with new motifs. It opens

Catherine prepares for the wedding in *The Scarlet Empress.*

with the camera tracking back from Catherine as she is dressed before a mirror. In the foreground of the image elaborate veiling is lifted up, so that she is completely surrounded; when the Empress walks in, she has to pick her way among the crowd of ladies-in-waiting and obsequious courtiers, the embodiment of power herself trapped and encumbered, as the victorious Catherine will be by flags and banners at the end of the film. The mirror is supported by an elongated statue of the Holy Virgin, who holds it in the crook of her left arm while balancing the Christ-child in her right hand; there is another Madonna-and-Child painted on the back of the hand-mirror Catherine holds—we see it periodically reflected in the large mirror during the scene. The dialogue revolves around the need for a male heir and the Empress's sense that she should have been born a boy. "We women are too much creatures of the heart, aren't we

Catherine?" she asks, and for Catherine's assent (beautifully delivered by Dietrich with a wistful yearning) von Sternberg cuts in to a closer shot of her reflected in the large mirror, framed, the living woman reduced to a "portrait."

The wedding is one of von Sternberg's greatest set-pieces. It brings to a head the religious imagery that gets so much emphasis in the film, and with it the sense of desecration (epitomized succinctly in the shot of the mad groom chewing delightedly on the holy wafer as if it were a bonbon). I do not think anyone will want to claim that the film expresses profound religious feeling—at least not in the orthodox sense. What is desecrated is natural feeling and natural response—human yearning, sexuality, motherhood—and the imagery needs to be understood in relation to this. Before examining the wedding sequence in detail it is worth pausing to consider the richness and complexity of effect achieved through the décor, which the "legendary" aspect of the film permits von Sternberg to develop so freely and lavishly. One may single out three distinguishable (but closely related) uses of statuary. Firstly, the chairs of the council chamber, above which rise huge, gaunt figures, holding their hands over their eyes as if unable to bear contemplating the squalid intrigues they have eternally to witness. Secondly, the madonna statues: the one already referred to, holding in her right hand the infant Catherine will be denied (her child is removed from her at birth) and in her left the mirror in which Catherine is reflected—increasingly forced to rely upon her own resources and create an "image" of herself; and the statue that surmounts the bridal bed, presiding over its ceremonial blessing and the prayer for fruitfulness—on which von Sternberg's comment is another slow dissolve from the madonna to a skeleton that holds up one of the dishes on the banquet table. Thirdly, the statues representing martyrdom: the images of an anguished Christ on the cross and, even more striking in the use to which it is put, the St. Sebastian beside the staircase, body twisted in agony and transfixed with arrows, visually prominent in several scenes, notably that in which Alexei endeavours to persuade Catherine to meet him clandestinely, shortly after her marriage. Von Sternberg's interest in Expressionism preceded his visit to Germany to make *The Blue Angel:* the deliberately cultivated influence is visible in his silent films. In his films of the thirties it becomes subtilized and diffused, completely assimilated into a personal style, but it is still there, and it seems legitimate to find in the St. Sebastian figure his means of giving powerful expression to all that is suppressed behind the impassive face of Alexei and the insistent insouciance of Catherine. Earlier, when Peter demonstrated his revolving soldier-toy, an extension of his madness, an expression of his militaristic fantasies, Alexei, standing by helplessly at this first stage of Catherine's disillusionment, was juxtaposed with another anguished statue.

The wedding sequence itself is marked off as a "set-piece" by its symmetry: it opens (as the Dowager Empress mounts the steps to her position of dominance) with the camera craning down and tracking left over the assembly, and ends with a shot that is almost a mirror-inversion of this. The symmetrical "enclosing" of the sequence might be felt formally to underline the stifling sense of entrapment it so powerfully creates. The décor is here at its most suffocating: the camera tracks past elaborate veiling behind which the congregation are only dimly visible, obscured; characters (especially Alexei) sit in confined compartments, hemmed in by flags and hangings; the crowns are like weights suspended above the bridal couple's heads. Two of the film's key motifs are here taken up in combination. Swinging censers insistently intrude into the foreground of the images, associated particularly with Catherine (one passes repeatedly across her face in certain of the big, long-held close-ups), recalling the earlier juxtaposition of bell-clapper and swing, reminding us that the wedding is a crucial step in Catherine's rise to power. The heart of the scene, again, is the exchange of looks between Catherine and Alexei. Their silent, and now deeply troubled, communication is again the outward sign of the only possibility of salvation but because it must remain silent and frustrated it acquires equally the idea of helplessness. In the sustained close-ups of Catherine, two expressive features stand out: the pleading so eloquently conveyed by her eyes, and the physical reality of her breath as the candle before her mouth repeatedly wavers and is almost extinguished: the effect is like watching the quickened beating of her heart. Alexei's location in the décor is never defined, though we know precisely where everyone else is. Partly, this is doubtless a matter of convenience: the cross-cutting makes it clear beyond dispute that we are meant to regard the frustrated lovers as looking at each other (her pleading answered by his impotence), yet for this to be physically possible Alexei would have to be seated roughly in the middle of the altar. The licence on the "naturalistic" level is made possible by the refusal to show him in the sequence other than in isolated close-shots; on another level, by defying naturalistic convention it emphasizes the special status of a relationship which will never exist as more than a shadowy defined potential: the "looks" transcend space.

The symmetry noted above is not exact: it gives particular force to the shot that breaks it. The sequence appears to be finishing as it started (but with the camera movement reversed) when von Sternberg cuts in to a final low-angle close shot of the Empress presiding in triumph over the ceremony, her face gloating with power and satisfaction, a large candle clasped in her fist. In retrospect, it might be said that the whole structure of the sequence demands this last shot, as explanation of the sense of suffocation, the helplessness and stasis (the long-held close-ups), the repression of natural impulse: the entire wedding is revealed as an act of the Empress's fixed will, of human drives perverted into the exercise of power. The candle, clutched like a sceptre, explains the impotence of the males: it is the imperial matriarch who wields the phallus. In the ensuing banquet scene she will mistake for her sceptre a large bone, and hold it erect in the same position.

The denseness of the film's imagery has by now perhaps been adequately suggested; tempting as it is to linger over each scene, economy forbids it. I move, therefore, to the first bedchamber sequence (which, like so much else in the film, will have its "echo" later): another sequence that knots together important threads of narrative and imagery, and once again presided over by the Empress, who conceives it as an object-lesson for Catherine and determines (one might say) its *mise-en-scène*. Candles again figure prominently, the recurring motif of their extinction (the candle almost blown out by Catherine's breath during the wedding, the extinction of light that concludes the wedding-night sequence, the candles extinguished by Alexei beside the great staircase as he tries to persuade Catherine to meet him) acquiring renewed force in terms of the "glorious destiny" that is also a progress into ever-deepening moral darkness. The successive stages in Catherine's rise to power are marked by the ringing of bells; certain key moments in the personal and private violation that accompanies the rise (as its inevitable corollary) are marked by the striking of ornamented clocks and by the visual motif of the little carved figures that announce the hour: a female figure lewdly opening her dress to reveal her nakedness (the wedding night); a grotesque figure with a club repeatedly striking a prostrate victim (prelude to Peter's assassination). The clock that strikes the hour for the arrival of the Empress's lover has the figures of torturers prowling across its face.

Set against the saints and holy men of the palace's public halls, the dominant statue in the bedchamber—holding a mirror, thus a macabre inversion of the earlier madonna—is a huge anguished devil, the central focus for the atmosphere of perverted sexuality. Its shadow is cast over the doorway to the secret passage, giving the opening a jagged outline like a monstrous vagina. The décor and action of the scene themselves imply a sexual conceit: the way to enter the Empress's chamber is up a dark secret passage-way from behind. Von Sternberg shows Catherine's horror and distress (after she has admitted Alexei and realizes who the lover is) by means of a lingering superimposition of her face: we never know exactly what, in literal terms, she is seeing (or imaginatively experiencing—she is on the other side of the closed door), but the sense of violation is intense, the superimposition suggesting the penetration of her being by the "vision."

The film's progress—essentially, the development of the theme of the frustration and perversion of natural impulse—can be traced through its intricate pattern of echoes and substitutions. It is convenient at this point to abandon chronology in order to disentangle the major motifs through which this progress is established.

1: *The pendant and the jewel.* When he talks to her on the staircase, Alexei gives Catherine a pendant on the back of which is a miniature of himself. Just as she, as a "creature of the heart," was reduced to a reflection in a mirror, so he—his feelings suppressed behind an impassive face and the words and manner of a cynical womanizer—can only be possessed by her as an image framed and behind glass. Von Sternberg stresses the ornament's glitter and triviality as it dangles in close-up. After the first bedchamber scene Catherine tries to smash this image by stamping on it, then flings it out of the window where it catches in the branches of a tree, slipping from twig to twig. When she goes out into the night to search for it she is intercepted by the captain of the guard whom she seduces and who becomes the father of the heir to the throne. The scene ends with the pendant slipping, forgotten, from her fingers (her wedding-ring also prominent) as she clasps her arms around the neck of her new lover. Thus her surrender to a series of trivial liaisons is marked by Alexei's slipping (literally) from her grasp. Bells and cannon promptly announce the birth of the heir; but it is the old Empress we first see in bed with the baby, as if she were its mother. Catherine, also in bed, her child removed from her care, is presented with a dangling, glittering jewel on a chain, a reward from the Empress for services rendered: taking up the previous imagery, the diamond becomes the substitute not only for her baby but for her relationship with the man who should (by natural inclination) have been its father. Von Sternberg ends the scene with a shot of Catherine through the veiling that surrounds her bed, as she gazes at the jewel dangling before her eyes: we see her half-obliterated.

2: *The cross and the veil.* A single brief scene succinctly sums up the theme of perversion. In the same décor in which Peter earlier showed off his "new invention" (the revolving toy), before the chest surrounded by bowed and aged figures and surmounted by huge phallic candles, Catherine and the Archbishop hold a consultation. He offers her the support of the Church; she tells him she has other "weapons." Von Sternberg cross-cuts between the old man fingering a small crucifix to Catherine suggestively fingering the veil she holds in her hands; the perversion of religion is symmetrically balanced by the perversion of sexuality, the abuse of each in the interests of power.

3: *Children's games.* Firstly, the swing scene near the beginning of the film gets its reflection in the scene of blind man's buff. The former was interrupted by the news that Sophia had been chosen to become Peter's bride; the latter is interrupted by the bell that chimes for the death of the old Empress. The décor of the former, though constricting and opulent, was spring-like; the décor of the latter, festooned with strangling creepers, is extravagantly decadent. The game on the swing has given place to far-from-innocent play with Catherine's favourite officers. Secondly, Peter's military toys and militaristic fantasies take increasingly sinister (while still childish) forms as he assumes power. He shoots down one of his own guards just for the hell of it; he "entertains" Catherine by beheading a doll in front of her (she was clutching a doll to her in bed as a child when the manservant read to her about executions and when she asked if she could become a hangman); and he parades his troops like wooden soldiers inside the palace on rainy days. This last scene, in which he uses the troops to menace Catherine, is once again charged with sexual symbolism: the royal cuckold and his multiply unfaithful wife are surrounded by antlered stags' heads; Peter has all his soldiers point their bayonets at Catherine's "lovely target"; when he threatens her with his own sword she ironically sticks her veil on its point.

4: *Straws and seduction.* Before the first bedchamber scene, Catherine (frustrated from seeing her mother, who has been sent home without her knowledge) keeps her rendezvous with Alexei in the stable. With the mixture of innocence, coquetry and erotic longing that characterizes her at that stage of her development, she first sways back and forth clutching a rope (the "hangman" motif again), then simultaneously provokes and frustrates Alexei's attempts to kiss her by repeatedly putting straws in her mouth. After the Empress's death she inspects the troops in their quarters, accompanied by Alexei. During the inspection she pulls a straw from the palliasse of one of the upper bunks: the reminder of the earlier scene (deliberate on Catherine's part—she is ironically taunting her frustrated lover) is underlined for the audience by von Sternberg's use of the same romantic music. The reminder given (and taken), she proceeds to decorate the captain for "bravery in action," using a medal she takes from Alexei's chest: it is the captain she seduced in the grounds at night, when she let slip Alexei's pendant—the father of her child.

5: *The tying of napkins.* Part of the wedding ritual involves the tying of the couple's hands together with a napkin. Towards the end of the film, after she has seduced the army (of which she makes, it is hinted, quite a thorough job), Catherine's decision to have her husband assassinated is signalled to her chosen officer during dinner by her tying a napkin in a knot: wedding-bond becomes death sentence.

6: *The second bedchamber scene.* As her revenge on Alexei and a demonstration of her power, Catherine stages an elaborate repetition of the scene where she was sent to summon him to the Empress's bed. Von Sternberg here associates Alexei closely with the devil-statue, using a dissolve to superimpose their heads. Alexei is, of course, a corrupted figure from the outset, but presented as a "fallen angel"; and, like Satan, he suffers (the face of the devil is as anguished as those of the martyrs elsewhere). The scene takes up once again the ritual extinction of candles and its central significance (central, I think, to the meaning of the whole film) lies in the final development of the motif of the exchange of looks. Catherine lies tantalizingly behind the veiling that surrounds her bed. Before she makes her intentions clear, she allows Alexei to kiss her. We see her hand clench on the net curtain as she responds despite herself, and pull it back so that their faces are briefly clear, unmasked; then the veiling falls back as she gives him his instructions, and she is obscured behind it throughout the remainder of the scene, the last expression of normal impulse perversely rejected and denied in favour of a sterile revenge; and the exercise of power. This extinction of the saving potentiality of the look is echoed even more eloquently in the treatment of Alexei at the end of the scene. After he has sent Catherine's current lover up the secret staircase, his face, in close-up, expresses his suffering more overtly than anywhere else in the film. The shot ends—and the deliberateness of the effect is beyond question—with the actor lowering his head so that his face disappears into heavy shadow: the look is obliterated. From there on Alexei plays no significant part in the action.

The ending of the film—the murder of Peter, and Catherine's

seizing of power—is the logical outcome of all that has preceded it: logical in its triumph, its tragedy and its irony, logical in the culmination of the unifying imagery. The moment that makes sense of the movement of the whole film is that when Catherine (dressed now as a man, in military uniform) ascends the stairs to ring the bell that is the signal for Peter's execution: the little girl who wanted to become a hangman has achieved her ambition, the enigma of the juxtaposed images of human bell-clapper and girl on swing is finally clarified, human energy and desire have been perverted into the brutal exercise of power. The moment also crystallizes one of the recurrent preoccupations of von Sternberg's cinema, the mystery of free will and destiny: Catherine's assumption of power (like Amy Jolly's walk out into the desert at the end of *Morocco*) appearing both a matter of deliberate choice and as predestined from the beginning, both triumphant and desolating.

The disturbing power of the last sequence arises from its complexity of tone and the ambivalent feelings aroused. On the one hand, Catherine has learnt how to survive in the world into which she was plunged (as von Sternberg struggled to do in the commercial cinema of Hollywood), has met it on its own terms and risen to supreme power within it (as von Sternberg almost did, before the decline of his prestige). On the other, her triumph over it is won at the cost of becoming identified with it: the wondering child of the start has become Russia's "most sinister" tyrant as the captions promised, a monstrous and dehumanized figure. The horses gallop through the palace and up the great staircase where Alexei pleaded for a meeting, their hooves clattering deafeningly in an astonishing exhibition of energy and desecration, von Sternberg tracking in at one point on the horribly contorted Christ on the cross now carried as a banner, at another allowing the agonized St. Sebastian again to dominate the foreground of the image. Catherine's face, the mouth exaggerated by make-up, has become a hideously grimacing mask, its expression recalling both the Empress's look of triumph at the end of the wedding sequence and the insane smiles of Peter, the "look" no longer directed at a human individual and no longer returned. By associating Catherine finally not with a lover but with a magnificent white horse, von Sternberg may conceivably have had in mind the legend (unsupported, apparently, by historians) of her death: that she died during attempted intercourse with a stallion which was accidentally let slip after being hauled into position. The legend's grotesqueness is quite in keeping with the figure—and the face—the film finally presents in what is perhaps the most extraordinary of von Sternberg's ironic "happy endings."

In attempting to "read" *The Scarlet Empress* I have accepted the narrative at its face value: it seems to me the surest way of doing justice to its detail and its tone. There are other levels—part personal, part allegorical—on which it can be interpreted without destroying its artistic coherence. It could be seen as an allegory (on whatever level of consciousness) about Hollywood and the star system: Sophia Frederica is groomed for stardom from infancy by her ambitious mother; "discovered"; taken to Hollywood (the court), where her name is changed and her mother becomes superfluous; is given a new image and presented to the public (the wedding); learns to take her career into her own hands and pursue power ruthlessly; ends up enshrined as "star" but finally imprisoned within her image, no longer existing as a private individual. Such a reading cannot be imposed consistently, but the overtones are strong enough for one to accept it as another level of meaning, nowhere at odds with the overt sense of the narrative. On a personal level, one can follow (though not entirely consistently) a process through the Dietrich films which may correspond to von Sternberg's feelings about their relationship. From *Shanghai Express* through *The Scarlet Empress* to *The Devil Is a Woman* there is a growing insistence on the impotence of the male and the ruthlessness of the woman. This ties in neatly enough with the "Hollywood" allegory, Alexei bringing Catherine to Russia as von Sternberg brought Dietrich to Hollywood, and finally becoming superfluous to her as she achieves "stardom." (Rumour has it that von Sternberg deliberately cast Lionel Atwill as the ultimate humiliated male in *The Devil Is a Woman* because of the actor's physical resemblance to him.)

Such overtones may help one to understand the nature of von Sternberg's emotional involvement in the films and his attitude towards their subject-matter; they do not, I think, affect in any important way one's sense of what the films actually are. Through the inter-relatedness of its motifs and the significant development of its imagery, *The Scarlet Empress* achieves the intensity of great poetry, in which nothing exists for itself alone but becomes charged with meaning from its context.

5

Ewig hin der Liebe Glück
Letter from an Unknown Woman

The foyer of the Vienna Opera; close-up of the placard announcing a performance of Mozart's *The Magic Flute*—an opera that sets beside the "absolute" love of Tamino and Pamina, and their progress through perfect union towards spiritual transcendence, the very earthly and relative desires of Papageno, who wants "Ein Mädchen oder Weibchen" and it does not much matter which or who. The camera tracks right, revealing the spectators during the interval between the two acts, moving about, talking. It picks up first one pair, now another, moving with each a little way then transferring to the next as if its attention had been distracted. The effect is dual, arising, one might say, out of a tension between content and style: the movement looks arbitrary, as if it did not matter which group or person the camera focused on (and none is a character with whom the fiction is concerned) or where it moved next; yet the movement (both of people and of camera) is so meticulously choreographed, so graceful and fluent, that we cannot but feel (even if subconsciously) that everything in the shot has been predetermined. Meanwhile, the off-screen voice of Lisa (Joan Fontaine) speaks of Chance and Destiny, telling us that nothing happens by chance, that our every step is counted. As she finishes, the camera in its peregrinations has arrived at the foot of the left-hand staircase that rises with its twin to unite on the level of the dress circle. Lisa and her husband come into view; as they mount, the camera cranes gracefully up to disclose the whole stairway, an ornate chandelier entering the frame, interposed between us and the characters. Lisa hears people talking about Stefan Brandt, the man she has always loved and (unknown to him) the father of her son. A moment later she will see him at the foot of the right-hand stairway and the course of her life will be abruptly changed.

It would be an exaggeration to say that the whole of Ophuls (or even of *Letter from an Unknown Woman*[3]) is contained in that shot: Ophuls's art at its best achieves a degree of refinement and complexity that demands that virtually every statement we might make about it be delicately qualified. It provides, none the less, in the centrality of its concerns and motifs, a valuable starting-point.

During Ophuls's career (which spans three decades and four countries), he evolved one of the most striking and instantly identifiable visual styles in the cinema: a style which, like Ozu's or Mizoguchi's, is inextricably linked with certain recurrent motifs, and which in itself embodies a view of existence. In that evolution, *Letter from an Unknown Woman* is poised stylistically midway between two films to which it is so closely related in theme and narrative movement that one might regard the three (though they are in different languages) as an Ophuls trilogy. In comparison, *Liebelei* (1932) appears less refined and less complex though it has a freshness of incidental invention that, while certainly not absent from the later works, is there more subordinated to structural precision; while *Madame de . . .* (1953), a great film and a masterpiece, appears just a trifle overblown. I had better add here, parenthetically, that the film most of Ophuls's champions single out as his greatest, *Lola Montes*, seems to me a failure, albeit a brilliant and distinguished one. It is easy to

---

3. One of British television's only unequivocal services to the cinema (apart from showing a lot of movies) was a series of BBC schools programmes devised and written by Victor Perkins. Perkins gave me a transcript of the programme on *Letter from an Unknown Woman,* and I am indebted to it for several specific ideas in the present essay. The debt is, however, more general: Perkins's script generated all my subsequent thinking about Ophuls, whom I had previously not valued highly.

see why it has been valued so highly: it has many of the marks of a final testament, a definitive statement. But no other film of consequence has suffered so disastrously from a central error or casting: the empty, doll-like figure presented by Martine Carol, in a role demanding the Dietrich of the thirties, the Dietrich of von Sternberg, leaves the film without a heart, and the humanity and passion of Ophuls's vision are at last overwhelmed by the proliferations of décor.

Though the method is somewhat artificial—a style being more than the elements that go to compose it, its essence created indeed by the interaction of those elements—it seems reasonable to approach Ophuls by listing some of the most striking stylistic features and recurrent motifs of his work. The list is not intended as exhaustive; far less are the examples offered as illustration, a complete catalogue of which would fill a book.

1: The tracking-shot (often with crane) and long take. It has become a commonplace that to discuss Ophuls is to discuss the meaning of his tracking-shots, and I shall return to this later. The tracking-shot is already established as a central stylistic strategy in the pre–World War II movies; it reaches its extreme (some would say excessive) elaboration in the post-Hollywood French films of the fifties. *Letter from an Unknown Woman* again represents a perfect mid-point in this evolution, the stylistic practice developed to a point of total expressive mastery but not yet to the point of domination it has reached by *Madame de . . .*

2: Staircases; movement up or down them, encounters on them, frequently accompanied by a crane movement. This is an important motif even in the Hollywood films on contemporary American subjects (*Caught* and, especially, *The Reckless Moment*) from which many Ophulsian "trademarks" are of necessity excluded.

3: Other places of transition; doorways, thresholds, entrances.

4: Bedrooms. Rarely the scene of passionate embraces (Lisa's

Lisa and Stefan in *Letter from an Unknown Woman.*

willing surrender to Stefan is exceptional); more often the set-ting for the expression of separateness (the conjugal bedroom scenes of *La Ronde* and *Madame de* . . . , the isolation of Lucia in *The Reckless Moment,* the imprisonment and delirium of the heroine of *Caught*).

5: Stations, trains, scenes of arrival and departure. There are obvious examples in *Letter* (three) and *Madame de.* . . (two); a particularly touching, almost wordless one in *Liebelei* (the er-rant wife seen off by her brother-in-law), where everything es-sential is communicated through the movements of hands; an important scene in *The Reckless Moment* is set in a bus station departure-room.

6: Carriages. Against the sterility of the husband/wife bed-room scene of *Madame de* . . . is set the passionate reunion of the lovers in a carriage; there are important carriage duologues in *Letter* and *Lola Montes;* the Lucia/Donnelly relationship in *The Reckless Moment* begins to develop in a car on a moving ferry.

7: Dances; the logical extension (in privileged cases, the perfect expression) of the "life-as-constant-movement" theme which the previous motifs combine to suggest. The supreme example is in *Madame de . . .* : the growth of the lovers' mutual passion shown through an unbroken succession of dances, the only circumstances in which they can touch. The dance as meeting-place also figures in films as diverse as *Letter* and *Caught.* (One wants also to acknowledge the potency in Ophuls's films of the negation of these recurrent motifs: the staircase in *Caught* which the heroine does not ascend, the ball in *De Mayerling à Sarajevo* from which Sophie and Franz-Ferdinand are—in effect—excluded.)

8: Music, especially Mozart, the Viennese tradition, the waltz. Paralleling the use of *The Magic Flute* in *Letter, Liebelei* opens at a performance of *Il Seraglio;* the pattern of relationships in the film (the "ideal" love of the principals set off by the frivolous affair of Theo and Mitzi) corresponds fairly clearly to the Belmonte-Constanza/Pedrillo-Blonde opposition in Mozart's opera. Gluck's *Orfeo ed Eurydice* figures in *Madame de . . .* , the heroine's feigned discovery of the "loss" of the ear-rings she has pawned to pay debts being accompanied by Orpheus's lament for irrecoverably lost love ("Che faro senza Eurydice?"), the effect at once ironic and anticipatory. Ophuls made a film version of *The Bartered Bride;* waltz themes by Oscar Strauss run through *La Ronde* and *Madame de . . .* as Liszt's "Farewell" waltz does through *Lola Montes;* even in *Caught* a character plays *Tales from the Vienna Woods* on the piano. Beyond such specifics, Ophuls's films can be regarded as possessing a metaphorical musical flow, as if the lilt and fluency of the Viennese waltz tradition and the simultaneous/ambivalent gaiety and pathos of Mozart were caught up in the movement of the films.

9: "Old Vienna" itself; a state of mind as much as a location. Ophuls made films in four countries and four languages but he returns repeatedly to his reconstruction of Vienna—*Liebelei, Leller, La Ronde*. The "feel" of *Madame de. . .* is so Viennese that one keeps forgetting it is ostensibly set in Paris. "Vienna, 1900" reads the caption that opens *Letter*, and at the beginning of *La Ronde* Anton Walbrook (in his capacity as *metteur-en-scène*) creates "Vienna, 1900" before our eyes, at the same time acknowledging his preference for the past, with neither the turbulence of the present not the uncertainty of the future.

10: Theatres, opera-houses, places of entertainment. *Divine* is centred on the theatre; *Liebelei, De Mayerling à Sarajevo, Letter* and *Madame de . . .* all contain key scenes set in opera-houses; Lola Montes dances in an opera-house taken over for that purpose by her royal patron, and ends her career in the circus-ring. As well as relating to the motifs of constant transition (Ophuls's characters often seeming most "at home" in an opera box or foyer) this also points to Ophuls's concern with role-playing, with the ambiguities of appearance-and-reality. The distinction between stage and box becomes blurred: both are stages, where actors are on view and must give performances. The dance-floors of *Madame de . . .* , the recurrent ceremonials and tours of inspection of *De Mayerling à Sarajevo,* are other related manifestations; so is Charles II's final entrapment in the royal role in *The Exile.*

11: Soldiers. Military men figure prominently among Ophuls's characters: *Liebelei, Sarajevo, The Exile, Letter, La Ronde, Madame de . . .* all contain important examples. The sympathy extended to them varies, but the stress is always on ceremony and performance, on the army as an extension of "theatre," the humanity of older and more high-ranking soldiers (*Madame de . . .* 's husband) in danger of becoming atrophied beneath their role.

12: Duels. Necessarily less frequent than most of the other

components in my list; but it is worth noting that *Liebelei, Letter* and *Madame de . . .* all culminate in fatal duels (implicitly in the case of *Letter,* but there, too, unambiguously) in which lover is shot by offended husband, the deaths (off-screen) in the first and third both established by the fact that there is no second shot fired. One might see the significance of the duel as the point where theatre and life fatally coincide, where one of the actors, at least, cannot get up to take a bow at the end of the performance.

13: Ornate and elaborate, often cluttered décor, at once opulent and suffocating; chandeliers, glass, mirrors, lights, glitter.

14: Objects intervening between characters and camera, especially during tracking-shots; bars, trellis-work, nets, foliage, pillars.

15: A fondness for framing the characters—in mirrors, in doorways, between pillars, in windows. We first see the face of *Madame de . . .* framed in a small, ornate mirror on her dressing table, after she has been indirectly characterized through her material possessions and her attachment to them; in *Sarajevo,* Sophie is caught motionless between two pillars at the moment when, in her role as governess, the secret mutual attachment between her and Franz-Ferdinand is discovered; examples could be multiplied indefinitely. Most typically, these arrests are momentary, occurring in the course of a tracking-shot, a point of brief stasis during a character's progress from room to room, from stage to stage, on the road to destiny.

16: Echoes and near-repetitions. Sometimes these take the form of refrains running through the whole film ("Who is it?"—"Brandt"—"Good evening, Mr. Brandt"; or the "Quelle heure est-il?" of *La Ronde*), a part of its "musical" rhythm, acquiring overtones of irony and poignance. More striking are specific echoes of scenes, situations, dialogue, that recapitulate the past in order to underline the distance the characters have travelled. Both *Letter* and *Madame de . . .* are largely constructed on "paired" scenes; in the latter, for example, two visits to the church, two visits to the jeweller, two scenes of farewell at the station, in each case the details of *mise-en-scène* (camera-movement, disposition of the actors) underlining the parallel.

17: Flashbacks. The sleigh-ride of *Liebelei* is recapitulated at the end after both the lovers are dead; *Letter* and *Lola Montes* (and *La Signora di Tutti*, reputedly one of Ophuls's greatest films) are structured in flashbacks; the repetitions in the latter part of *Madame de . . .* have the function of continually calling the past to our minds, evoking ghostly flashbacks as it were. The flashback structures of *Letter* and *Lola Montes* are not ingenious, decorative complications, nor are they merely nostalgic, but are essential to the film's meaning. One might say that the flashback or its equivalent is as central to Ophuls as it is alien to Hawks.

18: Circles; the merry-go-round of *La Ronde,* the circus-ring of *Lola Montes,* the recurrent foreign countries of the fairground "railway" in *Letter. Madame de . . .* opens with the camera moving in a semi-circle around the room as the heroine tries to decide what to pawn, finally returning (without a cut) to the ear-rings on to which it first directed our attention. The image of the circle—the return to the point of departure—is closely connected to the use of repetition and flashback as structural devices.

19: Chance, Fate, Predestination (according to taste); Ophuls's characters call it Fate, his style and method seeming partly to endorse them. Anton Walbrook in *La Ronde* unites various functions whose combination suggests a connection between style and theme, *mise-en-scène* and destiny. He is, he tells us, "anyone"—he is we, the audience, and can fulfil our desire to know everything; associated during the long opening tracking-shot with both stage and studio, he is also the *metteur-en-scène,* choosing the décor, positioning and directing the actors; and in so far as he is assimilated into the film's fiction, he is a "Fate" figure, controlling and helping to execute the characters' destinies. In this last function he carries the suggestion that Fate for Ophuls is not quite absolute: at several points, characters *almost* miss crucial appointments, the "ronde de l'amour" *almost* breaks down, it is not certain that the circle will be completed.

20: Time, clocks, watches. In their state of perpetual transition, Ophuls's characters are the prisoners of time and its passing. In the first half of *Sarajevo*, a watch becomes itself the instrument of Fate; in *La Ronde* (where this motif is most explicit and insistent), the characters are forever asking the time, and it is always later than they wish to believe; the husband/wife episode is dominated by the image of the clock, its pendulum ticking in the centre foreground of the screen, the couple in their separate beds disposed symmetrically to right and left.

21: The extinction of lights; a motif often unobtrusive, and only rarely raised to the level of overt symbolism, but remarkably consistent. The most striking and expressive instance is at the end of the suite of ball-scenes in *Madame de . . .* where, at the last dance, on a deserted floor, with the musicians packing up to leave, the lovers waltz with their coats on, Louise tells Donati that her husband returns tomorrow, and a servant walks round extinguishing the lights one by one, the single take (the camera seeming to dance with the actors in a continual suspension) ending on the harp as a black cover is placed over it. The darkening and deepening of tone at the end of *La Ronde* is subtly intensified by the extinction of a street-lamp as the Count comes out of the prostitute's house into the cold dawn.

22: Women. One cannot conclude such a list without noting the degree to which Ophuls's cinema is woman-centred: it is as unusual for one of his films to have a man as central consciousness as for one of Hawks's to be centred on a woman (the obvious Hawks exception, *Gentlemen Prefer Blondes,* in its characteristic presentation of women as aggressors, confirms rather than qualifies the generalization). Traditionally, the female principle has been regarded as passive, the male active, and, without wishing to suggest that Ophuls's films endorse any simplistic opposition of male and female roles, one cannot but feel a connection between the emphasis on fatality in his movies and his gravitation to woman-centred subjects. In *Liebelei, Sarajevo* and *La Ronde* interest is divided more or less equally between the sexes, though even here (especially in *Sarajevo*) one may feel an emotional gravitation to the female characters pulling against the scenario. The only Ophuls film I know which has a man as central figure is his first Hollywood movie *The Exile,* which was written and produced by its star, Douglas Fairbanks Jr., who clearly saw it as a vehicle for his own disputable talents. Ophuls decorates the occasionally risible masculine acrobatics with some beautiful camera movements, but one senses him wishing he could tell the story from the point of view of the Dutch girl (Paule Croset); and the most intimately Ophulsian sequence is undoubtedly that centred on Maria Montez. On the other side, the tally is imposing both in quantity and quality: of the films I have seen, *Divine, Letter, Caught, The Reckless Moment, Madame de . . . , Lola Montes* are all firmly centred on a female consciousness.

It is easy to relate all these components (grouping them accordingly) to certain basic assumptions (themselves interdependent) about existence: reality and illusion, life as dream, transience, destiny. But the recognition of the philosophical basis of an artist's work should never become an ultimate end: usually, reduced to this level of abstraction, the philosophy will be merely banal. In art, the underlying assumptions that make up an artist's "view of life" gain their validity from the precision, intensity and sensitivity with which they are concretely embodied in actual works, not *vice versa.* From the perception of an Ophulsian world-view, then, one returns to the realized detail of the films. No mere catalogue of motifs can do justice to the delicacy of tone and effect to which a conjunction of such motifs may contribute. Before focusing finally on *Letter from an Unknown Woman,* I offer one last example from *De Mayerling à Sarajevo,* at once one of the finest and most underestimated of all Ophuls's films.

The Countess Sophie Chotek, in love with the Archduke Franz-Ferdinand but unable to marry him, becomes governess to an aristocratic Austrian family. Franz-Ferdinand establishes himself as a regular visitor, letting it be assumed that he is courting one or other of the older daughters but actually using this as a cover for meetings with Sophie. In one scene we see a family group being posed for a photograph on the lawn of the chateau; Franz-Ferdinand is among them. Ophuls shows us this from a high angle in long-shot: we have the tableau posed as on a stage for the photographer (with Franz-Ferdinand, in particular, acting a role), and our own distance from this includes the photographer as part of the performance. The camera then moves back to "place" this group within the frame of an upstairs window, turning it already into a picture, and as the track backwards continues we suddenly have Sophie within the frame, looking down on the scene as a spectator. Our response is subtly modified with the change in perspective: we realize that we have been watching the scene on the lawn from her viewpoint, and at once the tone is coloured by deeper emotional resonances, the sense of distance separating the lovers, the pretence they must maintain in public, the contrast between private emotion and public performance. Ophuls thereupon cuts to a long-shot of Sophie from the other side of the room, emphasizing her aloneness and changing our perspective once again: it is *she,* framed in the décor, who now becomes a figure in a picture at which we are looking. Emotionally the sequence is central to Ophuls's world: the poignance of separation, or "ideal" love thwarted. What I want to stress here—to take up again in discussing *Letter*—is the delicacy with which Ophuls determines our relation to the action, and the shifts in that relation, the way in which our passing tendency to identify with Sophie, her mood, her actual viewpoint, is qualified by a cut that detaches us from her, making her appear as trapped and helpless from *our* vantage-point as Franz-Ferdinand appeared from hers. One might not consciously register the effect here as "ironic," but the pervasive possibility of irony is as essential to the Ophuls tone as his romanticism.

More must be said about Ophuls's tracking-shots. The Linz sequence in *Letter* can be taken as fairly representative: a relatively relaxed scene at a lower pitch of emotional intensity than those directly involving Stefan, hence exemplary of Ophuls's habitual practice. The first part of the scene consists of two long tracking-shots: One, Lisa, her mother and stepfather meet (by prior arrangement) a general and his handsome young nephew (a lieutenant), who it is hoped will become Lisa's suitor. They walk through the streets, the lieutenant questioning Lisa about Linz, slightly disapproving of her attachment to Vienna, attributing it to a fondness for music, and telling her they have good music in Linz too. The camera accompanies them through most of the shot, pausing to show the hopeful faces of the watching parents. Two, a shot that reverses the movement of the first, starting outside the church (the point the young couple had reached) where a military band is now playing in the square. The camera accompanies Lisa and the lieutenant as they walk past the band, pausing finally on the parents who are at the table of a sidewalk café expecting to celebrate the announcement of an engagement.

Apart from their unusual length in time and distance (but increasingly *usual* in Ophuls's later, post-Hollywood, films), the shots display a number of representative characteristics. Firstly, grace and elegance: the point at which traditional Anglo-Saxon criticism of Ophuls (represented, for example, by Karel Reisz, Lindsay Anderson, and by Richard Roud in an early monograph it is charitable to assume he would prefer to forget) begins and ends; the tendency was to regard Ophuls's film as sentimental novelettes over-decorated with frills. One should not, I think, over-react by denying the gracefulness importance in its own right: the delight in sensuous movement, the pleasure of creating beautiful and fluid images, is clearly a major factor in Ophuls's creative impulse. Secondly, connection: naturally inherent in a style based on camera-movement (see artists as different from each other as Renoir and Welles). In both shots we are led from group to group without a cut; the suggestion is of the interconnectedness of lives, the simultaneity of actions that impinge on each other. Thirdly, camera-distance. The characters are placed in an environment and in relation to each other, not isolated by cutting or by close-up. Further, the distance between camera and characters fluctuates during the take, so that our spatial relationship to them is not constant. Fourthly, the use of foreground objects intervening between camera and characters. Occasionally the effect is ironic (the workers' cart that rudely interrupts the pompous formalities of introduction); more usually the effect is of a graceful ornamentation and a subtle distancing, our view of the characters temporarily interrupted. Fifthly, "musical" form: the two shots are variations on each other, part repetition, part inversion. Sixthly, symmetry and circularity: the characters are brought back to where they started. But we are aware at once that time has elapsed and the situation changed: the lieutenant is about to propose.

The function of style in a work of art is not simply that of embodying the artist's vision; an important aspect of style is the defining of a relationship between the work and its audience: in the cinema, between the spectator and the characters and action on the screen. One can define the function and meaning of the Ophuls tracking-shot further by juxtaposing it with the camera movements of Hitchcock and Preminger. Since *Rebecca* (his first American film), one of the instantly identifiable characteristics of Hitchcock's *mise-en-scène* has been the *subjective* tracking-shot, that places us in the actor's position and gives us the sensation of moving with him; this usually alternating with backward tracking-shots of the actor moving. The device is a logical extension of the Hitchcockian principle of audience-identification, an expression of his desire to "put the audience through it." In the "classical" Preminger films of the forties and fifties, camera-movement has an opposite function, which can be briefly illustrated from *Laura*. Consider the famous sequence leading up to Laura's return—Mark McPherson's obsessive exploration of her apartment and personal belongings, his growing infatuation with a woman who is supposed to be dead. Here a subject that might well have attracted Hitchcock (think of *Vertigo*) is treated in a manner very different: instead of the fragmentation of Hitchcockian montage, Preminger uses as few takes as possible; at no point are we placed in McPherson's position or asked to see things from his (physical or mental) viewpoint; the only close-ups occur in the middle of takes, the character moving into close-up then out again into medium- or long-shot.

Subjective shots are very rare in Ophuls, and I can think of no subjective tracking-shots outside the scene in *The Reckless Moment* where Lucia Harper disposes of Ted Darby's body—a sequence that looks deliberately shot à la Hitchcock. In *Letter* there is a brief moving subjective shot from Lisa's position on the swing as she listens to Stefan's music; and there are the shots of Lisa from Stefan's viewpoint, notably as he turns at the gate to see her behind the glass of the door she has opened for him. The *Reckless Moment* sequence is interesting because of the ways (apparent *hommage* as it seems) that it is *not* Hitchcock: interspersed with the alternating shots of "person looking" and "what she sees" are shots that distance her from us, shots that use décor (the boathouse steps and struts) in a characteristically Ophulsian way, as a framing device.

Yet neither are Ophuls's tracking-shots really like Preminger's. For one thing, Preminger's, though polished and smooth, lack the actively expressive, "musical" dimension of Ophuls's; their main ambition is to be unobtrusive. If the subjective shot is infrequent in Ophuls, it is almost totally alien to Preminger. The camera in *Laura* moves to *watch* the character rather than to implicate us in his movements; having followed McPherson's tour of the living-room it not only stops to survey his progress to the next room in detached long-shot, it drops slightly so that a chair-back intrudes into the foreground of the frame. That chairback has nothing of the gracefully ornamental function of intervening objects in Ophuls; it is there simply to keep us at our distance. Ophuls's camera has a much stronger tendency to move with the characters, beside them and at their pace (in *Madame de . . .* , to waltz with them); though this is continually offset by intrusions into the frame, by the variability of camera-distance, by the (less frequent, but not uncommon) transference of attention to other characters, other groups. Equally removed from the audience-participation techniques of Hitchcock and the clinical objectivity and detachment of Preminger, Ophuls's camera-work achieves a perfect balance—in terms of the spectator's involvement—between sympathy and detachment. The sense of closeness without identification is essential to Ophuls's cinema: it is an aspect of that constant delicate intermingling of tenderness and irony that characterizes the Ophuls "tone." It relates similarly to a common structural feature of Ophuls's films: our intimate involvement with the characters is continually balanced by the fact that we always know more than they do. Our knowledge of historical facts in *Sarajevo* and *The Exile,* the flashback structures of *Letter* and *Lola Montes,* the merry-go-round symbolism of *La Ronde,* the obstinately recurrent earrings of *Madame de . . .* , all in their different ways place the spectator in a position of superior awareness.

The point can be further developed by reference to a crucial structural feature of *Letter:* the pervasive tension between subjective narrative and objective presentation. One can exemplify this most obviously by indicating the moments where Ophuls patently "cheats." The main body of the film is offered as a visualization of Lisa's letter; the question is, *Whose* visualization? Hardly Stefan's: the minor characters (Lisa's mother and stepfather, the lieutenant, etc.) whom Stefan does not know, are obviously not presented merely as he imagines them. The conventions of the first-person narrative in the cinema encourage us to accept the visualization as "how Lisa experienced it"; a moment's reflection will show us that much of the time Ophuls is taking great liberties with such an assumption. Consider the Prater sequence, where Lisa and Stefan, during their first evening together, visit a "world tour" railway in the funfair (the "train" remains stationary while backdrops of exotic countries move past the window), then dance together in a café. Throughout the sequence, we see that Lisa is completely enclosed in the world of her dream, aware of nothing except Stefan and the apparent realization of her fantasies. Ophuls, however, shows us a lot that is outside that world: the old man who works the levers that operate the backdrops, the old woman Stefan pays for the entertainment. While Lisa and Stefan dance together, Ophuls cuts in a bit of dialogue between the singularly unromantic women of the ladies' orchestra, who drink beer, chew sausage and complain of being kept late ("I like to play for *married* people—they've got homes"). All this, clearly, is outside Lisa's consciousness, and could not have been described in the letter. Despite the subjective narrative, Ophuls does not restrict us to Lisa's viewpoint. The tendency of the film to draw us into her vision is balanced and counterpointed throughout by a conflicting tendency to detach us from the "dream" and comment on it ironically, hinting at a prosaic reality that Lisa excludes, exposing some of the very unromantic mechanisms on which the dream depends. Ophuls's choice of music for the opera scene is very precise: as Lisa leaves her box, disturbed by Stefan's presence in the auditorium, and on her way to her fatal reunion with him outside on the steps, Act Two of *The Magic Flute* begins (incorrectly) with "Ein Mädchen oder Weibchen." The irony is clearly lost on Lisa; neither is it exactly simple. Papageno's desire for *any* girl or woman relates to Stefan's amorous pursuits and contrasts with Lisa's single-minded dedication to one man; yet, as the film reveals, Stefan's philandering has masked a search for the woman who might save him, the "unknown goddess" whom he failed (but, there are hints, only *just* failed) to recognize in Lisa.

Ophuls's love of near-repetition or echo itself becomes a distancing device even as it intensifies the poignancy of the action: again, we always know more than the characters. Sometimes, the discrepancy between their awareness and ours is slight. When Stefan Jr. leaves by train and repeats the words ("Two weeks...") his father called to Lisa just after his conception, we see Lisa herself react to the "echo." Yet we have more grounds for premonition than she: we know there is something amiss with the first compartment Stefan was put in, and as Lisa walks away we learn that there was a typhus case on the train. Ophuls's delicacy of effect might be represented by the shot of Lisa leaving the platform, the foreground of the image dominated by the spikes on the railings that form a barrier. Their harshness and gleaming coldness communicate a sense of the pain experienced by Lisa at that point, but the ominousness of the image conveys more than a subjective impression: we know from the beginning of her letter that she "may be dead," and we see her here as a trapped woman.

One might make a similar point with the two scenes involving white roses. In the earlier, during their first evening together, Stefan buys Lisa a single white rose from a friendly old lady; in the later, Lisa, visiting Stefan for what is to prove the last time, after she has broken her marriage and seen her son off at the station, buys a whole bunch from an old man who is "just closing up," but has "still a few flowers left." Again, the foreboding is experienced by Lisa but more precisely defined for the audience: the sense of "too late" associates itself with overtones of death—the anticipated death of Lisa, Stefan's impending duel, the typhus on the train.

Ophuls's fondness for "echoes" is not restricted to the "twinning" of scenes or incidents: it is expressed equally through the minutiae of *mise-en-scène,* the positioning of the camera, its angles, its distance, its movements. Occasionally, Ophuls creates a delicate irony solely through the use of the camera: about to leave for Linz, Lisa runs from the station at the last moment, intending to offer herself to Stefan. Finding him out, she awaits him on the stairs just above the door to his apartment. (The location has already accumulated certain emotional associations: it is where Lisa earlier crept during the night to listen to Stefan playing the piano.) Stefan comes home, but with another woman. We watch their entrance into the hallway (accompanied by the already familiar exchange with the hall porter: "Who is it?" etc.) almost from Lisa's position, the camera just behind her, looking down at them, panning right as they come up the stairs and disappear into the apartment. The effect is close to that of a subjective shot, encouraging us to share Lisa's disillusionment very directly: she leaves for Linz. Some years (though only about ten minutes of screen time) later, we have the sequence of Lisa's evening with Stefan: the visit to a café frequented by musicians, the gift of the white rose, the lobster dinner, the enchanted visit to the deserted, out-of-season Prater, the dance. Finally, Stefan takes her home with him: it is the ideal culmination and fulfilment of Lisa's romantic fantasy. Ophuls comments on it—and distances us again from Lisa's enchantment—by recapitulating the earlier shot's *mise-en-scène:* again we look down on the lovers from the stairs, again the camera pans to show them entering the apartment, and Lisa becomes but one woman in a never-ending succession—to Stefan, the suggestion is, scarcely distinguishable from the others, though the suggestion is qualified by other details in the preceding sequence.

I have so much stressed the delicacy of balance between identification with Lisa and detachment from her viewpoint because the film has so often been perceived (even by many of its professed admirers) as a sort of glorified "women's novelette" redeemed by Ophuls's taste and sensitivity. Such a distinction between subject-matter and treatment (besides doing grave injustice to Howard Koch's screenplay) is totally belied by the film. Its meaning is created by, and inseparable from, the detail of the *mise-en-scène* and the structure of the scenario, and it is there that one must look to account for the complexity of its total effect.

The fascination of certain films depends on our (often uncomfortable) awareness of the suppressed, ghostly presence of an alternative film saying almost precisely the opposite, lurking just beneath the surface. In some cases (Bergman's *Winter Light* and Chabrol's *Juste Avant la Nuit* are prime examples) this tension becomes so great, the suppression of the "alternative" film so precarious, that the conclusion can only be enigmatic, open to the most contradictory interpretations, the tensions left unresolved. This is not quite true of *Letter:* the ending, while complex in tone, ambivalent in its balancing of the tragic and the affirmative, represents a genuine, and deeply satisfying, resolution. Yet the more times one sees the film, the more one has the sense—it is a mark of its greatness—of the possibility of a film *against* Lisa: it would require only a shift of emphasis for this other film to emerge. It is not simply that Ophuls makes it possible for us to blame Lisa for destroying her eminently civilized marriage to a kind (if unpassionate) man, and the familial security he has given her and her son; it is also *almost* possible to blame Lisa, and her refusal to compromise, for Stefan's ruin. If the "echo" shot from the top of the staircase suggests that his night with Lisa is like all the others, this is qualified by other pieces of evidence: he does seem to recognize Lisa's difference (though fleetingly and never quite unequivocally), he *does* appear impressed by her perception that his playing reveals a man who has not found what he is looking for, he *does* go to the trouble of finding out where she works (and *after* she has spent the night with him, so this is not merely the compulsion of an obsessive seducer). One can admire the "absoluteness" of her refusal to have him notified of the birth of their child; one can equally (given the reflective distance from the fiction that Ophuls's style permits us) condemn the perversity with which she denies him his one chance to "realize" the glimpse of possibilities he has had, to confront responsibilities, to acknowledge the child who will die before Stefan knows he ever existed. Later, we see the Stefan who confronts Lisa on the opera-house steps as a desperate and haunted man—an image that his subsequent "cynical seducer" routine obliterates more completely for Lisa, perhaps, than for us. When she leaves his apartment, he has just declared that something she said the night before has been haunting him all day; she leaves without waiting to hear what it was, but Ophuls—as the camera lingers on the white roses and guttering candle—allows us to consider the possibility that a woman less devoted to an ideal might even at this late stage have been able to do something for a man not entirely beyond reach. The old flower-seller's remark (to which that last lingering shot of the roses might be felt to refer us back), for all its ominous overtones, can be taken as epitomizing this sense of fragile possibilities amid the encroaching darkness: there are "*still* a few flowers left." Lisa is in the mainstream of Ophuls's heroines and there is little doubt that the film is ultimately with her; yet its moral and emotional tensions can be suggested by saying that Stefan, on the other hand, has something about him of a male Lola Montes.

Ophuls's fondness for formal repetition and symmetry underlines the sense of destiny the films express: history repeats itself with variations, characters are returned to their starting-point that they may see how far they have travelled. I want to return, similarly, to mine: Fate, and the tracking-shot. One further comparison may give further definition to the significance of Ophuls's camera-movements. Like them, Renoir's tracking-shots, and his fondness for foreground/background counterpoint, suggest a view of life as constant flux, perpetual motion. The essential difference lies in the sense that in Renoir the camera is habitually at the service of the actors. One would not wish quite to declare the opposite of Ophuls—one never feels that the actors' movements are subordinated to an independently ("aesthetically") conceived camera-movement. But in Renoir the actors are free: one's impression is that the action is worked out in collaboration with them and the camera-movements (which rarely have the conscious elegance of Ophuls's) are determined accordingly. An Ophuls shot is a perfect unity of actor-movement and camera-movement. His people are in constant transition with little chance of standing still and taking stock: hence the importance in his work of staircases, doorways, stations, dance-floors. But at the same time they are trapped within the carefully predetermined movement, just as they are trapped within the clutter of the décor: they must move from *here* to *here* via *there*. Perpetually in motion, they are perpetually imprisoned—even as a piece of music, once it has begun, must move to its predetermined close. Ultimately, Ophuls's tracking-shots signify both Time and Destiny. In *Letter,* our sense of the inexorability of time is intensified by the flashback structure, which allows Ophuls to counterpoint the hours as Stefan reads her letter—the two time-schemes at last converging and uniting in the closing minutes, as Stefan finishes the letter and carriages arrive to bear him to the duel with Lisa's husband. The moment of bitterest irony in the film—given its force by the whole context of style and structure—is Stefan's remark to Lisa during their last meeting that "For us, all the clocks in the world have stopped."

The only escape from entrapment in time that Ophuls envisages is achieved through doubling back, re-living the past in order to transcend it. Hence the significance of flashback structures in his work. The ending of *Letter* is surely among the most poignant in the history of the cinema, at once desolating and exalting, tragic and affirmative. When Stefan, on his way to the duel, pauses and turns at the gate to see Lisa as she was the very first time he noticed her—but a Lisa, now, who fades, leaving only emptiness—we are intensely aware of the waste and loss: the loss not only of both their lives and of all Lisa has sacrificed for an impossible ideal, but of the relationship that might have been. At the same time it is a moment of supreme triumph: at the moment of recognition and remembrance, both the leading characters triumph over time, though one is already dead and the other on his way to die. Stefan's departure for the duel is at once suicide and redemption, the vindication of Lisa's romantic devotion, his acknowledgment of her vision. Should one finally talk of Fate or of Predestination? In France, Ophuls has had his Catholic interpreters (notably Claude Beylie), and *Letter* certainly permits a Catholic reading, with the first meeting of Stefan and Lisa presided over by a statuette of the Virgin, the crucifix dominating the room where Lisa's son has died and where she writes the letter, the appended note (the last thing Stefan reads) praying that God may have mercy on them both. Ophuls, I think, permits such a reading but does not demand it: the film is not inconsistent with the much more obvious ambiguity of *Madame de . . .* , where the similar religious motifs can be taken straight or read ironically.

Ophuls is ultimately (and because of, rather than despite, the pervasive irony) one of the cinema's great Romantics. The word has become so debased and simplified that it demands immediate qualification: there is, I have tried to insist, nothing simple or simplifying about Ophuls's commitment to Lisa's commitment, and it is never a matter of blind or uncritical identification. Lisa retains a yearning for a perfection unrealizable in life, yet the yearning confers upon life (even if posthumously) its highest dignity and value, and this Ophuls profoundly respects. The word "romantic" has many uses: one talks of a "romantic schoolgirl," and one talks of Keats as a "Romantic poet." The two usages have come to seem so distinct that it is worth remembering what they basically have in common: the romantic schoolgirl's yearning after an idol stems from the same urge as the Romantic poet's after the nightingale. So it is not impossible for Ophuls, dealing apparently with the former, to raise it through his art to the stature and significance of the latter.

6

Welles, Shakespeare and Webster
Touch of Evil

From what is known of Orson Welles's early life and background, one can select certain features of obvious and direct relevance to his films: as a child he knew long stretches of Shakespeare by heart and gave recitations in costume to audiences of doting relatives; before making *Citizen Kane* he worked in both theatre and radio; from childhood he has been fascinated by conjuring, performing feats of magic for his family and friends, entertaining the troops during World War II with a stage magician act. Part of the impulse behind the famous "War of the Worlds" broadcast was clearly the desire to amaze, an impulse present in most of Welles's film work, finding overt expression in the climactic pyrotechnics of *Lady from Shanghai,* movingly subjugated in *The Immortal Story.*

The fascination with Shakespeare has also proved constant. Apart from Welles's theatrical productions, there are the three Shakespeare films, *Macbeth, Othello, Chimes at Midnight,* and the long-cherished, still-unrealized project to film *Lear.* I am not concerned here primarily to trace particular links between *Touch of Evil* and Shakespeare, though a few (albeit somewhat tenuous) exist, the play in question being *Macbeth.* Most obviously, there is the blood on Quinlan's hand at the end, washed off in the dirty water but replaced almost immediately as he stands under Menzies's corpse; there is, more generally, the common theme of damnation, of the crossing of points-of-no-return; in such a context, one might see Marlene Dietrich's Tanya as a benevolent version of the witches: the purpose of Quinlan's second visit to her in the film is to be told his future.

And one might easily see the "night man" at the Grandi motel (Dennis Weaver) as a Wellesian equivalent for the Shakespeare clown—with as specific counterpart the "night man" of *Macbeth* who plays at being porter of hell-gate: he represents a grotesque parody of one of the film's leading themes, the moral complicity in evil of the "innocent" person whose innocence is dependent on a deliberate refusal to understand what is going on. Nor am I concerned here with the tendency of the dialogue to gravitate towards the rhythms of the iambic pentameter ("Have *I* still any credit left with *you*?"). Such details are more interesting for the ambitions and sense of affinities they indicate than in themselves.

What is important is Welles's evident partial identification with Shakespeare, manifested in the efforts to create a visual-poetic world equivalent to the "world" of a Shakespeare tragedy; in the constant reaching out for a tragic weight and grandeur; in the attempts to find a cinematic style that will fulfil a creative function analogous to that of Shakespeare's verse. When *Touch of Evil* first appeared, many critics saw in it—incredible as this now seems—no more than a commonplace cops-and-gangsters story, and bemoaned (not perhaps entirely without a certain malicious satisfaction in witnessing arrogance humiliated) Welles's degradation by the Hollywood system. This is rather like reducing (Shakespeare's) *Macbeth* to "Bad guy kills good guy and gets what's coming to him," in order to dismiss that as commonplace also. *Macbeth* is "poetic drama": the drama and the significance are in the poetry, which is not decorative clothing but artistic substance. To reduce *Macbeth* to its plot is quite simply to remove Shakespeare from it. For Welles, *mise-en-scène* is the cinematic equivalent of Shakespeare's poetry, an act of creation rather than interpretation. The meaning of *Touch of Evil* is no more reducible to its plot than the significance of *Macbeth*: its meaning is created by its style, the movement of actors and camera, the rhythms of editing, the recurrent and inter-relating image-patterns, that together build up a consistent and coherent world, not simply in the atmospheric sense, but in terms of a system of values, the embodiment of a view of existence.

Not that plot is irrelevant to *Touch of Evil* (any more than to *Macbeth*): I am not arguing for any "pure form" aesthetic nonsense. It is the case that any commonplace plot or situation, falling into the right hands at the right time, is capable of transformation into great art. (The converse is offered by Ken Hughes's *Joe Macbeth* which, by stripping *Macbeth* of its poetry without finding any cinematic equivalent, reduces it to the crudest banalities.) What Welles made of Whit Masterson's novel (*Badge of Evil*) is central to the recurrent thematic preoccupations of his films: the obsession with power and its corrupting effects. From *Citizen Kane* to *The Immortal Story* Welles has returned repeatedly to the figure of the man who usurps the functions of God in an effort to control his own destiny and those of others, a figure always viewed ambivalently as at once tragic-heroic and monstrously presumptuous.

If one studies Welles's movie career one can abstract a master-pattern on which individual films constitute variations (I do not suggest that it is necessarily the *only* pattern one might abstract). The pattern can be described thus: the relationship between two men, close friends, one old and corrupt, the other young and pure, the film moving towards the betrayal of the older by the younger; the older is always the film's true emotional centre, and he is played by Welles himself. Scarcely a single Welles film corresponds to this pattern *exactly*: in *Citizen Kane* the two men are roughly the same age, in *Confidential Report* the younger is far from pure, in *Lady from Shanghai* Welles plays (not very successfully) the young and innocent man, giving his own logical role to Everett Sloane, in *Othello* the corruption and purity are reversed, in *Touch of Evil* the two men are not friends. Yet if all these films are juxtaposed the pattern emerges clearly enough, and one film, later than any of them, expresses it completely and perfectly: *Chimes at Midnight*, where Welles's interest in the *Henry IV* plays is primarily an interest in the Falstaff/Hal relationship, the rejection of Falstaff by Hal becoming much more decisively the inevitable emotional climax than it seems in Shakespeare (where the interest is more complex and diffuse, and where Falstaff is more distanced). The pattern can also be seen as underlying *The Immortal Story*, and giving rise to its poignance. It might be argued that a strong homosexual undercurrent runs through Welles's work, the more potent perhaps for never being exposed to the light. Women are almost never central to his films and their roles are usually passive; the real tensions are between men.

Two riders need to be added to this theorem. Firstly, there is the curious case of *The Third Man*, written by Graham Greene, directed by Carol Reed, yet expressing the Welles pattern very strikingly. Rumour has it that Welles contributed both to the writing and direction of his own scenes—a rumour given some credibility by their style. It can scarcely be claimed that Welles invented Harry Lime, Holly Martins and their relationship, but his emotional involvement in the film, his personal gravitation to that situation, is eloquent. It is not unreasonable to claim for the film a peripheral place in the Welles canon. Secondly—and, *Touch of Evil* being in question, most significant of all—an early, cherished, never realized Welles project was a film version of *Heart of Darkness* in which Welles was to have played Kurtz. Readers of Conrad's extraordinary work will immediately recognize in it the archetypal Welles subject. It is not far-fetched to see vestiges of the project developed in *Touch of Evil*, with Quinlan as Kurtz and Vargas as Marlow.

Examination of the film's stylistic-thematic structure might appropriately begin with the opening shot, perhaps the most astonishing virtuoso crane-cum-tracking-shot in the history of the cinema, over which Universal saw fit to print the credits: no cut, from the first image of the hands in close-up adjusting the timing device on the bomb, to the moment when we hear the explosion off-screen. The shot decisively—even ostentatiously—establishes the film's two main characterizing technical means: depth of field and camera-movement. It must have been exceptionally difficult to organize and execute, with its complex movements of camera, actors, traffic, even a small herd of goats, all to be controlled and co-ordinated: so much easier to present the action in a series of short shots. One can begin by asking why Welles decided to do it that way.

There is, no doubt, a strong element of the showman-conjuror's desire to astonish: however many times I see it, the shot (supported by Henry Mancini's music, the ticking of the bomb taken up in the beat of the drums) remains one of the most riveting openings in the cinema, and a part of its effect derives from its sheer virtuosity, the sense of the impossible executed with apparent ease. Virtuosity, however, especially with repetition, becomes effective in direct ratio to our sense of its expressive potency, and the force of Welles's opening acts on deeper levels than that of the confidently executed conjuring-trick. One can "read" the shot most obviously in terms of the suspense generated and sustained: if we look carefully, we can see that the timing device on the bomb is set for it to explode in three minutes, and the strict continuity of the shot compels us to experience the passing of actual time. Cutting would (however subconsciously) undermine this: we are so accustomed to the use of editing to abridge the real duration of an action (character begins to mount staircase, cut to same character at top of staircase) that even the unsophisticated movie-goer quite unconscious of technical devices must be supposed to experience subconsciously the effect of suspension achieved by the spatial and temporal continuity.

At the same time, one must recognize that Welles's is not the only effective way of creating suspense. One can imagine the "master of suspense" himself, Hitchcock, shooting the scene very differently, breaking it up into a tense montage, returning our attention obsessively to the bomb, cutting repeatedly to the faces of the potential victims, using the rhythmic aspect of editing to tighten our nerves. Hitchcock's editing allows him to take frequent liberties with the actualities of time and space: the question with him would become, *When* will it go off? With Welles, if we are sufficiently attentive, we know approximately when, and the expectations set up are accurately realized (the opening shot lasts three minutes twenty seconds). Here, the suspense arises more from our sense of inevitability, coupled with uncertainty as to where the car will be and who will be near it at the predetermined moment. It is a matter of emphasis rather than of absolute difference. A style based on the carefully planned—predestined—movement of the camera, leading as much as following the actors from *here* to *there,* necessarily carries implications of fatality. The sense of Fate never becomes as explicit in Welles as in Ophuls and von Sternberg (at least, until *The Immortal Story*), but it is none the less there, supported by the strong Expressionist influence discernible in Welles's lighting, camera-placement and composition.

Beyond this, the stylistic choice in the first shot enables Welles to construct a pattern of movement in which is implicit one of the leading thematic/metaphysical concerns of the film: the idea of connectedness. The car starts, moves, is held up at an intersection, moves, is held up by a herd of goats, moves, is stopped at the frontier; a young couple (whom we may not recognize immediately, in long-shot and semi-darkness, as Charlton Heston and Janet Leigh) repeatedly pass it or are passed by it. The bomb will kill the couple in the car and drastically affect the lives of the other couple. In retrospect, the opening take can be seen as having a prophetic aspect. The two girls are visually connected by the fact that both are attractive young blondes. The girl in the car is an innocent victim of the bomb, which is not meant for her: she dies because of her involvement with the

Capt. Hank Quinlan in *Touch of Evil.*

man. Similarly, Suzie Vargas will suffer everything *but* death for
no reason except that she is Vargas's wife. Throughout the take,
the couples are linked in the minds of the audience by the common danger of which they are unaware; throughout the film, a
central unifying impulse will be the making manifest of connections (moral as well as actual) unrecognized or suppressed
by the characters. The vibrations from the explosion will sub-
side only at the end of the film, after the deaths of three more
men and the revelation of a complex pattern of interlocking
guilt and responsibility. The unbroken take, by its very virtuosity, its stylistic consciousness, its emphasis on spatial and temporal continuity, confers a potential significance on the action
beyond the simple, physical suspense inherent in it.

Certain other motifs, not dependent on the continuity of
the opening shot yet established within it, are also worth pick-

ing out for their significance in relation to the whole film. As the killer runs to place the bomb, the image is dominated by his shadow, moving huge across a wall; again and again in the film the image of people dwarfed by shadows—frequently their own—will recur. The use of shadows is one aspect of the nocturnal quality of the film. There *are* day scenes in *Touch of Evil* (whose action, in fact, covers a day and two nights), but, just as one thinks of *Macbeth* as a night play, so one thinks of it as a night film; it differs from Macbeth in that the shadows—the physical, mental, moral obscurity through which the characters move, the evil whose contamination (the "touch" of the title) no one escapes—will never be dispelled; the film's last image will be of a character disappearing into them. The film's very first image—the hands adjusting the mechanism—will be taken up in subsequent close-ups of hands adjusting car radios and, more significantly, of Vargas's hands adjusting the tape-recorder in the closing scene.

Finally, the opening shot establishes what is perhaps the key unifying image of the film, the crossing of borders. The border here is simple and literal, but one may note two things about it: its arbitrariness, half-way along a street in a town that looks much the same on either side of it; and the ease with which it can be crossed, a point emphasized in the scenes that follow, where Suzie will move from the American to the Mexican side and back ("Across the border again?"), and Quinlan ("Oh, *we're* tourists") will pass outside his area of jurisdiction, without opposition or interference.

The theme of connectedness is implicit also in the film's other celebrated long take, the interrogation of Sanchez in the apartment. Here, however, there is a simple explanation for the stylistic decision (it has been expounded by Charlton Heston himself): the five-and-a-half-minute shot represents the first day's shooting; Welles, virtually outlawed as a director by Hollywood, precariously reinstated owing, apparently, to a misunderstanding and to Heston's championship,[4] was bent on the vindication of his competence with the studio, and vindicated it in a characteristically flamboyant manner, by turning in two days' shooting quota in a single meticulously rehearsed take. The explanation, convincingly Wellesian, is half-satisfying: the single take is by no means necessitated by the dramatic content of the scene, nor is it entirely representative of the film as a whole. On the other hand, it is perfectly compatible with the style of the film (there are other, though shorter, interior scenes done in single takes), and Welles must have been well aware that he was asserting more than his viability as an economic proposition. One is struck here by the importance of his training in theatre and radio: though the dramatic effectiveness of every step in the scene's progress is determined above all by the framing and reframing as the camera moves, pauses, resumes its movement, the apartment is treated like a sort of multiple stage, the groupings revealing repeatedly a flair one might term "theatrical"; and the treatment of dialogue, rapid, overlapping, interrupted, the sound non-naturalistic (when Vargas and Schwartz talk in the bathroom doorway, the background conversation disappears for a time altogether, though it was perfectly audible from there earlier), as surely evokes the radio play: even a point as "cinematic" as the precise timing and "spotlighting" of the off-screen word "dynamite" to coincide with Vargas's upsetting of the shoe-box, suggests a director particularly conscious of the manipulation of sound.[5]

---

4. See interview from *Cahiers du Cinéma*, April 1965, reprinted in Andrew Sarris's *Interviews with Film Directors*.

5. Welles's expertise in radio may be partly responsible for the difficulties audiences notoriously have in following certain of his films, and consequently for their commercial failure: what would be perfectly intelligible in a broadcast, when all one's attention is concentrated on a single sense-stimulus, can become an incomprehensible gabble when part of our attention is diverted to visual events. The climax of *Lady from Shanghai*, where the entire explanation of an intricate murder-plot is given us at breakneck speed as off-screen commentary to a bewildering welter of fantastic images in a funfair and crazy house, is the most extreme instance.

On Quinlan's first appearance in the film, he and Vargas were established as antagonists of equal stature by their isolation in inter-cut close shots as they confronted each other. The single-take interrogation scene is centrally concerned with developing this confrontation as first one, then the other, dominates the frame, or as they are placed within the image in a precarious and temporary balance. The camera's movement throughout the take is like an invisible thread on which characters and incidents are strung in time and space. The spectator's eye is led relentlessly through each significant step in the unexpressed struggle for dominance that, rather than the interrogation of a suspect, becomes the real source of dramatic tension; a struggle interrupted by Vargas's departure to phone Suzie, to be resumed a few minutes later on his return, when it will centre on the discovery of the "planted" dynamite. Dramatic tension and opposition, however, can be expressed as effectively (as indeed they were earlier) by cutting; it is a sense of connection, as yet unexplained of the characters even in their antagonism existing on a single moral continuum, that is insisted on by the single take.

Camera movement connects, editing separates: the apparent truism, like most textbook rules, has some foundation in elementary practice but needs drastic qualification when confronted with the work of a major creative artist. In *Touch of Evil* Welles uses editing repeatedly to underline the sense of connectedness established by the camera style. Consider the sequence of shots that immediately follows the long take of the interrogation scene. The long take ends with Vargas in long-shot about to go out to phone Suzie; Quinlan, half-turned to him, dominates the foreground of the image, but the composition focuses our attention on Vargas. The complex action that ensues is recorded in three shots: one, cut to outside the door, Vargas, foreground, crosses the street, the camera moving with him. A car appears from around the corner in the background of the image and, although it is too distant for us to be certain we recognize the occupants, we may identify the car as Vargas's (in which Menzies has driven Suzie out to the motel), and our attention is drawn to it by the fact that one of the two men in it stands up and gesticulates on seeing Vargas; his build and mannerisms identify him as Grandi. As Vargas enters a shop opposite the apartment, we see the reflection of the car in the window, passing but slowing down. Two, cut to the interior of the shop, Vargas again in the foreground, which he shares with the blind shopkeeper, who tells him she has no directory and he should ask the operator for the number. The camera has swung across so that we can see, in long-shot, the street outside the window. The use of the window-frame almost as a screen within the screen directs our attention to the little pantomime, unperceived by Vargas, acted out within its space: Grandi and Menzies, entering from the left, arguing, the former driven on by the latter, who carries Quinlan's stick. Three, cut to outside the door of the apartment, Grandi and Menzies now in the foreground of the image, as Menzies chivvies Grandi into the flat.

Welles's composition and editing, whereby the background action of one shot becomes the foreground of the next, takes us from Quinlan to Vargas to Menzies and Grandi and back (in the next shot) to Quinlan, who is still inside the apartment. The sequence conveys important plot points: that Quinlan sometimes leaves his stick behind (rejecting the emblem of his physical infirmity, perhaps, as a symbolic refusal to acknowledge moral imperfection) and that Menzies returns it to him like a faithful retriever-dog. But the rationale behind the actual shooting seems again to be the preservation of a sense of continuity and connection: the close involvement of all actions, all characters, with each other, even when the involvement is not recognized.

On a verbal level, the theme of connectedness is expressed in the repeated references to "partners." Quinlan habitually calls Menzies "partner," emphasizing his complicity. We can piece together how they work as a team from various hints the film offers: when Quinlan is on a case, no one is allowed to search until he arrives on the scene ("We know better than that, captain—we were waiting for you"); he then plants the evidence which Menzies dutifully finds. The precise nature of Menzies's complicity is also implied quite clearly: he has never confronted the fairly self-evident fact that Quinlan frames his victims. His "innocence" is of the highly dubious kind that depends on the refusal of awareness: he cannot let himself know the inconvenient truth, or the partnership would cease to function.

The emblem of that partnership is Quinlan's stick: his "game leg" is the result of a bullet he received shielding Menzies. Welles has said that this was spelt out in a dialogue exchange cut by Universal, but it is a reasonable inference without this: at the end of the film, when Menzies shoots him, Quinlan says "That's the second bullet I've stopped for you, partner," and, given the law of artistic relevance, it is natural to associate the remark with Quinlan's only visible physical disability. It is around the stick that the denouement revolves, the emblem of mutual dependence becoming the instrument of betrayal. The irony is beautifully complex and complete. Menzies is shown to have two functions in relation to Quinlan: discovering planted evidence and retrieving the stick. Finally, after murdering Grandi, Quinlan inadvertently plants evidence against himself which Menzies dutifully finds: he leaves the stick behind. "Inadvertently" on the conscious level; but we are free to speculate as to whether Quinlan's forgetfulness has not a subconscious prompting in a desire to destroy himself: it is from the moment when he lets himself succumb to Grandi's temptation that his expressions of weariness become pronounced, and he begins to speak of his job (the only thing he now lives for) as "dirty."

In the course of the film Quinlan acquires an alternative "partner"—Grandi: the word is insisted upon in their scene of conspiracy in Grandi's bar ("You talk as if this was some kind of deal we were making, but no; in this we are *partners*"). Hence the murder of Grandi is another component in the pattern of betrayals: Quinlan betrays Grandi by killing him, Menzies betrays Quinlan by giving the stick to Vargas. The staging of the scene—it follows on from the later scene in Sanchez's apartment—in which Grandi leads Quinlan into partnership is particularly expressive, drawing on another recurrent visual motif, the receding line of three characters, one in foreground (usually right of screen), one in long-shot (left of screen), the third occupying a middle position. In some cases, this motif seems determined primarily by Welles's love of deep-focus images and the use of three-dimensional space: the spectator's eye is led not only across the screen from right to left but, simultaneously, from foreground to background. In the scene in question, however, the motif acquires a more precise significance. The sequence takes up visually the metaphor of crossing border-lines, Quinlan making the crucial transition from Menzies to Grandi. In the street outside the apartment, Menzies (right of screen) is abruptly dismissed as Grandi (left background) leads Quinlan across the road and towards his bar. The scene ends with a shot of Menzies watching sadly and anxiously from behind the window of the apartment, Quinlan and Grandi reflected, as they move away, in the glass that emphasizes Menzies's exclusion and helplessness. The essence of the following scene in the bar is again the crossing of a metaphorical border-line, Quinlan passing from candy-bars to liquor, automatically beginning to repeat his habitual "I don't drink" even as he realizes he has drunk Grandi's whisky—the alcohol he needs to weaken his remaining moral resources. A further ironic connection: the basis for the deal with Grandi was inadvertently supplied by Menzies; it was he who drove Suzie out to Grandi's motel.

The "receding line of three" motif emphasizes the notion of a moral continuum embodied here in the Menzies-Quinlan-Grandi triangle and in Quinlan's crossing from one to the other. We have seen that Welles repeatedly opposes yet connects

Quinlan and Vargas, as antagonists of great stature; it remains to be seen how Vargas relates to this moral continuum and to the crossing of boundaries.

Our first impression—influenced by the expectations set up by the casting and by the genre conventions—will probably be of clear-cut opposition, the pure Vargas against the corrupt Quinlan. Yet from the outset, even before Quinlan has appeared, Welles has undermined such assurances. The banality of the Vargas/Suzie dialogue during the film's opening shot ("... hot on the trail of a chocolate soda ..." "Do you realize it's over an hour since I kissed you?") would be easily acceptable within the strict functionalism of a B-feature crime melodrama, but is mercilessly thrown into relief by the aspirations of the Wellesian style. The counterpointing of visual intensity with verbal banality continues through the shots immediately following the explosion: rapid low-angle backward tracks, leading Vargas vertiginously on as he runs to the wreck, evoking the sense of instability, speed and confusion so characteristic of the world Welles creates for us, are combined with dialogue of stupefying obviousness ("Mike, what happened?"—"The car that just passed us exploded.... We'll have to postpone that soda I'm afraid"). The Vargas-Suzie relationship has come in for a lot of adverse criticism, on the grounds that the characters seem stereotyped and shallow. One certainly has the impression that Welles, in his re-working of the screenplay, has been content to leave them within the familiar conventions of the thriller, but this may, I think, be a deliberate strategy on his part: It is a way (whether an entirely valid or successful one is another matter) of qualifying any hero-villain opposition we may take as generically inherent in the relationship of Vargas to Quinlan. It is essential to the film's moral subversiveness that Vargas's moral rectitude have about it something rigid and priggish. Suzie's status as heroine, which likewise seems "generically" guaranteed, is thrown into question very early on, through her lack of understanding and sympathy for her husband's position, and through her mindless racism ("Lead on, Pancho"). Quinlan's racism is subsequently explained (excused?) by the fact that his wife was murdered by a "half-breed": the racism is a manifestation of his depth of feeling, while Suzie's is an aspect of her superficiality.

The necessary contrast, and the necessary parallel, between the two men is established through their attitudes to their respective wives. Both men are dedicated to their work; but where Vargas's dedication is presented as entirely idealistic and abstract, Quinlan's is revealed as psychologically motivated. Vargas's noble devotion to duty is consistently at the expense of Suzie and their relationship. The general point can be localized in another example of Welles's connective editing: the cut from the door of the motel room closing on Suzie's rapists to the door of the public records office opening as Menzies comes to interrupt Vargas's examination of Quinlan's past cases, a cut juxtaposing Suzie's violation with her husband's single-minded pursuit of an abstract-legal "truth." The ensuing scene, which sets that public morality against Menzies's personal loyalty, is very revealing of Welles's attitude. The *mise-en-scène* appears to endorse Vargas, giving the emphasis of close-up and a dramatic exit from the frame to his "clinching" point about the men Quinlan has had convicted ("Save your tears for them"). Yet the Vargas speech and its treatment remain rhetorical; it is the inward, helpless grief of Menzies (Joseph Calleia is superb throughout the film) that makes the real impression, and the moral dignity of Vargas's position is further undermined by our knowledge that Suzie is at that moment suffering gang-rape. Quinlan's remark in the climactic sequence of the film that it is the "starry-eyed idealists" like Vargas who cause the real trouble in the world would seem to be given oblique and insidious endorsement.

Against Vargas's commitment to duty, Welles sets Quinlan's corrupt methods coupled with his devotion to a dead wife ("I'm always thinking about her, drunk or sober. What else is there to think about?—except my job, my dirty job"). Welles unmistakably leads us to value this personal commitment above Vargas's dedication to a moral code. Further, there is the suggestion that all Quinlan's actions can be explained by reference to his wife's death. She was strangled, we learn, by a "half-breed" who evaded justice for lack of evidence against him, eventually dying beyond Quinlan's grasp ("the last killer that ever got out of my hands"); all of Quinlan's obsessively (and dishonestly) pursued convictions are acts of symbolic (though never satisfying) compensation. We are invited to interpret even Quinlan's most excessive criminal act, the murder of Grandi and attempt to "frame" Suzie for it, in this light. Menzies gives us the pointer ("Drunk and crazy as you were, I guess you were thinking of your wife"), and the apparent change in Quinlan's plan—the sense of irresistible subconscious impulse over-riding rational intention—is a further indication: his plan was clearly to shoot Grandi with Vargas's gun (stolen for the purpose from his briefcase, in Suzie's possession—the narrative logic is not entirely clear). The strangling of the heavily-built Grandi with Suzie's stocking renders the frame-up quite implausible, but represents a neat enactment of symbolic revenge: Quinlan's wife was strangled by a "half-breed," Quinlan now not only strangles a Mexican but makes it appear the act of a white woman and, what is more, a policeman's wife. The sense of confused, multi-levelled motivation (the execution of the plot against Vargas, the removal of the detested Grandi and the shame of their "partnership," the symbolic revenge, the desire for self-destruction) is typical of the unstable, nocturnal world of the film.

I suggested earlier a connection between *Touch of Evil* and Conrad's *Heart of Darkness*. The climax of Marlow's experiences up the Congo is his nervous breakdown as the boat returns, after the death of Kurtz: Marlow has recognized in Kurtz an obscure reflection of the darker potentialities within himself, within every man. Hence Conrad makes of the mature Marlow a detached and dispassionate observer who can no longer participate in life, only tell yarns about it. In *Touch of Evil,* Vargas begins to be a human being, and to be allowed a share of the audience's sympathy, from the moment he reveals himself as a potential Quinlan.

I am thinking of the sequences following Vargas's discovery that Suzie is not at the motel—sequences that again make significant use of the crossing of borders. Stylistically, these scenes carry to the highest intensity of expression "that sort of vertigo, uncertainty, lack of stability, that mélange of movement and tension that is our universe" (Welles, the *Cahiers* interview quoted above). The restless tracking and tilting camera movements as Vargas drives his car past the very hotel on whose fire-escape the wife he is frantically seeking screams for help, naked under a sheet; the rapid tracks and low-angled shots during the violent fight in the bar; above all, the cut from the sudden close two-shot on the word "Murder" as Vargas reacts to Schwartz's revelation of Suzie's arrest (the shot going abruptly out of focus), to the rapid low-angled forward track behind Vargas as he rushes down a corridor in the jail: all Welles's stylistic flourishes are dedicated to the sense of confusion, uncontrol, terrifying speed.

Vargas's drive recapitulates the opening shot in inversion: he passes the border-post again, in the opposite direction, without ceremony or legal formalities, scattering officials and pedestrians alike, all the superficial order and leisureliness of the opening destroyed. Most suggestive of all is the use Welles makes of the bead curtain in Grandi's bar: Vargas passes abruptly through it, crossing from his world of moral certitudes into the moral quick-sands of the Quinlan-Grandi universe, and the camera tracks laterally to the left, keeping the curtain between us and Vargas, indistinct beyond its shaking. "I'm not a cop now, I'm a husband," he shouts, making clear the implicit connection with

Quinlan, beating suspects to force a confession from them. The juke-box against which he beats the Grandi boy, shattering it, directly evokes the scene of Quinlan's fatal transition: the earlier scene in Grandi's bar, then deserted, ended with Grandi inserting a coin in the same juke-box as Quinlan clouded his consciousness with whisky.

The opening sequence of the film centred on a bomb; the close centres on a tape-recorder. The two are linked in our minds by the close-ups of hands adjusting dials, and by the furtiveness of the men who make use of them. The actions are further linked and linked also to another underhand activity, Quinlan's obsessive framing of suspects—when Schwartz reveals that Sanchez "was guilty after all": he planted the bomb to safeguard his marriage to Marcia, Quinlan's actions were motivated by a desire to avenge his wife's murder, and Vargas too is ultimately driven by the need to avenge what was done to Suzie and clear her name. The extraordinary climactic scene in which Vargas records Quinlan's inadvertent admissions to Menzies is characterized by an extreme use of deep focus that keeps speaker and auditor in frame, connected across the distances that separate them. At first Vargas is high up, viewing Quinlan from positions of furtive superiority, but as the scene progresses he is forced down, until he finally grovels in the muddy water under the bridge, the water in which Quinlan will die. The means by which he obtains justice, while not quite on a level with Quinlan's deliberate planting of false evidence, are underhand and morally dubious. And in the context of the moral priorities the film sets up, one is tempted to feel that the most insidious act of all is Quinlan's betrayal by Menzies, "the cop that loved him"—an act in terms of conventional morality entirely justified, even obligatory; in which paradox is epitomized the profoundly disturbing effect of the film as a whole. It is an act, of course, that Vargas is behind: a point given literal visual expression when Menzies falls to Quinlan's bullet, and Vargas is revealed behind him, with the tape-recorder.

One may ask where all this leaves us morally. Certainly in a world where nothing is stable, characterized by a "*mélange* of movement and tension": by the end of the film all our moral preconceptions have been undermined or subverted. One can ask whether the final effect is of compassionate understanding or of self-indulgent defeatism. It could be argued that the transference of our allegiance from the upright Vargas to the corrupt Quinlan is a salutary lesson in charity and the complexities of true moral sense. It could equally be argued that Welles's unsympathetic, even hostile treatment of Vargas and Suzie, his presentation of them as shallow, conventionalized figures beside the psychologically multi-dimensional Quinlan, is an unfair way of loading the dice, of *forcing* the spectator's sympathies to gravitate to Quinlan (with whom Welles is obviously much involved) and thus of excusing and even perversely justifying his corruption. The somewhat rhetorical, worked-up intensity of the motel scenes, especially the treatment of the gang-rape (the instructions to "hold her legs open," Mercedes McCambridge's request to be allowed to stay and watch) suggests an animus against the character of Suzie and a perverse relishing of her degradation. In fact, the identification of Welles the director with Quinlan the character is suggested by their mutual desire to discredit Vargas, without scruples as to the means employed. Quinlan's sense of the ingratitude of the "system" (the banquet at the start to which he was not invited, the oil-pump at the end pumping up the "money" with which he has not been rewarded) is obviously very personal to Welles, and the way in which personal loyalties are given moral precedence over any form of social morality follows on from this. One may note how, given the opportunity to make the film within the industry against which he feels such bitterness, Welles promptly surrounded himself with old friends, so that the film looks at moments like an "old boys reunion" from *Citizen Kane:* Joseph Cotten, Ray Collins,

Gus Schilling and Harry Shannon all appear in small roles. Yet Quinlan, however sympathetic a figure Welles encourages us to find him, is scarcely an admirable one, and the morally admirable qualities of Vargas are presented as unattractive and undesirable. We may feel that Welles ultimately drags the spectator down into the mud with Quinlan.

This impression is partly qualified, partly confirmed, by Welles's efforts to humanize Vargas in the closing sequences. The final Vargas-Quinlan exchange—immediately before Quinlan is shot by the dying Menzies—is one of the most quintessentially Wellesian moments in the film, Vargas's face expressing respect, almost affection, for the old man he is destroying (and who is threatening to shoot him). It is perhaps the moment in the whole film where we most like Vargas; at the same time a part of its purpose is further to ensure our sympathy for Quinlan—even Vargas ends by feeling a reluctant admiration for him. Again, the banal and perfunctory treatment of the Vargas-Suzie reunion (a quick embrace in the car followed by "I'm taking you home") acquires at least potential meaningfulness from its relation to Tanya's last words to Quinlan ("You'd better go home"), and our knowledge that Quinlan has no "home" to go to (except in the barest literal sense—his despised turkey-farm): a relation underlined by having Tanya (but not, I think, Dietrich!—the face is in heavy shadow) run past Vargas's car during the reunion. But "home" is a concept that (so important in *Kane* and *Ambersons*) scarcely exists for the later Welles, rejected and self-exiled, as more than a bitter irony: Quinlan's "home" is (or used to be) Tanya's establishment, just as Falstaff's only home is the tavern. For Vargas and Suzie, "home" would have to be defined in terms of their relationship, and Welles's failure (or refusal of interest) there leaves the banality of Vargas's last line un-transcended.

In assessing the film's total effect, a character I have hitherto largely ignored is crucial: Tanya. Not only is she given the film's epitaph on Quinlan to deliver (and its last word—"Adios"—as she disappears into the darkness) but her character is given a special status throughout. The casting—putting a star of Dietrich's already legendary eminence in so small a role—immediately establishes this, and the style and structure of the film confirm it. Tanya's relation to the world of the film is ambiguous: she is both of it and not of it. Her "establishment" became (we are given to understand) Quinlan's emotional home after his wife's death, where he went to get drunk. She is associated with nostalgia for the past (her pianola music set against Grandi's jukebox and the insistent pop-music on the motel radio) and with a kind of wisdom, the wisdom of resignation; she is also associated with a letting-go, a giving-up: Quinlan stopped visiting her when he made the transition from "hooch" to candy-bars. From a narrative viewpoint, Tanya is redundant: she contributes nothing to the action, to the development of the plot. She is placed outside the action, as "Fate" figure and clairvoyant (she "knows" Quinlan's situation, his lack of a future, and knows when he is dying and who shot him) and finally as choric commentator.

The style of the film changes abruptly every time she appears. I have noted the constant movement, the extraordinary mobility of the camera, the pervasive instability. When we enter Tanya's house, everything is still. In contrast to the twin devices of camera movement and deep focus that characterize the rest of the film, shots of Tanya have two main stylistic features: they are nearly always static, and frequently full-face close-ups from which background is virtually eliminated. Where other characters are repeatedly linked by camera-movement or composition (the "line of three"), Tanya is almost always isolated by a cut to close-up. The special status she is accorded gives clinching significance to her final speech, again isolated and underlined by a close-up. Tanya's "He was some kind of a man—what does it matter what you say about people?" may be a distant echo of Hamlet's "He was a man, take him for all in all / I shall not look upon his like again." The faint verbal similarity underlines the difference: where Shakespeare evokes a sense of tragic loss, Welles conveys a sort of metaphysical helplessness, a sense of futility and negation, of which Tanya's disappearance into darkness (the film's final image) is a fitting visual expression.

A great film, perhaps; an endlessly fascinating one, certainly; but one ends by finding it also somewhat worrying. Rather than Shakespeare, comparison with whom Welles has so consistently seemed to court, one might prefer to invoke Webster, in whose plays the Elizabethan creativity degenerates into morbidity and decadence. Shakespeare may make us feel that his Macbeth represents potentialities that exist in all of us, but he never sucks us into complicity with him, as Welles does with Quinlan—we are never invited to *condone* Macbeth's crimes. A concern with evil can shade imperceptibly into a fascination with evil, which in its turn can merge into a celebration of evil. Welles's film is never that: the profound moral and metaphysical unease it communicates resists any such simple definition. But the disturbance it leaves behind in the mind is not entirely free of distaste.

7
Images of Childhood

Like a fiend hid in a cloud
WILLIAM BLAKE

Peter Coveney's *The Image of Childhood* (Peregrine Books, 1967), an indispensable work of literary criticism by a historian, traces the development of the figure of the child in English literature from Blake and Wordsworth to the first decades of the present century. Its premise is that in Romantic literature the Child acquired a rich symbolic significance, representing the potentiality for growth and renewal in the individual and, by extension, in society. The book traces the development of this image from the visionary children of Blake to its final flowering in Lawrence (notably the children of *The Rainbow*), and shows how this development was counterpointed by decline and decadence, the Blakean symbol of universal rebirth dwindling into Peter Pan, the child who refuses adulthood. The figure of the Child, in this reading, reflects the condition of civilization, its health or sickness, as projected in the values and aspirations of its art.

Since the death of Lawrence the cinema has increasingly taken over from poetry and the novel as the central expression of creative energies. One might, then, expect to discover the further progress of the "Image of Childhood" in the images of childhood given us on the screen; and such expectations are amply fulfilled. A book-length sequel to Peter Coveney's work might well be undertaken; all I offer here is a sketch, suggesting areas for investigation, tentatively mapping lines of development. The complexities involved are multiplied by the universality of the medium: where Coveney could reasonably restrict himself to English literature, the accessibility of film makes it impossible to avoid confronting the cinemas of Europe and Hollywood, now part of our common culture.

The Neo-Realist Child

In the great period of Italian neo-realism, which gained so much impetus from World War II and its immediate aftermath, the precarious, shifting balance of despair and hope for renewal is repeatedly poised in the lives (and deaths) of children. The child at the end of *Bicycle Thieves* takes the hand of his humiliated father in a gesture that reaffirms the bonds of natural affection in a world where everything else has become uncertain; the partisan children at the end of *Rome, Open City,* having witnessed the execution of the priest, walk away grim but determined against Rome's skyline, the camera panning with them to stop when St. Peter's is in the centre of the image. Against these images of bleak affirmation must be set certain images of despair centred on children born or unborn, particularly strong in the first three postwar films of Rossellini. The shooting down of Anna Magnani in *Rome, Open City* gains its force from the fact that she is pregnant. In the Naples episode of *Paisa* a child (who recalls the boy in *Bicycle Thieves* except that he is bereft of parents and exists in even more desperate material circumstances) befriends a lonely negro soldier but knows that he will steal his boots as soon as the man falls asleep; in the final episode a baby totters screaming among the corpses of its family after a massacre. These intimations of the corruption of innocence and of irreparable loss and disaster come together in *Germany, Year Zero,* united in the central figure Edmund, the child perverted by Nazi doctrine, poisoner of his own sick father. The extraordinary last half hour of the film charts Edmund's progress to a casual, unpremeditated suicide amid the ruins of Berlin: Released

In *Germany, Year Zero*
(*Germania, Anno Zero*),
Edmund sits down in the
gutter while wandering the
streets of Berlin.

into solitude from the prematurely adult responsibilities of his
situation, he becomes a real child for the first time in the film,
playing desultory little improvised games; then, realizing he no
longer has anywhere to go, he throws himself from the top of a
devastated building.

The suicide of a child in a world that has nothing to offer it:
it is difficult to imagine a more desolate culmination. After it,
Rossellini moved towards a new affirmation expressed at first
though images of childbirth as triumphant vindication (Anna
Magnani in *The Miracle*) and pregnancy finally accepted (Ingrid
Bergman in *Stromboli*), and later manifesting itself as a search
for understanding and historical awareness through the series
of documentaries and historical reconstructions. This positive
note in Rossellini—active enquiry, vigorous analysis—sets his

development apart from that of his distinguished contemporaries. After *Il Grido,* children scarcely figure in the increasingly enervating films of Antonioni, the work of an artist narcissistically preoccupied with his own defeat. The de Sica of *Bicycle Thieves* and *Shoeshine* gave place to the commercial hack, and then to the de Sica who (by way of artistic "come-back") could use, in *Garden of the Finzi-Continis,* the extermination of the Jews as a vehicle for "aesthetic" self-indulgence. Fellini presents a more complex and interesting case, more central to the movement of the European cinema: I shall return to him later.

The Bergman Child

Bergman's art (with its striking anticipations in the plays of Strindberg) has tended strongly towards the "psychodrama"— the dramatization of internal tensions and conflicts, in which, the characters are partly to be viewed as projections of forces within the artist's own psyche. It is probable that all art that is in any sense personal—all art, in other words, worthy to be called art partakes to some degree of this tendency, even the most seemingly objective and extrovert artist revealing himself through the dramatization of recurrent preoccupations. In Bergman, however, because of the relative lack in his work of a socio-political dimension, because of its introspective nature, because of the pervasive evidence of its roots in personal neurosis (the presence of that "undigested clinical material" of which Andrew Sarris so tellingly complains), the degree is unusually high: films such as the "trilogy" (*Through a Glass Darkly, Winter Light, The Silence*), *Persona, Hour of the Wolf,* are the cinema's nearest approach to pure psychodrama. In such a context, the symbolic nature of the Romantic Child might be expected to reveal itself particularly clearly and strongly, and, although children play only a very small part in Bergman's total *oeuvre,* such is indeed the case.

The neurotic basis of Bergman's art is suggested by the presence of an obsessive structure of apparently unresolvable tensions, whose obstinate recurrence in film after film testifies to its psychological nature: like a Freudian dream-pattern, it adopts a variety of disguises and concealments in order to reach expression, and only becomes plain when one has analysed a whole succession of films into their basic elements. Its first complete expression seems to be in *The Seventh Seal*—that film, at any rate, provides a conveniently schematic starting-point. The opening sequences set in opposition the Knight (a tormented intellectual) and the materialistic Squire, and contrast with both the travelling players. Over all hangs the shadow of Death (the bird of prey of the first image, Death personified, the plague-stricken corpse). The pattern established here has certain important features: the Knight and Squire, though perpetually at loggerheads, are bound to each other apparently indissolubly; the family of players remain (throughout the film) quite external to this conflict, touching it only peripherally. Knight and Squire are introduced within a barren landscape expressive of the sterility of their conflict. Although they are not children (they have a baby) the players (Jof and Mia) are consistently characterized as childlike; they represent simple faith, positive acceptance, fertile relationship; with the supportive imagery that introduces them (verdure, bird-song, the vision of Mary and the Infant Jesus), they relate very directly and clearly to the symbolic significance of the Child in Romantic art.

The recurrence of this basic structure in subsequent Bergman films can be shown succinctly by means of a chart:

The central conflict in all these films is between the intellectual and the materialist, and the obstinacy of its recurrence, without much sense of progress, makes it appear unresolvable and sterile, the product of a neurotic complex never quite confronted as such, hence insusceptible to exorcism: the reason, surely, why even Bergman's admirers go through periods of dis-

Title	Spiritual/ Intellectual	Materialist/ Sensualist	Positive Acceptance	Presence of Death
WILD STRAWBERRIES	Isak/Evald	Isak's Wife/ Marianne	Sara I / Sara II and her boys	The opening dream
THE FACE	Vogler	Vergerus	Sara	Spegel
WINTER LIGHT	Tomas	Märta	Algot	Jonas's suicide
THE SILENCE	Ester	Anna	Johan	Ester's illness
PERSONA	Elizabeth	Alma	The boy	Vietnam (TV) / Warsaw ghetto
CRIES AND WHISPERS	Karin	Maria	Anna	Agnes's cancer

enchantment with his work. In terms of the characters' status as elements in a psychodrama, the peripheral nature of the "positive" characters is significant: either casually-encountered travellers or placed in subservient social roles (sexton, maid), they are offered as embodying a possible salvation, yet they can never seriously affect (let alone resolve) the central conflict. Their lack of integration and a certain externality in Bergman's presentation of them suggest that they represent a desire rather than a reality, a gesture towards an attitude to life forever beyond Bergman's grasp.

This impression is somewhat modified by the films of the trilogy. Algot, the crippled sexton of *Winter Light,* appears to offer Tomas more than the transitory relief represented by the wild strawberries which Mia gives the Knight in *The Seventh Seal.* Just *what* he offers is as lacking in precise definition as the character himself (Bergman called him an "angel," some find him slightly sinister—there is similar disagreement or uncertainty about Anna, the maid in *Cries and Whispers*), but the film reaches a convincing, if (perhaps because) very tentative and ambiguous, sense of resolution. One might feel that the child of *The Silence* grows out of this. Frail, sickly-looking, vulnerable, yet consistently enquiring and ready to learn, he seemed at the time to mark an important stage in Bergman's development. If the recent films have confirmed this only ambiguously, it remains significant that this component of the recurrent structure should have found incarnation in a child. For one thing, as Anna's son, Johan (though repeatedly pushed out into corridors, excluded from the sisters' intenser confrontations) is nearer the centre of the film's tensions than his predecessors, affected by and affecting his elders, ultimately judging them. For another, in a film that is one of Bergman's most manifest psychodramas, Johan's precarious aliveness, and readiness to explore and develop, within the decaying shell of the past (the hotel as symbol, perhaps, of the neurotic complex in which the "characters" are held, a building often representing the personality in Freudian dream symbolism), makes of him one of the purest manifestations of the Romantic Child in the menacing and disintegrating world of the modern European cinema.

One of the many disturbing features of *Persona* is that there the child (same actor—Jörgen Lindström—and still reading the book he had in *The Silence*, Lermontov's *A Hero for Our Time*) is pushed right outside the main action, existing in a no-man's-land somewhere beyond reality that makes explicit his symbolic nature but undermines his function as potential resolver of conflicts and agent of psychic progress. And after *Persona* children virtually disappear from Bergman's films: their absence or death, indeed, becomes a major motif of *Shame*. Yet in the films that follow *The Silence* a new exploratory quality makes itself felt which I associate with the presence of the child in that film—with the sense of vulnerable new life and a desire to look outwards. The stubborn structure, though it does not disappear, begins to dissolve, its components are broken down and reorganized in more complex forms. The embodiments of the "presence of Death" become both more concrete and more complexly suggestive (the war in *Shame*, the slaughter of animals in *A Passion*). It would be impossible to break down *A Passion* (which I take to be Bergman's finest film to date, wonderfully delicate, open and exploratory in style and structure) into the elements that would enable it to be added to my chart; the character here who most nearly corresponds to the "natural acceptance" syndrome—Johan, the pathetic and helpless victim of brutal prejudice—is at once more integrated in the total pattern (through the parallels established between him and Andreas) and more firmly recognized as providing no solution to the major tensions. *The Touch* (though the film is less successful) continues this dissolution of the recurrent structure. It is worrying, at first sight, that *Cries and Whispers* marks such a complete return to it; yet one might argue that the return is so complete as to be definitive, that Bergman has at last become fully conscious of the pattern, has mastered it by embodying it in its most stylized form, and is ready to move on.

The Fellini Child

The case of Fellini—another director whose work tends to the psychodrama—is particularly suggestive in the context of Peter Coveney's thesis. His entire development (or degeneration) is epitomized in the way child-figures are used in his films. Often, they are linked with the imagery of spontaneous release on which the affirmation of the early films centres: the grown child Gelsomina encountering the inexplicable circus band in *La Strada,* the child who leads the parade at the end of *8½,* the heroine's child-self set free at the end of *Giulietta degli Spiriti.* But the essential progress of Fellini's art can be summed up by juxtaposing two endings: the parallel between them is so clear that one feels Fellini himself must have been aware of it.

1: *La Dolce Vita.* The socialites, emerging at dawn from their abortive orgy, wander to the beach through the trees, where they find an amorphous sea-monster, a freak of nature as they are freaks of civilization, dragged ashore in a fishing-net. Suddenly Marcello becomes aware of the childlike young girl, the "Umbrian Angel" he briefly encountered earlier in the film, calling to him from across a stretch of water. Attracted by her innocence, so that he seems to lose awareness of his companions, he strains to hear what she is saying, but the distance is too great. (Fellini announced that his next film would be about what the "Umbrian Angel" was trying to say; in the event, it was *8½*, which is partly a film about the impossibility—for Fellini—of making such a film.)

2: *Toby Dammit* (final episode of *Tales of Mystery*, the Poe symposium-film). The dissolute, disillusioned movie-star (Terence Stamp) is haunted wherever he goes in Rome by an image of an "innocent" little girl who bounces a ball and smiles at him. After an hysterical drive through the streets at night in an open car, he pulls up at the brink of a chasm where a bridge is broken. Across the chasm he sees the child again, as tantalizing as Marcello's "Umbrian Angel." Determined at all costs to reach her, he backs the car then drives furiously forward to clear the gulf. The car passes, but the actor is decapitated by a wire stretched taut across the road; his head becomes the ball the little girl was bouncing, and her smile is revealed as an evil grimace. Fellini's films are avowedly autobiographical in nature, and the characters can be "read" as projections of potentialities, aspirations, fears in the protagonist/author. The transformation of the child-figure in his work from the "Umbrian Angel" to the demon-child of *Toby Dammit* succinctly accounts for the emptiness and sterility of his subsequent work, and his apparently final surrender to the futile and grotesque. Peter Harcourt points out (in his book *Six European Directors*) that even the children of the patrician couple in *Satyricon* who commit suicide rather than relinquish their humanity, are quite arbitrarily given the same sinister smile as the little demon-girl of *Toby Dammit*.[6]

If a tentative conclusion can be drawn from the preceding casual annotations, it is not a very encouraging one. The cinema of Bergman since *The Silence*, for all its creative forcefulness, could by no stretch of the imagination be regarded as optimistic about the future or even as unambiguously affirmative of positive values. If one accepts that the "Child" qualities find expression in a new exploratory freedom and openness, the absence of actual children from the narratives (apart from the daughter of *The Touch*, whose function scarcely extends beyond provoking her mother's guilt-feelings) has its significance in relation to the desperation that is still the films' predominant emotion. Children and adolescents figure prominently in Widerberg's films (one may, I think, include Sixten and Elvira in the category without stretching things very far), and contribute to their charm and freshness. The fact that the films are habitually set in the past, however, just as it seriously undermines any revolutionary fervour to which they might seem to lay claim, also (it is perhaps the same thing) renders somewhat questionable the potential for renewal or new development Widerberg's young people superficially represent: the dominant emotion is nostalgia.

As for the New Wave, one is struck, looking back, by the relatively minor role played by children in a movement that seemed at the time the most significant rejuvenating force in world cinema. There was, of course, the Antoine Doinel of *Les 400 Coups;* but perhaps the most that need be said of him in this context is that he grew up into the Antoine Doinel of *Domicile Conju-*

---

6. Since this was written, *Amarcord* (Fellini's rich and affectionate evocation of the world of his own childhood) has demonstrated that one should never be hasty in abandoning hope for an artist who has once produced distinguished work.

gal. The "affirmation through childbirth" of the end of *Le Beau Serge* seemed—in the light of the films that followed it—merely a false start: one would not have guessed, from the films from *Les Cousins* through to *Landru* and the "Tiger" movies, that children would come to play a crucial role in Chabrol's later work. That role cannot be separated from his extended investigation (from *La Femme Infidèle* on, but strikingly anticipated in *La Muette*) into the limitations, repressions, potentialities of bourgeois family life. The attitude was always ambiguous (characterized by the conflicting drives that produce that intensely personal and idiosyncratic "paralyzed" feeling of the last shot of *La Femme Infidèle* or the enigmatic ending of *Juste Avant la Nuit*), and leads to the increasing ambiguity of the child role, relatively straightforward in *La Femme Infidèle,* opaque to the verge of unreadability in *Les Noces Rouges.*

The relative freedom (relative to Hollywood) in which directors like Bergman, Chabrol and Fellini work, giving every opportunity for self-exploration and personal idiosyncrasy, makes it likely that generalization will be difficult, and the evidence is inconclusive. The most one can point to, perhaps, is a shared sense of crisis—of conflicts developing towards a point of breakdown or dislocation in which the child-role is but one feature: crisis and dislocation expressed most eloquently in films such as *A Passion* and *Nada.* It is, however, in Fellini's work that the Child becomes overtly sinister and destructive, and it is this development that is reflected, very disturbingly and on a scale that goes right beyond the personal, in the American cinema.

The Child in the American Cinema

The significance of children in American films is complex, determined by various interacting influences. The figure of the naturally wise child from whom corrupt or sophisticated adults can (and should) learn, and whose moral judgements the reader is encouraged largely to accept, has an important place in American literature, from Huck Finn to Salinger's *Catcher in the Rye*, a figure transmuted and subtilized (by the transatlantic crossing?) in James's Maisie. Such a concept of the Child is not uncommon in the American cinema, Capra's *A Hole in the Head* and Minnelli's *The Courtship of Eddie's Father* providing two splendid examples. It is a concept that can easily harden and degenerate into that of the "smart kid," the premature adult, a figure denied both childhood and maturity.

One finds a significant variation on this figure in the work of Hawks. Children play a minimal role in his films, yet one is struck again by the way in which an artist's world-view, and its limitations, are implicit in his presentation of childhood. Hawks's work, with its affinities with Hemingway, represents an important aspect of American art and bears an interestingly ambiguous relation to American ideology. The basic urge that unifies his apparently wildly heterogeneous oeuvre is the urge to escape from the constraints of established society, either by ignoring it (the adventure films) or by subverting and destroying it (the comedies). The grotesque little monsters who pass for children in his films (*Monkey Business, Gentlemen Prefer Blondes, The Ransom of Red Chief*) appear to be without families or (in the case of Lee Aaker's "Red Chief") are the means whereby traditional family feeling is ridiculed. The George Winslow figure of *Gentlemen Prefer Blondes* ("The child was the most mature one on board the ship"—Hawks) is the extreme case: a gruff-voiced, super-sophisticated dwarf whose age could be anything from eight to eighty. Such a view of childhood implies the absences that negatively characterize Hawks's world: the absence of a social sense, of any feeling for tradition, for a life with a past and a future, together with the absence of any real development in the corpus of his work.

I use Hawks here less for the intrinsic interest of his work than to highlight by contrast the central significance of the

Child in American films. The concept of Family—a motif that cuts across all genres in the Hollywood cinema, informing and structuring westerns, musicals, comedies, gangster films, melodramas alike is obviously basic to American ideology, and in the American film the Child has his full meaning only in relation to it. We have perhaps even now only begun to realize the interest and possible implications of the American "popular" cinema. Besides (though the two are not separable) its artistic richness, there is the growing awareness of the complex sources from which it is fertilized. While one must be wary of any simplistic assumption of a clear-cut correspondence between audience demand and the product supplied, it is impossible to resist the sense that the Hollywood cinema, by virtue of its collaborative and commercial aspects, reflects the desires, fears, aspirations, doubts, tensions, contradictions, not merely of the individual artist but of a whole people, and that it is possible broadly to deduce, from the development of genre and traditional motifs, the essential movement of a whole society: that a developed popular art, in which so much is taken for granted and which accordingly offers itself as the vehicle for all that cannot be overtly expressed, can be read as the projection of a national psyche.

There is material here for more than a thesis; no American film would be irrelevant to an exploration along these lines. I choose here, in the interests of economy, to go to the other extreme, juxtaposing two unrelated films made more than twenty years apart, and having nothing in common but that concern with the family which they share with a thousand others. From such a juxtaposition alone no safe conclusion can be drawn: perhaps not even a hypothesis, but merely a suggestion that I believe could be followed up, developed, qualified.

Meet Me in St. Louis (Minnelli, 1944) must clearly be a central point of reference for any discussion of the image of the Family in the American cinema and the significance of children within it. On the surface, the film is a hymn to American family life, and crucial scenes—like that in which an apparently temporary disunity is resolved as the mother (Mary Astor) accompanies the father (Leon Ames) on the piano in a nostalgically meaningful song, and the children are drawn back one by one to eat the slices of cake they previously rejected— are centred on the notion of family harmony and solidarity. Most people seem to experience the film as it is described in Leonard Maltin's *TV Movies* (a book which, while critically completely worthless, is a useful barometer of casual popular reaction): "Ames and Astor are heads of a wholesome American family, (Margaret) O'Brien an appealing little sister." In fact, the more one sees the film the more one is struck by the tensions on whose suppression this solidarity and "wholesomeness"—which could in 1944 still be convincingly and movingly depicted—depends.

I want to concentrate on the two magnificent scenes in which the "appealing little sister" "kills" substitute parent-figures. First, the famous Hallowe'en sequence: Hallowe'en itself having its significance as the annual occasion on which American children are licensed (under cover of "play" and make-believe) to express their frustrations and resentments by dressing up as demons, witches, etc. The film contrasts two sets of parent-figures (an opposition obviously rooted in fairy-tale and myth, fairy godmother and evil queen, kind king and wicked ogre). There are the benevolent parents of the family with whom the film is centrally concerned (the Smiths, to establish their typicality), and the childless and hated Brockhoffs, about whom dreadful rumours circulate among the children. Tootie (Margaret O'Brien), youngest of the Hallowe'en gang, undertakes to "kill" Mr. Brockhoff (by throwing flour in his face and saying "I hate you") in order to establish her right of membership. Her approach to the Brockhoff house is treated as a "suspense" set-piece: we are very close to the world of horror films, with darkness, deserted street, blowing leaves, isolated, terrified and vulnerable figure, disquieting and menacing music, and we may be reminded that the horror film and the fairy-tale share much common ground. With Tootie, we are given a glimpse of the Brockhoff ménage, seen through the front window: the burly, dominant, bearded figure of the husband (an archetypal "ogre"), the wife (who looks somewhat sullen and browbeaten), and in the place of children in the family group a ferocious-looking dog, a sort of animal extension of Mr. Brockhoff (it accompanies him to the door and stands beside him as Tootie performs the ritual "killing").

The Brockhoffs (the only other "complete" family group we see in the film) can be taken as a clear-cut reversal of the Smiths; even their name carries significant overtones, opposing the alien to the normal. The Brockhoffs are childless, whereas the Smiths have five children; where four of the Smith children are girls, Mr. Brockhoff has a defiantly male-looking dog; the Smith household is woman-centred and woman-dominated, the father a sort of tolerated breadwinner, the grandfather ineffectual, the son overshadowed by his sisters, whereas Brockhoff is clearly the master of his house. The significance of this pattern becomes clearer when one places beside it the second "killing" scene.

The main plot-line of the film concerns the father's decision to leave St. Louis, uprooting the family from their familiar environment, and move to New York, in the interests of his career. Throughout the film the father—apart from his function of satisfying the family's material needs—appears oddly superfluous; he is kept in ignorance of what goes on in his daughters' lives (even the cook being in their confidence and joining in conspiracies against him), and in so far as he asserts himself, he is a nuisance. His protests generally consist (in a manner familiar from the presentation of benevolent fathers in American family movies, though in Minnelli never merely comic—witness the much more overtly subversive and vitriolic *Father of the Bride*) of ineffectual outbursts of impotent rage, but his great attempt at self-assertion is the proposed move to New York, which the entire family opposes.

Tootie is responsible for the decisive action that changes his mind. The scene where she rushes out into the darkness in her nightgown to destroy her snow-people is rendered with an intensity that all-but-disrupts the overall tone of the film. (Such moments where suppressed tensions violently erupt are characteristic of Minnelli's work: a comparable instance also involving a child is the emotionally devastating "goldfish" scene in *The Courtship of Eddie's Father,* which also has in common with the snow-people scene the principle of psychological displacement.) The destruction of the snow-people is overtly explained in somewhat whimsical terms: Tootie can take everything (even the "dead" dolls whose funerals she takes a morbid pleasure in) to New York except them, and she does not want anyone else to have them. This in itself has its interest, as an example of capitalistic possessiveness in a young child; but if one accepts even the most rough and general analogy between the processes of art and Freudian dream, one can see it (in its very explicitness) as a "cover" for the real point of the scene, which is rendered visually. The snow-people, dressed in adult coats, hats and scarves, are fairly obvious parent-figures; Mr. Smith watches impotently from an upstairs window (as if from a box at the theatre) as Tootie hacks down with a shovel effigies of the father who is going against the wishes of the family and the mother who passively submits to this outrage. At the end of the scene the father, deeply shaken, goes quietly downstairs (standing aside while the sobbing Tootie is led back to bed), then abruptly summons the whole family to the living-room and announces that they are staying in St. Louis after all. Happy ending. But one could also argue that Tootie has killed more than her snow-people, and ask whether the real subject of the film is family harmony or family tyranny, the Leon Ames character a kind father or a castrated

one, his aspirations to an independent manhood and self-fulfil-
ment sacrificed to domestic cosiness and the *status quo.*

The ending of the film—experienced on the superficial level
as a hymn to provincial life and family wholesomeness—always
seems a considerable let-down. There may be a simple, material
explanation for this (one would need details of budget, shooting schedule, working conditions, etc.), but it is tempting to
justify it in terms of the film's unresolved tensions. All seems
set—as the family attend the long-awaited World's Fair—for a
big, clinching production number; all one gets is a brief display of coloured lights and the assurance that life could hold no
richer rewards. The curious lack of conviction might be felt as,
after all, expressive, the product of the implicit defeat that is the
price of the explicit victory. None the less, the film's continuing
(and richly merited) popularity must be largely attributed to
its success in containing its tensions within its celebration of
family life. I do not want at all to suggest that the film disinte-
grates—simply that the tensions, the complexities, are indeed
there. If one accepts the assumption that the popular cinema
offers a reflection of the inner life of the society that produces it,
one can go on to assume a correspondence between the ability
of the film to contain its tensions and society's ability to do so.

"Cut" to *Night of the Living Dead,* George A. Romero's exceptionally revolting little low-budget horror movie made more
than two decades later: a much rawer, less "realized" film than
Meet Me in St. Louis, but with an intensity and ruthlessness that
partly justify its status. The premise is that, because of some not
very interesting science-fictiony pretext, the unburied dead rise
up and begin to eat the living. The sort of fantasy of which more
than one interpretation is possible, no doubt; it is easy to see
the "ghouls" as representing the tensions on whose suppression
civilized society is built—"dead" yet very much alive, become
by virtue of their suppression ruthless, perverted and superhu-

manly strong. The film opens with a brother and sister visiting a graveyard, over which, prominent in the foreground of one shot, flies the stars-and-stripes. The visit to the grave of a father they barely remember is a duty, accepted by the girl, resented by the man. He teases, frightens and provokes her, imitating a monster, telling her "they're coming to get you, Barbara"; the first ghoul lurches forward, attacks her and strangles him, as if the product of the familial tensions. It is the "resurrected" brother who, towards the end of the film, leads the ghouls as they overwhelm and (presumably) devour his sister.

The main body of the film is set in an isolated house besieged by the ghouls, where a family—father, mother, sick small daughter—are discovered to be hiding in the cellar, where the child (who has been contaminated by the ghouls) is kept for safety. Later in the film the father, wounded, staggers down to the cellar and doesn't re-emerge. When the mother goes down, she finds the child (who has died and, because unburied, become a ghoul) eating her father's severed hand. The little girl then hacks her mother to death, *Psycho*-fashion, with a builder's trowel. Tootie's destructive fury can no longer be satisfied on snow-people.

It would be absurd, of course, to draw any specific connection between these two films in isolation. I offer them, in the interests of economy, against an understood background of the development of the American cinema since World War II. In that context, *Meet Me in St. Louis* and *Night of the Living Dead* appear at once exceptional (in quality or at least intensity) and representative (of general trends). One might test any suggestion one might be inclined to draw from this juxtaposition about the essential movement of American (Western capitalist?) civilization by moving for a moment outside films centred on children to consider the development of the western over roughly the same period.

Again, for the sake of economy I shall briefly juxtapose two films. Ford's *My Darling Clementine* (1946) is centrally concerned with the development of American civilization—the community establishing itself in the wilderness and (in the famous scene of the dance on the floor of the unroofed church) celebrating its establishment. The hero who rides in from the wilderness (a common western archetype) becomes integrated into the community (joins the dance), and this is regarded as mutually beneficial: the community acquires his "natural" goodness and strength, and he begins to acquire the refinements of civilization. As with *Meet Me in St. Louis,* the sense of harmony and wholeness is not without its inner tensions and contradictions (located particularly in the character of Doc Holliday, the "civilized" figure who has disintegrated in the wilderness), but the tone is predominantly optimistic: the church is dedicated, the townsfolk dance on its floor with dignity and energy under the stars-and-stripes and in the ennobling context of Monument Valley; Clementine (the girl from Boston) stays on to become a school-teacher.

"Cut" to *High Plains Drifter* (1973), directed by and starring Clint Eastwood, in himself an iconographic figure, who might be felt to be to America in the seventies what Henry Fonda was in the late thirties and forties. Again we have the hero who rides in from the wilderness; again we have the growing community establishing itself in the desert. Now, however, the community is regarded as irredeemably corrupt, founded in corruption; the hero (who may be the Devil incarnate) renames it "Hell" (on the signboard outside the town) and burns it to the ground.

High Plains Drifter is simply one of the most extreme of the apocalyptic westerns of recent years; the way it relates to *Clementine* parallels very strikingly the way *Night of the Living Dead* relates to *Meet Me in St. Louis.* If one is justified in finding in the popular cinema the dream-like expression of an American "collective unconscious," the signs for Western civilization are not encouraging—unless we feel that destruction and disintegration are a necessary preliminary to a new order. To return to Hollywood's images of childhood, in a cinema that has been much preoccupied of late with the Devil, I can hardly avoid closing this section with brief mention of *The Exorcist*—a film I do not particularly admire and which it is scarcely necessary to see: one has only to know it exists. The film offers itself, of course, as a vindication of Catholicism, a work concerned with the eventual triumph of Good over Evil. But what people go to see it for (and are encouraged to go to see it for) is its ultimate desecration of the image of the Child. In the forties, the American family could contain its tensions and unite to attend the St. Louis fair, and the settlers could dance on the church floor in hopeful expectation of a stable future. In the seventies, the family (now broken) produces a child who becomes the Devil, spewing filth (both verbal and literal) over the figures of order, and civilization, corrupt from the outset, is turned against itself, split apart, and obliterated; the flag that flew over the unroofed church flutters over the cemetery where the ghosts begin their revenge. Through its popular cinema, American civilization may be condemning itself to death and writing its own epitaph.

Godard's children

It may seem curious, even perverse, to conclude an essay on the cinema's images of childhood with a glance at the recent work of Godard. Children have been conspicuous in Godard's films largely for their absence; neither the little boy's brief monologue in *Une Femme Mariée* nor the presence of the little girl in the bath-tub in *Pierrot le Fou* (who gets read Elie Faure on Velas-quez) exactly impresses one with a sense of Godard's responsive-ness to children or to the values and aspirations they potentially embody. Indeed, one's reservations about Godard (the early films as well as the recent) might well be definable from that starting-point—coupled with his apparent inability to believe in reciprocal love, or at least to treat it with any confidence, and with his somewhat suspect gravitation to ruthlessness: suspect, because it seems so easy for him, and more a personality-trait (it is there from the outset) than a revolutionary principle.

But the logic of this essay leads inevitably to late Godard. To put it succinctly: I do not see how anyone who contemplates the implications of the development of the "bourgeois capitalist" cinema, whether in its "art-house" or "popular" manifestations, can *not* be interested in *Vent d'Est* and *Tout Va Bien,* whatever reservations he may have about them.

There is a sense, too, if we do not interpret the notion of childhood too literally, in which Godard's recent films have their appropriate place within the terms of my initial undertaking: his revolutionaries, while mainly of university student age, are in certain respects remarkably child-like. The emphasis of the films is repeatedly on the need to "return to zero," to unmake oneself in order to make oneself anew; the text, "Except you become again as little children, you shall never enter the kingdom of Heaven," seems not inappropriate, if one can translate it out of its Christian context. From the Maoist cell of *La Chinoise* to the student in *Vent d'Est* who gets sent away to learn to play the penny whistle before his performance is publicly acceptable, Godard provides a succession of children who must educate (or re-educate) themselves in a world where adults are uniformly discredited. And the lament for Gilles in *Tout Va Bien,* in its passion and tenderness, its outrage at the destruction of young life and its commitment to the redemption of the waste through positive action, unites many of the feelings and motifs clustered around the image of the "Romantic" Child.

The recurrent tennis-court scenes of *Vladimir and Rosa* can be taken as exemplifying what I have in mind: the more significantly in that the "children" here are Godard and Gorin themselves. The film—whose pretext and subject (or, more precisely perhaps, chief point of reference) is the trial of the Chicago Eight—is concerned (like *Vent d'Est*) with the problem of simultaneously making a film attacking conservatism and reaction, and confronting the question of how such a film can be made—how it can be most useful to those who see it, what methods and strategies it should employ. Its makers (we are explicitly told) are only partly in control—they are also part of a process. The tennis scenes, which interrupt and punctuate the extremely stylized "action" during the first half of the film, are explicitly self-reflexive, the film's makers commenting on and questioning what they are doing. A tennis-match is in progress (epitome of the complacent bourgeois world, wilfully ignorant of all but its own immediate pursuits?); Godard and Gorin walk up and down in the middle of it, on either side of the net (later, both on the same side, perhaps to indicate the partial resolution of their differences). They carry a tape-recorder and record their own debate as they walk. They talk like young children who scarcely know how to speak: both adopt severe speech-impediments. Just as the tennis-players seem quite unaware of, or indifferent to, their presence (they do not disrupt the game in any way, and never get hit by balls), so they completely ignore the players. They have the intentness of young children engaged in some wholly absorbing game, oblivious of the adults around them.

It is not the first time in Godard's work that he has presented adults as children: the somewhat less disarming precedent of Michelange in *Les Carabiniers* may give one pause, the seemingly very different cases linked by the common proclivity to the destruction of civilization. Peter Harcourt (in *Six European Directors*) draws the connection between the thug-outsiders of Godard's early period and the revolutionaries of the recent films. I agree with him in finding the similarities disturbing, but I think he fails to emphasize sufficiently the differences: whatever one may say about the revolutionaries, they are scarcely mindless or lacking in reflection. The tennis scenes in *Vladi-*

mir and Rosa indicate very precisely the status its makers see the film as having: they are children learning to speak, with all their teachers rejected, and the stumbling and awkward film, like their stammering speech, represents their efforts at articulation.

The most striking characteristic of Godard's "children" has not, I think, been commented upon, perhaps because it is too obvious: their family-less-ness. From the young Maoists of *La Chinoise* onwards, they seem to have come into being without parentage, to have no ties whatever with the past and only a very tentative sense of a future: as alien and frightening—and as lacking in love or compassion—as John Wyndham's "Midwich cuckoos," they are just as difficult to explain. It might be argued that this is just an aspect of the Godardian stylization, but I think it is more positively expressive, a defining characteristic without which they would not be possible. Their apparent unnaturalness is a necessary corollary of starting from zero.

The absence of any traditional sense of family has special significance in relation to the centrality of the concept of family in bourgeois ideology in general and in its most elaborate embodiment and means of self-perpetuation the Hollywood cinema (which Godard has, of course, progressively renounced) in particular. If, through that cinema, the collective unconscious of Western capitalism has expressed with what now looks like relentless and terrifying inevitability the breakdown of traditional family structure from its own internal tensions, the Godardian response becomes the logical one—if, to most of us, bleak, uninviting and impoverished.

There is, none the less, running through *Vent d'Est* (for all its effect of a sort of willed emotional constipation), an impulse it is not absurd to describe as Blakean. Indeed, the attempt to find a form which will permit continuous movement between different levels of meaning—combined with the insistence on the overthrow of repressive forces themselves conceived as acting on various levels, physical, social, psychological, sexual—has its most striking precedent not in Brecht but in the Blake of the "Prophetic" texts, the *Visions of the Daughters of Albion* for example. And Godard's attempt is in some respects more successful, perhaps because of the nature of the medium: where Blake's imagery (left to the visualizing imagination) becomes amorphous and unintelligible, Godard's images (given his refusal of all cinematic trickery) are always clear, whatever complexities of reference arise from their juxtaposition with the text.

Most Blake-like—because most resonant, less restricted to the rigours of a specifically Marxist analysis—is the progress through the film of the couple, that gives it the nearest thing it has to a narrative thread: their progress from helpless passivity (the chained bodies of the opening, that can do no more than clasp each other's fingers) to the symbolic liberation of the end, as they and the Indian emerge from the chasm and overpower their oppressors. By then, the three oppressed figures have accumulated complex connotations that sufficiently imbue them with a force of Blake-like generalization, at once precise and inclusive. The Romantic tradition may still be adopting new and unexpected disguises and transformations.

8
Reflections on the Auteur Theory

The status of the "auteur theory" as *theory* has always been somewhat dubious. To Truffaut, who seems to have invented it for the cinema (it is hardly new to the history of criticism, critics having on the whole agreed for several centuries that Shakespeare is the real author of *Hamlet*), it was rather "auteur *policy*," and meant simply that it is worth distinguishing between different artists (for what more does the once notorious remark that Renoir's worst film is more interesting than Delannoy's best amount to?). It is also obvious that its usefulness and interest exist within clearly defined limits, namely, the studio-dominated "commercial" cinema where the director is an employee. The proposition that (granted the social and historical determinants operative on *any* work of art) Bergman and Fellini are the real authors of most of their films is uninteresting because self-evident. The "auteur theory" is of value only where its validity is highly arguable.

Its value may, I think, prove to have been largely historical: what is valid in it is also obvious, and simply needed to be pointed out. Even Truffaut's original principle is scarcely beyond question: yes, I think Tourneur is a more distinguished artist than Mark Robson, but there are a number of Tourneur assignments that I would hesitate to prefer to the least unappealing of Robson's: the most one could say is that Tourneur's camera-style shows taste and reticence, qualities that become pallid and tenuous indeed in *Days of Glory,* and vanish altogether in his *Easy Living.* A great artist's failures are often interesting, certainly, but the interest lies in the light they throw on and the context they provide for the successes: that is to say, it is a passing interest. My interest in *Sergeant York,* for example, ceased when I felt I had understood its relation to Hawks's successful works—which is another way of saying, when I had accounted for its failure. I have seen *Rio Bravo* something like twenty times, and would see it again tomorrow; I have seen *Sergeant York* thrice, and have no particular desire to repeat the experience. One can blame Hawks or not for the failure of *Sergeant York:* either, "the material was uncongenial, Hawks was ill-at-ease," or "the failure of the film indicates clearly Hawks's limitations." Both seem to me true; it is the latter that gives the film its passing interest.

It still seems to me true that the director is the decisive determinant of the quality of the vast majority of films; but the statement must be qualified by important corollaries, which may at first appear contradictions. The first of these is that, the Hollywood cinema being in question, the presence of a given "auteur" is no *guarantee* of quality. It is not, of course, in any of the arts; yet *The Plumed Serpent* (which I take to be the worst, at least the most actively bad, of Lawrence's novels) retains many of the qualities of his best work, and this is more than one can count on in the cinema. The second is that films of excellence can (very occasionally) come into being independently of great directors. The third is that, given the complex determinants at work on a Hollywood film, a director's most "personal" films, the ones he "really wanted to make," need not necessarily be his best: *The Beguiled* is not necessarily superior to *Madigan, The Fugitive* is plainly *in*ferior to . . . (you name it!).

Rather than pontificate theoretically (a practice to which my readers will know I am little addicted, or indeed suited), I want here to consider briefly four films which strike me as, in their different ways, test cases for the "auteur theory," each of them, I think, excellent, each demanding or illustrating the sort of qualifications I have suggested. In each case the problems of authorship raised are only partly resolvable.

1: *Remember the Night* (1940) was scripted by Preston Sturges and directed by Mitchell Leisen. Most will agree (given the respective *oeuvres*) that Sturges was by far the more distinguished "auteur"; from the Leisen films I have seen I have difficulty in understanding, or feeling any sympathy with, the intermittent attempts to elevate him to "auteur" status. The interest of the over-rated *Midnight* can be safely attributed to its Wilder/ Brackett script and a very strong cast; *Easy Living* (not to be confused with the Tourneur film of the same name), the other Leisen movie with a Sturges script, is in effect a Sturges film, save for a certain stolidity in the *mise-en-scène;* films like *Death Takes a Holiday* and *Lady in the Dark* are, in their foolishness and vulgarity, beneath serious consideration as works of art. *Remember the Night* derives its qualities from a number of sources (or levels), of which the basic is that concern with home and family so central to American culture and ideology: the belief in the decisive formative influence on character of a secure and loving home, expressed here in the contrast between the homes of Fred MacMurray and Barbara Stanwyck, and, beyond that, belief in the redemptive influence of contact with the "right" sort of family. Secondly, the film is in the mainstream of the great tradition of thirties comedy, a tradition containing the full range from slapstick to tender sentiment (a range one might exemplify from the work of McCarey alone—from *Duck Soup* to *Love Affair*); a tradition so strong that it produced inventive and likeable films through generally undistinguished intermediaries (see, for example, W. S. van Dyke's *I Love You Again*). Thirdly, there is Sturges's presence as screenwriter; fourthly, the sort of cast that could almost be said, given substantial material, to direct itself—not only the two principles (Stanwyck is particularly fine), but the incomparable Beulah Bondi, plus Elizabeth Patterson and Sterling Holloway: players with clearly defined, pre-established screen *personae* playing variations on their familiar roles. Finally, there is the art direction: the richness of the central (and finest) section of the film is partly attributable to the marvellous, detailed creation of the Beulah Bondi home.

It is extremely difficult to speculate on the possible importance of Leisen's intervention in all this. Obviously, none of the determinants I have suggested would count for much on its own, and one can say, negatively, that a more self-assertive director might easily have ruined the *ensemble:* one can credit Leisen with being an effective and decently reticent co-ordinator. There are other considerations, however. For one thing, Leisen began his career as an art director, and décor is the most consistently interesting element in his films. For another, the scenario of *Remember the Night* is not entirely typical of Sturges: the warmth, tenderness and detail (in the acting as well as the décor) of the family scenes are not easy to parallel in the films he directed (*The Great Moment,* another less-than-completely-typical film, is perhaps closest in this respect); the cynicism which repeatedly undercuts the apparent "positives" of his work, giving it both its complexity and its ultimate hollowness, is absent from the Leisen film (though not from *Easy Living*). One would hesitate, in other words, to suggest that *Remember the Night* would *necessarily* have been even better if Sturges had directed it himself. It *might* have been. It would certainly have been different, for Leisen (see the account in *Hollywood Director* by David Chierichetti) discarded some of Sturges's scenes before shooting, cut others after shooting, and "shortened and simplified all of the scenes he shot."

2: One might wish to argue that Sturges was the real author of *Remember the Night.* Most people would be ready to assume that *North by Northwest* offers a clear-cut case of the obverse director-writer relationship: it seems so pre-eminently a Hitchcock film in plot, characterization, structure, themes, motifs,

The square dance of
Remember the Night.

style, that one might be forgiven for scarcely attending to the screenwriter's credit. I choose it, however, from the thousands of possible "clear-cut" cases, because the claims for Hitchcock's being considered its real author have been explicity challenged by the screenwriter himself—Ernest Lehmann, in an article published in *Sight and Sound* (Autumn 1960). Lehmann insists that *North by Northwest* is *his* film, that Hitchcock merely executed his script. Hitchcock has said elsewhere (interview in *Movie 6*) that he writes "quite a bit" of his scripts himself, and specifically lays claim to the line in *North by Northwest,* "That plane's dusting crops where there ain't no crops." But let us, for the sake of argument, concede Lehmann's point and assume he wrote the entire screenplay, including the shooting breakdown, directions for camera placement, movement, editing. The assumption admittedly strains the imagination somewhat, but it is certainly an excellent script, one of the best Hitchcock has ever shot, and Lehmann dearly deserves some of the credit for the film's excellence.

But is *North by Northwest* a Lehmann film or a Hitchcock film? It seems to me that one can clarify the issues (if not necessarily resolve them) by adducing two other films for comparison: *The Prize*, scripted by Lehmann, directed by Mark Robson; and the only film Lehmann has so far directed himself, the film version of *Portnoy's Complaint*, of which he also wrote the screenplay. The interest of *The Prize* lies in its incidental similarities to Hitchcock's film: similarities at times so great that one feels Lehmann might almost have sued himself for plagiarism. Specifically, two sequences strike one as close variations on two of the finest sequences in *North by Northwest:* the scene where Paul Newman is trapped on a deserted bridge by a car recalls the famous "crop-dusting" scene; the sequence where he evades capture by throwing into disorder an assembly of nudists recalls the scene in which Cary Grant disrupts an auction. The superiority of the Hitchcock sequences, considered as isolated set-pieces, seems too obvious to need arguing, though it could be demonstrated in minute detail in terms of *cinematic* construction—the shot-by-shot build-up of each sequence, the placing and movement of the camera, the editing—the areas in which the authorship of a film (as opposed to a scenario) is largely determined. If Hitchcock merely executed Lehmann's instructions, must one assume that Robson betrayed them?—or that Lehmann was this time working below par?

But the superiority does not end there. The description of the sequences in *The Prize* as "isolated set-pieces" seems perfectly adequate: they exist purely on a suspense-and-excitement level, and are introduced into the narrative quite arbitrarily. The corresponding scenes in *North by Northwest,* on the contrary, are completely integrated in the structure of the film, dramatically and thematically: both sequences gain some of their force from Grant's relationship with the equivocal heroine (she sends him out to get killed, the auction scene is centred on her presence); the crop-dusting sequence, functioning structurally as the film's centre-piece, gives us the formerly complacent hero stripped of all the civilized props on which he had relied, mercilessly exposed in an open landscape, thrown back on his own resources and his own resilience. One needs to account, then, not only for the film's superiority of *mise-en-scène* but for its superiority of construction. One can do this partly by saying that *The Prize,* made four years later (1963), is so obviously an imitation, and that imitations (even when the work of the same artist) seldom equal their originals. One is still left, I think, with a sense of very different *presences* behind the two films.

The interest of *Portnoy's Complaint* (in so far as that dreadful film can be said to have any) lies in its total dissimilarity from *North by Northwest.* It seems idle to argue simply that the subject matter is different and demands a different approach; the notion that the "real author" of Hitchcock's film went on to make it is scarcely more surprising than it would be to learn that Bresson came secretly to England to make *Carry On Nurse* under the pseudonym of Gerald Thomas. Questions of authorship become interesting only where work of some quality is under consideration, and fundamental to the concept is the tracing of links and relationships between this work and that; even the most disparate works of Hawks—disparate in quality as well as *genre*—reveal affinities of style, theme, attitude, areas of interest. It is impossible to discover any significant link between *North by Northwest* and *Portnoy's Complaint.*

What does all this prove? Nothing, perhaps, that was not already obvious. My conviction that *North by Northwest* is ultimately a Hitchcock movie remains unshaken; it would remain unshaken if Lehmann could prove that every camera set-up and every cut were indicated by him in the script. If such an assertion seems excessive or paradoxical, one has only to ask whether *North by Northwest* is conceivable *without* Hitchcock? If Hitchcock merely executed a meticulously detailed script, then it is evident that every detail in that script was conceived for *him* to execute. (One might even go on to claim that Hitchcock is the "real author," by a process of derivation, of what there is of interest or vitality in *The Prize.*) It is impossible, I think, on the strength of his screenplays, to make out a case for Lehmann as an "auteur," in the sense in which the term "auteur theory" is customarily understood. Richard Corliss, in his book on screenwriters *Talking Pictures,* seems to me virtually to concede this even as he tries to establish the opposite: "All *Sweet Smell of Success* and *North by Northwest* have in common are the craft, wit and story sense of their author"—that is not what makes an author an auteur. One might argue that it is Lehmann's contribution that makes *North by Northwest* one of the most completely satisfying of Hitchcock's films; but still Hitchcock's.

3: The case of Hawks's *Monkey Business* is more complex and indeterminate. In my book on Hawks (*Howard Hawks,* Secker and Warburg, 1968) I claimed it as the best (though not necessarily funniest) of his comedies: the most perfectly structured, the most satisfying. I hold to this opinion, but am less ready to give Hawks all the credit; I even think it could be argued that the film is more interesting in its conception than in its execution (brilliant as this generally is)—that Hawks, never a thematically conscious director, has not entirely realized (in either sense) the disturbing implications of the material. From this point of view one might distinguish the film from, say, *To Have and Have Not* and *Rio Bravo,* films whose qualities are entirely present in the realization, whose implications grow naturally out of the action and the way it is presented. The problem is obviously a delicate one. *Monkey Business* is thematically consistent with Hawks's other work; its particular flavour—indeed, its very character as a *comedy* rather than a tragedy or melodrama—is dependent on the fusion of Hawks's resilient humour with potentially devastating material. Yet the resilience is bought, one might argue, at the price of a certain insensitivity—the inability or refusal to confront the implications with full artistic seriousness.

It would be possible to relate *Monkey Business* in one way or another to numerous Hawks movies; it seems to me to bear a particularly interesting relationship to three. One of these is *The Thing,* made the previous year: there is the same attitude to science and scientists, the implicit assumption that a dedication to science tends to be accompanied by a corresponding failure of emotional development. The second is *Scarface,* made twenty years earlier, in which the central figure is implicitly or explicitly compared to a child and a savage (he is introduced as an ape- or neanderthal-like shadow on a wall). The collocation of these motifs is central to *Monkey Business,* which shows a learned and dignified scientist regressing under the influence of a rejuvenating drug to a state of joyous irresponsibility—the drug releasing everything he has suppressed in his life and in his marriage— associating himself finally with children and savages. Two of the three screenwriters who worked on the film were Ben Hecht and Charles Lederer; the former co-scripted *Scarface,* the latter scripted *The Thing.* One can see *Monkey Business* as the outcome of a fruitful interaction of talents in which the question of who contributed what becomes impossible to answer.

The third film to which I would relate it is *Hatari!* made almost a decade later, with neither Hecht nor Lederer involved. The attitude to regression in Hawks's films is always ambivalent: it marks a release of energies, a casting off of inhibition, and even the stunted and destructive *Scarface* becomes engaging in his ebullience and spontaneity. *Hatari!* can be seen as harmonizing all the tensions inherent in *Monkey Business:* animals, savages and "civilized" people co-exist without strain. In the established civilized order of *Monkey Business* Cary Grant's descent to painted savagery is violent discord; in *Hatari!*'s casual society of hunters, Elsa Martinelli can accept, albeit reluctantly, her initiation into membership of an African tribe, her paint implicitly compared, a scene later, to the "civilized" use of face cream. The tensions are resolved at the price of full adulthood: the society of *Hatari!* is essentially a gathering of kids, their childishness continually stressed. The link with *Monkey Business* seems strong enough to offset any sense the reader may have that I am trying to attribute the earlier film solely to its writers. Far from it: Hawks's intervention as, at the very least, a unifying and directing force, is evidently crucial in a way one would never claim for Leisen in *Remember the Night:* something more than a necessary point of intersection, if less than "absolute" author.

4: My last film, *The Reckless Moment,* presents a rather different facet of the "auteur" problem. It is the work of a director—Ophuls—whose "auteur" status no one, I imagine, would challenge: there is no artist in the cinema, save perhaps Mizoguchi, for whom I would make greater claims. The issue I want to raise can be made clear by placing the film beside *La Ronde.* Even a casual observer, with only a rudimentary knowledge of Ophuls's films, would probably identify *La Ronde* as being right in the mainstream of his work, both stylistically and thematically. The same casual observer might be forgiven for failing to perceive *The Reckless Moment* as an Ophuls movie at all. And such reactions are not merely the outcome of an only superficial acquaintance with Ophuls. The material of the Hollywood film is not entirely characteristic, and the various aspects of the Hollywood system (studio, genre, audience habituation, the conditioned assumptions of technicians) clearly imposed restrictions on Ophuls's style: if one knows Ophuls well, one finds his signature everywhere in the film, but nothing in it quite bursts the "classical" Hollywood mould, as the opening shot of *La Ronde,* for instance, would have done. The "auteur theory" has been concerned with identifying authors through consistency of style and theme, and one of its implicit assumptions is that the great auteur's finest work is his most typical, the work that most completely expresses him. While valuing Ophuls above almost anyone, I value *The Reckless Moment* above *La Ronde.*

If what one is interested in is the artist's "view of life," then one will go to *La Ronde* or, even more obviously, *Lola Montes.* But *The Reckless Moment* seems to me a more complex film than the former and a more successful one than the latter. I would explain both its richness and its success in terms of the fruitful interaction between the very striking and defined artistic personality of Ophuls and the framework of genre, convention and ideologically-determined concerns of Hollywood. *La Ronde* derives from a far more intellectually respectable literary source (Arthur Schnitzler, as against the *Ladies Home Journal*), yet its material seems thinner, lacking in complexity and inner tensions. Despite an astonishing opening and a last five minutes (centred on a performance of extraordinary refinement by Gérard Philipe) so disturbing as to cast a retrospective shadow over the whole film, suggesting a more troubled and troubling work than Ophuls has in fact given us, one may feel that here the Ophulsian "view of life" is reduced too much to a thesis. No thesis is deducible from *The Reckless Moment;* its organization is too complex for reduction.

What the film presents is not a simple case of a great artist transforming shoddy or indifferent material through personal artistry; the film's tensions are not of that kind, its unfailing fluency and control suggesting excellent working conditions, cooperation and teamwork. The presence of Joan Bennett as star, and her husband Walter Wanger as producer, doubtless has its importance: unlike so many Hollywood personalities with cultural aspirations, they seem to have been often guided by genuine intelligence rather than the lure of ostentatious "big subjects," working with interesting but not obviously "important" material and giving opportunities to some of the finest European emigré directors (Lang and Renoir as well as Ophuls). The presence of James Mason may also have its significance (apart from the excellence of his performance): Mason lent his prestige to a number of interesting ventures; without it we might not have had *Caught* (the Ophuls film that immediately precedes *The Reckless Moment*) and *Bigger Than Life,* the film on which a high estimate of Nicholas Ray can most convincingly be argued.

Much of the admirable detail that gives the film its richness and its life, while evidence of a delicate intelligence at work, is not inevitably identifiable: if one tends to attribute it to Ophuls's presence this is more through a general sense of its compatibility with the sensibility displayed in his other films than through a recognition of specific "fingerprints." There is, for example, the characterization of Ted Darby (Shepperd Strudwick) through the restless movements of his hands—his nervous fidgeting, during his duologues with Lucia Harper (Joan Bennett) and her daughter Bea (Geraldine Brooks), with tie, comb, paper decoration, cigarette. There is the sense of Lucia's aloneness (her husband is abroad throughout the film) conveyed by such unobtrusively presented details as her filling a hot-water-bottle from the tap of her washbasin. There is the utterly unsentimental treatment (contrary to the expectations the incident sets up) of Mason's gift of a cigarette-holder—the holder put aside for return to the store, the gift unrecognized. There is the treatment throughout the film of Sybil, the coloured maid, living in quarters apart from the main house, watching and intelligently observing, repeatedly though unostentatiously present in the background of shots, gradually emerging as the most perceptive and reliable member of the household—one aspect of the film's subtle subversion of the values and structure of American society.

Much other detail is, on the other hand, easily identifiable—especially the detail of the way things are shot. When at the beginning of the film Lucia goes to a seedy hotel in Los Angeles to talk to Darby, the camera, inside the lobby, follows her progress round the outside to the entrance as she passes from window to window; once she is inside, her progress to the bar is again shot from a distance, pillars, furniture, a covered double-bass intervening between us and the character as the camera tracks; in the empty bar, her meeting with Darby is distanced from us by the legs of piled chairs that intrude into the foreground of the image. These framing and distancing devices are not mere "applied" stylistic flourishes: they are essential to the tone of the film (which is to say, to its effect and meaning). A plot outline might suggest that Lucia is set up as a characteristic identification-figure of middle-class "women's magazine" fiction: the gallant housewife soldiering on while her man is absent, bravely coping with disturbing and dangerous situations. It is partly the style that determines the critical distance from which we view the character, hence making possible a complexity of attitude not only to Lucia but to the society and the ideology of which she is a representative.

Or consider the magnificent scene in the drugstore, in which Lucia, calling long distance to try to arrange for Bea to stay with an aunt, is forced to borrow a coin from the man who is blackmailing her. The scene, with its characteristic irony, unites most of the film's main elements; the world of family tensions, disturbed daughters, reluctant aunts, country rest-cures; the social world of small-town drugstores, family shopping, easy-going familiarity; the "under-world" of crime and moral squalor. Ophuls shoots the main part of the scene (excluding Donnelly's purchase of the cigarette-holder) in a single continuous take. We have Lucia's conversation on the phone in medium-shot, the character framed (imprisoned) in the glass booth (an image that will be taken up later, when she visits a loan office to raise the blackmail money, and which links with the imagery of imprisonment that recurs throughout the film). The camera then tracks left with Lucia across the store, the central display counter intervening between us and the character; after the conversation with Donnelly at the door, and the borrowing of the coin, this movement is repeated in reverse, the shot ending (with characteristic Ophulsian symmetry) with the resumption of the telephone conversation. The unbroken movement unites the various "worlds" in a single flow, insisting that all are aspects of the same world; it underlines the sense of growing connection—an involvement more complex than that of blackmailer with victim—between Donnelly and Lucia. Repeatedly prominent in the image, adding its own irony and its reminders of home, family, traditions, norms, is the decorated Christmas tree in the middle of the display counter; the implicit, unstressed connection between Christmas and commerce, the Family and capitalism, is central to the film's concerns.

In its thematic structure *The Reckless Moment* is highly complex. It can be read in terms of the characteristic Hollywood opposition of stable, "respectable" society (home and family) and a dark, precariously suppressed underworld of crime and violence—an opposition in itself never simple, though an archetypally "bourgeois" director like Wyler (*The Desperate Hours*) may strive to make it appear so. The film can also be read in terms of the characteristic Ophulsian opposition of romantic love and secure but unromantic marriage, with the emphasis reversed: while, for example, *Letter from an Unknown Woman* and *Madame de . . .* are centred on the love relationship, the centre of *The Reckless Moment* is the home. If, on the one hand, the genre ("Hollywood domestic melodrama") pushes Ophuls towards the exploration of areas not alien to his fully characteristic films but usually subordinate to his dominant preoccupations, he on the other inflects the genre in a very personal way, producing an extended critique of the American home-and-family ideal, emphasizing the liberating potential of romantic love. Central to the tone and significance of the film is a paradox from which springs an irony that affects, directly or indirectly, every aspect: Donnelly, while fully aware that Lucia's family imprison her, falls in love with her precisely because of her devotion to them; Lucia's attachment to Donnelly grows in direct ratio to her awareness of her entrapment and her glimpse of the possibility of freedom. By the end of the film, Donnelly is ready to sacrifice himself totally for her family, while Lucia has at last reached the point where she can contemplate sacrificing her family (or, at the very least, its good name which she has fought so determinedly to preserve) to save *him*.

Ophuls's intervention in *The Reckless Moment* gives point and precision to the ambivalent attitude to American society that seems to be inherent in the Hollywood melodrama genre: a society, the film suggests, dependent on the preservation of conventionalized and constricting images of human beings and their relationships. Ophuls's sensitivity to the predicaments of women produces in the character of Lucia a marvellously perceptive portrait of a woman trapped in an ideology which she herself (at least until late in the film) unquestioningly accepts, but from which we, through the distancing of Ophuls's style and the emphasis given by his ironic and unillusioned romanticism, remain detached. Her outward assumption of competence and of satisfaction with her role is constantly belied by her neurotic chain-smoking (on which Donnelly himself comments, the gift of the cigarette-holder being a further comment, at once tender and ironic), the tenseness in her dealings with her children, her insistent repressiveness towards David in the interests of an artificial and pointless propriety: signs that can easily be read as symptoms of sexual frustration and non-fulfilment. The contradictions in her role as wife-and-mother (a role at once venerated and ignominious), given authority over the home on condition that she consent to be its prisoner, are brought out sharply through the humiliation of her attempts to raise money, the descent through bank and loan office to pawnshop of a woman kept in comfort, security and respectability. This descent, together with the juxtaposition in the film of the upper-middle-class society of Balboa with the sordid or criminal world inhabited by Darby, Donnelly and Donnelly's senior partner Nagel, also exposes for us the dark underside of capitalism, the inevitable other face of a society based on values of material gain and financial security: a point epitomized in Donnelly's remark to Lucia about their respective imprisonments—"You have your family, I have my Nagel."

If I have stressed the film's subversive aspects at the risk of simplifying its complexity of attitude, that is because its acknowledgment of the strengths of American bourgeois society—a defined code (however restrictive) of moral decency, family solidarity, stability—is obvious enough and inherent in the genre. (People have been known to take the film at face value as conventional "soap opera".) The complexity of the response evoked can be suggested from the sequence that introduces Donnelly. Lucia arrives home, Sybil tells her a visitor is awaiting her. A single take leads Lucia from the brightly-lit kitchen to the living-room, where Donnelly stands in the shadows, which are intensified when the door is closed. The whole sequence plays on effects of light and darkness, light becoming associated with the family and the home, darkness with the menacing outside world and the intruder (who switches on a table-lamp that, while lighting the room, casts heavy shadows). The Ophulsian fondness for long-shot emphasizes Donnelly's isolation and strangeness in the décor of the home; the conversation is repeatedly interrupted by the intrusion of members of the family, ready to treat the visitor with frank friendliness as a guest who can be invited to stay for dinner, and by the carrying in of the Christmas tree. The simple response (family security threatened by sinister stranger) is gradually disturbed by our growing sense of Donnelly's humanity and charm, by *his* half-amused, half-tender response to all the manifestations of family life. The imagery also delicately suggests Lucia's entrapment: there is an archetypally Ophulsian shot (when she has run out to silence Bea who has read in the newspaper of Darby's murder) of Lucia half way up the staircase, suddenly arrested in indecision, framed between the pillars of the living-room décor. The sequence ends, marvellously, with Lucia drawn outside by Donnelly into the darkness, the two worlds of security and danger linked in the background and foreground of a single image as the two tensely discuss the blackmail demands outside while the family, visible through a window, settle around the brightly-lit dinner-table; the shot ending with Donnelly's disappearance into the shadows.

The same ambivalence is poignantly present in the final sequence in terms of material, fully representative of the way tensions are resolved in the Hollywood melodrama, but again given a particular poise and complexity by Ophuls's presence. The effect depends upon two identifiably Ophulsian features: repetition (which itself involves a group of motifs familiar from Ophuls's work—the bedroom as place of isolation, the staircase, the intervention of décor) and the simultaneous arousing of conflicting emotional responses, as at the close of *Letter from an Unknown Woman* (an effect deliberately—and successfully—recaptured by Demy in *Lola* and *Les Parapluies de Cherbourg*). The scene refers us back to the scene of Tom's phone call near the start of the film, before Darby's death. In both sequences dialogue, action, camera position, editing, follow a closely similar pattern: both begin in a bedroom (Bea's, Lucia's); Lucia is summoned to the phone by a call from Sybil; she descends the stairs; the family gather round as she talks to her husband, with no possibility of privacy, no chance to speak of the urgent matters that occupy her consciousness, so that the conversation becomes an exchange of reassuring platitudes. The similarities—as usual with Ophuls—are there to sharpen for us the sense of change. In the early scene, Lucia was handling a difficult but scarcely unfamiliar domestic problem (her daughter's rebelliousness) from a simple and unquestioning moral position; at the end, through her involvement with Donnelly, her perception of herself and her role has (by implication) changed, the blinkers have been removed. The final sequence starts with Lucia alone on her bed in the shadows, weeping helplessly: the setting intensifies the feeling of loss, and gives that loss the sexual dimension which Lucia consistently suppresses. As she descends the stairs, Bea and David return from the movies, with the news of Donnelly's death and the confession that finally blackens his name to save the family's; Bea is wearing her mother's fur coat, emblem of the rewards and servitude of domesticity—ironically suggesting here the chastened daughter's acquiescence in the traditional female role and the values the film has undermined, her acknowledgment that her mother was right. Lucia talks to Tom (who is phoning from Berlin) about Christmas and the tree they have chosen; the family gather round in solidarity, the security for which Lucia has fought and for which Donnelly has died reaffirmed. The camera descends so that Lucia, speaking on the phone at the foot of the staircase, is distanced and cut off from us by the banisters, the bars of the domestic prison to which she has voluntarily returned. The emotional effect arises from our response to the two levels on which this ending simultaneously operates: the conventional "happy end" of the domestic melodrama (reunion of family, reaffirmation of marriage), and the Ophulsian sense of tragic waste and loss that comments ironically on this without obliterating it.

What conclusions about the "auteur theory" can be drawn from these test cases? I prefer to draw no very definite ones, leaving my examples to suggest the complexities of authorship in the American cinema and the need for the greatest flexibility on the part of the critic. The validity of the "auteur theory," as generally understood, seems to me at once confirmed and qualified—there being, one might say, as many qualifications as there are movies. What I would like to see take place in criticism is a return from "auteurs" to films. Auteur theory in its more primitive and extreme manifestations has marked a phase through which it was necessary for film criticism to pass. Now that the notion of directorial authorship has become a commonplace, it should be possible to move away from the position that sees the identification of authorial fingerprints as an ultimate aim, to a position that regards the director's identifiable presence as one influence—probably the most, but certainly not the only, important one among the complex of influences that combine to determine the character and quality of a particular film. It is a position directly opposed, in its implications, to that expressed by Peter Wollen in his chapter on the auteur theory in *Signs and Meaning in the Cinema.*

9
Hawks De-Wollenized

An intellectual carrot—the mind boggles!
The Thing from Another World

Peter Wollen's *Signs and Meaning in the Cinema* (Secker and Warburg, 1969) is probably the most influential book on film in English of the past decade. I do not believe its seminal nature has been sufficiently acknowledged in print: the rehabilitation of Eisenstein, semiology, structuralism, the emphasis on Godard: it is all there, and more than embryonically. Probably its most *widely* influential (because most easily accessible) section is the chapter on Hollywood ("The Auteur Theory"). Wollen (to judge from the "Afterword" to the revised edition published in 1972) appears to have forsaken the interests defined in that chapter in favour of pursuing an avant-garde whose existence (with the exception, or perhaps the inclusion, of recent Godard) is largely theoretical, i.e., a non-existence; and of issuing lists of critical priorities to his fellows. But, although the present Wollen does not believe that "development of *auteur* analyses of Hollywood directors is any longer a first priority," the chapter continues to have its influence, and those of us not in the forefront of critical progress are still concerned with such fuddy-duddy issues as the stature of Ford and Hawks as artists, and the interpretation of their films. I want to focus first on Wollen's structural analysis of Hawks, and go on to question the general assumptions on which it is based.

As I am concerned here with the exposure of fallacies in a text I find less convincing every time I return to it, it is proper to begin by acknowledging a debt, the magnitude of which can be suggested by adding that there is no critical text to which I have returned more frequently. Readers of my books on Hitchcock, Hawks and Penn (all written before I had read Wollen's book) will, I hope, consider it a just claim that the general principles of Wollen's approach—the analysis of a director's work in terms of recurrent thematic motifs—were not entirely new or alien to me. They were, however, not at all rigorously or systematically employed. Wollen's chapter, plus an article by Alan Lovell in *Screen* (March/April 1969), taught me to apply "structuralist" principles consciously, though my treatment of them has always been sceptical and unorthodox. Articles I subsequently wrote on Bu̇el, Makavejev and Michael Reeves were consciously and directly indebted to Wollen and Lovell.

Alan Lovell's article took the form of a critique of my own work, focusing eventually on my account of Penn. The kind of unconscious previous relationship I had to structuralist criticism can perhaps be suggested by comparing his findings to my own. In my book on Penn I suggested that central to his work was a conflict between the conscious-rational and the spontaneous-intuitive, to both of which Penn is strongly drawn. Alan Lovell concludes that the recurring structural centre of Penn's films has been a conflict between a teacher/parent-figure and an unsocialized adolescent. The similarity of the two accounts will be obvious; I still regard my "model" as the superior one, because it allows for greater artistic complexity and critical flexibility, notably when the conscious/intuitive conflict is contained within a single character (e.g., Annie Sullivan in *The Miracle Worker*). The important difference, however, is in the status each of us gives to his "model": for Lovell, perception of the structural core is crucial, and everything else becomes dependent on it; for me, it offers one possible way of exploring the texture of Penn's films, the subject/style/theme synthesis they represent, the particular nature of each, which various circumstances and factors might contribute to determine. I would see no necessary correlation between the full realization of the recurrent structure and the quality of an individual film.

Two claims for "structuralist" procedure are either implicit or explicit in Wollen's and Lovell's pieces. First, implicit in Wollen is the notion of its interpretative and evaluative adequacy: by the end of his structural analyses of Ford and Hawks, he is ready to pronounce a confident verdict: while Hawks is merely "an undoubted auteur," Ford is a "great artist," and his superiority is proved by "the richness of the shifting relations between antinomies" in his work. Lovell is much more hesitant, wanting to postpone all attempt at evaluation until we understand the nature of the cinema better; but he finds it possible that *Bonnie and Clyde* might be regarded as one of Penn's lesser films because the father-figure who occupies a central position in the Penn structure is here pushed out to the periphery, making the film "simpler" and "less coherent" than its predecessors. The second claim—not, I think, made explicitly by Wollen, but implicit in the general thrust of his book and argued by Lovell in a rejoinder to my answer to his original article (*Screen,* Volume II, 4/5)—indicates the role structuralism plays in the general movement of contemporary film criticism: it forms part of the basis for a scientific-objective criticism that will make individual responses and individual voices redundant and supply a critical method and language no longer dependent on the individual sensibility. These claims may yet prove to be valid; but a theory is validated only by the practice which arises from it, and the record so far seems less than convincing.

Wollen's writing customarily suggests great haste, as if he can only function in a flurry of excitement; it may seem odd that a critic so committed to the intellectual should possess so little of the rational. The "auteur theory" chapter rests partly on a distinction between *auteur* and *metteur-en-scène* which cannot sustain much examination, as Wollen seems half to realize: "In concrete cases, of course, this distinction is not always clear-cut." In concrete cases it is *never* clear-cut, and could not possibly be, any emphasis in *mise-en-scène* implying an attitude, and a set of attitudes implying a thematic structure; therefore it has not much validity as theory. Nor is he always prone to factual accuracy: on one page he talks of "Macmahonism . . . with . . . its notorious text: 'Charlton Heston is an axiom of the cinema'"—a "text" coined by Michel Mourlet, whom the Macmahonists explicitly disowned; on the next he describes *Land of the Pharaohs* as a "Biblical" epic; and he subsequently conjures up a wife for Wyatt Earp in *My Darling Clementine.* The reader should be alerted to scrutinize his ensuing statements about Hawks with great care, but the sense of excitement with which Wollen writes, the air of authority and assurance, and the assumption of impersonality, in fact combine to impose his text as definitive.

If we insist, however, on careful scrutiny, we shall I think begin to raise a critical eyebrow at Wollen's very first statement about "values" in Hawks's movies: "Hawks, unlike Boetticher, seeks transcendent values beyond the individual, in solidarity with others." This introduces, of course, Wollen's discussion of "the group," clearly an important component of Hawks's films, which both he and Alan Lovell see as central to Hawks's values. If one ponders on what appear to be for Hawks "transcendent values," however, one will find that they are something inward and individual, achieved *through* "solidarity with others" perhaps, but scarcely adequately represented *by* it. That Wollen, however, sees no inadequacy in his account is soon confirmed: "For Hawks, the highest human emotion is the camaraderie of the exclusive, self-sufficient, all-male group." I am not entirely sure what "highest" means here (intensest? noblest? most highly valued?—a combination of the three?); and if we are to discuss the highest emotion "for Hawks" we would clearly have to take into account not only emotions expressed by his characters but the emotions generated in the spectator. With this in mind, I would suggest the following examples (not intended as exhaustive—others will of course have different lists) of supreme emotion in Hawks's films. One, in *Only Angels Have Wings* (a more overtly emotional film than almost any of the later works), Bat's triumph over cowardice and his regaining of self-respect, the death of Kid (his wish to be left to die completely alone, without even his best friend), Jeff's tears after Kid's death. Two, in *Ball of Fire,* Gary Cooper's attempt to explain his newly-awakened feelings, in the darkness of what he believes to be the room of one of his fellow-professors but is in fact the room of the woman he loves: feelings that set him apart from the activities and purposes of the group, making him aware of his individuality. Three, in *To Have and Have Not,* Harry Morgan's reaction to the news that the Fascists have taken Eddie, and his sense of moral outrage at the infringement of individual liberties. Four, in *Red River,* the intervention of Tess (the reincarnation of the girl Dunson lost at the beginning of the film) in the fight between Dunson and Matt, and the men's ensuing reconciliation. Five, in *The Big Sky,* Boone's decision to burn the scalp and return to Teal Eye, thereby at once establishing his adulthood and regaining the respect of his best friend. Six, in *Rio Bravo,* Dude's triumph over his alcoholism—the moment when, halted by the "Alamo" music from the bar across the street, he pours back the whisky he was about to drink. Seven, in *Red Line 7000,* the reunion in the purifying rain of Mike and Gaby, after he has taken his punishment from Dan—a reunion that marks his transcendence of the neurotic tensions that have driven him to attempt murder.

Most of these examples are connected (though in various and sometimes very tenuous ways) with the presence of a group, but that is scarcely the prime factor they have in common. Their variety, indeed, might at first suggest the irreducibility of an artist's work (especially an artist working in a collaborative medium) to a single structural pattern. Further thought reveals that they are all manifestations (taking very different forms, not all obvious) of the Hawksian belief in the individual's need for self-respect as an ultimate value. Not one of them is by any stretch of the imagination adequately summed up by the belittling word "camaraderie."

Belittling phraseology pervades all of Wollen's composite portrait of the Hawks group, which comes to resemble a gathering of neo-Fascist superman boy scouts. The description abounds in plausible falsifications, made possible by the fact that Wollen is offering an abstraction: it does not have to correspond to any *specific* instance in the actual films. "The élite group strictly preserves its exclusivity. It is necessary to pass a test of ability and courage to win admission." One can see how such an account might be defended, by pointing to this and that in the films; one can also detect the tendency of its tone, with such loaded terms as "élite" and "exclusivity." Hawks's groups are so varied that it is difficult to generalize safely about them: a complete view would need to account for the eccentric professors of *Ball of Fire;* the racing drivers of *Red Line 7000* are never a group in the same sense as the bomber crew of *Air Force,* who in turn are quite different from the *ad hoc* gathering of *Rio Bravo;* and do Humphrey Bogart and Walter Brennan (*To Have and Have Not*) constitute a "group"?—it is difficult to separate them from the *Rio Bravo* quartet. One can say, however, that each group undertakes an activity that requires certain skills or qualities (academic learning, driving aptitude, stamina) for its successful execution, and this necessarily limits membership (would a mail delivery service be "élitist" if it rejected an applicant who could not read?). This said, one would still wish to point out, as further qualification of Wollen's dictum, that Hawks's "exclusive," "élitist" groups do manage to include a mental defective (*The Big Sky*), a crippled alcoholic (*To Have and Have Not*), a cripple *and* an alcoholic (*Rio Bravo*), and, among *Hatari!'s* animal-catchers, an ex-cab-driver who is terrified of animals. This certainly suggests a qualification for membership beyond professional competence, though one may doubt whether passing "a test of ability and courage" quite describes it. Again, the examples are so different that generalization is not easy, but anyone who knows the films will see that the self-respect motif is again crucial: if a single qualification meets the bill, it is quite simply the *desire* to respect oneself, the acceptance of that as a central motivating value. Essentially, eligibility for group membership is a matter of Hawksian morality: it depends on an intuitive sense of moral integrity that can penetrate physical, mental and temperamental disabilities; it is intimately bound up with notions of friendship and personal loyalty, of the kind that has prompted Chance in *Rio Bravo* to buy back Dude's guns and preserve his clothes "until they fitted you again"; the same principle (though no group is in question) motivates the respect Marlowe develops for "Jonesey" (Elisha Cook Jr.) in *The Big Sleep*. The concept of eligibility is much subtler, finer and more flexible, that is, than Wollen indicates.

"The group members are bound together by rituals (in *Hatari!* blood is exchanged by transfusion) and express themselves univocally in communal sing-songs. There is a famous example of this in *Rio Bravo*." Again, I am not certain (apart from the *Hatari!* example given, which indeed points to something fundamental in Hawks, his fascination with the primitive) exactly what "rituals" Wollen has in mind. There is the repeated pattern of the exchange of blows leading to friendship (*The Big Sky, Hatari!*) and the shooting contest with the same result (*Red River, Hatari!*); there are various examples of relationships expressed or developed through the exchange, rolling or lighting of cigarettes (Grant/Mitchell in *Only Angels Have Wings*, Bogart/Bacall in *To Have and Have Not*, Wayne/Martin in *Rio Bravo*); there is the repeated examination of possessions after a death (twice in *Only Angels*, once in *Air Force*), with the line, "Not much to show for (twenty) years." None of these has much to do with groups or group membership: the first two are manifestations of personal relationships between a couple, the third both an expression of the Hawksian stoicism (as typified by the repeated burial speech in *Red River*—"You brought nothing into this world and it's certain you'll take nothing out") and a very private affair in which an intimate of the dead man's (friend and father respectively) mourns his passing. Most of the "rituals" (if that is the right word for them) in Hawks's films might be more reasonably related to the circularity and repetition that give his films their idiosyncratic rhythm and are central to their metaphysic.

"Plausible falsification" also seems to me a fair description of Wollen's treatment of the important motif of the shared song. Again, one is struck by the failure to distinguish between very different examples. Wollen's phrase ("express themselves univocally in communal sing-songs") clearly goes with the earlier "camaraderie" to evoke a "now-all-together-boys," scouts-around-the-camp-fire heartiness. It might just do for the example he gives subsequently from *Dawn Patrol* (though one would scarcely leave it at that, without qualification); it will not do at all for the "famous example . . . in *Rio Bravo.*" It is worth pausing on this scene briefly because it offers a beautiful example of the sort of complex significance (arising out of context, *mise-en-scène,* editing) which Wollen's analytical method tramples brutally underfoot. The scene consists of two songs: "My Rifle, My Pony and Me," started by Dude, developing into a duet (sung and whistled) for Dude and Colorado; and the traditional song "Cindy," sung by Colorado, with Stumpy and Dude joining in the refrain. It is not a mere quibble to insist that the first song is never "univocal," because its entire significance depends on this. The sequence marks the integration of Dude and Colorado into the group: Colorado has recently committed himself by direct action, Dude has triumphed over his alcoholism, and they have passed through rivalry to a balance based on mutual respect. The sequence opens with a close medium-shot of Dude as he begins the song unaccompanied, eyes closed, hat over his brow—he may, for all we know, be alone, the signs all suggesting that self-absorption that goes with his self-pity and alcoholism (earlier, he was overpowered by Burdett's men while peering at his own reflection in a horse-trough). The second shot shows Chance in the other room, getting himself coffee; it is only in the third shot that the camera pans on Chance's movement to reveal Colorado with guitar and Stumpy with his harmonica. The editing cuts between shots of the four until Dude signals to Colorado to take over the song; at which points Stumpy stops playing the harmonica and the editing is restricted to cross-cutting (the pace accelerated as the song continues) between Dude and Colorado. They never sing (or whistle) in unison, but overlap as a simple canon: they remain, that is, two individuals in a spontaneous give-and-take relationship, the song being closer to a love-duet than to a "communal singsong," the accelerated editing suggesting the growing intimacy. As such it relates very closely to other songs in Hawks's films: one thinks particularly of the Jim/Boone duet ("Whisky, Leave Me Alone")—again, treated as an overlapping part-song—in *The Big Sky*, and the Mike/Gaby shared song with the car radio ("Baby, Won't You Please Come Home?") again, partly whistled—in *Red Line 7000*. In all these cases, the song becomes a means of nonverbal (for the *words* are not important) communication on an intuitive level between two individuals who love each other and express their love in the interchange of the song, while retaining their individuality. In *Rio Bravo*, when the first song finishes, Stumpy asks for "something I can sing too," and the editing of the second song re-integrates the couple in the group: one might see this as epitomizing the way in which Hawks deals with the intimate man-to-man relationships that recur throughout his films.

Hawks also uses the sequence to define the relation to the

Rio Bravo's Dude, Stumpy and Colorado have a sing-along.

group of its leader. Throughout the scene, Stumpy, Dude and
Colorado form a circle which Chance remains outside; his exclusion is emphasized by the editing, which brings him back
into the image only at the end of the sequence. The moral infal-
libility he represents (and which is shown throughout the film
to be accompanied by human limitations) at once makes him
indispensable to the others as touchstone and example, and excludes him from their conviviality. Chance's position outside
the circle can also be felt to have a further meaning, harder to
argue (because never reaching overt dramatic expression) but
perhaps implicit in the overall movement of the film: Dude's
rehabilitation, and the expression through the song of his new
relationship with Colorado, release Chance from his responsibility to his friend, setting him free for the confirmation of his
relationship with Feathers. The transition from a male orienta-
tion to a heterosexual one is a recurrent movement in Hawks's

films: *The Big Sky* offers the most explicit example, but the ending of *Only Angels Have Wings* offers a particularly beautiful one, Kid's two-headed coin that was an emblem of his relationship with Jeff (*"That's* why I've been paying for the drinks all these years!"*) becoming, after Kid's death, the means whereby Jeff "asks" Bonnie to stay.

Wollen's habit of listing examples without indicating any discriminations between them leads at times to even stranger results. He discusses the Hawksian attitude to established society, "other people in general . . . perceived by the group as an undifferentiated crowd," the presence of which "is a constant covert threat to the Hawksian élite." The passage ends: "Often Hawks's revenge becomes grim and macabre. In *Sergeant York* it is 'fun' to shoot Germans 'like turkeys'; in *Air Force* it is 'fun' to blow up the Japanese fleet. In *Rio Bravo* the geligniting of the badmen 'was very funny.' It is at these moments that the élite turns against the world outside and takes the opportunity to be brutal and destructive." One may object here, firstly, to the lumping together of films in quite different genres, made under widely varying circumstances, with no sense of differences in the conventions they establish. *Sergeant York* is a film about World War I which attempts to reconstruct convincingly the look and feel of a battlefield and which makes much of physical pain and the horror of warfare (when it is Americans who are getting shot); I have always been distressed by the insensitivity of Hawks's treatment of the "turkey-shooting" of Germans, playing it for laughs, though it is worth pointing out that the basic attitude here has as much in common with other American war movies of the forties as it has with other Hawks adventure films. The same might be said of *Air Force* (which Hawks says he made as a contribution to the war effort), though the film is, I think, vastly superior if one can penetrate its superficial level of patriotic rhetoric. On the other hand, *Rio Bravo* is one of the most stylized of westerns, in which Hawks works out his own idiosyncratic variations within the most conventionalized forms, and in which the realities of pain and violence are scarcely an issue: the comic treatment of the dynamiting, the sense of it as a kind of celebration-fireworks-party for Dude's salvation, works perfectly within the genre framework. But Wollen is clearly little interested in what works and what does not: all is equally grist to the structuralist mill, or, to change metaphor, whatever cuts of meat one puts into the machine, out comes the same structuralist sausage. What is odder still is the way in which the Burdett gang and their hired mercenaries—a kind of crypto-Fascist group embodying the anti-Hawksian values of power and money-greed—here become equated by a sleight-of-hand that seems generally to have passed unnoticed, with the "undifferentiated crowd" of established society.

Wollen's description of Hawks's work bears, of course, a resemblance to it; I would define the relationship as one of parody—and essentially destructive parody. The parodic element is clearest in the "typical dialogue" (given as if it were actual quotation) which is meant to sum up Hawks's treatment of the role of women in his films: place it beside any of the exchanges it superficially resembles (the Kid/Bonnie duologues in *Only Angels* seem to be the closest) and its destructive intent (destructive of all the specific complexities and qualifications brought by context) will be apparent. But more important than the distortions in Wollen's account are the omissions. I have already suggested what I think are the crucial ones: the repeated emphasis on self-respect, individual dignity, personal integrity, as ultimate values; the dominant element of the spontaneous-intuitive in Hawks's positive characters and their relationships (hence the expression of feelings, attitudes, positions through actions rather than words, and the instant trust and equally instant antagonism the characters exhibit); the fascination with the "primitive"—animals, savages, simple communities or groups away from organized society, uncluttered Spartan bareness, elemental life-and-death situations—that relates the comedies to the adventure films not in simple opposition but as complements.

We can now return to the claims for the "structuralist" method that I suggested were implicit in the work of Wollen and/or Lovell. Firstly, any sense we may receive of "scientific" objectivity is manifestly illusory: Wollen's account of Hawks reveals as strong a personal bias as one will find in the most admittedly "subjective" criticism, the more dangerous for being concealed beneath an appearance of detached analytical method. As much as any other critic, Wollen sets his own personal value-system against the artist's in order to criticize the latter, as when he describes the Hawksian view of life as "desolate and barren" (Hawks clearly does not find it so—witness the joyousness and serenity of *Rio Bravo*), or sees the comedies as "the agonized exposure of the underlying tensions of the heroic dramas" (a description of *Bringing Up Baby* and *Monkey Business* that will startle most viewers responsive to the *tone* of a film). Wollen's account reveals, one may say, a strong, unadmitted, and largely unconscious animus against Hawks expressing itself as distortion and parody. The grounds for that animus are not difficult to deduce. Wollen is nothing if not an intellectual, and the positive values implicit everywhere in his work are those associated with intellectual activity: one may suppose him to set very high, perhaps supreme, value on the pursuit of knowledge. This does not mean, of course, that he can only do justice to artists who share such values (his account of Ford; while open to some of the same basic objections, is in a different class from his work on Hawks). But in confronting Hawks he is faced with a value-system not merely different from his own but diametrically opposed to it—a value-system centred on a commitment to the intuitive, the physical, the "primitive," and that shows no interest in concepts such as "progress." He responds with unconscious parody.

A film Wollen scarcely mentions, but which seems to me central in that it is the one film in the canon that presents the definitive Hawks villain, seems significant here: *The Thing from Another World*. The villain is the "Thing" itself: an extraterrestrial vegetable of extreme intellectual development, entirely devoid of emotion; it is also asexual, reproducing itself by dropping seeds from the palms of its hands. The leader of the scientific expedition, Dr. Carrington—who elsewhere in the film expresses the belief (roughly paraphrasing Bertrand Russell) that the only purpose of and justification for human existence is the pursuit of knowledge—regards it as an unequivocal advance on the human race: "No pleasure, no pain, no emotions.... Our superior, gentlemen, our superior in every way." Against the Thing is set the "camaraderie" of the group, and all that goes with it—human affection, mutual respect, sexual attraction. Peter Wollen is not exactly a "Supercarrot" (his writing, in fact, always seems to carry a strong emotional charge, a sense of excitement and personal pressure, that is either its weakness or its saving grace, depending on the point of view); but the Thing represents no more grotesque a parody of the values his criticism asserts than the account he offers parodies Hawks.

It remains to consider the status and value of the "structuralist" method, as exemplified here. I have indicated that I have myself found it very useful; I must add that its evaluative validity seems to me precisely nil, its utility strictly contingent upon other procedures (and ultimately on one's sense of values). In my answer to Lovell in *Screen* I pointed out that he unwittingly betrayed some uncertainty as to the status of structural analysis, calling it at times a "method," at other times a "tool." It is a tool, one among many, to be picked up and discarded at one's convenience, useful but not indispensable.

But perhaps this evades the ultimate question: the question of precisely what is to be evaluated. Are we interested in works of art, or in the abstractions that can be made from an artist's work? My answer is that for me art is concrete and specific: it is *Rio Bravo* in all its local detail, each little alive bit of business worked out between Hawks and his actors—not the "Homo hawksianus" or the "Hawksian heterocosm." I believe that a film's excellence is (in the overwhelming majority of cases) ultimately attributable to its director, but not at all in a simple "great artist reveals his view of the world" way. The term Wollen uses for anything that distracts our attention from the recurrent structural motifs, prevents our perceiving the structure in its abstract purity, is "noise," by which he appears to mean, primarily, the interference of producers or studio heads. Yet the distinction this suggests appears damagingly simplistic—damagingly, that is, in relation to any adequate sense of the complexities of "realized" art within a collaborative medium. The opposition structure/"noise" allows no means—to take the most obvious example—of discussing the intricacies of Hawks's collaborations with particular writers, though something of the quality of individual films clearly derives from this. One can trace through his work, for instance, a Ben Hecht–Charles Lederer weave and a Jules Furthman–William Faulkner–Leigh Brackett weave. Without being exhaustive, the former gives us *Scarface* (Hecht), *His Girl Friday* (Lederer, from a Hecht-MacArthur play), *Monkey Business* (Hecht and Lederer), *I Was a Male War Bride, The Thing* and *Gentlemen Prefer Blondes* (Lederer); the latter gives us *Only Angels Have Wings* (Furthman), *To Have and Have Not* (Furthman and Faulkner), *The Big Sleep* (Furthman, Faulkner and Brackett), *Rio Bravo* (Furthman and Brackett), *Hatari! El Dorado* and *Rio Lobo* (Brackett). The two "weaves" continually cross through Hawks's work, but never combine: there are no Hecht/Furthman screenplays, for instance, though each was involved in at least six Hawks scripts. While the impossibility of making clear-cut thematic distinctions between the weaves testifies to the pervasive and unifying presence of Hawks, each weave emphasizes and highlights characteristics the other plays down. The resulting richness cannot be adequately represented by means of a single schematic structure. Beyond that, there may be all kinds of complex forces working on a given film, a multitude of determinants with the director at its centre. It is far from inconceivable that a director's finest work may be his least typical, the one that least corresponds to any total structure or "heterocosm," a work in which circumstances (script, subject, actors, working conditions, *genre*) held in check his weaknesses and excesses. A work of art can transcend the personality, values, world-view of the artist; the greatness of a given film may be the product of an intricate interaction in which collaborators, circumstances of production, studio pressures, might all play their part.

Wollen, of course, would be the last critic to fall for the "Romantic" fallacy of equating the quality of a work of art with the artist's direct self-expression: he finds the significance of an *oeuvre* in the gradual, inadvertent revelation of a structure of "recondite" motifs of which the artist himself may remain unaware. One can grant the intellectual excitement of the search for such a structure; one can see that it may reveal interesting features in failed or inferior films (*Wings of Eagles, Donovan's Reef*)—though I personally cannot see that it reveals such films as, after all, successful works of art; most importantly, it can draw attention to some of the possible sources of a successful work's vitality. It constitutes, in other words, a potentially valuable preliminary to full understanding.

Mistaken for a valid method of evaluation, it leads Wollen to some very curious decisions. Hawks's interest lies, apparently, in the "structural" opposition between the adventure films and the comedies. Hence: "If we take the adventure dramas alone it would seem that Hawks's work is flaccid, lacking in dynamism." So what becomes of one's response to actual films, to the experience of sitting in front of one? Presumably, we endure flaccid, undynamic works like *Only Angels Have Wings, To Have and*

Have Not, Rio Bravo, feeling nothing but boredom and exasperation, until we have seen *Bringing Up Baby* and *Monkey Business* (also, I take it, of little interest in themselves). *Then,* however, "alongside every dramatic hero we are aware of a phantom, stripped of mastery, humiliated, inverted," and what was previously flaccid somehow ceases to be. It will seem to most people a very curious process, whereby we can only enjoy one film if we are thinking of another one while we watch it. In fact, an examination of *Rio Bravo* will show, I think, that the major tensions of Hawks's "world" are successfully and coherently contained within it: there is no need to place the comedies, or anything else, beside it for it to "become rich" and "begin to ferment."

Wollen's method rides roughshod over the internal delicacies and complexities of a work of art—the local significances that arise from the fusion of context and concrete realization. It is difficult to grasp, ultimately, what his valuation of Hawks actually is, or what it is based on. His structural analysis reduces the films to a scheme that, while it is assumed to convey Hawks's significance, appears trite, trivial and uninteresting; yet Hawks is included in Wollen's "Pantheon" of ten Hollywood directors at the end of the book (omitted from the second edition). I can see no justification for this high assessment in his text. As an antidote, and for the basis on which a serious case for Hawks might be built, the reader might look up an altogether more unassuming and less influential article by John Belton, reprinted in *Focus on Howard Hawks* (Prentice-Hall): it seems to me the best thing on Hawks I have read, searching out significance not in a simplified abstraction but in the concrete detail of the films.

To point to a constructive alternative—or at least counterbalance—to Wollen's parody, and to exemplify what I mean by the significance of concrete detail, without a sensitivity to which we cannot hope to "read" a work of art, I shall end by indicating two brief moments in *Rio Bravo.* Neither of them is accountable for in the terms of Wollen's structural analysis, though a more just and rational sense of the Hawksian value-system's finer aspects would certainly relate them to the concerns of the whole film and of Hawks's work in general. The first is the moment when Chance and Dude, patrolling the street at night, encounter the Burdett man set to watch the jail. Dude watches from across the street; Chance stands silently over the man (who begins to shuffle awkwardly) then speaks the words "Good evening," as only John Wayne can. The man mutters and moves away; Dude smiles admiringly. The incident established Chance's authority as essentially *moral:* the authority of the man who acts from inner principle over the hired mercenary. It also acts as an object-lesson for Dude: implicit in Chance's authority is the personal integrity and self-respect that Dude, in his lapse into alcoholic degradation, has forfeited and must strive to regain. He is separated from Chance by the street (and by the editing), a pupil-onlooker. Thus a mini-scene with only two words spoken encapsulates the film's leading moral and dramatic concerns.

The second moment, which occurs at the end of the "blood-in-the-beer" scene, again takes up the theme of authority and can be seen as both development and qualification of the first, hence exemplifying the complexity of attitude achievable without pretension or explicitness in a fictional narrative. The scene ends with Chance reminding Dude—now provisionally reinstated by virtue of his very un-alcoholic aliveness of perception and action—that he has still to deal with the man who taunted him by flinging a coin into the spittoon. Dude compels the man (by moral authority backed by the *possibility* of force) to retrieve it personally, with his bare hand. His comment is a succinct, "That's all for *me,* Chance." The comment clearly refers the spectator back to an incident earlier in the scene when Chance, as a punishment, struck a man savagely across the face with a gun-barrel. The moral centre of *Rio Bravo* is the developing comparison between the two men, the "infallible" leader, always refusing help yet constantly dependent on it, the extremely fallible, more human and responsive deputy. Dude's remark emerges as a criticism of Chance, a pointing of the human limitations and dangers that the role of infallible leader carries with it. The criticism is less one of physical violence *per se* than of motivation and role: Chance metes out punishment to an inferior, Dude demands his human rights through the enactment of a precise justice. Dude's participation in the song, in the democratic equality of individuals, and Chance's exclusion from their circle, are already implicit in that moment—the sort of moment one imagines developing, in a Hawks movie, out of the director's collaborative involvement with writers and actors, out of his sense of each actor's nature and what he can give. The life of a film is in its detail.

10
The Shadow Worlds of Jacques Tourneur
Cat People and I Walked with a Zombie

The series of horror films (for want of a better term) produced by Val Lewton in the forties can stand as at once a demonstration of the limitations of the auteur theory and its vindication. They are usually regarded, and with some justice, as essentially Lewton's films. Much of their taste, intelligence and discretion is attributable to his planning and supervision, and it becomes peculiarly difficult—in the last resort impossible—to sort out the precise contributions of producer, writer and director. Yet important discriminations remain to be made. None of the series, not even *Bedlam,* is without interest; and to be the producer of an interesting film directed by Mark Robson is in itself evidence of distinction.

Perhaps *The Body Snatcher*—which I thought on first viewing (mistakenly, as I now believe) the finest of the whole series—testifies best to Lewton's quality. It is a marvellously constructed film, a moral fable on the subject of dehumanization carefully structured in terms of its characters—brutalized body snatcher, experienced doctor tormented by his complicity yet too involved to extricate himself, young doctor in continual danger of getting drawn into the same trap—yet given considerable complexity by the varying play of sympathy elicited for each (Karloff's body snatcher remains disturbingly human). Yet, if one places it beside *Cat People* and *I Walked with a Zombie,* one cannot but be aware of a comparative crudeness of sensibility apparent in the realization. Insofar as it is a Lewton film, *The Body Snatcher* is a potential masterpiece (a *producer's* film cannot be more than potential); insofar as it is a Robert Wise film, it is inferior to certain of its companions.

Cat People and *Zombie* were both directed by Jacques Tourneur. Interestingly, they exhibit not only stylistic but thematic features that at once connect them with each other and distinguish them from other films in the series. And similar features are discernible in *The Leopard Man,* the other film Tourneur directed for Lewton. Though it contains several excellent—and recognizably Tourneuresque—sequences, *The Leopard Man* is notably inferior to its predecessors, striking one as at once over-explicit and under-developed, as if its makers had become *too* conscious of the thematic level of their work. I shall not discuss it here, as it does little that is not done better in the two earlier films, but it is useful in offering confirmatory evidence for the decisive influence on the films of Tourneur's personality. Decisive on their precise character and to some extent on their quality; and memories of *Curse of the Demon,* made later without Lewton, and exhibiting very much the same character and quality, tend further to support my growing sense of Tourneur as essential auteur.

But before going the whole auteurist hog and regarding *Cat People* and *Zombie* as Tourneur movies *tout court,* it is salutary to glance at some of his other work. My own experience here has been disconcerting. In the excitement of discovering Tourneur's Lewton films I managed to unearth six of his non-horror movies. With *Canyon Passage* and *Out of the Past* I began to wonder what Tourneur was doing outside Andrew Sarris's pantheon, and felt confident I had discovered one of the great unacknowledged masters of the American cinema; *Days of Glory, Experiment Perilous, Berlin Express* and *Easy Living* constituted four successive blows to that confidence.

Not that they offer any incontestable refutation: everyone makes bad movies sometimes (even directors with total control over their material and free choice of subject matter) and a Hol-

The presence of the zombie Carrefour
awakens Betsy in *I Walked with a Zombie.*

lywood contract director has the right to claim forgiveness for
any number of unredeemable fiascoes. One could not possibly
ask an artist of any intelligence and sensibility to interest himself passionately in the scenario of, for example, *Berlin Express,*
which is of a stupidity one would find unbelievable were one
not hardened by so many precedents.

What raises some doubt is the nature of the failure of these
films. Tourneur's visual style—characterized by a penchant for
long-shot and camera-movement—is intermittently recognizable in all of them (except perhaps *Easy Living,* overall the most
competent but least Tourneuresque of the four). But it is simply *applied* to the subject-matter externally, without in any way
transforming it. One begins to question, tentatively, the strength
and force of Tourneur's creativity; to ask oneself on which side
of the shadowy borderline between creator and interpreter he

belongs. An inability to enter deeply into not entirely congenial subject-matter, to penetrate its surface and transform it from within, is not inconsistent with the excellence of the Lewton films or of *Canyon Passage* or *Out of the Past*.

Related to this is one's general sense that Tourneur is not a particularly distinguished director of actors. In a Nicholas Ray movie, for example, no one ever gives a bad performance, not even Curt Jurgens or Robert Taylor. But in both *Cat People* and *Zombie* Tom Conway remains, unshakably, Tom Conway. If there are few really bad performances in Tourneur's films there are no great ones (with the possible exception of Mitchum in *Out of the Past;* and Mitchum, to adapt Michel Mourlet's famous remark about Charlton Heston, is an axiom). His best scenes are typically either atmospheric (certain sequences in the Lewton films discussed below) or ensemble scenes (the wedding in *Canyon Passage,* where the connecting camera-movement leads one to compare the status of the various couples present) in which individual performances are subordinated to a sense of relatedness between the parts.

It is obvious that all directors are dependent on their scripts; Tourneur appears unusually so. His chief qualities—words like "reticence" and "delicacy" come first to mind, rather than Sarris's somewhat belittling "gentility" (see his maddening, indispensable *American Cinema,* the most-thumbed reference work in my book collection)—are not necessarily negative ones but can easily become so. His bad films have nothing actively offensive about them; they are simply colourless and boring. Perhaps he could be fairly described as a born collaborator in search of someone with whom to collaborate. On the other hand, the humility that led him to accept whatever chores were thrown his way, however unpromising, is a quality that, in his best work, assumes great positive significance: *I Walked with a Zombie* is, in its masterly way, a lesson in humility.

Though I think it is Tourneur's contribution that distinguishes them from their companions in the series, I feel, then, that *Cat People* and *Zombie* should be regarded as group achievements, with due credit to Lewton and the scriptwriters—DeWitt Bodeen and Curt Siodmak respectively. Both films are beautifully planned and mostly (minus a few lapses into triteness) well-written; under Tourneur their implicit poetry reaches sensitive visual expression.

I have suggested that the two films are linked thematically as well as stylistically. Both are about honest, upright, uncomplicated Americans (in *Zombie,* in fact, a Canadian nurse primly commended by her employer and potential lover for her "clean, decent thinking") who are impinged upon by outside "foreign" forces at once sinister, mysterious and fascinating. The sociologically inclined will doubtless like to interpret the films in terms of American isolationism (as George A. Huaco in *The Sociology of Film Art* explains *Nosferatu* for us as reflecting "the growing economic crisis in 1922"). The treatment is in fact extremely complex and ambivalent.

Tourneur's father, Maurice, was not, as ignorant people like myself tended to assume, a director in France who emigrated to America to complete his career in Hollywood. It was precisely the other way round: from 1914 to 1926 he made films in America, then went to Europe where he continued making films, mostly in France, until 1948. Jacques, born in 1904, spent parts of his childhood in Europe and in fact began his career in France in 1931, where he made three films before settling in America in the late thirties. One would scarcely wish to claim him as a cinematic Henry James, but one can perhaps assume that the intermixture of American and European culture in his background gave him a particular sensitivity to the ambivalences inherent in the subject-matter of his Lewton films. (The presence, or at least the potential, of a similar ambivalence in the subject-matter of *Experiment Perilous* makes the failure of that film—Tourneur's inability, for whatever reason, to transcend the melodramatic banalities of the script—all the more disappointing.)

If the American protagonists embody a norm of straightforward decency, all the poetry emanates from the foreign elements; and in both films the decency is revealed as decidedly limited. One small, specific clue to Tourneur's sympathies can surely be found in the fact that the little song he gave Irena in *Cat People* is a French lullaby he remembered from his childhood. One is led to forget about geography and interpret the films in terms of an opposition between day-consciousness and night-consciousness, between a surface world of conventional and unimaginative "normality"—for want of a better word—and a far richer underworld of dangerous and fascinating dreams.

Some such opposition is, of course, a common and universal theme in the arts; it manifests itself in the American cinema with both frequency and intensity. It is there in *Sunrise,* in the comparison (implicit in the imagery) of the City Woman to a cat. (The fact that in that film sympathies are reversed, and the "underworld" is presented as almost exclusively evil and destructive, is more characteristic of German Expressionism than of Hollywood.) One need only mention—to suggest the variety of tone and manner, the range of genres in which it can clothe itself—*Bringing Up Baby* and *Marnie,* both of which use cats (leopard and jaguarundi, respectively) prominently in their imagery of the dangerous instinctual world on whose suppression bourgeois stability depends. Thematically, *Marnie* in particular offers fascinating and detailed parallels to *Cat People,* rendering explicit that film's psychological implications.

Confronted, however, with such delicate and reticent works, one wants to preserve a corresponding reticence in the interpretation. *Cat People* and *I Walked with a Zombie* both suggest, and in a more conscious and sophisticated way than is the case in the majority of horror films, that the myths they draw on are capable of psychological interpretation; neither is reducible

to clear-cut psychological allegory. They work by means of poetic suggestiveness rather than of clearly definable "meaning"
and any attempt to "explain" them beyond a certain point can
only do them harm. The sexual overtones of *Cat People* are clear
enough: Irena is afraid that her "cat" nature will be released if
she is sexually aroused, and it eventually *is* released by sexual
jealousy. Similarly, *I Walked with a Zombie* hints at an equation
between the zombie state ("the living dead") and emotional
death. But the film-makers have in both cases respected the poetic power of the myth. Psychological meaning remains a matter of suggestion; it is never insisted upon or spelled out. Rather
than attempt an allegorical interpretation (which would, inevitably, become an interpretation of the *script*), I want to examine
some of the films' poetic detail, or poetic *movement,* to show
something of their richness of suggestion.

The priest in Greene's *The Power and the Glory* regards ironically
the tendency of the good, and incorrigibly "innocent," Americans he meets to place cleanliness next to godliness—but only
just. *Cat People* opens (after an impressive-sounding quotation
about sin lingering on in the unconscious like fog in low places,
from *The Anatomy Atavism* by "Dr. Louis Judd," who turns out
later to be the glib and skeptical psychiatrist played by Tom
Conway) with a similarly ironic association of surface cleanliness with ignorance of deeper evils. Irena (Simone Simon) is
making her obsessive sketches, before the panther's cage in the
zoo, of a panther transfixed by a sword. When a discarded drawing fails to reach the litter basket, a young man (Kent Smith)
retrieves it and draws Irena's attention to the sign nearby: "Be
it not said, and said unto your shame / That all was beauty here
until you came." The same idea is referred to unobtrusively in
one of the film's climactic scenes: the build-up to the famous
sequence where Irena pursues Alice (Jane Randolph) along a
shadowy sidewalk at night is twice punctuated by brief scenes

in which a cleaning-woman meticulously flicks cigarette-ash off her uniform. The "cleanliness" motif consorts naturally with the "Protestant work ethic" epitomized by the song sung habitually by the man who cleans the cages in the zoo:

Nothing else to do,
Nothing else to do.
I strayed, went a-courting
'Cos I'd nothing else to do.

Honest toil and surface cleanliness are the safeguards against the dangers of sin and sexuality.

Such details point to the film's central opposition. Oliver, the young man at the zoo, is a draftsman in a ship designer's offices. As with Professor Cary Grant in *Bringing Up Baby,* the impersonal scientific activity represents a surface consciousness whose order depends on ignorance or rejection of the potentially chaotic world of unconscious forces and instincts; and, like Professor Grant, Oliver is involved with two girls, one who shares his work (it is nice that in both films she is called Alice) and one who embodies exactly those drives that threaten the surface order. But whereas Katharine Hepburn was content to own a leopard, Irena actually turns into a panther. Imagery derived from this basic opposition pervades the film. Even the apparently banal and incongruous moment when Oliver dismisses Irena-as-panther by brandishing a cross and exclaiming "in the name of God!" is partly redeemed by the fact that they are in the draftsmen's office and the cross is a set-square.

The film's delicate life is in the wealth of poetic invention. Oliver and Irena are in her dimly lit apartment. In the background an armchair casts its shadow on the wall. Oliver, lying on the sofa, declares his love for Irena. She draws back, disturbed, and her head becomes superimposed upon the shadow so that the uprights of the chair become cat's ears—the shape is very like that of the Egyptian cat-goddess beside which Irena pauses, later, in the museum. Characteristically, Tourneur does nothing to force the point—he neither cuts nor tracks in; the effect is conveyed solely through the actress's movement. Nor are such points underlined with music; credit for the discreet and sparing way in which music is used in these films (even truer of *Zombie* than of *Cat People*) doubtless belongs to Lewton as much as Tourneur, the score being one of the last things over which a Hollywood contract director is likely to have control. Later in the film, when Irena is spying on Oliver and Alice before her first attempt to kill her rival, Alice says, shuddering, as she and Oliver emerge from the building, "A cat walked over my grave." Tourneur cuts to Irena standing before the window of a flower-shop, with a wreath behind her. Most unobtrusive touch of all: the chain that bars Irena from the panther's cage during her nocturnal wanderings has, at the end of the film, when her animal nature has been released, mysteriously vanished.

But it would be false to give the impression of a series of isolated touches. To suggest how this delicate poetry pervades the movement of the whole film it is necessary to examine some extended sequences. Consider the sequence of the wedding night and the scenes that follow. During the celebration in the Serbian restaurant Irena is confronted by the cat-like woman who addresses her as "My sister." Afterwards, on the sidewalk outside Irena's apartment (where the couple are to live), she tells Oliver she cannot sleep with him yet, and asks him to be patient with her. Irena goes to the bedroom. We see Oliver standing helpless outside the closed door; cut to the other side of the door, where Irena is crouching, still hesitant. The mood is intensified by the snow falling outside the window in the background of the image. Irena's hand rises to the doorknob; the panther's cry comes through the night from the zoo; her hand draws back. Again, Tourneur's reticent style is crucial to the effect of the scene: a single, static shot, the camera at some distance from Irena at right of the screen, so that the darkness of the room behind her, the falling snow beyond the window in the left background, the distant, disturbing wail—all make, unforced, their contributions.

The next scene shows another of Irena's obsessive visits to the panther's cage and her dialogue with the keeper who, in response to her remarks about the panther's beauty, insists upon its ugliness and refers her to the Book of Revelations and the worst "Beast" of them all which was "like unto a leopard." The image of the snarling animal suggests both its beauty and its cruelty. The door that separated Irena from Oliver is paralleled by the cage that separates her from the panther: divided between two worlds, she is barred from access to either. The idea is taken up in the closing quotation—genuine, this time—from Donne's Holy Sonnet V: "But black sin hath condemn'd to endless night / My world, both parts, and both parts must die."

From this we are moved back to Irena's apartment. The sequence opens with an image that beautifully links what has gone before with what is to come: the painting of a black panther on a screen, over which falls the shadow of the cage of the bird Oliver has given Irena. The image provides a visual link with the previous scene, taking up the "caged panther" motif, and connects the panther with the bird. From this the camera moves back to take in Irena at her drawing-board, connecting her with the panther/bird image where cutting would have separated. She is working at a slick, commonplace fashion design, the image again suggesting the opposition between surface consciousness and unconscious forces. Irena stands back, and gives a little stretch, slightly drawing up her shoulders and curling her fingers, like a cat. Then she moves to the bird-cage, opens it, tries to take the bird in her hand. The bird flutters in wild hysteria, and an ambiguous smile comes on Irena's face: tender or sadistic? The bird dies of shock. The sequence ends with a long-shot of Irena standing desolate with the bird in her hand. In the foreground is the model of a ship, reminding us of Oliver and his work, balancing the expression of Irena's mysterious suppressed nature with the idea of conscious control.

There follows the scene where Irena takes the dead bird to the zoo and throws it to the caged panther, an action that crystallizes for us the ambiguity of her relationship to the beast. Most obviously (since Irena herself, at moments of crisis, assumes its form) it represents her *alter ego*. Yet it was emphasized earlier that it is a *male* panther; we may see it as an alternative potential mate to whom she is taking food, and the point is strengthened by the fact that the bird was originally a gift from Oliver. The action also suggests an act of propitiation, with the panther as some kind of dark god which Irena must appease with an offering.

Almost wherever one looks in the film one finds a similar accumulation of suggestive detail. The sequences of Irena's pursuit of Alice at night, and its aftermath, are particularly rich. Alice is alone in the draftsmen's office; Irena phones to ascertain that she is there, without herself speaking. The images of the two women, each with the receiver in hand, are very exactly balanced. Alice is lit from below by an illuminated table used for design work, Irena by a table-lamp. Beside Irena is the statue of King John of Serbia holding a speared panther aloft on his lance; beside Alice is a gentle domestic cat (called John Paul Jones). The sequence of the pursuit is a *locus classicus* of unnerving effects achieved with the utmost reticence and simplicity of means: movement, rhythmic editing, lighting, culminating in the film's one "shock" effect—the more startling for being unique—as the bus slides into the frame with a loud hissing noise just at the moment we expect the unseen panther to spring. This is followed by the shot of the dead, savaged sheep on which Irena has vented her animal fury (when we next see the panther, there is a leg of lamb in its cage!), with paw-marks deep in the mud; then by the simple, magical tracking-shot along the sidewalk as the paw-marks change, step by step, into the marks of high-heeled shoes and we see Irena walking slowly away, dazed—the juxtaposition recalling that of the panther-painting and the fashion sketch in her apartment. Later, when Irena has returned home, we see the base of her bathtub, resting on a foot shaped like an animal's claw, and the camera moves up to show Irena above, sitting in the bath, weeping, the unbroken camera-movement connecting her to the claw-foot, subtly underlining our sense of her divided self and of her poignant helplessness.

There follows the brief sequence of Irena's dream, one of the finest dream sequences in the cinema because so packed, complex and suggestive. Black panther shapes move outward gracefully and ominously towards the camera. From behind them emerges what at first appears to be an erect panther-figure but then reveals itself as Dr. Judd, the psychiatrist, dressed in chain-mail as King John the avenger. It was Judd who, earlier, at the zoo, brought to consciousness Irena's desire to steal the key of the panther's cage. In the dream, his sword becomes the key, and she wakes up knowing she must steal it. The dream is rich in ambiguities which relate to the role Judd plays but are characteristic of the manner of the whole film, at once concrete and mysterious, always eluding clear-cut definition.

Judd is ostensibly the doctor whose job it is to banish Irena's irrational fears, but he is also another potential mate. Therefore, in the dream he is both panther and avenging knight; he carries the sword which should destroy the panther but it becomes the key that will release it. The sword is also, of course, associated with the blade inside his cane which later transfixes Irena. Yet his identification with King John is always at least half-ironic: if he eventually kills the panther, he is also destroyed by it. The dream, in drawing together so many threads, concisely embodies the film's sense of life itself as a shadow-world in which nothing is certain, no issue is clear-cut, nothing is what it seems. The film's attitude to psychology is also very interesting. Coming somewhat in the vanguard of Hollywood's belated discovery of Freud as a subject for more than party jokes in the forties (it antedates Hitchcock's *Spellbound* and Lang's *Secret Beyond the Door* by several years), it suggests the possibility of psychological interpretation while regarding such interpretation with a healthy skepticism.

I am glad to find that Tourneur (in an interview in *Positif*, No. 132) considers *I Walked with a Zombie* the finer film of the two and, with *Stars in my Crown* and *Out of the Past*, one of his three best movies. He also claims it as (again with *Stars in My Crown*, which I have not been able to see) one of the only two of his films which he has been in on right from the original conception. Though Tourneur's claim that *he* had the idea of doing "Jane Eyre in the West Indies" is contradicted by DeWitt Bodeen (in *Films in Review*, April 1963), who says the idea was Lewton's, it does not finally matter. It is clear from the way Tourneur talks about *Zombie* that he regards it as one of his most personal works, and this is certainly confirmed by the film itself.

Tourneur's style, and the natural way it associates with Lewton's taste and intelligence, can be fittingly illustrated by *Zombie*'s most celebrated atmospheric set-piece; the scene in which Betsy, the Canadian nurse (Frances Dee), takes her patient to a nocturnal voodoo meeting in a desperate attempt to cure her. The women's departure is shown in a camera movement that spatially connects the central characters. We see the front of the house from a medium-shot position, the foreground of the screen in darkness, with the foliage of the garden suggesting the night world beyond the safety of the lighted house; the half-brothers, Paul (Tom Conway) and Wesley (James Ellison), are disclosed in turn, the former working, the latter drinking, in separate parts of the building. As the camera turns, the two women, in distant long-shot, emerge from the door leading to the tower where Paul's invalid wife is kept, and the camera follows them, still keeping its distance, as they move away from the possibility of male protection and towards the darkness. The shot combines all the functions of long-shot/camera-movement style: it connects different lives being lived separately but simultaneously. By placing the characters in an environment (where close-up would detach them from it), it enhances the atmospheric qualities of the scene; by keeping different characters in our minds simultaneously; and by preserving physical distance, it also encourages a certain *emotional* distance. We never become identified with Betsy or her actions, hence are free to consider their implications judicially.

The ensuing progress through the cane fields evokes memories of the sidewalk pursuit in *Cat People;* there is a similar delicacy and simplicity. The sequence is introduced by a medium-longshot, from a medium-low angle, of an unnaturally tall, gaunt negro standing in the shadowy moonlight at a crossing of paths in the middle of the cane-fields. The image has a dream-like quality—inexplicable, haunting, beautiful and sinister. It creates unease without any suggestion of a shock effect. It also gives us a sense that the journey to the voodoo meeting is a journey into dream. The women's movement is filmed mostly in medium-long-shot, often with foliage intervening between characters and camera; and the various sinister details en route, signposting the way, are introduced without over-emphasis, the entire sequence being notable for a total absence of music (until the voodoo drums become audible through the night). Especially characteristic is the introduction of the giant negro at the cross-roads: the camera follows the light from Betsy's torch as it moves forward along the ground, until it suddenly encounters a dark foot. There is no shock-cut, no crashing chord; the *frisson* arises from the simple process of discovery, without underlining. The sequence, recalling others like it in this and other Tourneur movies, is unlike the work of any other American director I can think of. The director it evokes, for me, irresistibly, is Mizoguchi—the Mizoguchi of *Ugetsu Monogatari.*

The theme of "clean, decent-thinking" North Americans impinged upon by disturbing outside forces—or of the relationship between the day-world and the night-world—is handled more subtly and complexly in *Zombie* than in *Cat People.* Leaving aside for a moment the film's supernatural elements, consider the use Tourneur makes of the calypso singer, Sir Lancelot. Though black/white oppositions play a characteristically ambiguous part in the poetic texture of the film, the racial issue never becomes a dominant theme. It is, however, touched upon, and has its relevance in the pattern of associations the film sets up: voodoo—darkness—the subconscious; zombiism—emotional paralysis—spiritual death; psychological repression—slavery—the continuing resentment of the black people towards the whites.

Tourneur in the *Positif* interview expresses satisfaction in the fact that he has always treated negroes with respect in his films, taking a stand against the pervasive tendency to restrict them to undignified roles; and his satisfaction is certainly justified. There cannot be many Hollywood movies of the early forties in which a coloured character is permitted to make sly, malicious fun of whites who are neither comic nor villainous—with the film's at least partial endorsement—and get away with it. One could, I think, find Tourneur's use of Sir Lancelot more acceptable, in its unobtrusive way, than the pious (hence insidiously condescending) treatment of blacks in the later forties movies that began to handle racial issues explicitly.

The end of the sequence in which Sir Lancelot appears draws together several threads of the film. As the singer approaches Betsy and the unconscious Wesley (he has drunk himself to sleep at the table) out of the darkness in a slow, threatening advance, singing his insultingly personal calypso, he becomes associated with the mysterious, disturbing forces by which Betsy feels herself menaced. Yet the fact that, previously, his dignity, intelligence and irony have engaged our sympathy serves to detach us further from Betsy; we cannot simply share *her* awareness of him as a threat. Although, obviously, she is the heroine of the film, our consciousness of the overall action is never limited to her point of view.

The superiority of *I Walked with a Zombie* over *Cat People* is primarily one of structure: of—in so far as the distinction is possible—poetic structure rather than narrative structure. The linear progression of the earlier film, the development of its story, leaves nothing to be desired; but in *Zombie* the poetic resonances, the suggestive ambiguities and uncertainties, are more meaningfully organized. It is by no means a matter of explaining, resolving or simplifying them—if anything, the contrary. In *Cat People* the opposition between the "day" characters and the "night" world remains clear-cut. Only Oliver's attraction to Irena implicates him in the mysterious urges she embodies; he never reveals anything corresponding to them within himself. But in *Zombie* such barriers are dissolved. The night-world pervades everything and implicates everyone, even Betsy. To analyse the film is but to define its ambiguities.

At its centre are two related figures: T-Misery and Carrefour. T-Misery is the name the blacks give to the figurehead (now a statue in the garden, streaming with water like tears) from the boat that brought the first slaves. He is himself an ambiguous figure, fusing the film's oppositions. All stuck with arrows, he is St. Sebastian, the Christian martyr; yet he is also unmistakably negroid, and to the blacks the embodiment of slavery. Carrefour, the guardian of the cross-roads, bears a striking facial resemblance to him. He is a zombie, and, as his name suggests, the intermediary between the two worlds, the messenger the night-world sends to claim its dues.

The clue to reading the film is given us in Paul's speech on the boat that brings Betsy to the island (itself called St. Sebastian). He tells her that the beauty she's admiring is illusory, the phosphorescence that makes the ocean seem alive is produced by a myriad of dead and decomposing creatures, she is coming to a world where nothing is what it seems. By the end of the film *everything* has proved to be other than what it seemed—even the motives of clean, decent-thinking Betsy herself.

The quiet, intense poetry of the film is evident in the scene of Betsy's first encounter with her patient, Jessica. It opens with a shot of T-Misery, and with the sound of weeping (seeming at first, disturbingly, to emanate from the statue) which awakens Betsy. She crosses the courtyard to the tower door, from which the crying is issuing. When she has climbed the stairs she is pursued by Jessica, unnaturally tall and gaunt, moving like a sleepwalker. The heroine threatened by a sinister figure—yet Betsy is in black, Jessica in white.

This poetic ambiguity is developed in the cane fields sequence, where each woman is given a lace badge that will allow her to be "passed" by Carrefour and will gain her admittance to the voodoo meeting; Betsy, in black, has a white badge (which catches, unnoticed, on the foliage as they push their way through), Jessica, in white, a black. The weeping is subsequently explained. It was the maid mourning the birth of her sister's child; for the tradition has been handed down through generations of slaves that one mourns birth, rejoices at death.

Uncertainty, ambiguity, the reversal of expectations, pervade every aspect of the film. Who is responsible for Jessica's state? Betsy's lover, Wesley, with whom she was about to run away? Her husband, Paul, who (according to Wesley—and Paul's treatment of Betsy offers some confirmation) destroys all sense of beauty, all feeling for life? Their mother, Mrs. Rand, who believes herself responsible for Jessica's being a zombie, deadening spontaneous instinct to preserve family unity? What is Betsy's real motive for persuading Paul to give permission for Jessica to have insulin shock treatment (which the doctor warns may kill her), or later, for taking her to the voodoo meeting? Does she (already in love with Paul) want to cure Jessica (as she clearly believes she does) or to kill her? She is, in Paul's words, the "nurse who's afraid of the dark"—which means, in the terms suggested by the film, afraid of her own subconscious.

I remember, during my first viewing of the film, at the end of the "insulin" sequence, thinking, "But don't Tourneur and Lewton realize that Betsy probably wanted Jessica to die?"—as she and Paul are expressing their disappointment that the treatment has had no effect. At which precise moment Wesley stepped out of the shadows and accused them of just that. Which shows how one can still underestimate the possible subtleties of an unassuming little Hollywood thriller. The ambiguities come nearest to explicitness in the revelation of Mrs. Rand's involvement with voodoo. Is she Christianizing voodoo or voodooizing Christianity ("I should have known there's no easy way to do good, Betsy")?

The shadows and half-lights of the film's haunting atmospheric quality are in fact but the expression of its moral and spiritual world, in which nothing is fixed or certain, nothing is as it seems: a world subtly dominated by the subconscious, a world of shadows in which we can do no more than cautiously and hesitantly grope. The last, magical, sequence of the film beautifully and movingly unifies many of its poetic motifs. The emotional paralysis that deadens the lives of the characters is dissipated not by the exercise of conscious reason but by a cathartic gesture activated by the subconscious: Wesley at last kills Jessica, and then himself. He kills her by driving through her heart an arrow plucked from T-Misery; his actions are subconsciously induced by voodoo. He carries her body out into the sea, which in Paul's speech on the boat became an embodiment of simultaneous beauty and horror, and drowns himself. As he carries her down the shore, he is followed by Carrefour, arms outstretched; and it is Carrefour who bears Jessica's body back to the house when it is retrieved by fishermen, at night, their spears and torches adding a visual poetry to the poetry inherent in the ideas. The film ends with a track-in on T-Misery. *I Walked with a Zombie* is a small masterpiece—perhaps the most delicate poetic fantasy in the American cinema.

11

The Ghost Princess and the Seaweed Gatherer
Ugetsu Monogatari and *Sansho Dayu*

> He had taken a Chinese drawing of geese from the boudoir,
> and was copying it, with much skill and vividness. . . .
>   "But why do you copy it?" she asked. . . .
>   "I want to know it," he replied. "One gets more of China,
> copying this picture, than reading all the books."
>   D. H. LAWRENCE, *Women in Love*

A colleague told me recently that he would not feel qualified to talk about Ozu and Mizoguchi; that he would not know how to approach them; that he could do so only in terms of *mise-en-scène*. In the context of the conversation it was clear that this was a covert reprimand rather than an expression of humility: my colleague meant that he did not know enough about the circumstances of production within which the films were made (the Japanese film industry, social-political-cultural conditions at the time) or about the conventions on which they draw and the cultural tradition within which those conventions developed; and he implied (correctly) that I knew no more than he. I think we were both aware that fundamental principles were involved, though neither of us pursued them: fundamental questions about the nature and function of art and the status of individual works: art as art, or art as social process. My own position with regard to movies from "alien" cultures is implicit in earlier essays in this book. I think any knowledge one might acquire about cultural background and circumstances of production is potentially useful, but also potentially dangerous: useful, as a test of one's own perceptions; dangerous, because such knowledge of a culture which must necessarily remain alien however much information we acquire, can easily influence our reading of individual works disproportionately: we begin to see "Japanese culture" instead of Mizoguchi. A "realized" work of art will, by and large, carry its explanation within itself, for anyone willing to trust (however provisionally) his instincts and imagination.

Around the same time, one of my students told me, during a seminar, about Yin and Yang. Yin and Yang are, in Japanese tradition, the passive and active principles respectively; they correspond to the moon and sun, woman and man, water and fire. My student applied them (resourcefully, I thought) to the water and fire imagery of *Sansho Dayu*. I like Yin and Yang; I find them immensely reassuring. They confirm for me that I had understood *Sansho Dayu* before I heard of either of them. They figure, I think, in most mythologies (e.g., Diana and Apollo) and in the novels of D. H. Lawrence (e.g., *The Rainbow*). They help me to make my point: that (give or take a few details) the essential significance of *Sansho Dayu* can be deduced from the specific realization of the film; that, at most, one needs a knowledge of a few other Japanese films from the same period in order to confirm one's deductions. How many westerns must one see before one can confidently interpret *Rio Bravo* or *The Searchers*? A few, I think: perhaps four or five. I am aware (and could, I think, have deduced without being told) that the styles of Ozu and Mizoguchi derive from various traditional elements in Japanese art—particularly drama and painting. I cannot imagine how a more detailed knowledge of these elements than I have would significantly affect the way in which I read the films.

An attempt to define the art of Mizoguchi can usefully take as its starting-point comparison with his great contemporary Ozu. It must be said at once that any general definition must be tentative in the extreme, being based on only a small proportion of each director's work: about a dozen Mizoguchis and only half

In the opening shot of *Sansho Dayu*, the boy Zushio and his family
move through the forest toward his exiled father.

as many Ozus, mainly late works in both cases. The enterprise
is further complicated by the great range of subject-matter and
expression within Mizoguchi's work. Rather than attempt to offer generalizations that would cover even all his accessible films,
I am limiting this essay to only two, though they seem to me the
greatest and most completely representative of those I have seen:
Sansho Dayu and *Ugetsu Monogatari*. They are closely related to
each other, and the other late works—including those with a
modern setting like the magnificent *Uwasa No Onna* ("Woman
of Rumour") and even a film as different in obvious ways as
Street of Shame—can be seen to relate significantly to them: one
might reasonably claim that they represent, together, a central
core within Mizoguchi's late period, though others might wish

to make similar claims for *Shin Heike Monogatari* or *Yang Kwei Fei*.

Although Ozu and Mizoguchi, when juxtaposed, appear in many ways polar opposites, both have been placed in opposition to the more Western- (and "western"-) influenced Kurosawa. Kurosawa's work is studded with adaptations of Western literature; his films not only show the influence of the Western cinema but lend themselves in turn to adaptation, so that at least four have been re-made in Hollywood or Italy. No one seems to be rushing to re-make *Tokyo Story* or *Sansho Dayu* in an American setting, though the subject-matter of neither would present insuperable difficulties. The films' tone and style are felt as somehow indigenously Japanese, though it is difficult to link them beyond a somewhat loose application of the adjective "contemplative." Mizoguchi's style shows greater affinities with that of Ophuls on the one hand and Rossellini on the other than with that of any other Japanese director within my experience, yet one does not think of him as in any sense deriving from European cinema: any resemblances seem fortuitous, a matter of spiritual affinity rather than influence in either direction. One guesses that the late styles of both Mizoguchi and Ozu are the product of a long period of evolution within the Japanese cinema, and, beyond it, within Japanese culture.

Ozu's visual compositions are dominated by the square and the rectangle; Mizoguchi's are characterized by an equally striking and pervasive emphasis on diagonals. The tendency of Ozu's cinema is towards a series of "stills." His characters either face the camera directly or sit or stand at right angles to it. The square or rectangular patterns of the décor—walls or doorways or windows—often frame them as if to enclose each in his or her separate compartment. Each image takes on the quality of a framed picture, as if cut off from any outer world beyond the confines of the screen. When characters enter or leave the frame during a shot, they do so behind an intruding screen or partition; the unity of the image and enclosedness of the frame are carefully preserved. The spectator's eye is directed always towards the figure at the centre of the composition, almost never towards the periphery.

The composition even of static dialogue scenes in Mizoguchi is habitually built on diagonals cutting across the screen. The characters are placed at oblique angles to the camera, and so are the mats on which they sit; where Ozu tends to place his actors squarely against walls or doorways, Mizoguchi typically uses a corner as focal point. However beautifully organized the composition (and there are no more beautiful compositions anywhere in the cinema), the diagonals invariably lead the eye outwards, always implying a world beyond the frame. What is true of interiors is equally so of exteriors. Paths cross the screen diagonally; in *Ugetsu* the boat bearing the dying fisherman emerges through the mist at an oblique angle to the boat poled by Ohama; in *Madame Yuki* a speedboat and its wake cut a diagonal line across the image.

This contrast is reinforced by the totally opposed camera styles of the two directors. In late Ozu the camera virtually never moves; to cut from static image to static image is to detach and separate little segments of the world as objects of contemplation. In late Mizoguchi the camera moves in the great majority of shots, and the movements are frequently long and elaborate; to move the camera so that one part of the world is excluded while another is framed, is to unite, to make connections. If "Cinema of Contemplation" is a phrase applicable to the work of both directors it is a much more adequate description of Ozu than of Mizoguchi: the contemplative aspect of the latter's work is continually balanced, and at times superseded, by its dynamism. Ozu's characters (in the late films) almost never touch—an abstention that confers great importance on even the simplest hand-clasp, by virtue of its rarity. Mizoguchi's characters, on the other hand, always relate to one another physically, often with great intensity: witness any of the emotional climaxes in his films. And a general observation about the content of their respective *oeuvres* is relevant here. Both deal recurrently with the theme of the Family; but where characteristically Ozu's people are finally separate, alone, Mizoguchi's move almost invariably towards union, mystical rather than physical, even when some of them are dead. The stylistic differences are clearly related to—if not actually expressive of—this opposition in overall movement.

An example will help to clarify the part played by the contemplative in Mizoguchi's style. Consider (as representative rather than exceptional) the brief scene in *Sansho Dayu* where Zushio, seeking redress for the horrors Sansho has perpetrated, attempts to confront the minister with a petition and is overcome and dragged away to prison by guards. The tracking-shot that accompanies Zushio's desperate efforts to be heard is far from contemplative: it involves the viewer very directly in the scene's hectic movement, in the urgency and near-hysteria of the young man. Mizoguchi does not cut away to show us the guards approaching—they suddenly irrupt into the frame from all sides. This is immediately recognizable as a recurrent motif in Mizoguchi's films: other striking examples are the mother's attempted escape from the island of Sado in *Sansho* and the rape of Ohama in *Ugetsu*. The sudden intrusion of hostile, menacing forces into the foreground of the image, surrounding and overwhelming the protagonist, forcefully expresses the director's sense of the precariousness of things, the continual imminence of disaster, his characters' terrible vulnerability. It also suggests the dynamic nature of his style, the sense of a world beyond the frame, the compositions never final, subject to continual variation and modification. But equally striking, and equally typical, is the sudden cut to long-shot at the climactic moment as Zushio is overcome, the action abruptly distanced, the foreground of the shot occupied by a large, decorative, bushy tree.

The violence, and the hero's frenzied screams, are suddenly placed in a context of stillness and serenity. The opposition is central to Mizoguchi's art, and to his vision of life.

Or consider the shot, after Ohama's rape in *Ugetsu,* of her sandals (which have fallen off in the struggle) on the beach. It is in some ways a fairly close equivalent to those series of shots of landscapes or townscapes that punctuate Ozu's films, generally used as transitions from scene to scene or from one time of day to another, having something of the function of establishing shots, but serving primarily as points of meditation, the action of the film suspended, the eye and mind given an emotionally neutral view—or, at least, a view not directly related to the immediate narrative—on which to rest for a moment. But herein lies an important difference: the shot of the sandals provides, certainly, a still point of meditation after the emotional and physical turmoil that have preceded it, yet it is by no means divorced from the action nor emotionally neutral. The stillness and emptiness of the shot emphasize, by contrast, the journey structure on which the film is built; its desolate effect arises from a complex of contextual implications, chief among which is our sense of her husband Tobei's responsibility for Ohama's fate. Where Ozu's "punctuating" shots are still points of pure contemplation, the shot of the sandals encourages in the spectator that precise balancing of contemplation and involvement characteristic of Mizoguchi.

The vivifying impulse in Mizoguchi's late films is towards wholeness and unity, and this is expressed in stylistic detail as surely as in overall movement. It is an impulse that necessitates the maintenance of a certain emotional distance between artist and material, the purpose of which is not to deny or diminish the emotional intensity inherent in the action, but to place it in a wider context, a context both spatial and temporal. An event in a Mizoguchi film is never felt as isolated. We are not allowed to respond simply, with the immediate emotional reactions the event might provoke: we are encouraged to view the event within a cosmic perspective. If this sounds mystical (and we are perhaps too ready, in the west, to distrust mysticism, or confuse it with mere vagueness), it can be pinned down in the concrete detail of Mizoguchi's *mise-en-scène*. Consider two scenes where the emotional content is inherently very powerful, the kidnapping in *Sansho*, the mortal wounding of Miyagi in *Ugetsu*. Both can stand as representative of Mizoguchi's method, though they are in some respects stylistically dissimilar: the underlying assumptions about life, about values, about the function of art, about the relationship between the spectator and the action on the screen, are the same.

Sansho: Tamaki and her two children Zushio and Anju, on their way to join their exiled husband/father, are sheltered and fed by an elderly priestess who persuades Tamaki to continue the journey by boat. She in fact betrays them: Tamaki and the children's old nurse are carried off in the boat while the priestess and another boatman hold the children; the nurse, too old to be a valuable commodity, is thrown overboard and drowns, the children break away and rush to the water's edge but are swiftly recaptured. Stylistically three aspects stand out: dynamic movement, whether of the camera or within the frame, communicating the intensity of the protagonists' struggle against separation; a preponderance of long-shots that place the violence, grief and turbulence of the action in a context of natural tranquility—smooth water, still sky, motionless rushes and bare tree; superb deep focus images. At the beginning of the sequence the boatmen are introduced in an image dominated by the leafless, thorny tree left of screen but centred on the fire, beside which the men rouse to sinister alertness as they become aware of the family's approach: the juxtaposition of fire and water is a unifying motif to which I shall return.

The emotional distance implied by the use of long-shot has nothing of coldness or complacency: the extraordinary intensity with which the action is staged amply testifies to Mizoguchi's readiness to enter fully into his characters' anguish. The use of long-shot is of course inseparable from the use of deep focus. The effect is to hold the action at a distance while consistently emphasizing its reality. Nowhere in the cinema has the reality of physical space been used to more eloquent effect. Mizoguchi cross-cuts between boat and shore, but never fragments, never destroys our sense of the unity of the action: from the boat, Tamaki in the foreground, we can see the children struggling to escape, straining towards her; from the shore, children in the foreground, Tamaki's frantic efforts to return are shown in crystal-clear long-shot. From shot to shot, the widening of the distance separating them is rendered with scrupulous precision, and the distance is always physically there on the screen, shore and boat in the same image. The style here implies the essential theme of the film, the tension between physical separation and spiritual unity, the family forcibly held apart yet united by Mizoguchi within the frame.

Ugetsu: Miyagi, trying to return home with her child, is attacked on a mountain path by three starving outcasts (perhaps deserters) who steal the rice-cakes she has been given. When she protests, one of them drives a spear into her. Her little boy still on her back, she staggers on, supporting herself on a stick. Here, there is no cutting: the scene is a classic example of what the French call the *plan-séquence,* the "sequence" organized within a single shot. But the preservation of spatial reality within the image, and the preservation of the spectator's distance from the action, are again crucial to the total effect.

For the great majority of directors, the temptation here would be to go for impact: one "could invent a breakdown of the scene into twenty or so shots—close-ups of the men emerging from the hut, of Miyagi's frightened face, of the spear driven in, of the screaming, terrified child, of the woman in agony, of the men, showing their callous indifference—which could be immensely powerful in its force and directness. Mizoguchi's long take holds the spectator at a distance throughout, preserves the unity and continuity of the action, and preserves the sense of environment of the action situated in a real world governed by the realities of time and space. We are not asked to respond simply and directly to the physical horror of a spear entering a woman's belly, but to an event existing in a context. The detachment with which the camera compels us to watch the action makes the emotion it evokes much less immediate and overwhelming, but also much finer and deeper: we are free to contemplate the scene's wider implications, to reflect on the events that have preceded it and its likely consequences.

The organization of the complex action over a large area within a single take is remarkable: one would call it virtuoso did not the word carry connotations of display, the technique here being self-effacing in the extreme. The staging has many of the features one thinks of as characteristically Mizoguchian. The camera position is slightly above the action, in the interests of clarity: from it, we can see not only the path and the hut, but down into the valley below. The path crosses the screen diagonally. As Miyagi walks along it, the child on her back, the men emerge from the sides of the screen, eventually surrounding her—our minds are led back to the parallel scene of the rape of Ohama. The men steal the food, one of them wounds Miyagi, they disappear down the slope. Miyagi struggles to her feet and staggers on; the camera tracks with her, revealing the stick she takes to support herself, which lies at right angles to the path, hence making another diagonal to the frame—all the composition's main lines point outwards to the world beyond the screen. As Miyagi and the camera move on, we can see the men again in extreme long-shot in the valley, quarrelling and fighting over the meagre bits of food, their movements providing a strong if distant visual counterpoint to Miyagi's. The pain of the woman is placed in a context of universal disorder and suffering; our horror at the men's indifference is qualified by a sense of a world in which human beings starve to death and are degraded to an animal-like struggle for survival.

It is known that Mizoguchi had problems with *Ugetsu:* specifically, he was forced for box-office reasons to change his conception of the sub-plot. Originally, Tobei and Ohama were to have progressed, ironically, to great material prosperity and worldly fame as samurai and courtesan respectively; the ending would therefore have balanced worldly gain/spiritual loss (Tobei and Ohama) against worldly loss/spiritual gain (Genjuro and Miyagi). The film's actual ending provides a contrast that is much less sharp. In material terms, both men are back to square one, but Genjuro has developed spiritually while Tobei has merely accepted his lot; Genjuro and Miyagi achieve ideal union, though on opposite sides of the grave, while Tobei resigns himself guiltily to the aggressive domination of a very much alive Ohama. The resolution of the action works well enough, but the last-minute alterations in the scenario may be at least partly responsible for one's sense that the two plots are not very successfully integrated in the second half of the film. A worse flaw seems to me the awkward and arbitrary introduction of the Buddhist priest who "sees" Genjuro's fate in his face, though it is not impossible that there is a cultural barrier here, a convention operating to which Japanese audiences would know how to respond. Relative to *Sansho,* one must judge *Ugetsu* structurally flawed, though it is still possible to value it above almost every other work in the cinema. Two elements in the film seem to me to demand attention if one is to offer some justification for so high an estimate; Mizoguchi's magical evocation of the supernatural in the central scenes, and the reconciliation with reality, with "normal" human experience, towards which the whole film moves.

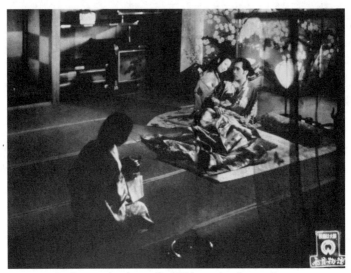

Genjuro under the spell of Wakasa, the ghost princess,
in *Ugetsu Monogatari*.

No film-maker in my experience—not even Tourneur or
Dreyer—has treated the supernatural with such delicacy and
respect, with such subtle force of suggestion and so rigorous a
refusal to sensationalize or vulgarize. Strikingly, the treatment
involves the complete eschewal of all camera trickery and "special effects"; Mizoguchi refuses to tamper with the reality within
the image, restricting his eerie effects to what décor and lighting
can achieve and the camera record. Hence the suggestion that
the Princess Wakasa's mansion exists in a world outside time
is conveyed by our being shown it, unobtrusively and without
comment, in three different conditions: first, derelict and decaying, the garden overgrown, the broken gate swinging on its
hinges; second, magically restored and revivified by Genjuro's
entry into it, the garden neat, the walls, windows and panels as
new, servant-girls emerging with candle-flames; third, as ruins,

a few blackened sticks and struts (over which lie the kimonos Genjuro bought for Wakasa) rising out of apparently uncultivated grass. The film's other great "supernatural" effect—the apparition of Miyagi to welcome her husband home—is even more remarkable. The camera is inside the house as Genjuro approaches, looks in at the window, opens the door and enters. The room is quite bare and unkept. He walks across it hesitantly, calling Miyagi, and the camera pans left with him, excluding the right hand part of the room. He goes out through another door, left, and we see him through windows walking round outside, back to the front entrance. The camera accordingly moves back with him; but this time, as the rest of the room comes back within the frame, we see that its décor has been miraculously restored and that Miyagi is in the middle of it, cooking over a fire, awaiting Genjuro, who sees her as he re-enters, the camera now having returned to its original position. The *frisson* this moment excites is due largely to the simple technical fact that there has been no cut, no dissolve, no editing of any kind: the impossible has happened before our eyes.

The respect Mizoguchi accords the supernatural stylistically, also involves rejecting any temptation to rationalize it. If we are led to find symbolic meaning in *Ugetsu*'s ghosts, it is by a process of suggestion that never destroys or undermines our sense of wonder. The "meaning" is suggested, I think, by the parallel my above description implies. In both scenes, the house is, as it were, brought back to life by the man's entry into it. The scene with the ghost Miyagi clearly associates this with the restoration of marital and family union; but the ghosts of the central sequences, Wakasa and her nurse, were also motivated by the desire that Wakasa be fulfilled through marriage. The resemblances encourage us to connect the scenes in our minds, but the purpose of the parallel is clearly to make us aware of major oppositions. The Wakasa world, outside time, is associated with illusion, with the dream-fulfilment of unrealizable aspirations (the pottery vessels that Genjuro recognizes, somewhat hesitantly, as his own, were clearly never made by him in the "real" world), and ultimately with death—the only condition wherein the desire to escape from the stresses and responsibilities of reality can be fulfilled. Mizoguchi creates its seductive beauty in a style that contrasts with that of the rest of the film while remaining recognizably Mizoguchian: the compositions are still built on diagonals, the camera still moves fluently, but the images look much more consciously and artfully composed, the camera moves away from one such beautiful composition precisely to frame another. We are also, here, brought in much closer to the actors than elsewhere in the film: even in the culminating erotic scene on the lawn, there is a sense of oppressiveness. Wakasa urges Genjuro to stay with her and perfect his art—the art represented by the delicate objects she has presented as his creations, "art for art's sake," rarefied and out of touch with the outside reality where Miyagi suffers. At the end of the film Genjuro, mystically united with his dead wife, is turning a pot under her spiritual guidance, a pot as different from the *objets d'art* of the Wakasa world as it is from the crudely functional, mass-produced "commercial" vessels we saw Genjuro making and selling earlier. The new dedication he brings to the work comes across as the outcome of assimilated experience: the artisan has become an artist, in the full Mizoguchian sense, the sense, that is, defined by the style, structure and significance of the late films. The fineness and depth of Mizoguchi's sensibility can be gauged from the way in which, having created for us the Wakasa dreamworld with such richness of sensuous beauty, he can lead us to find greater beauty in Genjuro's ultimate reconciliation with the real world and the processes of life-in-time.

From the film's last sequence I want to single out two shots in which the assimilative impulse of Mizoguchi's art finds perfect expression. One is the shot of Genjuro at Miyagi's grave. He asks why she had to die; her voice tells him softly that she is there beside him. The camera has already begun to track back, and as Miyagi speaks we see first the empty space beside Genjuro and then their son, kneeling at the graveside—the child in whom both parents are reunited, who represents what is perhaps the only immortality to which men should presume to aspire: immortality through continuity, and through what is transmitted. The second shot is the last of the film. In the background, Genjuro is tending his kiln, the pots so lovingly created, conceived as the joint work of man and wife, are baking; in the foreground, Ohama gives the child a bowlful of the rice she has been cooking. He runs off to the right, and the camera tracks with him to Miyagi's grave. He places the rice before the grave as if his mother were still alive, and the camera cranes up away from him to reveal again the landscape with which the film opened, with two men in the distance at work in the fields. Several factors contribute to making this one of the most poignantly beautiful last shots of any film. First, the continuity of camera movement that connects all the components of the scene: the pots baking, the child moving between father and mother, the underlying sense communicated of the triumph of the spirit over death, of the family mystically reconstituted and reunited, new life developing out of this reaffirmed unity. Second, the sense of continuity hinted at in the two labourers (for the film opened with Genjuro and Tobei leaving for the town), the sense of other lives being lived, similar to those whose progress we have watched yet different, each unique. Third, the shot formally reverses the opening shot of the film, which started on the same landscape and moved left and downwards to show Genjuro with his cart. It is not just a case of a satisfying formal symmetry: having shown us Genjuro's story, Mizoguchi turns us outward, to the world, and the potentialities for experience it offers every individual. The total effect is to universalize the action, to suggest that the narrative we have watched unfold is at once unique and typical, that the path towards spiritual acceptance and assimilation is there for each man to tread in his own way.

I have hinted that in certain respects *Ugetsu* can be read as Mizoguchi's artistic testament. The three kinds of pottery with which Genjuro is associated, and more particularly his attitudes to them and the personal developments with which each is linked, are very suggestive from this viewpoint, especially in conjunction with the stylistic contrast I have noted within the film. Mizoguchi through his narrative rejects commercialism (the pursuit of easy money separated Genjuro from Miyagi) on the one hand, and "ivory tower" aestheticism (the claustrophobic though alluring world of Wakasa) on the other, in favour of a progress towards an art that will truly express the assimilated experience of life, art that resolves the dichotomy of "personal" and "impersonal" by growing out of experience yet commanding that experience through understanding and acceptance. *Sansho Dayu,* made a year after *Ugetsu,* can be regarded as the perfect equivalent for the pottery Genjuro is making at the end of the earlier film. The parallels between the two films are in some ways very close. If one regrets the absence from *Sansho* of the supernatural dimension that gives *Ugetsu* its uniquely haunting and suggestive quality, this is more than compensated for by the later film's undeniable superiority in structure and by the poetic density its structural perfection makes possible; for by "structure" here I wish to imply not only something that could be schematically worked out on paper but the delicate inter-relationship of all the parts down to the smallest details.

The inter-relationships are so intricate, so much the product of a supreme creative genius at its most alive (the aliveness a matter of the free intercourse between the conscious and the intuitive), that complete analysis seems neither possible nor desirable: it would quickly become unwieldy. Looking for some way into the film that will make it possible to suggest its nature without laborious over-explicitness, I fasten on its recurrent fire and water imagery, as an aspect conveniently limited yet clearly central. I use the word "imagery" (rather than "symbolism") advisedly: the most cursory consideration of the film should suggest at once the undeniable unifying significance of fire and water and the lack of any rigid schematic meaning attaching to them. Water is frequently associated with the women, and with the concepts of patience and passive endurance; fire is often linked with violence and active cruelty. But the opposition is by no means inflexible. The sea is associated naturally with danger ("Is the sea safe?" Tamaki asks the treacherous priestess the night before the kidnapping), separation (Tamaki helplessly calling to her children from the cliff on the island of Sado) and natural disaster (the tidal wave that has drowned great numbers of people referred to at the end of the film). Mizoguchi never imposes symbolism on the action. Accordingly, the significance of the recurrent imagery is to be interpreted flexibly, in relation to the events with which it is linked; as the film progresses, it accumulates complex emotional overtones from the shifting juxtapositions, until by the end the visual presence of the sea makes emotionally present for us all the past events with which fire and water have been associated, becoming one of the means by which Mizoguchi deepens and intensifies our response to the last scene as the point to which every impulse in the film has moved. At the beginning, mother and young children are walking beside a stream; at the end, mother and adult son are reunited in view of the sea.

The scene of Anju's suicide—visually, among the most exquisite (I mean the word in no pejorative sense) things the cinema has given us, the visual beauty being the expression of spiritual depth—offers a convenient point of entry. It is a perfect example of Mizoguchi's ability to create images that are at once intrinsically beautiful and expressive, and rich in accumulated resonances. His characteristic delicacy and reticence are there in the choice of long-shot and the sharply focused tracery of foliage that part-frames, part-screens the girl's slow progress to the water. The cross-cutting between Anju and the old woman who has helped her bring in another recurrent and complexly treated motif of the film, the opposition between enclosure and openness, slavery and freedom: the old woman is standing in the gateway to the slaves' compound as Anju descends to the freedom of death. That "freedom" is not entirely ironic. The tranquility of the setting and the sense of ceremony in Anju's gesture of obeisance to her old helper confer serenity upon her action. At first, in long-shot, the water looks like mist, into which Anju seems to merge, suggesting a gentle dissolution into the harmony of nature, the soul diffused into its native element. We may connect the stillness of the water with the name Anju was given in the compound: Shinobu, which means patience. Anju's death is dignified—in Mizoguchian terms, or in the film's total context, made sacred—by its purpose. She sacrifices herself to facilitate Zushio's escape, and because she knows she would reveal his whereabouts under torture, and the aim of his escape is to reunite the dispersed family (and incidentally save the life of Namiji, the sick slave-woman who was kind to them earlier because they reminded her of her own lost children—the ramifications of the family theme and its extension into loyalty-to-the-past reach everywhere in the film). The water into which Anju disappears links her with her mother: Tamaki is consistently associated with water, from the image early in the film of her scooping it from the stream to drink (which inaugurates one of the flashbacks showing her unity with her husband) to the final reunion with Zushio by the sea. The image, inevitably, recalls the scene of the kidnapping (the dispersal of the family), but it also, less obviously, anticipates the scene of Zushio's visit (his escape successful) to the father's grave in Tsukushi, shot against a background of distant water. Our sense of interconnectedness is intensified by Mizoguchi's use of Tamaki's song

("Zushio, Anju, I long for you . . .") on the soundtrack as fitting accompaniment to the girl's suicide, half-ironic, profoundly poignant. Her descent into the water is framed between a flourishing bamboo to her left and a leafless, stunted shrub to her right. The last shot of the scene sums up its emotional ambivalence, that characteristic fusion of the tragic and affirmative: the water has closed over the girl's head, but the ripples are still widening across the surface, Anju's sacrifice is both an end and a beginning. The scene seems very close, in its economy, lucidity and complexity, its extreme concreteness of imagery and its mysterious aura of suggestivity, to the spirit of the haiku.

The essential difference is that a haiku exists in isolation, self-sufficient, while a detail in *Sansho* reverberates subtly through the whole structure. The final image of the water dissolves to the darkness around the temple where Zushio has sought refuge, a darkness almost immediately penetrated by the flaming torches of his pursuers. The progression is repeated later: from the scene of Zushio at Anju's memorial by the water, after the overthrow of Sansho, Mizoguchi takes us directly to the freedom celebrations of the released slaves, around a bonfire which eventually burns down Sansho's mansion. The fire imagery is more consistent in significance than the water imagery, though the visual artist in Mizoguchi is always ready to seize on fire simply as the focal point for a composition. In general, fire is associated with violence and evil: the boatmen-kidnappers are introduced huddled around a fire, and earlier our first view of the priestess has been introduced by a flame appearing disturbingly out of the darkness. In particular, fire is linked with Sansho, the principle of active cruelty and tyranny, as against Tamaki's endurance, Anju's patience, and the strength of memory and fidelity. Almost every scene in which he appears has a fire blazing; his habitual punishment for slaves is branding with a red-hot iron; his house is consumed by fire. Zushio's spiritual development in the central part of the film is from his brutalization under Sansho's dominance to his resolution to escape and reunite the family when a combination of circumstances recalls him to himself by making his sense of family real to him again. It can be traced from his acceptance of the duty of branding the old man who attempted to run away, to his decision to run away himself and take Namiji with him: in the shot where he lifts her to carry her off, water-drops suggesting tears of compassion are splashing from a spring at the left of the image. One may comment here in passing on the consistent purity of Mizoguchi's treatment of violence on the screen, which avoids the opposite pitfalls of sadism and softening. The horror of the brandings is by no means diminished by the fact that in both cases they are just off-screen. The scene in which the brothel-keepers cut Tamaki's Achilles' tendon to prevent further attempts at escape is especially reticent visually (the act concealed behind trellis-work), yet extraordinarily powerful: Like the other women present, we want to avert our gaze, despite the fact that nothing horrible is shown on screen. But the crucial point here is the treatment of Sansho's downfall. Mizoguchi refuses to indulge any vindictive desire we might feel to watch this monster meet a violent, messy death: he is simply denounced, bound and sent into exile.

As in *Ugetsu*, the essential movement of *Sansho* is towards the assertion of spiritual triumph over time and space, towards that poignant fusion of affirmation and tragic loss. This movement, centred on the theme of family unity, is implicit in the film from the beginning, finding especially beautiful expression in the introductory flashbacks. Mizoguchi implies the continuing present-ness of the past by dissolving from Zushio as adolescent to Zushio as child, running in the same direction from the camera. Even more beautiful is the linking of wife and husband across time: from Tamaki scooping water from the stream we are carried back to her husband making the same gesture as he raises a drinking vessel to his lips. Most beautiful of all is the sense that the memories are shared. The last of the flashbacks, showing the father's farewell, his gift of the symbolic statuette (the goddess of mercy) to his son, and his passing on of precepts about the brotherhood of human beings, begins as Tamaki's memory, but at its close we are returned to Zushio, handling the statuette around his neck and repeating the precepts. What we took to be the mother's memory of the father proves to be simultaneously his: the spiritual communion of the family could scarcely be more subtly or more tellingly expressed.

I want to examine the last sequence of *Sansho* in some detail: no scene is richer in accumulated resonances. First, however, it is important to have clear the film's political implications. Learning of his father's, then of Anju's death, Zushio renounces the power he has achieved—which he has in any case jeopardized by his grand gesture of overthrowing Sansho and freeing the slaves, a gesture that affronts the entire social and ideological structure of the time. The treatment of authority and rebellion in the film is characteristically complex and comprehensive. While the film's ideology is clearly traditionalist and aristocratic (much is made of inheritance and continuity; progress is achieved by the heroic actions of individuals of noble descent), it is also progressive and even, within limits, revolutionary. One is invited to compare and contrast its three father-figures: Zushio's father, Sansho (who almost becomes an alternative father to him), and the minister to whom Zushio presents the petition. Mizoguchi offers no simple explanation of human goodness: Zushio, the son of a humane and noble father, is corruptible, and *almost* becomes a second Sansho; Taro, Sansho's son, has an innate humanity inexplicable in terms of heredity. Yet Zushio's strength is seen as at least partly derived from, and sustained by, parental example: when he frees the slaves, he is conscious of "following father's path." Taro has no such example to give his actions force and conviction: though outraged by his father's behaviour, he can never stand up to him—can only depart surreptitiously;

he fails to right Sansho's iniquities, and retires into the passive, contemplative life of a monastery. The minister, another compassionate figure, reminds one of Zushio's father—a connection underlined by the respect he expresses to Zushio; yet his humanity functions only within the limits determined by the *status quo;* he is an essentially conservative figure, his passivity contrasting with the defiant progressive acts of father and son. Because of this, he is able to retain power and to continue doing limited good of the kind that will never bring about radical change; Zushio and his father both go into exile.

The film implies a further distinction between the radical acts of the father and son. Zushio's action in freeing the slaves (which the film unequivocally—though not simplistically—endorses) is much more extreme and outrageous, more overtly passionate and defiant, than his father's support of the peasantry; as in *Shin Heike Monogatari,* the strength the son draws from allegiance to an inherited moral code enables him to go much further than his father would have done. His renunciation is correspondingly more extreme: where the father rode into exile in his ministerial robes and remained a venerated authority-figure in Tsukushi (the peasants there keep his grave fresh with flowers), Zushio casts off all outward signs of authority and leaves for Sado as a pauper, alone. The attitude to Zushio's action, while complex, is very precisely defined. He achieves no widespread transformation of society, and the implications of his resignation are, on the socio-political level, extremely pessimistic; yet his action destroys one petty tyranny, ends the "earthly hell" of Sansho's estate, makes more bearable the lives of a few individuals. His revolutionary gesture, therefore, is presented as neither futile nor reprehensible; and I do not feel that the treatment of the slaves' freedom celebrations—the clumsy, drunken dance filmed in a single tracking-shot in which the camera serenely surveys the chaos and wreckage, finally rising slightly to look down on it—radically contradicts this. The sequence-shot here exemplifies that constant tension between style and content that characterizes Mizoguchi's late work: the presentation of a violent, disordered world from a viewpoint of compassionate contemplation and an achieved serenity totally devoid of complacency. It marks a realistic acknowledgment that the liberation of a people kept in ignorance, squalor and misery (the old man Zushio branded is prominent in the scene, personalizing the general conception) cannot produce instant utopia. Someone told me that Zushio resigns because he realizes that his action has merely led to further disorder, and that the despair implicit in this (a despair seen as going with, and justifying, an inherent conservatism) represents Mizoguchi's position, but this is a demonstrably incorrect reading: Zushio has already written his resignation when he is told that Sansho's house is burning. It is clear, I think, from his words to his mother at the end of the film, that he *must* resign: the prevailing system cannot tolerate the sort of radical action he has performed.

The effect of the final scene is partly dependent on the sociopolitical pessimism: Zushio has gone as far as he can go in terms of political action; the system will close its ranks, there will be (doubtless *are*) other Sanshos; the final emphasis is less on the limited social good Zushio has achieved than on the personal integrity, the triumph of humane feeling, the achievement confirms. The apparently very different conclusions of *Ugetsu*, *Sansho* and *Shin Heike*—the first essentially conservative, the third defiantly radical, *Sansho* offering a point of balance between them—are doubtless partly determined by their historical contexts and source material; that maturity should be associated in *Ugetsu* with resignation and contentment with one's lot, in *Shin Heike* with active and passionate defiance, can be explained by the fact that the hero of the former is a peasant (hence quite unable to affect destiny on a political level), of the latter a samurai. Yet, beneath the differences, the three endings are consistent in their emphasis on self-determination within the available pos-

Zushio is reunited with his mother—now blind and lame—
at the end of *Sansho Dayu*.

sibilities—on the protagonist's achievement of awareness of the
world, awareness of self, on his definition of his own identity
which is also a definition of relationship to the past. It is this
achievement of awareness—present ubiquitously in the style of
the late films—that represents the supreme value of the Mizoguchian universe.

The last sequence is prefaced by a sequence-shot without
dialogue whose immediate narrative function is simply to record Zushio's progress towards his mother, but which is rich
in emotional associations. Having enquired for Tamaki in the
brothel district of Sado, where he learns (though reports conflict) that she was drowned in the tidal wave that devastated the
area two years previously, he nevertheless presses on around
the cape, impelled either by desperation (for if she too is dead,
the entire progress of his life, and of the film, is merely towards
the discovery of futility) or by some profound, quasi-mystical

instinct: the two are not incompatible, and the context (which is no less than the entire film) makes both relevant. It is that context, indeed, that the sequence-shot evokes. The camera records Zushio's progress along the cliff from which, earlier, Tamaki, lamed, called to her children across the sea. Her crying of their names echoes through the film, the very first shot of which (after the "foreword") established two of its main motifs: the journey towards reunion (as the family moved through the forest towards the exiled father and the boy Zushio ran forward along a fallen tree that cut the screen diagonally) and the mother calling to her son (the first word of dialogue). The "call" motif was taken up in the sequence where the children gathered brushwood for the night's shelter, and it was the enacted repetition of that scene (when, as adults and slaves, Zushio and Anju gathered sticks and reeds to build a shelter for the dying Namiji) that was crucial in recalling Zushio to himself after his Sansho-dominated lapse into brutalization—the scene that culminated in the moment where brother and sister heard, or seemed to hear, the mother's voice calling to them across space and time. The visual presence of the cliff—again, we are facing out to sea—evokes all these associations, making real for us the notion of spiritual journey. What is lacking is the melody of Tamaki's song—the song that, sung by the young girl-slave from Sado in Sansho's compound, became the children's one intimation that their mother might still be alive. The melody accompanied Tamaki's cries across the sea; it also accompanied Anju's suicide. Now, at the point where we would logically expect a further recapitulation of it (to the extent that I actually invented one in the original version of this essay), the silence is broken only by a strange (to Western ears) flute-cry. In *Ugetsu,* when Genjuro, on his way to deliver his pots at the Wakasa mansion, paused before a cloth salesman's to imagine Miyagi admiring the fine kimonos, a holy man passing in the background played an instrument that emitted similar sounds, so the flute-cry may have religious overtones. But it also (one can say more confidently) "stands in" for the cries of Tamaki in the earlier scene; and our expectations of the accompanying melody are aroused here so that their delayed fulfilment may be, when it eventually comes, the more moving. The sequence-shot ends with the camera turning to show Zushio moving down towards the little bay that was the scene of Tamaki's attempted escape, when, desperate to rejoin her children, she tried to bribe a boatman to take her away, before being recaptured by her pursuers from the brothel. The fact that the two earlier scenes (the cliff, the bay) are evoked here in reverse order subtly intensifies the sense that Zushio is moving *back* towards reunion with Tamaki.

The last scene of the film, to which this evocation of the past is the necessary prelude, consists of eleven shots marked as a sequence by the near-symmetry of the first and last, both of which link the three participating characters in a single camera-movement, the first moving left to right, the last right to left. The sequence uses every camera position from extreme close-up to extreme long-shot, and every kind of camera movement (as well as the static camera)—panning, tracking, craning: the fact suggests Mizoguchi's stylistic flexibility and command of expression. The action can be broken down as follows: (Shot 1) It is low tide; Zushio questions an old man who is spreading seaweed out to dry from a large pile he has collected. The old man has just told Zushio that Tamaki is certainly dead when her song, faint to the verge of inaudibility, drifts across in a frail, cracked voice. (2–7) Zushio makes himself known to his mother, who is now blind as well as lame, but she rejects him, preferring hopeless resignation to the further dashing of vain hopes; she has been deceived too many times. (8–10) Zushio convinces her that he is indeed her son by giving her the little figure of the goddess of mercy; he tells her of the deaths of his father and Anju; after a moment of bitter grief, the two cling together, reunited.

The overall effect of the last scene, like that of *Ugetsu*, is to balance the sense of loss and tragic waste with an affirmation of spiritual unity; if in *Sansho* the effect is somewhat more desolate, the affirmation more penetrated by irony, this is partly accountable for by the absence of a child, though I shall argue that concepts of continuity and renewal are subtly present in other ways. The obvious comparison is with the late plays of Shakespeare (and their great forerunner, the father/daughter reconciliation scene of *King Lear*), and Mizoguchi is perhaps the only film-maker who would not suffer from such a juxtaposition; the recognition scene of *Pericles*, in which the presence of the sea is also crucial, offers the closest parallels. We see Zushio, like Marina with her father, restore Tamaki to life by reawakening within her the desire to live: a movement expressed in the action, the editing and the imagery. Tamaki's blindness (unlike the lameness, given no narrative explanation) has a symbolic dimension: she has withdrawn into herself, away from life and light; her almost tuneless chanting of the song ("Zushio, Anju, I long for you . . .") has become automatic, expressing fantasy without hope, lacking all outgoing purpose, as ineffectual as her feeble beating with the switch in her hands. Like Lear ("You do me wrong to take me out o' the grave"), she resists Zushio's revelation of his survival, scornfully rejecting him: the paralysed despair in which she exists is easier. The sequence opposes two backgrounds, each dominating four shots of the eleven: the sea (1, 3, 7, 11), associated now with Zushio and life, open, calm and bright, gleaming in the gentle sunlight; the hovel (4, 5, 8, 10) into which Tamaki tries to withdraw, merely a dark enclosure (we make out nothing of its interior).

Central to the action and significance of the sequence (hence of the whole film) is the figure of the goddess of mercy, whose special status is underlined by a cut-in to close-up (shot 9) that echoes the earlier cut-in of Zushio's written resignation (both objects lying diagonally across the image). The figure evokes particular associations for Tamaki (the father, his moral precepts, past family unity) and more for the spectator (the saving of Namiji, the recognition of Zushio by the minister); its accumulated significance, as well as its intrinsic meaning, draws together all the threads of the film at this climactic point. Tamaki's fingers, in the close-up, trace its outlines as, in the next shot, they will trace the features of Zushio's face—as if she were tracing there the features of the child who was dragged from her or the husband whom she was following into exile. The significance of the statuette as a life-renewing emblem is defined very exactly by the *mise-en-scène:* in the eighth shot of the sequence, Tamaki hobbles into the darkness of the hut, almost disappearing from view; Zushio follows her (their backs are towards us) and as a last resort gives her the figure; clutching it, she turns, and moves out again into the sunlight, towards the camera, where she examines it with her fingers.

The force of affirmation is partly derived from the contextual sense of the spiritual presence of the father and Anju: in performing a noble, altruistic deed (but one in which family feeling—the desire to rescue Anju—also played its part) before renouncing temporal power, Zushio has indeed followed his father's path (as the film's first scenes showed him doing literally), and Anju's death has contributed to the reunion of mother and son. Although two members of the family are dead and a third blind, lame and decrepit, the sense of loss and waste (the devastation of the tidal wave, the monstrousness of human cruelty) is counterbalanced by that of achieved mystic unity, the past alive in the present, the dead living on in the survivors, the transmitted values reaffirmed and validated: "You followed father's words," Tamaki tells her son in the film's last line of dialogue; "that is why we can meet here like this." In the world of conflicts, cruelty and violent disorder that Mizoguchi so vividly creates for contemplation, the survival of humane, *human* feeling ("Without compassion, man is but a beast"—one of the father's precepts), defined in terms of a complex and living relatedness to family and tradition, is itself a triumph to be celebrated.

There remain for consideration the two shots involving the seaweed-gatherer, the sequence's symmetrical framework and culmination. The symmetry, it is important to note, is not exact: in shot 1 the camera tracks and cranes, in shot 11 it cranes and *pans*. The distinction is not merely pedantic. In the first shot, the tracking camera carries us along *with* Zushio, emotionally participating in his movement; in the last shot, the camera cranes up from the embracing mother and son, revealing sea and sky, a world opened up to us as if re-created, and pans to show the old man still at work, laying the seaweed out to dry. The seaweed, a reminder of the sea's power and potential for devastation, will be used either as food or fertilizer, to sustain life and foster new growth: the symbolism, quite unobtrusive, is profoundly satisfying as a summation of the film's progress, implying continuity and renewal wrested out of disaster; and this effect is underlined by the fact that the action has reached the point of completion, the pile of seaweed has disappeared. The crane up (to a greater height than the first shot, giving us a more panoramic view) communicates most movingly, like the last shot of *Ugetsu*, a sense of spiritual uplift; the fact that the camera now pans detaches us from the characters, conveying a sense of a heightened, contemplative and serenely accepting perspective on life that is wholly lacking in sentimentality. Style in *Sansho Dayu* is the convincing embodiment of the cinema's supreme intelligence and sensibility.

12
Notes for a Reading of *I Walked with a Zombie*

With this, the third issue of *CineAction!* it is becoming clearer that the magazine's position is in certain respects uneasy and problematic. We want on the one hand to remain accessible—or at the least relatively so (we don't write for people who just want to be entertained). On the other, we want seriously, and we hope formidably, to challenge the current theoretical hegemony, the structuralist/semiotic/Lacanian school. It doesn't take much reflection to realize how difficult it is to do both. Yet the two undertakings are also interdependent: our prime objection to the Lacanian school is its apparently relentless inaccessibility, and our sense that it has lost whatever political thrust it once had by becoming increasingly hermetic, self-involved, "academic" in the worse sense. This necessitates a third undertaking, introducing further problems: to rescue from the structuralists (they might prefer "steal") those concepts and aspects of their methodology that we value, and try at once to incorporate them in an alternative system and render them comprehensible to intelligent readers who have resisted the structuralist hegemony.

I believe myself that structuralism has revolutionized the analysis—"reading"—of films: simply to ignore the movement is automatically to render oneself obsolete. To be overwhelmed by it, on the other hand, is (as so many cases have demonstrated) to lose one's own voice and much of one's potential audience by adopting a convoluted jargon that frequently has to be translated back into English before it reveals its (often quite simple) meaning.[7] (In certain extremist structuralist/Marxist circles, the desire to preserve one's own voice will be instantly suspect; but I think we need not take very seriously a Marxism that has neither place nor respect for individual utterance, and no theorization of its—I was going to write "validity"—*necessity*. It is precisely when Marxism rejects all intercourse with humanism that it becomes dangerous.) I want in this article to appropriate certain concepts and procedures from the work of Roland Barthes. Strict semioticians will frown upon the appropriation, complaining that I am to some degree diverting the procedures from their original ends, diluting them, and assimilating them into a more traditional aesthetic. But no text, no concept, no procedure is sacrosanct: the critic has the right to appropriate whatever s/he needs from whatever can be found, and use it for purposes perhaps somewhat different from the original ones. And if I, to some degree, transform Barthes, it is at least equally true that Barthes transforms me: it is impossible to adopt his methodology, in however modified a form, without simultaneously modifying (and extending) one's own.

The text that interests me here is *S/Z*. This is far from being the first attempt to apply the "codes of realist narrative" to the reading of a film.[8] I lay no claim to originality, but neither am I merely imitating: both my method and my results are to some degree idiosyncratic. I shall preface the reading of *I Walked with a Zombie* (Lewton/Tourneur, 1943) with my own account of what have come to be known as "the Barthes codes" (though they were his discovery rather than his invention) in the hope of rendering them and the reading accessible to those who

---

7. An example ready to hand is an essay on *The Pirate* ("Vision, Desire and the Film Text") in *Camera Obscura 6*. Extreme but not altogether untypical is the author's definition of the fiction film as "a textual mode which privileges the scopic and the auditory." Translation: "Films are seen and heard."

8. See, in particular, Julia Lesage's analysis of *La Règle du Jeu* in *Jump Cut*, preceded by Judith Mayne's explication of the codes.

have not read *S/Z* (and in the further hope of making the book more accessible too). Those already familiar (perhaps beyond the point of saturation) with Barthes's work can of course skip, though they may wish to check up on my (mis)representation of this distinguished and important figure.

S/Z

The main body of *S/Z* consists of a reading of Balzac's novella *Sarrasine*. One should first distinguish between "reading" and the more traditional "critical interpretation." The latter usually starts from the critic's sense of what the work in question is, what it is about, what it *does,* and the interpretation will aim to establish the work's coherence (or criticize its failures to become coherent), supported by quotations of what are regarded as particularly significant passages. A reading, on the other hand, attempts to account for everything, and will be more concerned with process (the work of construction) than with establishing a definitive, coherent meaning. (There is of course no guarantee that a reading will not also start from the critic's sense of "what the work in question is.") The reading of Balzac's 33-page novella occupies 200 pages (not counting the introductory material and the appendices), and every word of Balzac's text is quoted and annotated in the form of "lexias" or units of reading. Barthes attributes to the classical narrative a "limited plurality," and seeks to demonstrate this in his reading of *Sarrasine*. On one level I find this misleading: what finally emerges from the reading is as coherent an overall sense of the novella as any "traditional" interpretation would be likely to produce, largely free from the internal conflicts and contradictions that the promise of a "limited plurality" might seem to suggest. *S/Z* has been widely held to mark a decisive and irreparable break with traditional notions of interpretation; it seems to me that it can just as easily be regarded as demonstrating its continuity and compatibility with them. What *S/Z* uncovers is not so much a plurality of meanings as the intricate and multi-layered nature of the activity of reading itself. Here the adoption of the word "text" for any art work (book, film, painting, piece of music) is important. "Text" suggests "texture," and a texture is composed of many interweaving strands. The analogy with weaving has a further implication, that of an intricate coherence: a texture that did not cohere would simply disintegrate.

The Five Codes

In his reading of *Sarrasine,* Barthes discovers that the entire novella is constructed (woven) according to the operation of five "codes": "There will be no other codes throughout the story but five, and each and every lexia will fall under one of these five codes." (In fact, most of the lexias turn out to fall under several simultaneously, and this will also be the case with *I Walked with a Zombie.*) Though Barthes doesn't actually say this, the implication appears to be that all classical narratives are structured upon these five codes and only these. I have accepted this assumption in my reading on the film, but I think the acceptance should only be provisional. As I shall show, there are important differences in function and status among the five codes (so extreme in the case of one that it seems scarcely to belong with the other four, and some alternative form of categorization may prove desirable). It also seems uncertain that the five in themselves account for *all* the possibilities of classical narrative: the case, for instance, of narratives within narratives, where the "truth" of the internal narrative may be in question, produces problems that cannot be easily resolved within the Barthesian methodology (Ophuls's *Letter from an Unknown Woman* offers an extreme example, *I Walked with a Zombie* a minor one). I miss particularly the inclusion of an *authorial* code, that would allow for the annotation of all those points (so important a feature of the "pleasure of the text") where we recognize an author's imprint (whether thematic or stylistic): Barthes was of course committed to a view of art that virtually obliterates the notion of individual authorship, so the omission is understandable if not excusable.

The clearest way to elucidate the codes is by means of examples. I have chosen to concoct my own sentence (to be imagined as the opening of either a story or a chapter of a novel), not because it is beautiful prose but because I can ensure that it exemplifies all five of the codes:

> The day of the picnic, awaited by Max with his usual youthful eagerness, began under the auspices of Phoebus, but little did he guess in what darkness it would end.

As a transition to film, I shall take as second instance the opening shot of *Letter from an Unknown Woman,* chosen because (a) it is probably familiar to most readers, and (b) it also happens to exemplify all five of the codes very clearly and precisely.[9] Here, then, are the five codes of realist (or classical) narrative.

1. The *Proairetic* code (from the Greek for "actions"): the code that gives us the series of actions upon which the narrative is

---

9. For those unfamiliar with Ophuls's film, the content of the first shot is as follows: A rainy night in a cobbled city street; a horse-drawn carriage is approaching a long-shot; the caption "Vienna, about 1900" appears over the image; a clock is striking two. As the carriage draws near and stops outside iron gates, the camera moves in so as to frame the man who gets out (Stefan/Louis Jourdan) in the rectangle of the far window. Brief dialogue with the two men who remain inside the carriage: "So you're going through with it?" Stefan (shrugs): "Why not?" "Well, for one thing I hear he's an excellent shot." Stefan: "Oh, It's not so much that I mind getting killed. But you know how hard it is for me to get up in the morning." One of the men tells him that they will return at five o'clock, adding, "And if I were you, no more cognac." The carriage continues on its way, and we see Stefan approaching the gates.

constructed: in the above sentence, the action of "the picnic." Immediately, we must face a possible objection from those hitherto innocent of semiotics, an objection to the term "code." Everyone knows that a narrative consists of actions and could not exist without them; every schoolchild can follow the actions through a narrative. The term "code" implies the work of decoding, and no such work is necessary here—we are not idiots, thank you. The answer is, first, that the act of decoding is so long-ingrained and so familiar as to be entirely automatic, but, second, that such an act does indeed take place. My sentence does not merely convey the fact that a picnic is to take place, it alerts us (because of our familiarity with other narratives) to an implied process of narrative structure: an account of the picnic will follow; it will occupy at the very least a paragraph, probably a chapter, perhaps several chapters (or, if this is the beginning of a story, the entire narrative); the account will probably be subdivisible into numerous stages (preparations, departure, events on the way, choice of a site, events during the picnic, etc.); eventually we shall be told what happened, the action will be concluded and (if this is part of a novel) will give rise in turn to other actions.

The proairetic code is indeed the fundamental one on which the narrative edifice is built: without actions even the most elementary narrative would be impossible (provided we understand "actions" in the widest sense, to include for example the act of thinking or sleeping). What needs to be stressed here is the interweaving of actions in classical narrative: there must be no hiatus, one action must be prepared as one is completed. Even if, as in certain Victorian novels, the action is suspended while the author moralizes, the logical chain will be resumed as soon as the moralizing ceases. Usually, however long the work, there will be a *dominant* action overarching and encompassing the entire structure. For example, a novel might begin with a ship leaving Southampton and end with it docking in New

York: the dominant action would be the "trans-Atlantic voyage." In between the departure and the docking, however, we shall be led through the narrative by a continuus, often overlapping, series of subordinate actions: A and B will fall in love, C will be murdered, D will be unmasked as an enemy agent, the captain will go insane, a gaint man-eating spider will be discovered in the boiler-room. . . The typical dominant action of classical narrative (linking *War and Peace* to *The Sure Thing*) is the construction of the "good" or "normal" hetrosexual couple. (It is likely that, in our hypothetical novel, this will coincide with the end of the voyage, after all the threats have been systematically eliminated.)

The opening shot of *Letter from an Unknown Woman* offers us two actions (one shown visually, the other introduced in the dialogue): the arrival home, the duel. The latter is indeed the dominant action of the film—it has not even been concluded at the end, though we know by then what its outcome will be. The former is the first small, finite action in a *proairetic chain*—arrival home, preparations for departure, interruption, reading the letter—which will guide us through the film.

2. The *Hermeneutic* code (from the Greek for "enigmas"): the proposal, development and eventual resolution of puzzles, questions, mysteries. In my sentence, "little did he know . . ." immediately presents an enigma, providing the reader with knowledge to which poor, eager, unsuspecting Max does not have access, but not too much knowledge: we know that something frightful will happen, but we shall have to wait (perhaps for a hundred pages) to find out what. The privileged site of the hermeneutic code is clearly the detective novel: someone is found murdered on page one, and 200 pages later the great detective expounds the solution, unmasks the culprit. Again, we find a *dominant enigma* ("Who done it?") encompassing the whole narrative, with a continual play of enigmas (clues, mysterious utterances,

anonymous letters, red herrings) interweaving throughout. But every classical narrative plays on suspense and curiosity to some degree. One might certainly argue that the proairetic code, every time an action is introduced, implies an enigma ("What will happen?") automatically. This shows how intimately the two codes are interrelated, but it seems reasonable to follow Barthes in reserving the hermeneutic code for the stronger and more explicit introduction and pursuit of specific enigmas. One might make the distinction by suggesting that, while actions are essential to a narrative, enigmas (in the strict sense) are not, and one might construct a (very boring) narrative without any ("I went for a walk. I met a friend. We talked about the weather. We said goodbye. I went home.").

The *Letter* shot is particularly rich in enigmas, all surrounding the action of the duel: Why is it being fought?—Who is the opponent?—Will Stefan fight?—Will he be killed? All these are answered, but not until the very end of the film, during its closing minutes. This gives us another (almost) absolute principle of the hermeneutic code: that, just as every action must be concluded, so every enigma must be resolved. (I shall argue that it is one of the distinctions and eccentricities of *Zombie* that one of its enigmas, a crucial one, is left disturbingly unresolved.) We may also notice another common feature of the *hermeneutic chain,* that of *apparent but false* resolution (I call it "blocking," in preference to the standard translation "jamming") in order further to postpone the true one: the question as to whether Stefan will stay to fight the duel is apparently answered in the negative in the following scene ("Pack my things.... Enough for an indefinite stay."). Typically, this takes the form of a kind of teasing: if we really believed, beyond doubt, that we had already been given the "true" solution, we might be tempted to close the book, walk out of the movie, then and there (compare Hitchcock's audacity, bitterly resented by many spectators, in supplying us with the true solution to *Vertigo's* dominant enigma, beyond any uncertainty, two-thirds of the way through the film). In the example from *Letter*, we are not really convinced that the film's male protagonist, played by a prominent star, will not fight the duel. We shall encounter excellent examples of "blocking" in *Zombie* (even in the opening credit-title shot).

Clearly, the proairetic and hermeneutic codes belong together: they continually intertwine and supplement each other, their joint task is to push, guide, lure us step by step through the narrative, always focusing our attention on the future ("What will happen?") so that we read on; they are the codes that "tell the story." We can designate them as the *linear* or *horizontal* codes (in contradistinction from the other three). In the classical Hollywood cinema (and most post-classical) they are always dominant (audiences go to Hollywood movies "for the story" and on the rare occasions when their dominance is challenged (*Heaven's Gate*) the work is considered inept. They also represent the level at which the work of producing and reading narratives is likely to be most fully conscious, on the part of the censorship (literal and symbolic, external and internal). Hence, in the classical Hollywood narrative, the tendency of the linear codes will almost always (there are very few exceptions) be ideologically conservative, leading us, with endless repetition, towards the restoration of the patriarchal-capitalist status quo ("normality") and its attendant value-system. (Critics and theorists who dismiss the Hollywood cinema outright habitually reduce Hollywood movies to the operation of the linear codes, ignoring the rest).

3. The *Semantic* code (from the Greek for "meanings"): corresponding roughly to what traditional aesthetics would call the "thematic" level of narrative. Barthes tells us that this is most commonly attached to characters, and reflection proves

him correct (in *Hamlet* and *Macbeth* respectively, the themes of indecision and ambition are clearly introduced and developed through the protagonists). In my sentence, "awaited by Max with his usual youthful eagerness" suggests the themes (or "meanings") of anticipation, youth, innocence: themes that may or may not prove to be important in the total structure of the work, but which are here attached to what may be its main character. The *Letter* example offers most obviously the theme of *decadence* (the men are returning from some kind of nocturnal debauch, at 2:00 a.m.), attached especially to Stefan (he has been over-indulging in cognac, hates getting up in the morning, and is cynical about death and honor). We may notice also, however, the theme of *time* (the clock, the men's promise to return at five), which is not a part of the characterization but will be a major preoccupation of the narrative. There will of course be "meanings" that are merely transitory and incidental, dropped as soon as introduced—"meanings" that never become "themes," the defining characteristic of a theme being recurrence. We may say in general that the more frequently a theme recurs from lexia to lexia (perhaps in a variety of forms and modes, from serious to comic, from emphatic statement to glancing allusion) the more important it will prove in the total structure.

4. The *Symbolic* code. We are familiar with the notion of symbolism. Barthes demonstrated very impressively (though the idea is scarcely new to criticism—see, for example, F. R. Leavis's concepts of "symbolic drama" and "dramatic poem" extended to works of fiction generally) that symbolism is not something applied occasionally to a work like cherries on a cake but a major structuring principle. He shows that the symbolic structure of a work typically organizes itself in terms of *oppositions*. In my sentence, the obviously "symbolic" use of "darkness" implies one of the fundamental symbolic oppositions of our culture:

light/darkness, day/night, happiness/tragedy, good/evil. The *Letter* shot plays on much the same opposition: the *night* and *rain* in which the film opens will be replaced in the precisely symmetrical last shot (the carriage drives away from the same gates) by *near-dawn* and *no-rain,* expressing the film's progress from confusion to enlightenment, from the dominance of worldliness and corruption to the triumph of spirituality. The symbolic oppositions will not be arbitrary or haphazard: all will relate to all (though the relationship may be complex).

It swiftly becomes clear that, just as the proairetic and hermeneutic codes are more or less inextricably interconnected and interdependent, so too are the semantic and symbolic codes (and more rather than less). The themes of a work will inevitably be drawn into its pattern of oppositions (Hamlet's indecision against the promptness of Laertes, the murderous ambition of the Macbeths against the loyalty of Banquo and Macduff): even within my sentence, Max's eager anticipation has its answer in the threat of disaster, and these correspond to the *symbolic* opposition of day/night. In *Letter,* Stefan's disillusioned decadence will be answered by Lisa's idealistic purity, and these are taken up in the rain/no-rain, night/near-dawn oppositions. One could of course equally put it the other way around: the symbolic oppositions invariably have a thematic dimension. Consequently, in my reading of *Zombie,* I have not been too scrupulous about distinguishing these two codes: as a theme encounters its opposite I have tended to gather them in symbolic code and speak of the film's *semantic/symbolic structure* as an entity (which does not mean that it is monolithic or free of internal tensions). The relationship of this structure to the linear structure produced by the work of the proairetic and hermeneutic codes can range from the simply supportive (in our rudimentary narratives) to the highly complex. In general, the semantic/symbolic structure of a work is likely to be far less accessible to consciousness (of the maker, the veiwer, the censorship) than the progress of the linear code ("the story"). One can therefore at this stage posit the possibility that the two pairs of codes may develop in a state of permanent tension (perhaps contradiction) rather than in simple co-operation or mutual support. I shall go on to declare that such is indeed the case with large numbers of distinguished Hollywood films, and this is why those critics who reduce the films to the progress of the linear codes are quite simply wrong.

5. The *Cultural* code (Barthes also calls it the code of *reference*): reference to shared, familiar knowledge within the culture, such as proverbs, common sayings, mythology, topical events, famous people. In my sentence, we have to know that Phoebus is the Greek sun-god if we are to grasp the meaning. Barthes acknowledges that in a sense *all* the codes are cultural: we have to learn to read narratives, though the learning took place so early in our lives that the process has become entirely naturalized. However, he retains the cultural code for the annotation of specific references. It seems to me that this "code" does not really belong with the other four, its function being entirely different: they are structual codes, this is not (except in so far as the references are drawn into the semantic/symbolic structure, in which case they can be grouped under those codes). Analysis of the cultural code belongs, in fact, to a simpler (though very important) stage in the development of semiotics, that represented by Barthes's earlier *Mythologies:* the exploration of a culture's "myths" through its specific individual artifacts and practices (wrestling, steak-and-chips, Garbo's face, etc.). As I am concerned in this paper with structure, I have ignored the cultural codes *as such* altogether, preferring to group many of its instances under the canopy of the semantic and symbolic codes. It is probable that *all* manifestations of the cultural code can be

Besty and the "Isle of the Dead" in *I Walked with a Zombie*.

grouped in this way: the obvious one in the *Letter* shot, for example (the caption "Vienna, about 1900"), immediately evokes not only the music (from Mozart to popular waltzes) that plays so important a part in the film's thematic development and its analysis of class, but also the connotations of "fin de siècle" that attach themselves to the theme of decadence. Or take two striking examples from the décor of Jessica's bedroom in *Zombie*, the harp and Böcklin's painting "The Isle of the Dead": both belong within the cultural code (we have to know not only what a harp is but also its association with angels, hence with a certain cultural myth of woman), but they equally belong to the semantic/symbolic structure (the harp standing in opposition to the voodoo drums).

Is It Worth It?

Finally, the reader may ask what is gained by a method of analysis that requires such an elaborate exposition. First, quite simply, it helps one to notice (be aware of) so much more: take a sequence from any film, look at it again in relation to the four (or five) codes, and see how many details that previously passed by uncommented suddenly relate, make sense, form patterns with other details across the film. Beyond that, the method greatly heightens one's awareness of structure and the *process of structuration.* Beyond that again, it makes possible a rigorous and systematic investigation into what has proved by far the most fruitful concept in recent approaches to Hollywood, the concept of *ideological tension or contradiction.* I hope these claims will be substantiated by the (admittedly skeletal) reading that follows.

To make that skeletal method clear, I close this introduction by showing how the two examples I have used can be succinctly annotated.

> *My sentence:*
> PRO.: "picnic" (statement of action).
> HER.: "little did he guess . . ." (enigma).
> SEM.: "awaited . . . with his usual youthful eagerness" (themes of anticipation and innocence).
> SYM.: "auspices of Phoebus," "in what darkness . . ." (opposition of day/night, light/darkness, happiness/disaster).

> *The* Letter *shot:*
> PRO.: arrival home; duel (dominant action).
> HER.: Why is the duel being fought?—Who is the antagonist?—Will Stefan fight?—Will he be killed?
> SEM.: decadence (cynicism, cognac, "fin de siècle");

time, passing of time (three hours).
SYM.: rain and night (answered at end of film by no-
rain and near-dawn).

Why *I Walked With a Zombie*?

A complex of reasons. First, I needed a film to which I had easy
access (the analysis demanding prolonged and intensive work)
and which is in distribution (it has also been repeatedly shown
on pay-TV) so that interested readers might have access to it
also. Second, I wanted an unquestionably distinguished film
with a very rich semantic/symbolic structure, but one which
nevertheless was securely contained within the bounds of classical Hollywood narrative, a film at once representative and exemplary. Third, I wanted a film as short as possible, for obvious reasons. (This article is already lengthy enough—imagine
the method applied to *Duel in the Sun* or *The Deer Hunter*!) I
should add that I have loved *I Walked with a Zombie* for many
years: this is not an "objective" academic exercise carried out
upon a film whose title was produced out of a hat (an exercise
of which I think I would be absolutely incapable).

The Reading

This is an attempt to outline the basis for a complete reading of
a specific classical Hollywood narrative (one of great distinction), and to suggest, at the same time, how classical Hollywood
narratives work, the process of their construction. The major
omission is a very serious one: there is no adequate attention
to the operation of the "codes specific to film"—camera placement, camera movement, camera angle, editing, lighting, framing, etc.—but to attempt this as well would make the exercise
virtually interminable!

The film, just under 70 minutes long, consists of 509 shots. I have broken it down into 46 segments, roughly along the lines of Metz's *Grande Syntagmatique*.[10] In most cases the "autonomy" of the segment is clearly marked (change of location, time lapse, cinematic punctuation such as fades or dissolves); in a few cases my divisions are more questionable, especially that between segments 28/29 (which occurs in the middle of a shot). The great majority of the segments are, in Metzian terminology, either "scenes" or "ordinary sequences," and I have not bothered to specify these, noting only the more unusual types.

The figures in brackets denote the number of shots in each segment (I have tried for perfect accuracy, but there may be errors).

1[1]. *Title, credits, opening shot.*
Diegetic[11] ambiguity: though seemingly "realistic," the shot has no logical place within the narrative. purely "poetic" status?
Title: PRO.: the walk (specific reference to canefield
                  sequence?)
           HER.: the zombie

---

10. The *Grande Syntagmatique* was Metz's attempt to construct a syntax of the narrative film, specifying the possible types of sequence (or syntagma). Its usefulness is very limited (problems arise almost every time one tries to apply it), but it has provided a rough means of breaking a film down into its "autonomous segments." Only a few of Metz's categories are relevant to *I Walked with a Zombie:* the *scene* is a sequence in which the action is perfectly continuous in time and space, without ellipses; the *ordinary sequence* is like the scene but omits stretches of time unnecessary to the narrative (e.g., the walk through the canefields, segment 28). These two syntagmas account for most of the segments into which I have divided the film. There is also a *descriptive syntagma* (No. 6), a sequence of shots outside any clear chronological progress establishing a location, etc.; a *sequence shot* (No. 26) in which an action that might normally require a sequence is filmed in a single take; and an *alternate syntagma* (I prefer "alternating sequence," No. 31), in which two actions taking place in different locations are intercut.

11. The *diegesis* is the complete fictional world created within the film, its illusion of reality, including for example the action, the characters, the settings, atmosphere, realistic detail . . .

Visual: PRO.: the walk (an impossible one).

HER.: the zombie (blocking of enigma: the zombie referred to in the title is Jessica, not Carrefour).

SEM.: freedom, space; harmony between races (deception).

SYM.: land/sea (the figures walking along the boundary between); black/white (race, clothing—the black cape).

NOTE: Beginning of Betsy's narration.

2[7]. *The Office.*

Establishing shot: "Parish and Burden"

SEM.: Connotations of religion and slavery.

The scene:

PRO.: the interview (completed here); the journey—i: announcement; the job (continued to end of film).

HER.: Who is Betsy's employer? Nature of wife's illness? Question about witchcraft?

SEM.: Betsy as nurse (service, dedication, purity); Betsy's rationalism (witchcraft); Betsy's romantic aspirations (fantasy of West Indies); dominant position of male, submissive position of female.

SYM.: Canada/West Indies, medicine/witchcraft, rationalism/superstition.

3[13]. *The Ship.*

PRO.: journey—ii. the ship; the relationship between Paul and Betsy (beginning—the dominant action of the film?).

HER.: Why does Paul behave like that?

SEM.: bitterness, destruction of illusions (Paul's character); deceptiveness of appearances; romantic aspirations (beauty, the ladder, the stars); death ("Everything dies here"); dominance (male over female, master over workers, white over black).

SYM.: development of semantic connotations into structure of oppositions: Canada/West Indies, white/black, master/slave, male/female, illusion/reality, life/death, beauty/horror.

Note: Betsy's reaction to Paul ("Clean, honest") will be echoed in segment 33 by Paul's words to Betsy ("Clean, decent, thinking").

4[3]. *Disembarcation.*
        PRO.: journey—iii: arrival at St. Sebastian.
        HER.: Paul's absence (SEM.: aloofness).
        SEM.: cultural difference.

5[5]. *The carriage.*
        PRO.: journey—iv: driving to Fort Holland.
        SEM.: cultural difference; Betsy's rationalism ("You mean
            a figurehead"); domination and oppression (linked
            especially to the name "Holland," hence indirectly to
            Paul, not Wesley); deceptiveness of appearances ("If
            you say, Miss . . .") again linked to "beauty"; black
            subservience.
        SYM.: white/black (race); rationalism/ superstition; power/
            oppression.
Note: Ti-Misery introduced as emblem of oppression and black ("his
black face").

6[13].   Fort Holland. The sequence is unclassifiable within Metz's
        categories as it moves from chronological narrative into an
        a-chronological "descriptive syntagma" and back again, the
        transitions linked by Betsy's narration.The three sub-
        sections are:
  a.   Characterized by Betsy's POV (7 shots):
        PRO.: journey (concluded): arrival.
        SEM.: rationalism undermined in this new world ("like a
            dream").
        SYM.: Ti-Misery/St. Sebastian, uniting white/black,
            Christian/ non-Christian.
  b.   "descriptive syntagma": the rooms (three shots linked by
        dissolves).
  c.   Return to chronology: Betsy preparing for dinner (three
        shots).
        PRO.: dinner: i.—preparation.
        SEM.: shadow-patterns, evoking notions of uncertainty,
        ambiguity, confusion; deceptiveness of appearances (sinister
        shadow is merely the servant announcing dinner).

7[6]. *The dining-room.*

> PRO.: dinner. ii—the family.
>
> HER.: enigmas surrounding Mrs. Rand (runs dispensary but not a doctor; doesn't live in her own home); Jessica (Wesley's tone of voice).
>
> SEM.: male authority—the two fathers (Holland/capitalism, Rand/religion, both names carrying connotations of South Africa, imperialism, oppression of blacks).
>
> SYM.: the system of oppositions: the half-brothers, dominance/subordination ("Master of the house").

8[16]. *The dining-room [later]*

> PRO.: dinner: iii—completion.
>
> HER.: reasons for Wesley's hostility to Paul, and for his heavy drinking; the tower, the obscure door, Jessica's dinner.
>
> SEM.: Wesley's weakness, bitterness, envy and enmity; deceptiveness of appearances (the work-drum and "voodoo").
>
> SYM.: the half-brothers (British/American, dominant/sub-ordinate); Christianity/voodoo (the drums linked to mention of Mr. Rand as missionary).

9[7]. *Betsy's bedroom*

> PRO.: preparation for bed, first sight of patient.
>
> HER.: Jessica, the tower, her illness.
>
> SEM.: association of Jessica with darkness, nature, mystery, beauty.
>
> SYM.: light/darkness (the abrupt switch from clearcut image to criss-cross of shadows, in which Betsy herself is included).

10[39] *The tower.*

> PRO.: Betsy's job, encountering her patient.
>
> HER.: Jessica's strangeness, her unnatural height, threatening movements; nature of her illness.
>
> SEM.: deceptiveness of appearances, cultural difference (the crying). The crying also signifies oppression, with several forms linked together: (a) Ti-Misery (the visual image), (b) Jessica (who Betsy thinks is the

source), (c) the black slaves and their descendants.

> SYM.: white/black (race—the two united in Ti-Misery);
> white/black, Jessica in white; brunette/blonde:
> reversal of conventions, undermining of expectations.
> Hence:

> SEM.: Betsy and Jessica are inverse mirror-images.

> SEM.: the real attitude of black servants to white masters
> (Alma's sarcastic remarks about Betsy: compare next
> segment).

11[9]. Betsy's bedroom.

> PRO.: breakfast in bed.

> HER.: Jessica's illness: explanation i ("She was very sick,
> and then she went mindless"): explanation vague and
> unsatisfying, developing rather than resolving the
> enigma.

> SEM.: cultural difference (method of awakening; the
> brioche/puff-up); deceptiveness of appearances (the
> brioche; Alma's obsequiousness—compare previous
> segment); class division, Betsy's indeterminate place
> as Jessica's nurse; the dialogue connects Jessica and
> Betsy (the past and future Mrs. Holland).

Note: Jessica referred to as "doll" ("It's just like dressing a great big
doll"): compare the "Jessica-doll" of the voodoo scenes.

12[3]. *Paul's workroom.*

> PRO.: the Betsy/Paul relationship.

> HER.: Jessica's illness: explanation ii ("a mental case"):
> parial, misleading.

> SEM.: Betsy's uniform (whiteness, purity, service); fear of
> "the dark" (commonest symbol for the unconscious).

Note: The watch-pendant (visual motif) introduced here.

13[8]. *Jessica's bedroom.*

> HER.: Jessica's illness: explanation iii ("tropical fever"):
> false resolution ("blocking"); introduction of notion
> that Jessica is a zombie (the truth disguised as a joke).

> SEM./CUL.: the harp (white culture; woman as angel).

> SYM.: harp/voodoo (talk of the zombies).

> SEM.: "Isle of the Dead" (Böcklin's painting, also the title of

the last of the series of Lewton-produced horror
films): borderline between life and death.

14[6]. *The veranda.*
>PRO.: Paul/Betsy relationship.
>
>HER.: Paul's actual feelings for Betsy; reasons for his
>bitterness.
>
>SEM.: deceptiveness of appearances (what is "beautiful"?).

15[2]. *St. Sebastian.*
>PRO.: day off, visit to town—i: meeting Wesley.
>
>SEM.: cultural difference, white as aliens.

16[20]. *The café: day.*
>PRO.: visit to town—ii: drinks.
>
>HER.: the song, hints of family scandal, of the background
>to Jessica's illness and Paul's bitterness.
>
>SEM.: tensions and disunity within the family; deceptions of
>appearances, problems of interpreting behavior:
>(a) singer's subservience barely concealing insolence
>(compare Alma); (b) Paul and the word "beautiful";
>(c) Paul's motivation—using Jessica to see Wesley
>"squirm."
>
>SYM.: white/black (race), calypso and "the British
>Grenadiers"; whites as concealers of truth, black as
>revealers of truth.

17[14]. *The café: night.*
>PRO.: visit to town—iii: concluded.
>
>HER.: Jessica's illness—explanation iv: the conclusion of the
>song links it to adultery, suggests it may be a punish-
>ment for immorality.
>
>SEM.: woman as bringer of discord—parallel between
>Jessica and Betsy, past and future trouble, in the song;
>hence:
>
>HER.: will both brothers fall in love with Betsy, repeating
>past history? (false enigma).
>
>SEM.: family tension (the song); Mrs. Rand introduces
>herself as "*Wesley*'s mother" (she is also Paul's),
>suggesting favoritism, a further reason for rivalry/

resentment.

SEM.: singer paralleled to Jessica as threat (approaching Betsy out of the darkness); association of Jessica with the blacks (racial oppression, gender oppression).

SYM.: light/darkness (the CU lamp, the night); white/black (singer and darkness).

PRO.: Betsy to help Wesley (alcohol); Betsy/Paul relationship (hints of Betsy's influence); hence:

SEM.: Mrs. Rand's knowledge, and:

HER.: Where does she get her information?

18[5]. *Fort Holland.*

PRO.: helping Wesley: Betsy speaks to Paul.

SEM: uncertainty of motivation (Paul's refusal).

SYM: clarity vs. confusion or obscurity: silhouette image followed by faces shadowed with lines.

19[20]. *The dining-room.*

PRO.: helping Wesley (no decanter); the Betsy/Paul relationship (Betsy's influence).

HER.: voodoo (conch, drums); question of Paul's treatment of Jessica, secrets in the past.

SYM.: white rituals/black rituals (formal dinner, voodoo ceremony); home/houmfort (the "home" is also a "Fort").

20[16]. *Paul's room.*

PRO.: Paul/Betsy relationship: growth of intimacy, mutual attraction.

HER.: Jessica's illness—explanation v: the quarrel (note parallel development of dominant action and dominant enigma). Again, the "false" explanation juxtaposed with hints of the true one (the drums, association of Jessica with voodoo).

SEM.: Chopin's E major Etude, but more familiar to audiences as "So deep is the night . . ."

SYM.: piano/voodoo drums, white culture/black culture.

21[2]. *The Sea.*

PRO.: Betsy's recognition of her love for Paul and her decision to help him determines the entire chain of subsequent actions to the end of the film: the insulin treatment, the visit to the houmfort, the "voodoo" invasion of the white world. It can therefore be claimed as the turning-point of the film.

HER.: What exactly will Betsy do? Can she save Jessica? Does she really want to?

SEM./SYM.: the sea, already established in segment 3 as image of uncertainty, deceptiveness of appearances, linked here to doubts about Betsy's motivation.

Note i: symmetry of classical narrative: the sea at the beginning (segment 3) and end (segments 44–45) of the film, and also at this near midpoint.

Note ii: end of Betsy's narration (because she can no longer control a narrative that calls into question her own motivation?)

22[3]. *Jessica's room [day].*

PRO.: saving Jessica—i:a. insulin shock treatment.

SEM.: danger (Jessica may be killed—question of Betsy's true motivation).

23[4]. *Jessica's room [night].*

PRO.: saving Jessica—i:b. failure.

SEM.: uncertainty of motivation (Wesley's speech makes this explicit); darkness and the unconscious.

SYM.: light/darkness.

Note: the threatening figure (here Wesley) approaching out of the darkness, recurrent motif (compare Jessica in segment 10, calypso singer in segment 17).

24[20]. *The veranda.*

PRO.: saving Jessica—ii: voodoo: a. suggestion ("*better doctors*")

HER.: witchcraft; will Betsy take Alma's advice?

SEM.: uncertain motivation (here, Alma in relation to Jessica: help her, or get her to the houmfort for "test"?)

SEM./SYM.: the drawing together of major components of the system of oppositions: white/ black, science/voodoo, rationalism/superstition. The collapse of Betsy's

rationalist certitude is linked to her troubled, unclear
motivation (loss of self-image).

Note: visual motif: the brooch for Ti-Victor (compare Betsy's watch-
pendant).

25[4]. *The dispensary.*

　　　　PRO.: saving Jessica—ii: voodoo: b. proposal.

　　　　HER.: the houmfort and possibility of danger.

　　　　SYM.: Christianity/voodoo ("one foot in the church and
　　　　　　one in the houmfort"); science/voodoo; church/
　　　　　　houmfort, dispensary/houmfort; rationalism/super-
　　　　　　stition (psychological explanation for Mamma Rose's
　　　　　　cure).

26[1]. *The garden:* sequence shot.

　　　　PRO.: visit to the houmfort—i: departure.

　　　　SEM.: continuous camera-movement to connect Paul,
　　　　　　Wesley, Betsy/Jessica, Alma and Ti-Misery: theme of
　　　　　　interconnectedness, breakdown of clear divisions,
　　　　　　female transgression.

　　　　SYM.: movement from light to darkness (the black exit).

27[2]. *Outside the gate.*

　　　　PRO.: visit to the houmfort—ii: directions.

　　　　HER.: will they get lost?—what will happen?

　　　　SYM.: light/darkness (complex image with Alma, flour,
　　　　　　flashlight, Betsy's black cape); the voodoo patches
　　　　　　(compare Betsy's watch-pendant, Ti-Victor's brooch);
　　　　　　black/white (race and clothing), dark/fair.

　　　　SEM.: "Carrefour" (French for crossroads)—passing from
　　　　　　one world to another; female transgression.

28[31½]. *The canefields.*

　　　　PRO.: visit to the houmfort—iii. the walk.

　　　　HER.: will they get lost?; significance of the various sinister
　　　　　　objects.

　　　　SEM.: voodoo (conch), death, the "living dead" (Jessica
　　　　　　linked to images of death, her dress brushing past
　　　　　　the skull, etc.); Carrefour—passing the crossroads
　　　　　　(point of no return?).

SYM.: white/black (clothing, patches), rationalism/
        superstition; passage from "white" world to "black,"
        from science to voodoo, from conscious to uncon-
        scious (the darkness as the world of the unconscious).
Note: I have segmented the film here according to precise locations;
Betsy and Jessica pass from the canefields to the site of the voodoo
ceremonies, marking the transgression of another boundary, within a
single shot, half of which belongs to this segment, half to the next.

29[16½]. *The houmfort.*
        PRO.: visit to houmfort—iv: the ceremony.
        HER.: significance of dance, danger for intruders.
        SEM.: subjugation of women, phallic power (the dancers);
            possession; Betsy and Jessica linked in frame, like
            doubles (female transgression).
        SYM.: development of interlocking systems of oppression:
            white/black, master/servant, male/female.

30[8]. *Outside the door.*
        PRO.: visit to houmfort—v: plea to Umbala.
        HER.: the door, what is behind it?
        SYM.: medicine/voodoo; Betsy as white nurse involving
            herself in irrational practices associated with blacks.

31[22]. Alternating sequence: inside and outside.
        PRO.: visit to houmfort—vi: revelation, failure. Beginning
            of attempts to reclaim Jessica as zombie.
        HER.: resolution of some enigmas (Betsy's danger, what is at
            houmfort, etc.), development of others (nature of
            Jessica's illness—she doesn't bleed—partial revelation
            of "true" explanation).
        SEM.: compromise, corruption, ambiguity ("there's no easy
            way to do good, Betsy"—compare Betsy's own
            behavior and motivation); female transgression
            (theme connecting Jessica, Betsy and Mrs. Rand).
        SYM.: some of the structural oppositions abruptly drawn
            together in the ambiguous figure of Mrs. Rand:
            science/voodoo, Christianity/voodoo; darkness/light.

32[2]. *The canefields.*
        PRO.: visit to houmfort—vii: the return journey.
        HER.: will they be pursued?

33[4]. *Fort Holland: the garden.*
        PRO.: visit to houmfort—viii: homecoming; Betsy/Paul
            relationship: deeper understanding.
        HER.: Paul's real feelings about Jessica (explanation).
        SEM.: "the nurse who's afraid of the dark"—fear of dark-
            ness, the unconscious.
        SYM.: white music (Chopin theme on soundtrack) con-
            trasted with voodoo drums of preceding segments;
            "clean, decent thinking" vs. unconscious motivation.

34[8]. *The garden [day].*
        PRO.: visit of commissioner.
        HER.: reason for visit?; connection with visit to houmfort?;
            danger of voodoo?
        SEM.: class/race difference—the white lady's knowledge of
            horses; male/female relations (leading horse without
            looking at him); horse as representative of (male,
            white) authority (commissioner, police, Paul);
            uncertain motivation (Alma's "stupidity" as possible
            cover for eavesdropping?).

35[1]. *The houmfort* [anticipation of 37].
        PRO.: getting Jessica back—i: ritual.
        HER.: witchcraft, meaning and effectiveness of ritual.
        SEM.: male domination of women; Jessica as "doll"
            (compare No. 11).
        SYM.: white/black, rationalism/ superstition.

36[3]. *Jessica's room.*
        PRO.: Paul/Betsy relationship: mutual respect.
        HER.: relationship between Jessica and voodoo? Paul's guilt?
        SEM.: male/female relations: male authority, female submis-
            siveness (deviousness?).
        SYM.: harp/drums.

37[5]. *The houmfort.*

>PRO.: getting Jessica back—ii: the agent.
>HER.: precise meaning of ritual? Carrefour as zombie?
>SEM.: the "living dead": connection between Jessica and
>   Carrefour.
>SYM.: white/black: blurring of boundary.

38[5]. *The garden.*

>PRO.: Paul/Betsy relationship: confession of love, need for
>   separation.
>HER.: will Betsy return to Canada?
>SEM.: male authority/female submissiveness (deviousness?);
>   male desire to dominate/destroy women—Paul's fear
>   of his own impulses.
>SYM.: Canada/West Indies.

39[43]. *Jessica's room—garden.*

>PRO.: getting Jessica back—iii: the agent, failure.
>HER.: Carrefour as zombie: is he dangerous? will he
>   succeed? basis of Mrs. Rand's authority over him?
>SEM.: Mrs. Rand's authority, her usurpation of power,
>   transgression of male order.
>SYM.: home (Fort)/houmfort—transgression of barriers;
>   harp/shadow of Carrefour.
>SEM.: "Isle of the Dead."

40[34]. *The living-room.*

>PRO.: investigation, confession.
>HER.: Jessica's illness: explanation vi: the "true" explanation,
>   immediately blocked by Dr. Maxwell (Jessica never
>   died), followed at once by new enigma (Mrs. Rand's
>   "of course").
>SEM.: family tensions; repression/punishment of female
>   sexual desire; ambiguity of Mrs. Rand's position (she
>   destroyed Jessica in order to protect the patriarchal
>   system within which women are subordinated, siding
>   with the "firstborn," Paul, for whom she never shows
>   any affection, against Wesley, whom she loves); the
>   oppressed become in turn oppressors.

SYM.: the "white" system (patriarchy, the family) and the
    "black" system (voodoo) joined as oppressive sys
    tems; the major oppositions undermined in Mrs.
    Rand.
Note: recurrent visual motif: Mrs. Rand's pocket handkerchief as
voodoo-patch.

41[17]. *Houmfort, garden* [alternating sequence].
    PRO.: getting Jessica back—iv: another ritual.
    HER.: Jessica's illness: explanation vi confirmed (removal of
        "block" by revelation of coma; Jessica's response to
        ritual).
    SEM.: voodoo as black male power.
    SYM.: the half-brothers, the "righteous" and the "sinner,"
        on opposite sides of gate (Paul's scepticism, Wesley's
        belief in voodoo); echoed by Betsy/Jessica opposition.
Note: recurrent visual motif: the pocket handkerchief as voodoo
patch, here associated most prominently with Paul, the apparently
"righteous" brother who doesn't believe in voodoo; hence:
    SEM.: undermining of moral certainties.

42[6]. *The garden, the veranda.*
    PRO.: "freeing" Jessica—i: Betsy's complicity sought.
    HER.: what will become of Jessica?
    SEM.: Betsy's "integrity": she can't do deliberately what she
        has tried to do unconsciously (eliminate Jessica).
    SYM.: Ti-Misery (the white/black opposition undermined).
Note: Recurrent visual motif: watch pendant as voodoo-patch.

43[12]. *The garden, the houmfort* [alternating sequence].
    PRO.: "freeing" Jessica—ii: Wesley as agent.
    HER.: Jessica's fate.
    SYM.: the oppositions joined in Wesley (acting as another
        "zombie"); use of arrow from Ti-Misery.

44[27]. *The seashore.*
    PRO.: "freeing" Jessica—iii: "death."
    HER.: resolution of problems.
    SEM.: oppression involving both worlds, white/black,
        Christian/voodoo, rational/irrational: the problem-

atic of transgressive sexual desire (especially *female* desire) and its punishment or elimination to maintain the patriarchal order.

SYM.: white/black: possession of Jessica (Wesley/Carrefour).

45[7]. *The sea.*

PRO.: recovery of bodies—i: the sea.

SEM.: the sea, as signifier of uncertainty, deceptiveness, ambiguity (compare segment 3)

SYM.: voice of minister (black, Christian) begins on soundtrack; hence:

SEM.: undermining of oppositions; continuance of oppression.

46[7]. *The garden.*

PRO.: recovery of bodies—ii: procession home; resolution of Paul/Betsy relationship.

SEM.: a. the "happy end."

b. continuance of themes of oppression, ambiguity, undermining of clear-cut oppositions: the black minister, Mrs. Rand, Ti-Misery (on whom the film ends).

Appendix I: Beyond the *Grande Syntagmatique*

A number of critics (notably Raymond Bellour) have pointed out that, while it makes a useful starting-point for segmentation and analysis, Metz's *Grande Syntamatique* can have the unfortunate side effect of exaggerating the autonomy of the so-called "autonomous segments"—that the individual segment is invariably contained within larger patterns of alternation, repetition, and symmetry that structure the entire film. It is scarcely possible here to demonstrate this systematically and exhaustively; I have selected three examples which at once illuminate particular aspects of *I Walked with a Zombie* and illustrate the working of classical Hollywood films in general. The first two concern the film's overall structure, the third exemplifies the patterns of symmetry and asymmetry within a segment larger than Metz's classification allows for.

1. *The sea.* As indicated in the foregoing reading, the image of the sea is used symmetrically to mark the beginning and the end of the film and the turning-point of its actions. But this is not to be seen as a *mere* formal device, *mere* pattern-making: at the outset of the film (segment 3) the sea is invested with a specific metaphysical meaning ("deceptiveness of appearances," etc.) which has resonances throughout a film in which nothing is what it seems, and in which most of the main characters (Paul, Jessica, Mrs. Rand, Betsy herself) turn out to be ambiguous in various ways.

2. *Night/Day.* The most obvious structuring principle operating across the film as a whole is the alternation of day and night. Clearly, this has its significance in relation to the film's complex structure of "symbolic" oppositions indicated in the "reading" above (Canada/West Indies, white/black, science/witchcraft, Chrisianity/voodoo, conscious/unconscious, etc.). The alternation can be set forth as follows (the numbers refer of course to the segments in the reading):

Day:	1, 2,		4, 5,	11–16,	18,		22,		24, 25,		34,		40,	
Night:		3,		6–10,		17,		19–21,	23,			26–33,	35–39,		41–46

It will be obvious that the alternation is neither consistent nor symmetrical; the imbalance takes on great resonance in relation to the overall thematic and dramatic movement of the film. In the earlier part, there is a fairly even distribution of day and night scenes; in the latter part, night progressively takes over. From segment 26 (the departure for the houmfort, very strongly marked as the film's only true sequence-shot), only 2 of the 21 segments are set in daylight.

3. *Symmetry within a larger segment.* The formal principles of symmetry, alternation, repetition operate within classical Hollywood cinema at all levels. The arrangement of shots within an individual sequence will show a frequent tendency to a rough symmetry. An example from *I Walked With a Zombie* chosen at random: segment 3 (the ship), composed of 13 shots, begins and ends by cross-cutting between Paul and Betsy in isolation, separated on the boat; the central shot (No. 7) is both (a) by far the longest take in the sequence and (b) the shot in which Paul moves into Betsy's space, so that they are in frame together.

Here, however, I want briefly to indicate the tendency to symmetry over a larger segment than a single sequence. I have chosen the visit to the houmfort, because it is the core of the film. The segment divides between four (continuous) locations, which we may identify as follows:

A. The garden of Fort Holland.
B. The canefields.
C. The site of the ceremony (dance).
D. The interior of the houmfort.

From segment 26 to segment 33 (inclusive), this gives us the progression A B C D C B A. The central movement (in certain aspects, central to the whole film), the revelations of Mrs. Rand's position, is marked further (within a segment predominantly characterized by darkness) by the abrupt switching-on of a lamp. (It will be noticed that the symmetrical use of locations is qualified by the asymmetry of duration: the recurrence of locations C and B after D is much briefer than their initial appearance).

Appendix II: The Operations of the Codes

We can, finally, draw some conclusions from our tracing of the four codes throughout the film (though the reading of a complex work can never really be concluded).

First, the two linear codes (Proairetic, Hermeneutic): they are dominant (though not always to the same degree) in every classical Hollywood film, whose first aim and duty has always been *to tell a story*. Every story, and every telling, depends for its success on the logic of its chain of actions and the maintaining of interest and curiosity through its chain of enigmas. It is not quite possible to imagine a narrative film that entirely lacks a semantic/symbolic structure: as soon as you introduce a good character and a bad character you have the beginnings of one, and even the most childish and simple "B" western will produce its set of oppositions (*good* cowboy wears *white* hat, rides *white* horse, *bad* cowboy wears *black* hat, rides *black* horse, etc.). But on that rudimentary and banal level, the only interest of the film is likely to be on the level of what-happens-next (usually quite predictable, also). One might venture the proposition that, the richer and more complex the semantic/symbolic structure, the finer the film.

At the same time, the linear codes represent—in the overwhelming majority of cases—the *conscious* level of Hollywood film-making: even the greatest Hollywood directors (for example, Ford and Hawks) tend to discuss their films predominantly in terms of the story, the action, the characters, apparently being (at most) only vaguely aware of the semantic/symbolic dimension of their work. What is also crucially important is that it is on the level of the linear codes that Hollywood films have always been most vulnerable to censorship in various forms (from studio decisions to the strictures of the Motion Picture Production code, elaborated to guard against subversion of the dominant norms of society in any form), simply because that is the level of which censorship is conscious, the level that must be seen to conform to the demands of "the dominant ideology." In Hollywood film, then, the level of the linear codes—roughly, the level of the "plot"—is likely to be (superficially, at least) conservative, the "restoration of order" at the end being the restoration of the status quo, patriarchy and the conventional morality that serves it.

One can see this clearly (and typically) in *I Walked with a Zombie*. We have specified the "dominant action" as the development of the Paul/Betsy relationship, and the "dominant enigma" as the problem of Jessica (her illness, its cause, its nature, what can be done with her?). One can trace, through the reading of the film offered, the interdependence of the two and their perfect correlation at the end: with Jessica at last dead, and her enigma explained, Paul and Betsy can embrace. To put it another way: the film moves, in a way paralleled in countless other narratives, towards the elimination of the "bad couple" (Wesley, Jessica), who have transgressed the patriarchal moral code, in order finally to construct the "good couple" (Paul, Betsy).

What interests me here above all is the ambiguity of that relationship between the operation of the linear codes and that of the semantic/symbolic structure, which supposedly sustains them but in fact undermines them: I want to claim that the whole linear progress of the film towards its apparently conformist, conventional, reactionary resolution, effectively collapses under the weight of semantic/symbolic implication. One can suggest how this comes about by listing the dominant themes that are established, reiterated and developed: deceptiveness of appearances, uncertainty of motivation, oppression (on many levels, in many forms), female transgression . . . etc., etc. . . . and by tabulating the intricate structure of binary oppositions indicated as forming the film's symbolic structure:

Canada	West Indies
white	black (race)

white	black (clothing)
day	night
science	witchcraft
Christianity	voodoo
home (Fort)	houmfort
light	darkness
conscious	unconscious
harp, piano	voodoo drums
rationalism	superstition
etc., etc. . . .	

One must then go on to indicate (as I have done in the reading of the film) how the apparently clearcut nature of the oppositions (in a *simple* narrative they would be reducible to "good"—left-hand column—and "evil"—right-hand column) is systematically undermined as the film progresses, so that all moral certitude is lost; and also to indicate how all this affects our reading of the characters and their actions. I suggest here a few points where linear and non-linear codes intersect.

1. *Jessica's illness.* We are clearly meant to take explanation vi (Mrs. Rand's confession) as the "correct" one, yet it is clear that it complements rather than disqualifies the preceding ones: Jessica was engaged in an adulterous affair with Wesley; she and Paul had a violent argument in which he said terrible things to her; she fell ill, succumbing to a tropical fever; only then was Mrs. Rand able to intervene. In other words, all the family is implicated in Jessica's condition.

2. *Betsy.* Signified heavily as the "pure," "innocent" heroine ("clean, decent thinking," etc.), Betsy is in fact drawn into the web of moral ambiguity (repeatedly suggested visually, by the intricate lighting effect): the insulin shock treatment and visit to the houmfort (both of which she has been assured are extremely dangerous) can be read as (unconscious) attempts to eliminate Jessica, not save her.

3. *Paul.* Interestingly, one enigma is left conspicuously un-resolved, what one might call the chicken-and-egg question of Paul's character; certain elements in the film suggest that he be-came bitter and cynical because of his wife's infidelity, others suggest (more emphatically and more convincingly) that he was always like that (which can be read as the motivation for Jessi-ca's desire to run away with Wesley). The film's nominal "happy ending" in no way *guarantees* happiness: as Betsy and Jessica are frequently paralleled in the film, we are free to believe that Betsy's fate will be similar to that of her deceased patient.

4. *The Voodoo patches.* The canefield sequences associate the woman's protective voodoo patches with the recurrent theme of ambiguity (white on black, black on white). But this is taken up in the visual motif that runs through the film: Betsy's watch pendant, the brooch she gives to the baby (segment 24), the pocket handkerchiefs, of which Mrs. Rand's (40) and Paul's (41) are especially prominent, all figure as subtle reminders of the transgression of boundaries, the uncertainty of accepted val-ues.

5. *Ti-Misery.* Arguably, the central symbolic image around which the whole film is organized. Introduced in segment 5 (by verbal reference), he is visually prominent in segments 6, 10, 26, 43, and 46. Combining white Christian saint and black slave, he becomes a generalized image of oppression, transgressing the boundaries between the film's oppositions: it is fitting that the film ends with a tracking-shot in on him.

13

Creativity and Evaluation
Two Film Noirs of the Fifties

For Simon, my son, from whom I have learnt so much

To surround anything, however monstrous or ridiculous, with an air of mystery, is to invest it with secret charm, and power of attraction which to the crowd is irresistible. False priests, false prophets, false doctors, false patriots, false prodigies of every kind, veiling their proceedings in mystery, have always addressed themselves at an immense advantage to the popular credulity, and have been, perhaps, more indebted to that resource in gaining and keeping for a time the upper hand of Truth and Common Sense, than to any half-dozen items in the whole catalogue of imposture.

CHARLES DICKENS, *Barnaby Rudge*

This article began as a very modest project, both in length and ambition: during a course on film noir I screened, in consecutive weeks, *The Big Heat* and *Kiss Me Deadly;* I became interested in the many parallels between the two films, and, as a direct consequence, in what seemed the importance of making certain discriminations between them; I then decided to work up my notes into a short article. At the same time, however, I became conscious of a certain uneasiness, as if the simple exercise I was undertaking were somehow suspect or invalid. This led, in turn, to some wider ranging meditations on the function of criticism and what has become of it during the past two decades, accompanied by a kind of indignation that I should allow myself to feel guilty for trying to fulfil that function. F. R. Leavis consistently saw evaluation as the ultimate aim and justification of criticism. I still think he was right. This belief has survived over 20 years of theoretical positions that have regarded evaluation as either superfluous, unimportant, or actively reprehensible. The opening of a new decade provides an appropriate moment for defending it.

Hostility to evaluation (at least, seriously argued hostility) begins with *Movie* in the early '60s. The original team of founders/editors/writers were quite explicit about this; when I wrote for the magazine I was very conscious of warily slipping in value-judgements, testing the ground to see how far I dared to go. My name has consistently been linked to the early *Movie* and its critical practice, and certainly I wrote for it often, but although I remain proud of the connection I never felt a part of its critical core. That I was a frequent contributor is due more to generosity and tolerance of its founding members, who found they could peacefully coexist with me, than to any sense of comfortably shared critical principles. They viewed Leavis with considerable mistrust. *Movie*'s rejection of evaluation always seemed to me somewhat rhetorical, more apparent than real. It seemed based on an honourable but misguided notion of the "democratic": to offer an explicit value-judgement was to attempt to force that on readers, an act of coercion, and the critic then became a kind of dictator of norms. Instead, it was the critic's task to *describe,* as accurately as possible; the reader, his/her own perceptions fortified or corrected by this "accurate" description, would then be in a position to reach an enlightened response to the work in question. Such was the rationale. The fact remains that the *Movie* critics only described films that they loved (apparently a description of a film you disliked would be biased and misleading, a regrettable weakness from which "positive" descriptions were somehow mysteriously immune): their descriptions, while usually scrupulously "accurate" in terms of the factual information they conveyed, plot, camera-style, editing, etc., were, when they were worth reading, animated by that love. The evaluation was there, but pretending it wasn't: invisible, under the cloak of "objectivity."

Essentially, *Movie* criticism retained its links with the traditional function of art, as it has always (with a very wide range of specific cultural/historical variations) been perceived and experienced. By the end of the decade those links have been brutally shattered and evaluation declared either retrograde or merely beside the point. I had better at this stage define what I take the traditional function of art to have been (and what for most of us it still is, all intimidations to the contrary). Perhaps I should write "functions," in the plural, though the various partly distinguishable functions intricately interact, merge into one another. First, then, there is the simple function of giving pleasure, the forms of "pleasure" ranging from casual amusement to the most intense religious exaltation, the varieties of pleasure asked of art, in any particular time and place, depending on cultural/historical specificity. The pleasure given by art is (potentially at least) extremely complex. There is the pleasure of recognition and familiarity, always reassuring (at lowest, the enjoyment of a joke that flatters one's own prejudices); there is the pleasure of novelty, of difference, of being told something we didn't already know or had never thought. It seemed probable that the richest works of art developed out of an interaction between those two phenomena (the operas of Mozart and the plays of Shakespeare would be obvious examples). One of the finest pleasures of art is that of extending and expanding one's own experience, by growing to understand and embrace other people, other sensibilities, other cultures, the expansion of our own emotional and intellectual potential. I can testify to the crucial importance to me—growing up in an oppressive, emotionally and intellectually constricting British middle-class environment—of discovering, during my adolescence, classical music. Whole worlds of experience suddenly opened up to me, accessible though previously unimaginable: the successive discoveries—Tchaikovsky,

Beethoven, Stravinsky, Bach, Mozart—completely haphazard, accompanied by no sense of cultural determination or historical background, totally transformed my life, awakening me to the sense of human potential beyond anything that my immediate environment recognized or could cope with. I am glad no one informed me at that time that all I was experiencing was various assemblages of culturally constructed signifiers. Central to all these forms of pleasure is the sense of sharing, of participation and identification: learning, often slowly and painfully, to share the experience of the maker or makers of the work, and to identify imaginatively with that experience.

Obviously, the experience of sharing, of participation, of identification (which we know can never be perfect, always coloured by our own subjectivity) depends upon a strong sense of personal authorship. With the rise of semiotics, personal authorship—or individual creativity—was declared to be no more than a fatuous illusion: works of art are not products of the individual's drive to create, but of ideology. As soon as one accepts this, the whole traditional function of art as I have described it collapses. The problem is that it is not easy to accept—or even to *grasp*—the function that is supposed to have replaced it. A work of art is not—we are not to believe—produced by the artist's desire to satisfy her/his creative impulses and share experiences, attitudes, values, with others; it consists merely of a collection of signifiers (preconstructed, seemingly, by the culture) more or less intricately combined. The organic has been replaced by the mechanistic, the artist struggling to comprehend, cope with, and if possible resolve urgent problems of living has been replaced by a child building a structure with a mechano set. It seems that we should not even express a preference for one of these structures over another: if evaluation is "out," then presumably the implication is that all such structures are of identical value, for if their value is *not* identical why are we supposed to find the qualitative differences not worth discussing? The question of function remains somewhat obscure: if it is not what we had supposed it to be, then what is it? Why have we been so stupid as to allow ourselves to become emotionally involved with a set of preconstructed signs? Why have people like Beethoven and Van Gogh been so stupid as to believe they were producing personal statements that also had cultural significance, that spoke for both themselves and their culture? I have not seen this question tackled within the semiotic tradition, perhaps because the implicit answer to it would seem slightly absurd were it to be spelt out: "works of art" (mechanistic, predetermined) are produced in order to give semioticians (superior, knowing, *not* predetermined) at best the opportunity to deconstruct the ideology of their culture, at worst the opportunity to show off.

It has come to seem to me but another manifestation of the incredible sickness of our civilisation. *Are* we trapped in a universal death wish?—Do we really all *want* to be dead? On the one hand the building of a nuclear power, the pollution of the environment, the spread of conservatism with all its concomitants—the endorsement of wealth, the proliferation of poverty, the deliberate erosion of woman's rights, native American rights, the sharp increase of racism (all of which go together in intricate interconnection); on the other (in so far as it still matters—having complacently accepted its social role of "the academic" it has forfeited much of its significance), the perverse denial by intellectuals of everything that *fundamentally* matters, that gives life meaning, the only force that could rejuvenate and transform the civilisation: creativity. When I first encountered the semiotics movement (in England in the early '70s, when semiology became the official methodology of *Screen*), it seemed—although perversely abstruse, mystificatory and jargon-ridden—-genuinely progressive and political. Today, I understand that there are university courses in "postmodernist" semiotics that are explicitly anti-feminist and anti-Marxist, and that teach the new generation of potential revolutionaries that nothing can be done and all action is meaningless. Within the present cultural circumstances, to give one's students the sense that they can't change anything is probably the vilest crime any teacher can commit. But even aside from what I charitably assume are atypical aberrations, who really, in academic circles, cares any more, since the decisive moment when we learnt that everything can be deconstructed? It gives us a nice, secure, impregnable position: Everything is mechanistic, everything is determined, so we can sit back and enjoy our yuppie affluence, meanwhile churning out scholarly papers that pay dutiful lip-service to feminism and political liberation, but prove ultimately that everything is really hopeless and we can all sit comfortably on our fat asses mourning the pity of it all and relishing our *filets mignons,* along with the wives and servants who have prepared them for us. I've been there for 20 years now: I've seen it all.

It is not difficult to see why academic film study allowed itself (aside from a few isolated pockets of resistance) to be appropriated, overwhelmingly, by semiotics. In the early days, semiotics promised so much, and with such confidence: it was to be the answer to all critical/theoretical problems, transcending every theory of film that had hitherto been proposed, rendering obsolete all other types of critical discourse. Consequently, it conferred upon film study a convincing academic respectability: unlike previous discourses on aesthetics, it was "scientific," its findings were verifiable. And no semiotician, once "hooked," seems ever to have suffered from doubts: doubts, especially, as to what was the cost of this new hegemony, doubts about the omissions and suppressions on which it was constructed. Academia had always had problems coping with art (the history of which goes way back to the struggles to include "Literature" other than "Classical"—i.e., Greek and Latin—literature in the university curricula). Art is by definition not "scientific," and no attempt to encompass it in a "scientific" discourse, though it may have its provisional uses, can ever be adequate (the basic crime of semiotics was it pretence to adequacy). The function of art, both personal and social, is deeply involved with our emotional life; emotions are not merely "unscientific," they are also unacademic. University professors are not supposed to discuss the feelings (elation, despair, disturbance, etc.) that a given work arouses in them: in other words, they are expected to eliminate from their professional discourse all relation to art's real function. Students, correspondingly, are taught to suppress their feelings (that is to say, their active engagement in "reading" the work adequately) in favour of the elaboration of statements that can somehow be regarded as verifiable, as opposed to the type of provisional agreement/disagreement (Leavis's "This is so, isn't it?"/"Yes, but . . .") that characterizes the finer types of critical discourse/collaboration. That these "verifiable" statements rest upon a structure of theories that are both unproven and unprovable is a point that is conveniently ignored. This is why most papers read out at conferences, and most student essays, are so boring: all the potential life has been deliberately and perversely forced out of them. Film study once had the potential to challenge the whole constricting and oppressive concept of "the academic," to be the vanguard of a revolution within that concept; instead, it has sold out to it.

If university students ever feel inclined to start a new revolution (it could hardly develop in isolation, only as part of a general movement in the culture), it could well begin as a revolt against the "academic": the restrictions on thought and feeling that the university curriculum imposes, in the content of its courses, in the careful regulation of the students' interests and desire in the imposition of essay topics, in the demand for a certain "correct" style, for constricting rules of essay construction, for the deployment of currently fashionable jargon and the thought-patterns it reproduces. Why should students—the future of civilisation, if indeed, it has one—*follow* courses? Why shouldn't they *lead* them? Students would do well to regard university professors as their own employees, and treat them as such: after all, in strict economic terms, it is the students, ultimately, who pay their salaries, either directly (in fees) or indirectly (by agreeing to participate in higher education). It is the students who should design the curriculum calling in the professors in an advisory capacity whenever they feel they might be of use (very seldom, if my estimate of many of my ex-colleagues is accurate and representative).

Any valid revolution must come from below, as a popular movement; a revolution can never be imposed. That is why an "academic" revolution would have to come from the students. I think many teachers would be ready to join it: it is not only the students who are oppressed by the system. The pressures of conformity are extreme. It is only in my last year that I have taught a course which I can remember with some pride though my own contribution to it was extremely tentative, and what I am proud of is my ability, at last, to "let go," to take a relatively passive role. The course—my own project—was an interdisciplinary Fine Arts course on some of the major currents of the 20th century culture, with reference to film, music and literature (the only fields in which I can claim expertise). Although I produced, at the outset, the requisite list of books to be read and works to be studied (partly to satisfy the bureaucracy)—we began with Mahler and Tolstoy, and ended with *A Question of Silence, Life Classes,* and the symphonies of Sallinen—I really made up the course as I went along, feeling my way from week to week, asking both myself and the students the fundamental questions: What in the contemporary crisis of our civilisation, perhaps of *any* civilisation, when the future of the planet itself may be in jeopardy—what is important? What should be discussed, in context of the arts? What *matters*? I gave the students total freedom in what they wrote or produced (a few did largely non-verbal graphic presentations). If they asked me what I wanted, I told them that the only condition was that their work should respond to the question, What does it mean, how does it feel, to be alive in the 20th century? and I quoted Diaghilev's famous demand to Cocteau: "Astonish me." They did: I have never before received such an amazing assemblage of original and exciting work. Several of the essays moved me to tears.

Universities should be run by and for the students. At present, they seem to be, predominantly, places where pompous people with Ph.Ds can develop their own sense of self-importance though the wielding of power. The first reform: no lecturer, professor, etc., should have the power of awarding grades for a course. This simple and material function is in fact the whole basis for professors' alleged "authority" (as opposed to the valid "authority" of someone who has something urgent to say): it's as basic as that. Deprive a professor of his/her power to award a grade for the course, and the only criterion for that course would be the ability to interest students: to most academics, a terrifying thought. I can see a number of my ex-colleagues having fully justifiable nightmares over it. Yet how humiliating, to feel in your heart that your students fill your classroom, not because they want to hear and discuss what you have to say, but because they hope for a B+. And how shameful to be complicit with that form of blackmail: to stand in front of a class knowing that most of the students present are listening to you, not because they care a damn about what you are saying, but because they are anxious about their degree and feel they must reproduce what you tell them in order to pass your course. Students should be willing to sit and listen to a professor only so long as they sincerely believe that what s/he is saying is important and relevant—relevant not just to the immediate topic or the course content, but to "life," and *their* lives: and only so long as he is ready to listen to *them,* without condescension (they may not have so many facts and dates at their fingertips, but they may know a hell of a lot more about "life," which is the point). One of the finest compliments I have ever been paid—and simultaneously, one of the most damning indictments of university education in general—occurred at the end of my last course, when a student (a film major) came up and told me that this was the first course he had taken where the instructor had not made him feel stupid and "talked him down" when he tried to give his own view of a film. If students would only realize the power they have—without them, a university could not exist—they might cease to tolerate such situations, and such teachers.

There has always been a certain, and necessary, gulf between artist and critic, the artist understanding his work in one way, the critic in another, which the artist may not be able to recognize (in some cases justifiably, in others as a perhaps necessary defense). But in recent years the gulf has become unbridgeable: it seems unlikely that any true artist could see his work in the way proposed by semioticians, which denies creative function altogether. If s/he did, then why produce it, as it no longer constitutes a creative act or personal statement but must be read (or "deconstructed") as a kind of automatic "writing" authored by the culture ("The author does not write, he is written")? What artist wishes to be reduced to the status of scribbling automaton? I certainly believe that artists are not able to understand fully the implications of their own work, and I think in many cases it is important to them that they don't: total self-consciousness has not shown itself particularly congenial to the production of great art. Creativity (which is all that we are ever likely to know of "god," whatever the phenomenon might be) works in very mysterious ways, most of them quite beyond the reach of semiotics. Yet any artist when s/he authorizes publication of a work, thereby accepts a personal responsibility for it. Here I am clearly on the artist's side: a critical theory that has deliberately cut itself off from the recognition of creativity, individual achievement, and personal responsibility, automatically invalidates itself. It may produce important incidental insights, and be valuable for that, but it cannot pretend to interpret the whole of the artistic process or the meaning of the works that process produces.

If the purpose of this article (which, transcending its origins, can be read as a companion piece to the article on Alice Miller that appeared in the last issue) can be summed up in a single, simple formula, I would say that it is to reinstate the word "creativity" in the available and acceptable critical vocabulary. If we don't believe in our own creativity—which is essentially a *religious* belief, in the widest sense of the word—then I don't understand what we are living for. To lose touch with the concept—I would prefer to say the *reality*—of our creativity is to become detached from the sources of life and the motivation for action. Only the creative forces can save our world: that is why it is necessary to attack the enemies of creativity at every level, wherever they manifest themselves, within the organized religions, within national and international politics, in gender politics, in the educational system, in academia . . .

The notion of creativity solves a number of problems. For a start, it resolves that tedious old opposition, source of much futile wrangling, art/entertainment: Ingmar Bergman is an "artist," Howard Hawks an "entertainer," but both must be seen as intensely, obsessively "creative": the difference is simply between the ways in which the creativity is mediated (the area in which semiotics becomes helpful), as all creativity—all human emotional and intellectual activity—must be. I have argued at length, in the introduction to *Hitchcock's Films Revisited* (reprinted elsewhere in this issue), for a reinstatement of concepts of personal authorship, suitably modified in the light of experience, and I shall not repeat the argument here. It does, however, seem pertinent to insist again on the harmfulness of the either/or opposition that semiotics has set up: *either* works of art are produced by individual geniuses out of their God-given imaginations, *or* they are cultural/ideological products. Neither term of the opposition is remotely acceptable in itself. Works of art are produced by people whose creativity has crystallized into a specific drive, working within, and partly determined and restricted by, specific cultural formations; they have been formed by the culture, and use its available conventions, but they are not its slaves or puppets. The art that wishes to assert that it is produced outside cultural determination, that wants to be perceived as unmediated personal expression (i.e., certain forms of avant-gardism), has never interested me, though it occasionally produces innovations that can be incorporated into mainstream art. The richest art has always accepted the inevitability of mediation and gladly made creative use of the available conventions, frequently developing them to the point where they are transformed (Shakespeare, Mozart, Mizoguchi . . .).

The widespread contemporary critical/theoretical hostility to mainstream cinema is, by implication, a hostility to the traditional concept and function of art itself and a desire to replace it with a different function. I think this enterprise rests upon misconception and confusion. The new concept cannot possibly *replace* the old, because the function of the "art" it gave rise to would be completely different: one can't "replace" a lawn-mower with a hair-dryer. This new concept has two (often distinct, sometimes overlapping) components: the notion that art should have *direct* social/political effect (the "agitprop" component); the notion that every work of art, to be significant, must be formally innovative, deconstructing the existing conventions. In fact "innovative" is in this context an inadequate term. Beethoven's "Eroica" symphony was certainly innovative, but it can easily be demonstrated to have developed out of what preceded it, particularly the late symphonies of Mozart and Haydn: Beethoven simply achieved an unusually long and audacious leap. The concept of innovation current today seems to involve doing something entirely different from anything done before—a virtual impossibility, hence the desperate lengths to which its practitioners have been driven, e.g., John Cage's "composition" consisting of five minutes of silence; hence also the difficulty of building any steadily evolving avant-garde tradition (a contradiction in terms, since "tradition" is precisely what such work seeks to destroy).

I am frankly not interested in this second component. The rationale behind most of its products has been the exploration of the material properties of film, and the result has been to demonstrate quite convincingly that the material properties of film are not *in themselves* very interesting and that any art form built strictly upon them is likely to be extremely limited and impoverished. I am not of course hostile to innovation, provided one doesn't make a fetish out of it: anything that offers artists more tools, a wider range of materials, more possibilities of expression, is to be welcomed on principle. An innovation—technical or formal, or simply an extension of admissible subject matter—is valuable in relation to its use. Haydn was "innovative" at many points in his long career, but many of his symphonies, quartets, etc., capitalize on innovations he had already introduced, and they seem in no way inferior to the works that actually introduced them: often, they are richer. Bach in his day was regarded as a conservative in comparison to composers who are now forgotten outside academia (they have become "of historical interest"): he simply made incomparably intelligent and resourceful use of the innovations of others. An "innovative" work is not *necessarily* of any particular artistic value: the *innovation* may be valuable (because of the ways in which it can be used), while the work may not be. It remains true that the important innovators—Haydn, Beethoven, Mahler, Schönberg, for example—have generally been great artists as well, creativity having the tendency of pushing against boundaries, often impatiently; but the great artists are not necessarily important innovators. It can certainly be argued that the greatest single achievement of the so-called "Second Viennese School" is Alban Berg's *Wozzeck,* which draws upon the innovations of Schönberg and uses them, on the whole, in a more conservative way than their great instigator.

I must also take issue here with another contemporary critical perversity (as I see it), the until recently fashionable assault on the "dominance of narrative" that mainstream cinema has foisted upon us so oppressively. The "dominance of narrative" has reprehensively impeded the full flowering of the potential of film as a medium, that potential consisting, apparently, of a set of formal/technical devices the development of which should be an end in itself, outside the dominance of anything else. (This is essentially the view, as I understand it, of Noel Burch in his formalist period and of the "Wisconsin neo-formalist school" in its remoter reaches of speculation. It should be added, in fairness, that neither seems now to stand by his/its earlier theoretical excesses, to judge from the "revisionist" introduction to the later edition of Burch's *Theory of Film Practice,* or David Bordwell's recent book on Ozu.) It will be seen that this view merges easily with the view of innovation discussed above.

I think myself that narrativity, though not the only potential of cinema, was and remains the most important and the one still capable of the richest and most complex developments. It is certainly a potential inherent in the medium itself, and not dismissible as an imposition on it of bourgeois ideology. Narrative is already inherent, potentially, in photography, and in representational painting: a picture of a tree tells us, to adapt Christian Metz, not merely "Tree," but "here is a tree." The beginning of a narrative? rather, perhaps the middle of a narrative. The tree has a history: a past, when it was a seed, and a future, when it will be timber, or a fertiliser for subsequent trees. It also has a more circumscribed history, imaged at a specific time of day or night. As soon as you move into film, the *potential* narrative becomes actualized: a shot of a leaf stirred by a breeze is already a story.

One might, of course, postulate a narrative cinema that eliminated or marginalized human beings (a cinema that Ozu and Mizoguchi, despite the posthumous theorizing of the formalists, happily never succeeded in realizing). Such a cinema might be a beneficial reminder of "Otherness," but it could never play a central role in western culture (for better or worse). It doesn't appear, so far, to have been developed in *any* culture, and certainly not in Japan. (There is a lot more to say on that subject: I propose to devote an article to Ozu in a later issue of *Cine-Action!* wherein I shall endeavour to rescue his work from the clutches of neo-formalism.) The West must, I am afraid, pursue its own destiny, for better or for worse. We certainly have it in our power to affect that destiny, but not by deflecting attention from human interaction (also known as "narrative").

It has been customary, since the early days of the semiological takeover, to denounce me as a "humanist," and the foregoing paragraphs will once again confirm this view. If humanism is defined as "Having a primary interest in human life, human potential, human creativity, human relations—personal, social, political," then I plead guilty and remain unrepentant. This interest also seems to me to provide the subject-matter of significant narrative art—again by definition.

If I am skeptical about the value often attributed to the "formalist innovation" side of avant-gardism, on the other hand I fully acknowledge the value of "agitprop": the attempts of artists to make a *direct* intervention within a specific set of social/political circumstances, in order to effect or at least influence immediate change. The function of agitprop is, however, quite distinct from the function of the art with which, as a critic, I am primarily concerned (though both may, in specific circumstances, be produced by the same artist). The difference can be seen clearly if one considers the criteria for evaluation that are relevant to the two categories. The criteria by which one judges a piece of agitprop are: (1) Is it on "my" side? and (2) Is it likely to be politically effective in influencing people here and now and promoting a specific definable end? Certainly, there are sets of political circumstances of such urgency (one could instance many in the world today, and might well argue that they have become all pervasive) in which the production of agitprop becomes top priority and the production of art almost frivolous. (For an intelligent defence of art in a period of social crisis, see Hindemith's opera *Mathis der Maler.*) When a piece of agitprop has fulfilled (or failed to fulfil) its function, it becomes of merely historical or merely aesthetic interest.

The criteria by which one judges works of art are quite other, and resist any simple definition of this kind: the *aim* of art is not susceptible to pat summary (which is its strength, not its weakness). The criteria would include terms (none of which must be taken as absolute or prescriptive) such as complexity, intelligence, sensitivity, emotional generosity, relevance to "life," as well as (and in close and necessary conjunction with) the aesthetic criteria of form, structure, style. The significant fusion of these two sets of criteria is what Leavis sums up in his indispensable terms "enactment" and "realization."

It will be objected (quite rightly) that the above is still too simple, that the opposition art/agitprop is often not so clear-cut. (I leave aside here the question of "propaganda": I assume that the distinction between propaganda and agitprop is that the former is produced by those in power and the latter by those who wish to overthrow it. My argument therefore has no room for propaganda.) *Middlemarch* is a work of art, the graffiti "NO TO HOMOPHOBIA" which is still, at time of writing, on prominent display at York University is a piece of agitprop. But what of, for example, Marleen Gorris's admirable *A Question of Silence:* art or agitprop? Clearly, it contains elements of both. What I am trying to define, however, is a difference in *function,* and there is no reason why two distinct functions should not in certain circumstances be combined, become fused. In general, it is not the function of art to effect direct and specific social change: if it does, it does so incidentally. Works of art (not necessarily good ones) that have had direct, discernible, statistically demonstrable social effect are very rare indeed: it was reported that many people joined the Campaign for Nuclear Disarmament after seeing *On the Beach* (how long the impetus lasted is less easily verifiable); and *Oliver Twist* reputedly influenced changes in the Poor Laws in Victorian England (as the most disgraceful poverty—disgraceful from the viewpoint of the culture that permits it—is still very much with us and around us, the changes, though obviously valuable for their time and place, cannot be held to have been very radical). There does not seem to me to be any contradiction in applauding these works for the effect they produced while insisting that *On the Beach* is by no stretch of the imagination a great film and that *Oliver Twist* is very far from being among Dickens's greatest novels. This does not mean that art has no social effect: simply that it is impossible to measure it. *Dombey and Son,* which formally "enacts" and "realizes" its themes in ways of which the Dickens of *Oliver Twist* was incapable, remains today one of the greatest *feminist* novels in the whole of literature, because its analysis goes much deeper than anything likely (even today) to be ratified by law.

Agitprop is for a fixed and definable purpose; art is not. That is its weakness (if you like), but it is also the definition of its importance, and why, even in an age as desperate as ours, it continues to merit our attention and commitment. It is not easy to defend art from any practical, immediate, political viewpoint, and one can certainly understand the impatience with it of people who want to see everything change and change quickly (I hope it will be clear that I strongly sympathize with them). Art can be appropriated for all sorts of purposes (and by all classes or groups of people), many of them reprehensible in the extreme. We are all familiar, for example, with the use of opera as a social event for the wealthy to display their clothes, wives, their wives' jewels and of course their "culture"; but does anyone who grasps the significance of Verdi's operas wish to relegate them to that function? Then there is the oft-quoted case (it doesn't matter whether it is fact or myth, as it is perfectly plausible) of the concentration camp commandant who used to relax after the onerous duties of the day by playing Schubert on the piano. The answer to that one seems to me as simple: to use Schubert merely as an escape is to demonstrate one's total inability to understand him. The disturbing fact remains: art always offers that licence. You can choose to ignore its meaning and imbibe it as "culture"; you can read *Dombey and Son* "just for the story," and take nothing else away from it. This is not because the artist "compromises," "sugars the pill," etc. It is rather because great art does not deliver messages or tell people exactly what they should do, but attempts to represent, explore and criticize human experience as fully and honestly as possible, and the more complete and adequate the representation, the easier to ignore or minimize the criticism, since experience is always many-sided and ambiguous.

The answer to these perplexities seems to me not the rejection of art but its redemption, which is synonymous with its appropriation for radical purposes. Such an appropriation is perfectly valid and intellectually justifiable as it is based (unlike the social displays of opera-goers or the relaxation of concentration camp commandants) upon a recognition of art's true nature. A great work of art is by definition (whatever its more superficial meanings, which could be extremely conservative) an embodiment of human creativity; and it is human creativity (the phenomenon that all the dominant forces of our epoch, on every level, are bent upon repressing, destroying or denying) that is the basis, validation and impetus of all resistance to oppression, all protest, all justified revolution.

Creativity has perhaps never been understood, acknowledged, and valued at its worth within capitalist culture: as the supreme value of human life, no less. A culture founded upon greed, competition and money-values must at bottom be terrified of it, whatever lip-service it pays to "art," "individualism," "expression," etc.: a *liberated* creativity could only be deeply threatening. At some deep level our culture acknowledges the threat, and responds to it: we live in an age when creativity is being systematically destroyed or perverted at every level, both by the capitalists and by the intellectuals who profess to be their enemies. Only a few voices, today, speak for life, and they are in constant danger of being drowned out. Who can realize his/her creativity, and what form can creativity assume as its flesh, in a world in which it is confronted on all sides by moral and aesthetic ugliness and squalor, and where these—the values of consumer-capitalism—are raised up as the values by which people are supposed to live? You have only to ride, with open eyes, on a subway train in any of our cities, and examine the advertisements that surround you, to recognize the simple truth of this assertion. It becomes difficult to understand how anyone, leafing through the pages of his/her daily newspaper, does not draw the obvious conclusions and become committed to the necessity for revolution: it is unlikely that any page will not contain evidence of some horror *directly attributable to the conditions and structures of our culture,* whether it be national or international, general or personal, from yet another instance of child abuse through an exposure of yet another political scandal to the report of yet another environmental hazard produced and condoned by "businessmen" who love their children and grandchildren so very much but basically don't care whether they grow up in a world in which it is possible to even survive, provided profits continue to accumulate.

I want to develop the argument for the radical appropriation of art, and I shall argue it at its most difficult, taking as my example not the cinema (the political dimensions of which—from melodrama to screwball comedy, from musical to film noir, from western to horror film—should by now be obvious enough), but the apparently abstract, non-narrative, art of classical music, where one cannot point to such obviously "political" features as the presentation of character-relationships, etc. And I shall make things even more difficult for myself by concentrating on the most seemingly abstract of all great composers, the man who, at one stage of a long and varied career, actually declared that music, by its nature, is incapable of expressing anything. I am thinking less here of Stravinsky's early ballets (the so-called "Russian period," where the major influence was Debussy) than of the extraordinary succession of the assured, mature masterpieces produced from the '20s on—roughly from the Wind Octet to *Agon.*

Stravinsky is an especially useful figure to evoke in the context of semiotics, because no composer has had a stronger sense of music as a sign-system, or series of sign-systems. In his mature works he deliberately employs the conventions, the idioms, of virtually every period of western music, from the Middle Ages to Schönberg, from Bach to jazz. The result is neither parody nor pastiche, though it has been mistaken for both: although wit and humour play important roles in the music, we are never invited to laugh at or feel superior to the conventions it employs; although the past is always present in the music—by reference at least—there is never a sense that the past is being reconstructed. Every work is astonishingly *new,* even when it quotes (see, for instance, what Stravinsky does with the theme of the *Barber of Seville* Overture, in the "third deal" of *Jeu de Cartes*)—innovative in the best sense, rooted in tradition but pressing forward to new discoveries. Hence, Stravinsky's insistence that he was not a "composer of music" but an "inventor of music." Every work—even the relatively slight ones—asks to be heard as (whatever else besides) an embodiment and celebration of creative energy, of the joy of liberated creativity, a creativity fuelled by the rediscovery of the past. The creativity manifests itself, above all in the music's extraordinary fusion of the physical and the spiritual (perhaps its strongest, most constant characterizing feature). No music is more intensely physical. If chance initially involved Stravinsky in the ballet, it was not chance that took him back to it repeatedly, through all the transformations of his career. Every Stravinsky work—not only the ballets or those that build explicitly on dance forms—consistently evokes bodily movement. (It is very difficult to keep still while listening to the *Dumbarton Oaks* Concerto!) At the same time, the music is perhaps unique, in our *angst*-ridden century, in its *convincing* embodiment of spiritual qualities, such as serenity, joy, exaltation. This is, perhaps, why Stravinsky was regarded so often with distrust, as some kind of charlatan: his music is so at odds with the spirit of the age that one can easily feel that it has no right to exist. Yet the spirituality is never spurious, willed or facile: prolonged acquaintance with the music makes it impossible to doubt its authenticity. It is not, of course, at all the kind of "spirituality" to which common usage has accustomed us: it is a spirituality express through emotional toughness, wit and energy, the capacity to sustain an apparently unquenchable sense of joy from one's inner resources, in the face of the most daunting odds.

Let me specify one moment out of the hundreds one might choose as emblematic: the magical moment in the first *pas d' action* of *Apollo* where the theme (or more precisely a segment of it)—in itself a melody of unsurpassable beauty—is played in counterpoint at four different speeds simultaneously by the different sections of the string orchestra. The technical *tour de force* is important, and it is important that the listener be aware of it: the sense of extraordinary human skills fulfilling their potential is a significant factor in the effect. Closely related to this is the moment's formal satisfaction—the sense that certain potentials of the material are being fully realized. There is the seeming paradox that this high point of form and technique is emotionally a point of relative relaxation, ease, serenity. There is also the sense of a satisfying order and control: a benevolent control, a non-repressive order. It is one of the transcendental moments of modern western music (though there are at least half-a-dozen others in the same score!)—a *utopian* moment, an emblem of utopia.

Stravinsky's mature music makes nonsense of any simplistic opposition between personal expression and cultural production. In fact, the opposition seems to depend for its plausibility on the construction of a parody, an absurdly naive notion of "personal expression": Mozart was feeling a bit gloomy one day so he composed his G minor symphony; a few days later he cheered up and composed the "Jupiter." Every great artist carries within him/her the capacity for recalling and drawing creatively upon the widest range of human emotional experience, and knows how to use the culturally available signs, idioms, conventions as a medium for its expression. Bergman's statement that he couldn't have made *The Silence* if he hadn't been, at the time, a happy man is pertinent here.

Against the utopian experience of Stravinsky's music that I have tried to describe, I want to set another experience: that of wandering the streets of San Francisco at night and seeing the homeless huddled in doorways and alcoves under blankets, rags and newspapers. Does the latter experience invalidate the former, render it frivolous, escapist and morally reprehensible? I don't think so. The crucial question is the use we put it to, for what end we appropriate it. Does one separate the two experiences, or juxtapose them? It is very easy to see how Stravinsky's music, which in general has no explicit or obvious political connotations, could be used as an escape, a refuge: with its apparent denial of engagement with the social realities it lends itself to that. It depends, in the last resort, on whether one experiences it as an escape or a utopia. If the latter, then it provides a touchstone and context within which the monstrous and unpardonable enormities of our culture can be seen for what they are: instead of a refuge, it becomes a further spur to action. The realized sense of human potential, of human creativity, a unified physical/spiritual transcendence, when juxtaposed with the reality of actual *and remediable* human misery, becomes a virtual plea of revolution, for the overthrow of the domination of the greedy, the selfish, the materialistic, the seekers after wealth and power, the petty-minded, the essentially ignorant . . . the people who at present determine the development of our culture and its future, if it has one.

Or take Mahler. The 3rd symphony is perhaps the most comprehensive celebration of nature and humanity's relation to it in all music: coarse, refined, brutal, tender, raucous, gentle, banal, sublime. To listen to it within the context of the blind and brutish devastation of the environment by capitalism and Stalinist communism alike—the pincer forces of the universal death wish—has certainly become a political experience, beyond anything Mahler could have envisaged. And to listen *seriously* to Janacek's Glagolitic Mass, one must either be or become a revolutionary.

The construction of emblems of utopia—embodiment of human potential and human creativity at its highest—is one of the most important possible functions of art; it is by no means the only one. There is the strictly complementary function (each acquires its validity in part from the coexistence of the other), the examination and analysis of human existence as the artist understands it: not the unmediated depiction of some personal vision of universal "reality," "human nature," "the human condition," but the reality of social structures, social relations, the values and norms of the culture—the kind of critical inquiry found in classical Hollywood film at its finest. There is also art of protest, related to agitprop but more personal, less public, in its nature and ambitions, art that may seem (lifted out of its social context) to amount to no more than an impotent protest against life itself, but which (restored to its social context) reveals itself as protest against the most impossible and crippling social conditions. Against the utopian art of Stravinsky one might set the distinctly non-utopian art of Shostakovich, music characterized by despair, rage and sarcasm. One can readily see it as the denial of the utopian potential, and its very intensity testifies to the terrible deprivation that results from that denial: the human need for the availability of the utopian vision is made the more poignant and authentic by its absence.

Consider the astonishing creative energy that produced, say, the 8th symphony. One can relate it, certainly, to influences (the past of Russian music, Mahler, and, yes, Stravinsky at times; and isn't that Nielsen behind long stretches of the last movement, beginning from the bridge passage that leads into it from the Largo?—one would love to know whether Shostakovich was actually aware of the Great Dane) and to social circumstances (the suffering of the 2nd World War, rage against the rise of Stalinism). Does this mean that the symphony is yet another arrangement of signifiers?—that it doesn't correspond to anything that Shostakovich, as a human being in a given cultural/historical situation, thought and felt and *meant*?—that the composer did not compose, he was composed? The very idea is stupid, pettyminded and insulting: it could be advanced only by an impertinent and undistinguished mind bent on a malignant destructiveness toward everything that is of value in human life and toward all the significant achievements of human civilisation.

The semiotics movement began (in England at least) as a revolutionary movement committed to the analysis and exposure of the manifold forms of oppression; it has ended by declaring all human endeavour meaningless. One question urgently needs to be asked and answered: why has a whole generation of intellectuals, apparently dedicated to transforming culture radically by undermining its dominant norms, been so perversely preoccupied in expressing its discoveries (of which the basic and most important ones are not particularly obscure) in language impenetrable to all but the initiated? What can possibly be the *political* justification for such a strategy? Surely this weird phenomenon can be explained only in terms of a paralyzing ambivalence: the sense of the need for a total transformation of the social structure from its base upward, involving not merely changes on the level of politics and economics but in personal relationships, gender roles, taken-for-granted social institutions such as marriage and the family, all our social and sexual arrangements in all their comforting familiarity, is countered, rendered impotent, by a fear lest such a change actually come about, lest words (of which we have had so many) be converted into action. So let's keep the news safe, the possession of the intellectuals, wrapped up in esoteric language that only a small élite will understand. Finally, the movement has produced its necessary and ideal solution: the necessary change is proven to be impossible. Eureka!

To move forward from the impasse one must first move back; if, searching for a route to a new and vital future, one has taken a wrong turning and finds oneself up a dead end, one must first retrace one's steps to the point where one went wrong. I believe that point to be the moment when the intellectuals jettisoned the notion of human creativity. To correct one possible misunderstanding of what I have written so far, let me say here that I intend the term in its widest sense. Doubtless the highest manifestation of creativity, its most concrete, tangible and irrefutable embodiment, is in the great achievements of art, but these are but the highest expression of something far more general, constitutive of human-ness itself. What I have in mind is the sense in which we commonly speak of "creative emotions" or "creative relationships," and the force of this will be immediately clear if we remind ourselves that the opposite of "creative" is "destructive."

I take it as axiomatic that *all* authentic manifestations of creativity are of value, though the degree will vary enormously from instance to instance. Because it goes necessarily—by definition, one might say—with a high degree of sensitivity, creativity is extremely vulnerable, easily damaged, warped, perverted, disguising itself for protection in coldness, negativity and denial. This is how I see the work of Lynch and Cronenberg: that their films are currently held in such high esteem testifies to the frightening strength and pervasiveness, in our era, of the forces of negativity. Here the artist's creativity—while its authenticity is not in question—has been cruelly stunted, the life-affirmation which is central to the creative impulse perverted into attitudes of cynicism and disgust, attacking the roots of life itself. This is what is meant by defining the interest of such works as *Blue Velvet* and *Dead Ringers* as that of the "case": they are certainly not devoid of either interest or distinction, and there are always ways in which they can be found useful, as testimonies to the harm our culture can (and pervasively does) do to the potential of the human psyche.

If what one values in art is the manifestation of human creativity (the embodied movement of thought and feeling, intelligence and sensitivity), then the importance of evaluation as the ultimate aim of criticism—the careful arguing of value-judgements that are at once responsible and provisional—automatically follows. Semiotics has a perfectly valid and useful, but strictly subsidiary and humble, function to perform (its problem being that it has developed unwarranted and finally destructive delusions of grandeur): the analysis of the conventions and structures of non-creative artifacts (the *merely* conventional, *merely* commercial, inert and mechanical) in order to establish the background against which truly creative art can be seen for what it is. A semiological analysis of a Roy Rogers western, a television sitcom, a shampoo commercial, can be (if it is not blunted by Emperor's New Clothing of pretentious and mystificatory jargon) extremely useful. On the other hand, a semiological analysis, *if it pretends to adequacy,* of a *Heaven's Gate,* a *Celine and Julie Go Boating,* or even (descending somewhat in the scale of achievement) a *Touch of Evil,* is merely presumptuous. "If it pretends to adequacy": I grant, by that qualifying clause, that semiotics can be useful in analysing *any* work of art, as a means of establishing a work's deviation from or transcendence of the norms, rather than (as has usually been the case) reducing it *to* them: a means of establishing the degree of a work's generality and conformity, in order to highlight and foreground the important thing, the degree and nature of its specificity and distinction, which will *always* be traceable to the creativity of an author or authors. The valid task of semiotics, in order words, is to serve the critical function by clearing away the deadwood, facilitating the examination of vital growth. From this viewpoint, the entire purpose and raison d'ètre of Stephen Heath's celebrated reading of *Touch of Evil* (which remains, for all its perversity, among the most distinguished achievements of the semiotics movement in the area of film) should have been the demonstration of the extent to which Welles's creativity (with all its flaws) triumphs over and transforms the inert conventions that continue partly to structure the narrative.

Leavis always insisted upon the inseparability, in any value-judgement, of aesthetics and morality; I would turn this duo into a triumvirate by adding politics: a valid value-judgement must be at once moral, aesthetic and political. I am sometimes confronted by the perplexing—I would say intrinsically non-sensical—objection that an interest in questions of morality is in some mysterious way incompatible with, even antagonistic to, an interest in politics. I can only ask, in response, if a political judgement is not a moral judgement, then what is it?—what can it possibly mean and what can be its basis? The choice between socialism and capitalism, or between feminism and non-feminism (by which term I mean an indifference to feminism; *anti*-feminism, which can rest only on bigotry and blind stupidity, does not merit serious consideration, despite its current hideous re-emergence), is a *moral* choice: a choice, in my view, between morality and immorality.

Before passing to specific examples of the kinds of critical value-judgement that seem to me worth attempting. I shall sum up the first part of this article by reiterating certain key points. They seem to me obvious, but the obvious continues to be conveniently ignored by those who find it inconvenient.

1. The reason for the rejection of the concept (or reality) of creativity (one of the most *necessary* terms in the critical vocabulary) is doubtless partly that it inevitably brings in its wake other concepts (personal authorship, spiritual values, "religious" experience) that are anathema to our self-professed "scientific" Marxists (to the disastrous impoverishment of Marxism): like creativity, they have to be rejected as mere bourgeois illusions, despite the fact that they have, in their infinite manifestations, animated every known culture since that of the cave-dwellers, and continue to animate our own (in so far as it is still capable of being animated—one should not mistake its convulsive mechanistic jerkings for creative energy), despite concerted efforts to repress or deny them.
2. Creativity, though it must be taken as one of the defining characteristics of humanity, central to any concept of "life," if "life" means more than mere inert or mechanical existence, can only express itself—embody itself—in ideological forms. This is presumably why semioticians manage to reduce it to some kind of ideological manifestation or function: creativity becomes "an effect of the text," not the force that animates it.
3. Creativity is fostered or stifled by specific cultural conditions.

Given the realities of our contemporary civilisation, it is amazing—and a tribute to its tenacity, its "inextinguishability," to borrow a title from the great Carl Nielsen—that it survives at all, especially as so many of those who should be passionately defending, preserving and nurturing it (the true function of criticism) seem perversely bent on denying its reality.

4. The kind of use the creative artist makes of the available forms—her/his attitude to those forms—will depend very much upon the whole complex of existing cultural conditions. It has been possible, in certain phases of our civilisation (frequently those that have been richest in the production of art) for artists to feel comfortable within the available forms and able to develop and enlarge them from within: Bach, Mozart, Haydn, Shakespeare were all of this type, and so were certain of the great directors of the classical Hollywood period (Hawks and Ford, for example). At other times the nature of the artist's creativity and her/his situation within the culture will make it impossible to work comfortably within the available forms; the moulds will quickly shatter from the strain, and new forms will rapidly evolve: Blake and Berlioz are obvious examples. Stravinsky, an extreme case, swiftly discovered that the tradition into which he was born was really of no use to him whatever: even *Fireworks* owes more to Debussy than to Rimsky-Korsakov, and each of the three early ballets, though still in some ways conspicuously "Russian," constitutes a leap away from his immediate musical inheritance. He eventually felt compelled to construct his own tradition, out of his progressive discoveries of the European past.

I want to safeguard myself against one other possible conception: the notion that the critical practice I am upholding here has as its function the validation/celebration of "supreme works," "immortal masterpieces," the establishment of a "Pantheon" with (as its corollary) the summary dismissal of everything that falls short. I think one needs touchstones (they are likely to vary widely from person to person): works that embody what one feels to be most valuable. Otherwise, one can get carried away by the pleasures of the moment. I watched *Turner and Hooch* the other night, and found it a decent, amusing little movie: at least, it wasn't hateful, in the manner of most contemporary Hollywood movies. If I had seen nothing *except* contemporary Hollywood movies, and read nothing except Micky Spillane, and heard no music beyond Billy Joel, I think I might have formed the opinion that it represents one of the peaks of artistic achievement. Placed in a context that includes *Anna Karenina* (Tolstoy, not Clarence Brown), the B minor Mass, and *Tokyo Story,* it appears negligible (which is not to say that I am ungrateful for a pleasant 100 minutes). On the other hand, I can see some point in devoting ten minutes to arguing for the superiority of *Turner and Hooch* to *K-9* (though I do not propose to do so here). My point is simply that discriminations are worth making at all levels of artistic aspiration. I think my own record is sufficiently clear on this: when I have argued in the past for the interest and distinction of *Fast Times at Ridgemont High* and *Eyes of a Stranger* in relation to the general run of teen sex comedies and slasher movies, I don't think I can have been taken as offering Amy Heckerling and Ken Wiederhorn as the contemporary Hollywood cinema's equivalents of Rembrandt and Leonardo. But the objection continues monotonously to recur, the simplest way of attacking a position of whose validity you don't wish to be convinced, remaining the strategy of constructing a parody of it and attacking *that.*

Consider, then, a comparison that occurred to me recently during a performance by Marianne Faithfull in a San Francisco club: W. H. Auden's "ballad" "Miss Gee"; the Beatles' song "Eleanor Rigby"; and "The Ballad of Lucy Jordan" by Shel Silverstein, made famous by Faithfull in her album *Broken English,* the rendition subsequently taken up by Makavejev for the soundtrack of *Montenegro*. (Faithfull repeats it in her new album *Blazing Away*, with immensely clearer diction—one can at last get all the words!) It might look at first sight like a simplistic and trifling exercise: the work of one of the 20th century's most "brilliant" intellectual poets placed beside a couple of (presumably) ephemeral pop songs. In fact, it is "Miss Gee" and "Eleanor Rigby" that seem to me to belong most significantly together (though there, too, there are discriminations to be made), with "Lucy Jordan" definitively "placing" them both. I am also not troubled by the fact that we are comparing works in different media (a poem, two songs): clearly, one cannot separate "Eleanor Rigby" and "Lucy Jordan" from the familiarity of their respective performances (so that authorship becomes problematic), but my concern here is with overall effect, and with the nature of the intelligence and sensibility in evidence. Obviously, the nature of the audience implicitly being addressed is of prime importance.

"Miss Gee" and "Eleanor Rigby" are linked, for all the disparity in authorial ambition and the audience addressed, by the fact that they are both by men, about women, and by their condescension toward their subjects—far more obnoxious in Auden than in the Beatles. Auden's poem, indeed, is the kind of object one wishes to hold at arm's length, one's fingers on one's nose. Even its form and manner seem condescending: the great intellectual poet goes slumming, generously reaching down to the level of those who are (understandably) baffled by the determinedly crabbed and convoluted obscurities of his "serious" work. Auden's intellectuality (a characteristic never to be confused with intelligence) has in general as its main object the establishment of his superiority to his readers (the intellectualizing proving, on inspection, to be in most cases devoid of significant substance, a mere exercising of cerebral tissue). In "Miss Gee" Auden's need to establish superiority is extended to his subject, a function for which Miss Gee is the ideal construct: to what, more than to an "old maid," could a male (even, somewhat shamefully, a gay one) feel more grandly superior? Miss Gee suffers from the Freudian cliché of producing a cancer instead of a baby (she is a victim of sexual repression, the only reason why a woman might wish to remain unmarried), and ends up, coldly dissected, as a medical specimen. On the level of conscious intention Auden apparently wants to convey his outrage at such callousness; yet the callousness is shared, unambiguously, by the poem, which dissects Miss Gee just as coldly, reveling in its own smartness. Consider, in relation to any possible expression of compassion, the tone, diction and movement of this representative quatrain:

> They laid her on the table,
> The students began to laugh;
> And Mr. Rose the surgeon
> He cut Miss Gee in half.

One could, I think, argue seriously (without making any extravagant claims) that the Beatles in their brief heyday, and within their cultural context, represented a more interesting *kind* of creativity than is embodied in the works of Auden. Many of their songs (including "Eleanor Rigby") significantly extended the range of expression and subject-matter of which "pop" music was capable. "Eleanor Rigby" remains, for me, somewhat distasteful—perhaps because "expression" and "subject matter" haven't quite jelled and the chirpy, jaunty tune is at odds with any socially aware compassion one might find in the lyrics. Compassion, in fact, is again what the song lacks, and the effect is once again of condescension, and the establishment of a superiority bordering on (perhaps passing over into) contempt: "All the lonely people" are not being offered for our understanding (the question, "Where *do* they all come from?" receives no answer, and there is no sense that the song's audience expects one) but for "us" (that is, the youth community) to feel reassured that we are not like them, we are not lonely, we can all come together and cheer at Beatles' concerts. And of course we can also have sex, unlike poor Eleanor. At least she is spared the grosser indignities of cancer and public dissection, but there remains the sense that, an "old maid," the loneliness is her just desert.

The essential difference lies in social context and in the audience being addressed: the *cultural* meaning of "Eleanor Rigby" is significantly different from that of "Miss Gee." It is not entirely clear to me just how the Beatles' audience, by the time of *Revolver* (the album that introduced "Eleanor Rigby"), is to be defined: certainly it had become much more amorphous than the audience for their early songs. The songs up to *A Hard Day's Night* (and of course including that album's title-song) seem addressed primarily to a *working-class* youth audience. Fame changes all that. And of course movie stardom: one can see the change enacted in the transition from *A Hard Day's Night* (the movie) to the very different *Help!* where the Beatles lose their class connotations and become generalized emblems of "liberation" (the film was compared by some critics to those of the Marx Brothers). By the time of *Revolver* the audience has become "youth" in general; and the middle- and upper-classes can afford to buy more records. The album seems to mark the phase of transition, a midpoint in the shift in subject-matter from the fatigue and sexual energy of working-class men ("A Hard Day's Night") to psychedelic experience ("Lucy in the Sky with Diamonds," in the *Sergeant Pepper* album). By the time of *Revolver*, also, the Establishment had begun to decree that the Beatles were "important": they could enlist the aid of Alan Civil, the leading horn-player of the Philharmonia Orchestra who had recently recorded all the Mozart horn concertos with Otto Klemperer (see *For No One*), and it would not be long before music critics were comparing them (not to their disadvantage) to Schubert. I remember that it was around this time that my wife and I (an archetypal bourgeois couple) began to collect Beatles albums, having crinkled up our noses in disgust at their earlier efforts . . .

The working class tradition from which the Beatles came, and the generalized youth audience they ended up addressing, scarcely offer more progressive attitudes to the unmarried woman (aka "old maid") than the audience for poems by fashionable intellectuals prior to the emergence of militant feminism. What makes "Eleanor Rigby" so much more acceptable than "Miss Gee" is, nonetheless, its social context. The question is of who is being invited to feel superior and why. At the heart (though it doesn't have one) of Auden's poem is the ridicule of a woman who failed to fulfil her "true" biological function, produced with smug calculation for an intellectual èlite (we needn't be *too* impressed by Auden's new-found "simplicity"—the desire to reach a wider audience never amounted to more than the vaguest gesture) assumed to share the attitude. (It is important that Miss Gee is not only an "old maid": she inhabits the spectral netherworld that is neither working-class—we mustn't ridicule "the workers"—nor successfully bourgeois.) The Beatles' song, on the other hand, is addressed primarily to a disaffected younger generation ready (up to a certain point) to reject the values of conservative bourgeois "respectability," though without any clear idea of what might replace them; its animus is directed as much against organized religion (as depicted in the figure of Father Mackenzie and his "sermons that no one will hear") as against old-maidness. Its appeal, that is, is to a *potential* anti-establishment solidarity (we are in the age of the "hippie" movement), even at the moment when the Beatles themselves were becoming an Establishment institution. That seems far less reprehensible than the knowing flattery of an èlite.

The first thing to be said of "The Ballad of Lucy Jordan" is that it is the only one of the three examples (having the advantage of a latter date) to view its subject from a feminist perspective: which is to say, showing an awareness of the realities of its female protagonist's social position. The second (closely related) is that it alone does not have as its creative motivation the desire to establish superiority to its subject. It is also the only one that is the work of women. (I know nothing about Shel Silverstein, but am assuming she is a woman—Shelley? It would be nice if she turned out to be a man,[12] because it seems so important, from every point of view, that men should become feminists; that one feels, from the internal evidence of the song, that this is very unlikely to be the case testifies to the distance most men still have to travel before they can achieve real empathy with a woman's viewpoint.)

The question of audience, and the song's relation to its audience, is again crucial. Faithfull's audience cannot be assumed to have been composed exclusively of militant feminists. Her fame initially rested upon her ignominious status as Mick Jagger's lover, and subsequently on her struggle to overcome her drug problems and on her growing self-awareness (and, with it, social awareness). The great respect that I think her work commands is due partly to the fact that she never exploits this directly personal background in any self-serving way: if certain of her songs refer to it, the tone is never either self-pitying or self-congratulatory. She assumes that her listeners "know" all about her, but she consistently maintains a distance both from them and from herself, an impersonality even when she is most "personal." One might say that her performances evoke Dietrich rather than Garland. This gains a special significance from the fact the audience at the performance I recently attended, while it included many women, was predominantly male. Of the three works I am considering, "The Ballad of Lucy Jordan" is the only one that *challenges* (as opposed to indulging) its audience.

---

12. He is!

It is impossible to separate the song from Marianne Faithfull's inimitable rendering of it (I have never heard it sung by anyone else): she has made it hers as much as its composer's, the extraordinary fusion of anger and compassion belonging as much to the performance as the text and melody. At the same time, it is obviously important that here text and melody are fully integrated: there is nothing of that sense of jarring dislocation between music and subject that one experiences when listening to "Eleanor Rigby." But the song belongs to Faithfull rather as *Now, Voyager* belongs to Bette Davis. Behind it (as performed) lies an authentic pain and struggle, for selfhood, but also for survival itself. Lucy Jordan, the bourgeois housewife and mother, whose "case" is so remote from Faithfull's own, and who never achieves selfhood, withdrawing instead into attempted suicide and insanity, is neither condescended to nor sentimentalized; the rendering establishes, simultaneously, imaginative empathy and detachment. Unlike Miss Gee and Eleanor Rigby, Lucy is presented as trapped within a clearly defined context of male control, from the "nursery rhymes she memorized at her Daddy's easy-chair," through her preordained role as housewife with its real and fantastic options ("She could clean the house for hours / Or rearrange the flowers / Or run naked though the shady streets, screaming all the way"), to the glamorous wish-fulfillment fantasy, clearly media-inspired, of riding "through Paris, in a sports car, with the warm wind in her hair," into which she finally and irrevocably withdraws. The song traces Lucy's progress through the sterile cleanliness of her world, in a single day, from her waking "in a white suburban bedroom in a white suburban town," to the moment when she is led down from her rooftop by a man (to whom she dutifully "bows and curtseys") to "the long white car that waited past the crowd": the sense of wasted potential, and specifically of *women's* potential in a male-constructed culture, could not be more devastatingly conveyed. Between them, Silverstein and Faithful have produced a small masterpiece. Were one working with film students one might move usefully from "The Ballad of Lucy Jordan" to an analysis of *The Reckless Moment.*

Before passing to the comparison that provided the initial impetus for this article, I want to stress that the reader's agreement or disagreement with the judgement I have reached above seems to me of incidental importance. I offer it, in any case, merely as an example, which could of course be multiplied indefinitely. What is of primary importance are the premises and principles involved:

a. If art matters to us *as art,* and not merely as cultural data for "scientific" deconstruction—if we take it as an activity that engages, challenges, affects, modifies our sensibilities—then discrimination becomes an essential part of our critical activity as we experience a given work (at whatever level, conscious or unconscious, that activity operates).

b. The criteria by which we evaluate a work will differ somewhat not only on a basis of individual proclivity but culturally and historically, dependent upon the specific set of circumstances in which we find ourselves. My own criteria, for example, cannot be quite the same as Leavis's, not just because I am a different person but because I live in a different age and a very different cultural situation. (This is not to say that there is no correspondence whatever; simply that the two sets of criteria, while overlapping, are not and cannot be identical.) My aim, therefore, is not to compel the reader to share my view (though it is obvious that, however fallible it may be, the *type* of judgement I have arrived at follows on from the premises), but rather to engage in an ongoing activity in which the activity itself (the complex process of experiencing, testing, weighing, comparing, pondering the work in its total context—authorial, generic, cultural, the audience it appears to address) is more important that the actual judgement reached.

c. A value-judgement must be at once moral, aesthetic and political, inseparably—though the last is given a particular edge by the contemporary crisis of our civilisation. The above comparison of "Miss Gee," "Eleanor Rigby," and "The Ballad of Lucy Jordan" is an attempt to exemplify this, and the comparison of *The Big Heat* and *Kiss me Deadly* that follows is another.

If these premises and principles are accepted, then they restore to art a valid and important role and function: as Leavis repeatedly insisted, judgement about a work of art is a judgement about "life."

In the course of which I screened the two films, we discussed at great length the historical antecedents and development of film noir; the somewhat tedious and "academic" question of whether it was a genre or a style; its relation to American (and, more widely, patriarchal capitalist) ideology; its relation to other genres, either precedent or contemporary (screwball comedy, the musical, the horror film, the World War II movie, the woman's melodrama)—the areas of difference and overlap . . . All of this proved profitable and important of course, but I found myself, increasingly, wanting to argue for the importance of discrimination between different works on quite traditional grounds that always came back, in the end, to the question of personal authorship: discriminations that drew necessarily on terms like "intelligence," "sensitivity," "complexity." I have mentioned the vague sense of guilt and uneasiness that this induced. It can be traced, I think, especially, to a fashionably dominant trend in film theory/criticism, the notion that what one should attempt to "read" (or initiate a reading of, the process being by definition interminable) is the entire text in all its endless determinations. (John McCullough's article on *The Big Sleep*—"Pedagogy in the Perverse Text"—in the last issue of *CineAction!* than which you cannot get more fashionable, is a useful example). I think the attempt to decipher texts as cultural products without boundaries, interweaving infinitely with other texts both cinematic and non-cinematic, is very interesting and potentially very profitable. It is not what I personally wish to undertake, but I am certainly not "against" it, on principle. What angers me is the arrogance of the assumption that this is now the "only" way in which we "must" read texts. McCullough's tone, in the article cited, clearly tells us that it was very reprehensible of Michael Walker to offer an "auteurist" reading of *The Big Sleep:* "we" know better now (and, whatever he might have intended, McCullough's "we" sounds suspiciously like the "Royal We" to me). Why an attempt to read a film in one way for one purpose should invalidate attempts to read it in another way for a completely different purpose is a logic that escapes me. We are back with the "either/or" syndrome, or, to take up my earlier comparison, with the desire to replace a lawn-mower with a hair-dryer: if I possess both hair and lawn I can use both. There remains, of course, the question of what is most important within a given text. I can only repeat that, if a text is alive, it is animated by personal creativity, and it is the text's aliveness that interests me.

One evaluative comparison that arose on the course was between Altman's *The Long Goodbye* and Penn's *Night Moves;* but I have already made what seem to me the necessary points in the essay on Altman reprinted in *Hollywood from Vietnam to Reagan,* and (although it was written 15 years ago) seeing the two films again in close juxtaposition fully reconfirms my judgement then. I turn instead to *The Big Heat* and *Kiss Me Deadly.*

The outcome of the comparison (to avoid any suspense)—that Aldrich at his best was a very interesting director, Lang, when working with congenial material, a great one—will cause little surprise (and will presumably, to semioticians, amount to no more than a boring irrelevancy, if indeed it is allowed even to carry any meaning). What seems to me important is the grounds on which it can be based: especially in view of the fact that Aldrich's film is clearly the more "satisfying" (i.e., coherent) of the two.

The comparison rests on the fairly close parallels between the two films. Both belong to the '50s, and are characterized by the period's mounting paranoia and potential hysteria, with the threats of nuclear power and the cold war in the background (with *Kiss Me Deadly* one might rather say the foreground). They consequently belong to what one might see as the first (partially) revisionist period of film noir, wherein the figure of the investigator (clearly the moral centre of the '40s Hammett/Chandler adaptations) is subjected to scrutiny and criticism. (The second, far more drastic, revisionist period is the '70s, with *Night Moves* and *The Long Goodbye* as prime instances.) The threat in both films is the greed for power: Lagana in *The Big Heat* wants to control the city; virtually all the characters of *Kiss Me Deadly* are trying to gain possession of "the Great Whatsit," which turns out to be nuclear energy itself, no less. In both, the hero's integrity/moral stature is called into question (ambiguously in Lang, unambiguously in Aldrich), and the criticism of the hero is articulated primarily through the women's roles. The dénouement, in each case, involves the downfall of the film's most prominent villain through a woman's violent actions (Debbie/Gloria Grahame revenges herself on Vince/Lee Marvin; "Lily Carver"/Gaby Rodgers shoots Dr. Saborin/Albert Dekker) before the hero intervenes. A crucial step in the early stages of each narrative involves the murder of a woman (Lucy, Christina) precipitated by the fact that she has given the hero information, and made possible by the fact that, because of his contemptuous attitude toward her, he offers insufficient protection.

One of the most impressive things about Aldrich's film is its relationship to Mickey Spillane's thoroughly obnoxious novel,

Dr. Saborin and "Lily Carver" in *Kiss Me Deadly*.

of which the film constitutes a drastic critique. Spillane's totally unreflecting fantasy—identification with Mike Hammer, as there seems no critical distance whatever between author and character—is unambiguously rejected in favour of what amounts to a systematic discrediting of him.

The critique of the hero is clearly central to the progress of both films. In Aldrich this is far more devastating and uncompromised—but only because the overall vision is altogether simpler and cruder. Lang plainly dislikes Bannion/Glenn Ford, but cannot simply *denounce* him, as Aldrich can Hammer, because (a) he sees him as necessary to a culture that may not be entirely unredeemable (Hammer/Ralph Meeker is as necessary as a pain in the ass) and (b) he realizes that Bannion's virtues and flaws are inseparable from each other (Hammer *has* no virtues, he is all flaw). Bannion's virtues and flaws can be summed up in a single word: he is an idealist, always a problem for a pragmatic materialist like Lang. Hammer, on the contrary, is a mere *vulgar* materialist, like virtually everyone else in the film: the case is as simple as that. He is motivated by a greed that makes him indistinguishable from the nominal villains, and the means he employs are as callous and devoid of human caring as those of the FBI. The extraordinary, irresistible force of Aldrich's film is achieved at a certain cost: the elimination of all complexity of attitude.

In both films the critique of the "hero" is effected primarily through the female characters. It is characteristic of *Kiss Me Deadly* that there this is achieved by direct and explicit denunciation: Christina/Cloris Leachman near the beginning and Velda/Maxine Cooper towards the climax, are both given speeches whose functions is in effect to tell the audience what they are to think of Mike Hammer. Neither speech seems very clearly motivated in terms of characterization and situation of the speaker: Christina has only just made Hammer's acquaintance, so that her insights into his character, while certainly valid, seem somewhat abrupt and rhetorical; Velda has been thoroughly complicit with him (to the point of prostituting herself at his instigation to incriminate errant husbands in divorce cases), bolstering his egoism, and her only reason for turning on him appears to be her recognition that this time he is involved in something much more dangerous than usual. At least the film never applauds her for "devotion to her man," but it is also clear that the women in the film, although they suffer in various ways and degrees, carry absolutely no moral weight. Both Christina and false Lily Carver die because, like everyone else, they are pursuing "the Great Whatsit"; as for Velda, what moral substance can we grant a character who devotes herself single-mindedly to the "hero" the film despises and condemns?

The case is very different when we turn to *The Big Heat*. Here, the critique of the hero—itself a far more complex matter: Bannion, unlike Hammer, is a moral crusader from the outset, and subseqently motivated by his outrage at Katie's death—is dramatically enacted, not explicitly stated in somewhat arbitrary speeches: the evidence, I would claim, of Lang's far surer, finer, more complex grasp of his theme, the token of a finer mind and sensibility. Consider how our attitude to Bannion is defined (or more precisely redefined: hitherto we have seen only the idealism) in the scene in "The Retreat" with Lucy Chapman early in the film. In retrospect from it, Bannion's automatic readiness to take Bertha Duncan on trust develops a fresh significance (we saw it earlier, I think, simply as an aspect of his moral goodness). With the confrontation with Lucy (for whose death Bannion is clearly responsible—he offers her no protection despite the fact that she has given him "dangerous" information, and treats her with undisguised contempt because she doesn't measure up to his standards of bourgeois respectability) Lang shows us the other side of the idealism, a type of idealism that is usually a "given," an unquestioned positive, but is here subjected to astringent analysis: a self-righteous priggishness, class-based, that judges people purely in terms of their social position, and which blocks Bannion from any finer insights into character. (One might comment here, as an aside, on the perfect casting of Glenn Ford).

Lucy, shortly after she gives our idealist hero the crucial information he needs to start him on the track, and is summarily dismissed for her pains, is tortured to death. Her fate seals what is already clearly there in the scene in "The Retreat," our detachment from Bannion as an identification-figure: for Lang ensures that *we* see Lucy very differently from the way in which *he* sees Lucy. The critique of Bannion is developed though his dealings with and attitude to Debbie Marsh/Gloria Grahame (another instance of perfect casting!). I discussed this at some length in an article mainly on *Rancho Notorious* in the *Film Noir* issue of *CineAction!* (No. 13/14), and shall try not to repeat myself more than is necessary for my argument. Consider, however, Debbie's death scene near the end of the film. Earlier, Debbie, in love with Bannion (or, more precisely, in love with his perceived idealism, his moral integrity) has asked him to talk to her about his dead wife Katie/Jocelyn Brando, and Bannion, seeing her as a "fallen woman" contaminated by her involvement with gangsters, in contrast to Katie's flawless, if somewhat artificially constructed, bourgeois purity, has shrunk in revulsion from doing so. At the end, he is able at last to grant Debbie's wish for three reasons: (a) Debbie has murdered Bertha Duncan for him, with the gun somewhat pointedly left with her, thereby exposing and destroying Lagana; (b) she has been instrumental in the arrest of Vince Stone; and, most important, (c) he perceives that she is dying: she can be safely sentimentalized, without the consequences of any awkward involvement or responsibility.

Between the death of Lucy Chapman and the death of Debbie Marsh (for both of which Bannion has a responsibility he never, in his smugness, allows himself to fully recognize, permitting the former by his negligence—Lucy is, after all, "just a B-girl," not a policeman's wife like Katie or Bertha Duncan—and precipitating the latter by insinuating Debbie into performing for him an action he is too "moral" to perform himself) comes the brief but crucial appearance in the film of another female character, Selma Parker/Edith Evanson, the crippled woman who works for Dan Seymour's car-wrecking company. Her one scene (apart from a very brief reappearance when she identifies Lagana's henchman Larry for Bannion) occurs around the midpoint of the film, and provides the narrative with its turning-point. Without the slightest ostentation or underlining of "significance," Lang privileges Selma's intervention. Although she appears briefly in the background of the scene in her boss's office—and her reaction to Bannion there impresses itself—the image I think everyone retains is of her hobbling on her stick between the rows of wrecked cars toward Bannion, who is on the other side of the chainmail fence. She defends her boss (who, out of fear, has refused to give Bannion information)—he "isn't

Lucy Chapman gives Bannion "dangerous" information in *The Big Heat*.

a *bad* man," and after all, who else would employ a woman like herself?—before risking her own life (we know that she could easily join Lucy Chapman in the morgue) by telling Bannion what he needs to know. It's an extraordinary little scene—understated, almost thrown away: Selma is the one character in the film whose motives are absolutely pure. Lucy talks to Bannion because she was in love with Tom Duncan; Debbie acts because she is in love with Bannion. Selma has everything to lose and nothing whatever to gain, except self-respect. While Lang admires the other women, I think he invites us to put Selma (and what a little gem of a performance!) in a special category. *The Big Heat*, consistently, reveals a sensitive awareness of the social position of women, and offers a moving, unobtrusive tribute to their resilience, courage and tenacity, that *Kiss Me Deadly* needs, but entirely lacks.

The three female victims of Dave Bannion (if Selma survives, it is not *his* doing) are roughly paralleled by the three female characters of *Kiss Me Deadly*. If Aldrich's film offers an equivalent for the death of Kate Bannion, it is the death of Nick, Hammer's devoted "best buddy." This points to what is surely the film's most interesting aspect, a dimension lacking from *The Big Heat* and from Lang's work in general: its pervasive suggestion that the American construction of "masculinity" (together with its accompanying paranoia) is built upon the repression not only of the male's "femininity" (which would account for Hammer's hatred of/contempt for women, the film's major debt to Mickey Spillane), but his innate homosexuality. It is a theme that Scorsese was to "realize" fully and magnificently a quarter of a century later in *Raging Bull;* in Aldrich it remains a flickering, tantalizing implication, a "subtext" in the strict sense. Yet it is worth recalling that an interest in the ambiguities of gender and sexuality recurs spasmodically throughout Aldrich's work (and never in Lang's: the one apparent exception—the suggestion of homosexuality in the psychopath of *While the City Sleeps*—is treated entirely negatively, as no more than pathological symptom). *The Legend of Lylah Clare, The Killing of Sister George, The Choirboys,* are overt examples, but even a film like *All the Marbles,* with its "tag team" of female athletes under an "apathetic and non-athletic" manager, is relevant here. Aldrich's treatment of this theme is not notable for much complexity or sensitivity (the sledgehammer sensibility that is both the strength and limitation of *Kiss Me Deadly* prohibits any nuance), but its presence (which is perhaps, in subterranean forms, more pervasive than the few examples cited suggest) is partly responsible for the distinctive quality of his work.

It can certainly be argued (and I shall not dispute it) that *Kiss Me Deadly* is much the more striking of the two films. It has a force, directness and impact that one is never likely to forget, and isn't this the outward manifestation of an intense creative energy? Fair enough: such a description acknowledges the film's undoubted distinction and testifies to its authenticity as a response to the contemporary cultural climate. With it must be considered the film's stylistic progressiveness (beside which *The Big Heat* appears decidedly conservative): "Years ahead of its time, a major influence on French New Wave directors," as Leonard Maltin's TV Movies guide (an indispensable barometer of contemporary taste) succinctly puts it. The influence seems to me unproven: the *Cahiers* critics adored the film because it demonstrated again what could be achieved within a generally disreputable Hollywood genre, but I can't see that, when they made their films, they learnt much from it directly. It is one of those films that *appears* stylistically innovative, because it employs devices that one was not then accustomed to meeting within the general run of "private eye" thrillers. In fact, its pervasive "baroque" rhetoric (deep focus, strikingly extreme low- and high-camera angles) derives entirely from Welles and Toland: the "innovation" lies in applying it to film noir (from whose world it was never entirely alien). It is certainly an audacious film; I don't think this is a valid reason for preferring it to a movie that is content to utilize (with great intelligence) the shooting/editing codes dominant in the Hollywood cinema. *The Big Heat* proves yet again (how many demonstrations does one need?) that those codes can be put in the service of subversive and radical purposes. Lang at his best (as he is in *The Big Heat*) is among the cinema's subtlest and most subversive moralists; Aldrich's moral sense does not lend itself to the finer discriminations—which, it is worth insisting once again, are as much political as moral.

If both films depict a culture in which corruption is virtually all-pervasive, the world of *Kiss Me Deadly* is *just* corrupt, and there is little more to be said about it. Hammer is allowed one moment of grace: his grief over Nick's death, as he gets drunk in a bar: a moment that eloquently confirms one's sense that the emotional centre of the film is homoerotic (Hammer nowhere evinces this concern over women). Otherwise, the simplicity—the lack of complexity, of delicate exploration—of Aldrich's vision actually makes it much easier to enjoy *Kiss Me Deadly* on the superficial level on which genre movies are generally offered, the level that we call "entertainment." The to-hell-with-all-this, blow-it-all-up attitude to American civilisation actually provides a relatively easy excitement, satisfaction, exhilaration. (The studio, which added a final shot still there in some prints showing Hammer and Velda standing amid the waves, apparently safe, need not have worried: audiences generally seem to derive a lot of pleasure from the fact that Aldrich blows up *everybody.*) Lang's cautious, probing attitude that qualifies every judgement makes an easy satisfaction impossible (we would get no satisfaction from blowing up a civilisation that contains Lucy Chapmans, Selma Parkers and Debbie Marshes). One is left with a sense of discord and disturbance—with the sense of a culture to whose problems there will be no easy solutions: a disturbance crystallized in the film's last line: "Keep the coffee hot."

14
Responsibilities of a Gay Film Critic

In "To Have (Written) and Have Not (Directed)" in the first volume of Movies and Methods, *Robin Wood extracted elements of Hawksian vision from a film that had numerous contributors and constraints. The article was a model of auteur criticism. Since the mid seventies, Wood has shifted his critical emphasis and actively identified his writing with the politics of gay liberation. Along with other gay critics, such as Lee Atwell, Richard Dyer, Vito Russo, and Thomas Waugh, Wood has worked to establish a significant body of gay criticism both in academic and popular journals and in the gay press (for example,* The Body Politic, Christopher Street, *and* The Advocate*).*

At a slight lag, this criticism parallels the development of feminist film criticism. It constitutes an important countercurrent in its lively effort to merge personal and political concerns on the terrain of the social production of sexual identity and the cinematic representation of sexual politics. Gay criticism begins from a social perspective and proceeds to investigate the workings of culture in relation to that perspective, a procedure that often generates remarkably insightful results.

Here, Wood returns to his earlier auteur criticism, retaining the subject matter but radically changing the perspective. (In that respect, Wood's shift contrasts revealingly with Metz's, where the transformation from structural to psychoanalytic theory does not require a reassessment of earlier work.) This change in perspective compels Wood to address issues of ideology and sexual politics that have direct import for everyday life, and they become uppermost in his evaluations of Renoir, Bergman, and Hawks.

Wood now finds an ambiguity in Renoir and Hawks that he could not identify with precision before. In each case, it has to do with monogamy and sexual identity. Renoir focuses on the tension between human desire and existing social practices, while Hawks conveys the tension between these practices (namely, male camaraderie or domestic family life) and an indefinable chaos that lurks beyond the existing alternatives. Ingmar Bergman's explorations of human anguish pose a different problem by presenting anguish and neurosis as the human condition for which there is no alternative. His films foreclose the possibility of actively achieved change. In each case, Wood examines the director's oeuvre not in relation only to gay themes or the gay movement but in relation also to the interrelationship between aesthetics and ideology. By placing this question in a personal frame that minimizes theoretical abstractness, Wood shows us that thought and ideas can actively reshape our lives and that we do not have to repeat the misperceptions learned in a society that seeks to preserve its traditional forms. "Our emotions have to be educated," Wood writes, and it is to this valuable goal that Wood dedicates his recent writings.

First, my title. I intend equal emphasis on all three terms: *Gay Film Critic*. Critic: one concerned in problems of the interpretation and evaluation of art and artifacts. Film critic: one who makes the central area of that concern the cinema. Gay—not just the word and the fact it points to, but the word and fact asserted publicly: one who is conscious of belonging to one of society's oppressed minority groups, and who is ready to confront the implications of that for both his theory and his practice.

I can define what I mean here in relation to two types of gay critic who reject this equality of emphasis. First, the critic who for whatever reasons (many different ones are conceivable, of widely varying respectability) resists the public revelation of his gayness, arguing (either as defensive self-justification or as a sincerely held principle) that it has nothing to do with his view of art—the view conceived as "objective," and art conceived as something out there that one can be objective about. I cannot afford to be too contemptuous of this type, as I belonged to it myself until quite recently, and in my case I was always half aware that the defensive self-justification was of the flimsiest. A gay subtext is intermittently discernible running through my early work; a number of people, including some who hadn't met me, have told me that they deduced that I was gay long before I came out. But if these early writings are worth analyzing at all from the gay viewpoint, it could only be as an analysis of self-oppression—an alternating pattern of peeping out of the closet door and then quickly slamming it shut, and pasting over the chinks with placards on which words like *Marriage, Family, Health,* and *Normality* were loudly displayed—and with self-oppression becoming, as it always must, the oppression of others. (See, especially, the treatment of homosexual relations in the account of *Les Biches* in the book on Chabrol I co-authored with Michael Walker, for the most embarrassing moments of which I must accept responsibility.)

The other type of gay critic places the emphasis strongly, sometimes exclusively, on "gay," and concerns himself strictly with works that have *direct* bearing on gayness, approaching them from a political-propagandist viewpoint: do they or do they not further the gay cause? He will find it necessary to review Fassbinder's *Fox,* but will probably ignore Godard's *Tout Va Bien.* My choice of examples here is not arbitrary. The objection to such criticism is not merely that it is aesthetically restrictive but that it implies an inadequate, and insufficiently radical, grasp of what the Gay Liberation Movement stands for at its best, of its more general social significance. Godard's film, in which gayness is nowhere alluded to, seems to me to have far greater positive importance for Gay Liberation than Fassbinder's sour determinism, with its incidental reinforcing of gay stereotypes for the bourgeois audience ("the truth about the homosexual milieu," as the English Establishment critics greeted it).

Positively, I am able to point to two British colleagues who amply fulfill, in their very different ways, my conception of the gay film critic's responsibilities: Richard Dyer and Andrew Britton. The latter's article on Eisenstein in the forthcoming *Framework* strikes me as exemplary in this respect.

The change in my critical position and practice which many people have noted—some with favor, some with dismay—has been centrally determined by my coming out, and by the changes in my personal life connected with that. Critics are not, of course, supposed to talk personally. It is regarded as an embarrassment, as bad taste, and besides it is an affront to the famous ideal of "objectivity." The typical bourgeois Establishment reaction to any form of personal revelation might be typified by a remark by Philip Strick in his ignominious review of my last book in *Sight and Sound*—a review that managed to trivialize every issue in sight—where my coming out in print was described as "telling us about his love life." Yet I believe there will always be a close connection between critical theory, critical practice, and personal life; and it seems important that the critic should be aware of the personal bias that must inevitably affect his choice of theoretical position, and prepared to foreground it in his work.

I don't believe that any theory exists in a vacuum or as Truth. Every theory is the product of the needs of particular people within a particular culture at a particular stage of its development, and can only properly be understood within its context. Our gravitation, as human individuals within, and determined by, our culture, toward one or other of the available critical positions, will depend upon our personal needs, on the way we wish to lead our lives, on the sort of society we would like to build, on the particularities of our involvement in the social process. Such a view presupposes a constantly developing, dynamic relationship between criticism and art, between individual and work. There is in a sense no such thing as "the films of Ingmar Bergman," existing as an entity that criticism could finally and definitively describe and interpret and place in the museum. Rather, the films exist as experienced and perceived by the viewer, with the precise nature of the experiencing depending on the viewer's position in society and within ideology. Our sense of the *use* of art generally, and of the particular uses to which particular works allow themselves to be put, will vary from generation to generation, shifting in accordance with our sense of personal and social needs.

What I propose to do is, first, define what Gay Liberation means to me, the kind of significance I attach to the movement, the kinds of social intervention I see it capable of making; and then reconsider certain films and directors (not necessarily or centrally concerned with gayness) that already meant a great deal to me before my coming out, in an attempt to indicate the nature of the shift in my critical practice, the somewhat different kinds of interest and emphasis I would now bring to an interpretation and evaluation of them.

As most commonly expressed in the newspapers, periodicals, etc., of our Establishment (not to mention various Gay Society discussions I have attended), the aim of the Gay Liberation Movement would appear to be read as that of gaining acceptance and equal rights for homosexuals within existing society. My basic argument is that such an aim is totally inadequate. Acceptance of the homosexual by society has its obvious corollary and condition: acceptance of society by the homosexual. To see the incongruity of this, one has only to consider the dominant ideological norms of the society within which we live. As far as love and sexuality are concerned, the norms are marriage (in the form of legalized heterosexual monogamy) and the nuclear family (with the alternative, at once complementary and incompatible, of exclusive romantic love). Between them they offer homosexuals the terms on which they might be acceptable: the aping of heterosexual marriage and family (with poodles instead of children) or *l'amour fou,* preferably culminating in suicide or alcoholism.

Of crucial importance to Gay Liberation is its very close, logical connection with Women's Liberation. The present status of both has been made possible by the increasing public acceptance of birth control, with its implicit acknowledgment that the aim of sex is not necessarily procreation, and its consequent undermining of the tyrannical and repressive norm of monogamy and family. The common logical aim of both movements must be, it seems to me, to attack and undermine the dominant ideological norms on all levels. This offers the gay critic a brief that is enormously more open and comprehensive than the examination of the ways in which homosexuals have been represented on the screen (though that might of course become a perfectly legitimate focus on her or his attention, provided the wider implications were always kept in view). The attack, for instance, could—indeed, should—be directed at the economic structures of capitalism that support the norms, as they are embodied in the structure of the film industry itself as well as in its products. Being neither a practiced political nor a sociological thinker, I am going to restrict myself to questions of sexuality and love.

When dealing with ideology it is always necessary to ask not only what it *ex*presses but what it *re*presses. The opposed, largely contradictory, ideological positives our culture offers (monogamy and family, romantic love) have one obvious feature in common: the insistence on exclusivity and mutual possession, with "fidelity" thought of basically in sexual terms and sexuality mystified as "sacred." Beyond this, there is the furtive extra-marital affair, with its penalties of tension, secrecy, distrust, recrimination, etc. What is repressed is the possibility that people might relate freely to each other, on a non-pairing basis, without imposing restrictions on each other's liberty. The dominant ideology has a word for this: promiscuity, a term loaded with pejorative connotations. According to ideology's double standards, there is some difference between male promiscuity and female promiscuity. A heterosexual man who is promiscuous acquires a certain glamour and is a Casanova; a woman who is promiscuous is a bitch, a tart, a slut, or a whore. By and large, however, ideology has no place for promiscuity (or, as I prefer to call it, relating freely to one another) as an asserted life-style or a possible norm.

My shift in terminology is also a shift in meaning. "Promiscuity" is always exclusively sexual, and the notion of it within ideology has the function of separating sexuality from love. "Relating freely to each other," on the other hand, involves potentially the whole person—*including* his or her sexuality, without which the relating wouldn't be free, but not *restricted* to it. (This is not to denigrate the pleasure of quite casual sexual relations, or to suggest that every relationship should be "complete," whatever that might mean.) Much the same distinction could be made if one substituted for "promiscuity" the term "permissiveness"—a term popularly understood almost entirely in sexual terms rather than in terms of free human relationships. The term has the added objectionability that it implies that someone or something ("society") is doing the permitting; and to acknowledge society's right to permit is to acknowledge its right to prohibit. In general, ideology's method of dealing with the unthinkable notion of free relationships is to trivialize or dirty it, so that it becomes difficult to imagine what it might actually entail or how it might work.

In *Life Against Death*, Norman O. Brown defines the central characteristic of capitalist man as dissatisfaction, with anxiety as its inevitable companion: the desire to own more, coupled with the fear of losing what one has. Anxiety, or insecurity, certainly seems fundamental to the possessiveness that characterizes most of our sexual relationships. Parenthetically, as a person whose personal insecurity reaches proportions one might describe as grotesque, I must stress that I don't wish to appear to speak from some superior "liberated" position wherein I have solved all life's problems within my own life. On the contrary, I speak as one struggling and floundering amongst the mess and confusion of sexual relationships as they currently exist; I am prey to all the contaminations of the jealousy, possessiveness, and exclusivity that I attack. One must, however, recognize—otherwise there could never be any progress—that ideas must always outstrip emotions. Our emotions have to be educated, and emotional education is the most painful of all processes, because the education is resisted at every point by what we call our instincts but might more reasonably think of as our ideological structuring. Only with ideas can we confront ideology.

I shall move in a while to two strongly contrasted directors with whose work I have, as a critic, been associated—Bergman and Howard Hawks—attempting to suggest ways in which their work might be re-read from the perspective I have outlined. I shall not spell out in detail the differences between my approach now and my books on these two directors, as this would be deducible for those who have read them and boring for those who haven't, but I hope for the former group a critical reflection back over my past work will be implicit. First, however, I want to talk briefly about a film that, long among my favorites, has grown in meaning and in richness for me over the past year: Jean Renoir's *The Rules of the Game*. I have come to re-read the film precisely in the context I have defined: our entrapment in ideological notions of love and sexuality, with their emphasis or pairing, choice, and exclusivity; and the continuously repressed but insistent vision of the potential loveliness of genuinely shared relationships, in which none of the participants feels excluded, in which love is recognized as a life-principle that transcends the exclusive romantic attachment. To anticipate, one can evoke here one of Renoir's favorite words, and the force it gets from the context of his work: generosity.

Two general or recurrent features of Renoir's work must be made present here. One is the notion (influenced perhaps by the childhood described in *Renoir, My Father,* and the background of French Impressionism) of life as continual flux. He quotes Antoine Lavoisier's "In nature nothing is lost, nothing is created, everything is transformed" as one of his favorite texts. The other is the recurring relationship-pattern in his films (at once an extension and a questioning of the "eternal triangle") of one to three—usually one woman to three men (*The Golden Coach, Elena et Les Hommes, Diary of a Chambermaid, French Can-Can,* and *Rules of the Game* itself, where there are in fact four men if one counts St. Aubin), though in *The River* there is one man to three women. The addition of a third option crucially affects the significance of the triangle, which in our culture has always been firmly associated with exclusivity and the necessity for choice (usually, the conflict is between marriage, family and romantic love, the opposed and complementary ideological poles). If three, why not four, five—or twenty?

The film was initially received (and is still, by some people) as virulent social satire, an attack on a decadent ruling class on the eve of its inevitable dissolution. Confronted with this view, Renoir's own response was one of amazement: "But I love those people. . . . I would love to have lived in that world." It is consistently analyzable, I think, in terms of a tension between the two impulses these responses suggest.

There's another way of looking at the film's rich ambiguity of effect: it can be read as a film about people who go too far, or as a film about people who can't quite go far enough. Many have commented on the difficulty of defining what, precisely, *are* the rules of the game. In fact, every character has his or her own rules, or a personal variation on an implied complex of rules. In only two characters do the rules appear clear-cut and rigid in their application: Schumacher (Gaston Modot) and Lisette (Paulette Dubost). One aspect of the film's astonishingly complex yet precise formal organization can be suggested by pointing to three things about them: (1) they are husband and wife; (2) the rules they enforce are the most strongly contrasted of any represented in the film, indeed diametrically opposed; and (3) it is the dual action of their application of their rules that produces the climactic catastrophe. The rules of Schumacher, the gamekeeper from Alsace (who is deliberately presented, in 1939, as an embryonic Fascist), are centered on strict and repressive notions of marital fidelity, the ownership of wife by husband, that give him the moral right to shoot both wife and lover in the event of discovered infidelity. The rules of Lisette, the Parisian ladies' maid, are centered on notions of free sexual play as long as it remains frivolous and unengaged. When it comes to seriousness, the priorities are narrowly social-ideological; Octave (Renoir) is too old for Christine (Nora Gregor), and couldn't afford to keep her in the luxury she's used to.

Between these two—with their equally defined and entrapping, if opposite, sets of rules—come the film's central characters, who all exist in states of varying uncertainty and confusion as to what the rules are. And Christine's uncertainty is significantly the most extreme. From her point of view, the ambiguity of the film can be put another way: the story of a woman trying desperately to understand what her role should be or the story of a woman who can't quite accept that all roles are traps and refuse them all—with the roles defined in terms of the relationships available with particular men. It is important to recognize that the society Renoir depicts is inhabited almost entirely by outsiders: the Marquis is Jewish, Christine is from Vienna, André Jurieu (Roland Toutain) is from the modern world of aeroplanes and public heroes, Octave is a perpetual outsider wherever he is. The character who seems chiefly to embody our idea of a stable aristocratic society is the General, an old man whose constant refrain is that everything is passing away.

It is a society in which all order is at a stage of potential or imminent collapse; and this can be seen either in terms of a closing down or an opening up (the film encourages both readings). "I don't want fences, and I don't want rabbits," the Marquis tells Schumacher, and the remark has very clear parallels with the paradoxes of the characters' sexual behavior throughout the film. I have no knowledge of the actual domestic commitments of rabbits—their familial organization may be as impeccably bourgeois as it appears in the books of one of my favorite authors, Beatrix Potter—but in popular imagery rabbits always have connotations of promiscuity; "breeding like rabbits" doesn't refer merely to the number of offspring but to presumed sexual habits. The emphasis through the hunt is on the mindless slaughter of rabbits, the detailed imagery evoking the strongest sympathetic response toward what is being destroyed.

The tension that I have described can be illustrated succinctly with the beautiful little scene in which, after her discovery of her husband's adulterous relationship with Geneviève (Mila Parély), Christine confronts her rival in her room and enlists her in an ambiguously motivated complicity. On the one hand, Christine's reaction to the shock (she had previously believed completely in her husband's fidelity) is to play what she takes to be "the game" by rejecting all seriousness; she wants Geneviève to keep her husband occupied, not so that she can develop her relationship with André—whom she describes at this point as "too sincere"—but so that she can play around. On the other hand, the possibility of freely shared relationships is nowhere closer to the surface of the film than in this scene, which culminates in a moment of relaxed conviviality and exchange between two women (the demonstrations of how Tyrolean dances go) of a kind very rare in cinema, where women are habitually seen from the male viewpoint as rivals for the man, their possible uniting repressed. The whole film can be read as structured on continuously shifting couplings (I don't intend the sexual meaning here) which cut completely across all the divisions of sex, class, social role; virtually all the characters have a "duet scene" at some point in the film. The obvious exception is André and Geneviève—the two Octave suggests near the beginning that it would be most convenient to pair off.

Renoir's method and the film's visual style are crucial to its meaning. His creative collaboration with actors—*all* the actors—is well known. The camera style emphasizes the structure-patterns of the scenario by never allowing us more than transitory identification with one character at the expense of others. The constant reframings, in which the camera excludes some to include others, the continual entrances into and exits from the frame, the division of our attention between foreground and background—the style might be aptly described as perpetual visual promiscuity, quite breaking down the traditional one-to-one relationship of spectator to protagonist to which the cinema has habituated us. The Renoiresque principle of emotional generosity is everywhere frustrated in its free functioning by the characters' insistence on sexual pairing, and everywhere expressed and celebrated through the "promiscuity" of the camera style and the direction of actors.

Ultimately, *The Rules of the Game* is circumscribed within the ideological assumptions about pairing (Renoir never overtly questions this on a sexual level), yet it is precisely such assumptions that provoke every disaster in the film. It hovers continuously on the verge of a new acceptance. Hence the final ambiguity of effect. The film is at once an elegy to a lost society and one of the most progressive ever made. The world it creates is of the past, yet it everywhere points toward a possible future.

If I were to rewrite my early books now, the one on Bergman (published in 1969) would certainly cause me the greatest problems, and be the one in need of the most drastic revision. When I wrote it, my sense of identification with its subject was extraordinarily intense. Beneath the apparently happy surface of a firmly traditional marriage-and-family situation, I was experiencing the sort of anguish and desperation that Bergman's films so compellingly communicate, and accepting it as unchangeable, as "the human condition." Now, it is precisely this tendency of the films to impose themselves as "the human condition" that most worries me. In a supremely revealing moment of the interview-book *Bergman on Bergman,* the filmmaker asserts his innocence of any ideology, a substance by which his films are apparently completely uncontaminated. He seems to be using the term in a sense somewhat different from that in which it is usually employed in current film criticism; he means by it a *conscious* structure of social-political ideas. Yet the innocence clearly extends beyond that. There is no awareness that an ideology might exist in one's work, and centrally structure and determine it, without one's being conscious of it. The lack of an explicit social-political dimension to Bergman's work has often been noted; ten years ago I quite failed to see the force of such an objection, my own work as a critic having precisely the same lack.

Another, related way of considering the limitations of Bergman's work is via Andrew Sarris's objection that the films are repeatedly flawed by eruptions of "undigested clinical material." The obstinate recurrence of certain narrative and relationship structures in Bergman's work (structures which, I have argued elsewhere, are basically psychological, the characters representing projections of the artist's inner tensions) is plainly neurotic, and testifies to that central principle of neurosis: resistance wherein the neurosis defends itself against cure. What the films repeatedly assert, with impressive intensity and conviction, is that life under the conditions in which it is lived is intolerable, therefore . . . At which point a shutter comes down. The "therefore" should continue: "therefore we must strive to change the conditions." The shutter asserts, "the conditions are something called 'the human predicament'; they can't be changed."

In Bergman's films, neurotic resistance goes hand in hand with the resistance to any concept of ideology. Since I wrote my book he has made what I consider two of his finest films, *The Passion of Anna* and *The Touch*—though neither seems to be in general very highly regarded, and my admiration for them is not without reservations. Both films contain important elements, both in style and narrative structure, that suggest a desire on Bergman's part to open out his work, to pass beyond the stalemate in which it constantly threatens to get trapped. An extended analysis of these films would take the form of examining the conflict between these innovative elements and the resistance to them. More briefly, one can assert that nowhere more than in *Passion* has the intolerability of possessive relationships—the lies, subterfuges, resentments, frustrations, jealousies, eruptions of "psychic and physical violence," the ultimate mutual destructiveness—been more ruthlessly or vividly analyzed. Yet the films continue, doggedly, to assert all this as a fact of life, as the human condition, rather than as ideologically determined. Even *Passion*, with its relatively open structure and its excitingly spontaneous, exploratory style, can never seriously envisage the possibility that things might be changed.

In any assessment of Bergman's work I would not wish to give much prominence to *Face to Face*, which seems to me one of his very worst films, actively offensive in its self-indulgence. If I focus on it here, it is because it is his first work to deal openly with gayness, and because its treatment of gays provides so precise an index of the limitations of Bergman's work.

Near the beginning of a film devoted to portraying the inner anguish of an individual, defined in terms of personal psychology, the notion of "world revolution" is reduced in passing to a game for 14-year-olds; no possible connection is suggested between the two. Of the three gay characters, two are presented as stereotypical. (The treatment of the actor, Michael Stromberg, is more detailed and sympathetic in the published script, which one might read as a sign that Bergman was actually repressing his own sense of other possibilities in the finished film; the sympatheticness, however, takes the form of suggesting that the character shares in the general anguish.) The third, the character portrayed by Erland Josephsson, is presented favorably by Bergman, the penalty for which is that his gayness is essentially monogamous—a minimal adaptation of the dominant ideological assumptions about relationships is firmly put down. We are left with the familiar Bergman pattern: the heroine, tormented in adulthood by her experiences as a child, moves toward forgiveness and reconciliation across the generations. In Bergman's world, as nothing can be changed, all that people can hope for is to learn to forgive each other for the pain they inflict.

I suspect that, were I to re-read my early books, the one on Hawks (1968) would embarrass me least. By and large, I continue to admire the same Hawks films I admired when I wrote it, for some of the same reasons, and my delight in them is undiminished. My way of seeing them, however, has changed and widened somewhat.

First, I want to consider the ambiguous relation of Hawks's work to the dominant ideology: sexist (they celebrate masculinity and, however aggressive the women may be, male dominance is always reasserted at the end) and racist (white Americanness is a taken-for-granted token of superiority, and foreigners are either comic or subservient, and frequently both). These are more Hollywood than Hawks, though of course one can't clearly separate the two; they could be paralleled in the work of most mainstream American directors. Though they have to be noted, it seems legitimate to place the emphasis on the Hawksian particularities, the features that distinguish him.

The films might be said to belong loosely to an alternative American tradition (represented at its best by *Huckleberry Finn* and at its worst by Hemingway) which says no to established society, to the development of civilization conceived as the supreme good. What is striking is the almost total absence in the films of home, marriage, and family—and not only concretely but as concepts. The opposition between the adventure films and the comedies has been perceived in various ways, but both have in common the rejection of established order. The adventure films create an alternative order, cut off from mainstream civilization, centered on the male group; the comedies subvert order, throwing everything into chaos. The two sets of films are by and large very different in tone and rhythm. The adventure films are leisurely, measured, with an overall serenity that grows steadily up to *Rio Bravo* and *Hatari!* and then decreases abruptly in the films of Hawks's old age; the comedies are fast, frenetic, tense, with hysteria constantly threatened and sometimes taking over. In both sets the concept of chaos is important, but it is quite differently defined. In the adventure films it is *out there* (the Andes mountains, the Arctic wastes, etc.) and menacing; in the comedies it is *inside,* a positive force awaiting its chance to disrupt the established order, appalling yet also exhilarating and liberating.

The role of women in Hawks's films is always problematic. In many respects they remain male fantasy-figures; no one would wish to claim them for the Feminist cause, despite their aliveness and independence. With very few exceptions (*Red Line 7000,* for example), the women are always hostile to each other, unable to unite, conceived as instant, automatic rivals for the male, as in *Only Angels Have Wings* and *To Have and Have Not*. Their great interest—apart from the intensely vivid and dynamic, if male-orientated, performances Hawks usually gets from his actresses—lies in the total absence, in the adventure films at least, of any logical role for them. The point becomes very clear if one juxtaposes them with John Ford's women, who have a very well-defined, thoroughly traditional role: they are wives and mothers, mainstay of the home, at once the motivation behind the building of civilization and the guarantee of its continuance and transmission. In Hawks there is no positively conceived civilization, no home, no marriage. Woman becomes problematic by her very presence—which in Hawks is always a very insistent presence, far removed from the little lady left waving tearfully goodbye at the start to await the hero's return at the end. Hawks's solution (always uneasy, never satisfying, but central to the vitality of the films) is to break down as far as possible the division between male and female; always, in the adventure films, by making the woman aggressive and "masculine."

Many critics have noted a gay subtext running through Hawks's work, constantly suppressed, yet always insisting on some form of ambiguous, half-grudging expression. It goes right back to the silent period. *Fig Leaves* contains a remarkable scene in which a man "acts" a woman in a mock courtship with his friend; *A Girl in Every Port* (which actually ends with the woman ousted and the male relationship reaffirmed at her expense) was the first of two films Hawks has described as "a love story between men." He has of course never acknowledged gayness in his films and would repudiate any suggestion of it; nonetheless, one might see the term "love story" as a giveaway.

There are obvious examples of male relations so close as to become at least sexually ambiguous: Thomas Mitchell's feeling for Cary Grant in *Only Angels Have Wings,* or Kirk Douglas and

Dewey Martin in the other "love story between men," *The Big Sky*. There is also, from the forties on, a whole procession of young male actors, usually playing second fiddle or sidekick to the hero (but the relationship always characterized by an underlying tension or conflict—that conflict in which, according to *Bringing Up Baby*'s psychiatrist, the love impulse expresses itself), who are fairly obvious gay icons in appearance and behavior, if not always in offscreen actuality: Montgomery Clift, Dewey Martin, Ricky Nelson, the young James Caan.

In view of this continually present, half-suppressed, sexual ambiguity in both male and female roles, the notion of chaos in Hawks—and the films' ambivalent attitudes to it—takes on a new interest. It is closely connected to one of the most striking, consistent, and peculiar features of his work: the fascination with role-reversal. This takes a great variety of forms. In *Gentlemen Prefer Blondes* and *The Ransom of Red Chief* (Hawks's episode in *O. Henry's Full House*), the reversal is between child and adult; in *Monkey Business* and *Hatari!* the sophisticated and the primitive change places, becoming reversible, the distinction blurred. Most striking here is Elsa Martinelli's initiation into the Warusha tribe, and the subsequent scene where her tribal paint is replaced with cold cream. *Hatari!* also reverses humans and animals; it opens with truck and jeep converging on a rhinoceros, and ends (almost) with baby elephants converging on a woman. Most bizarrely and puzzlingly, one has in *The Thing* the reversal of human and vegetable.

But most pervasive—and surely the crucial and explanatory instance—is the reversal, in film after film, of male and female. Existing within sexist ideology, the films never manage to assert equality: it is funny for men to dress as women, but generally attractive for women to dress as men (and they are in uniform, not drag). Yet the notion of potential reversibility is very strong. One small, intriguing point: the interchangeability of Angie Dickinson in *Rio Bravo* and James Caan in *El Do-*

rado. Both are conceived in terms of their relationship to John Wayne, a relationship based on both affection and antagonism; both are gamblers; both are seen doing the same bit of business with a pack of cards; both are identified partly by their idiosyncratic adornments (Dickinson by her feathers, Caan by a picturesque hat); both follow or stand by Wayne after they have been dismissed—in the long tradition of Hawk's heroines. And both have the same line of dialogue, addressed in both cases to Wayne: "I always make you mad, don't I?"

The logical end of the characterizing tendencies of Hawks's work is bisexuality: the ultimate overthrow of social order, and the essential meaning of the chaos the films both fear and celebrate. Ultimately it is always contained (Andrew Britton would say "repressed") within Hawks's classicism, which is also the classicism of pre-sixties Hollywood. Yet is seems to me nevertheless the secret source of the oeuvre's richness, vitality, and fascination.

SELECT BIBLIOGRAPHY

Chierichetti, David. *Hollywood Director.* New York: Curtis, 1973.

Corliss, Richard. *Talking Pictures.* New York: Overlook, 1974.

Farber, Manny. *Negative Space.* London: Studio Vista, 1971.

French, Philip, ed. *The Films of Jean-Luc Godard.* London: Studio Vista, 1967.

Harcourt, Peter. *Six European Directors.* London: Penguin, 1974.

Kitses, Jim. *Horizons West.* London: Thames and Hudson, 1969.

Leavis, F. R. *Nor Shall My Sword.* London: Chatto and Windus, 1972.

McBride, Joseph, ed. *Focus on Howard Hawks.* New Jersey: Prentice Hall, 1972.

Maltin, Leonard, ed. *TV Movies.* New York: New American Library, 1975.

Perkins, Victor. *Film as Film.* London: Penguin, 1970.

Sarris, Andrew. *Interviews with Film Directors.* London: Seeker and Warburg, 1971.

Steiner, George. *Language and Silence.* London: Faber and Faber, 1967.

Wollen, Peter. *Signs and Meaning in the Cinema.* London: Seeker and Warburg, second revised edition, 1972.

INDEX